"A bright, informative history of zoos in general. With Gold's vivid images in mind, a visit to any zoo will never be quite the same."

—*Chicago Tribune*

"Gold details the frustrations and pleasures of operating a zoo—from lions who escape their lairs to the monkey business of the primates. That's why reading *Zoo* is truly a learning experience, for it gives one a new perspective on zoos and their importance in our lives."

—Lawrence Hall
Newark Star Ledger

"The animal cast runs from inscrutable deadly spitting cobras to infant gorillas that tug your heartstrings. But the new twist in this book is not in its marvelous anecdotes of animal personalities but in its focus on the zoo staff. The result is an informative and candid look into daily zoo operations."

—Mark Rich
Chicago Sun-Times

Other books by Don Gold:

Letters to Tracy (1972)
Bellevue (1975)
The Park (1978)
Until the Singing Stops (1979)
The Priest (1981)

ZOO

A Behind-the-Scenes Look at the Animals
and the People Who Care for Them

DON GOLD

CB
CONTEMPORARY
BOOKS
CHICAGO · NEW YORK

Library of Congress Cataloging-in-Publication Data

Gold, Don.
  Zoo : a behind-the-scenes look at the animals and
the people who care for them.

  1. Zoo animals.   2. Zoo keepers.   I. Title.
QL77.5.G65   1989   570'.74'477311   89-15834
ISBN 0-8092-4258-3

Quotation from *Cancer Ward* by Alexander Solzhenitsyn,
translated by Nicholas Bethell and David Burg. Translation
© 1968, 1969 by The Bodley Head Ltd. Reprinted by
permission of Farrar, Straus and Giroux, Inc.

Illustrations by Joe Hindley

Published by Contemporary Books, Inc.
180 North Michigan Avenue, Chicago, Illinois 60601
Manufactured in the United States of America
Library of Congress Catalog Card Number: 88-23761
International Standard Book Number: 0-8092-4617-1

Published simultaneously in Canada by Beaverbooks, Ltd.
195 Allstate Parkway, Valleywood Business Park
Markham, Ontario L3R 4T8 Canada

For
Alexander
and
Lola

CONTENTS

If we stop loving animals, aren't we bound to stop loving humans too?

—Alexander Solzhenitsyn
The Cancer Ward

1

Zoo:
Ark and Covenant

For animals, humans have been loving, threatening, and often unreliable friends. Fickle, opportunistic, needy, they have petted animals and slain them, built monuments to them and eaten them. People have covered their chilled bodies with animal fur and fitted animals with sweaters to guard against the wicked winds of winter. It is no wonder that some animals cling to humans and others run wildly away from them.

It is not surprising, either, that the history of zoos is strewn with ambiguities. To look at zoos is to look at the ways in which humans have confronted animals. A search into the distant corners of history can be revelatory.

From the murky past, some scraps emerge. As early as 4500 B.C., in what is now Iraq, pigeons were kept in captivity. Groups of elephants were assembled in India in 2500 B.C. During that same period, hoofed animals—antelopes—wore collars; they can be seen in drawings in Egyptian tombs. We know that the Egyptians treated some animals as sacred: lion, baboon, ibis, among others. Ani-

1

mal parks existed in that ancient society; the prevalent attitude toward animals was reverent.

By 1000 B.C., there were zoos in China. Halfway around the world, the biblical King Solomon was fond of the apes and peacocks given to him as tribute every three years; he was a part-time zoologist. He was not the only ruler with a passion for animals. Assurbanipal, who ruled Assyria (669–633 B.C.), and Nebuchadnezzar, the King of Babylonia in the sixth century B.C., sponsored royal zoos.

The Greeks had been displaying captured animals several centuries before Aristotle wrote *The History of Animals* in the fourth century B.C. Aristotle, wise in many matters, knew about zoos; so did his pupil, Alexander the Great, who caught animals on his expeditions and shipped them home.

The Romans joined in centuries later. But their use of animals was not benign. Their devotion to blood sports led to the slaughter of animals. Bull elephants fought each other, to the delight of Roman spectators. Big cats were tossed into an arena to destroy each other. Peacocks, sacred in other cultures, were roasted and served. In one series of games that lasted four months, 10,000 gladiators did battle, and 11,000 animals were killed.

Charlemagne, in the eighth century A.D., proudly displayed captured animals. In England four centuries later, Henry I opened a zoo near Oxford; in it, he displayed lions, lynx, leopards, and camels. In France, Philip VI opened a zoo, with lions and leopards, in the Louvre in 1333.

When Cortez arrived in Mexico, he discovered a zoo (in 1519)—a massive collection served by more than 300 keepers and a corps of nurses serving as veterinarians. There were birds in huge aviaries, iguanas, monkeys, bears, and jaguars. Other explorers seized animals to stock urban zoos in Europe and North Africa. In 1665, animals were on display at Versailles; it was an early case of animals as the basis for scientific research and education. Eventually, that zoo was moved to Paris.

In 1752, the Imperial Menagerie was founded at the

Schonbrunn Palace in Vienna. It was officially opened in 1765 and is still open today. It was built by the Holy Roman Emperor Francis I for his wife, Maria Theresa, who had a fondness for dining while surrounded by camels, zebras, and elephants.

Ten years later, a zoo was opened in Madrid. By 1793, the Muséum d'Histoire Naturelle was flourishing in Paris.

For centuries, animals had been herded into cages for the pleasure of rulers and governments. The welfare of the captured creatures was secondary to the delight of the observers.

Then, in 1826, a pivotal development occurred. The London Zoological Society was founded, the first of its kind, and a major trend toward scientific inquiry was begun. Other societies were to follow; meetings were held regularly, publications were born.

In 1828, a zoo was built in Regent's Park in London. In 1847, the term *Zoological Gardens* (in London) was shortened to *zoo*, and the word quickly became universal. The United States Congress funded a National Zoological Park in Washington, D.C., in 1890.

In 1907, another crucial development took place that was to influence zoos everywhere. Carl Hagenbeck, an animal dealer in Hamburg, took a chunk of his profits and opened his own zoo in Stellingen. Hagenbeck was a man with a vision. His zoo did not resemble any other zoo.

He described his mission: "I desired, above all things, to give the animals the maximum of liberty. I wished to exhibit them not as captives, confined to narrow spaces, and looked at between bars, but as free to wander from place to place within as large limits as possible, and with no bars to obstruct the view and serve as a reminder of captivity."

Hagenbeck's dream proved to be contagious. The traditional tile cages with cement floors and bars persisted, and still do, but zoos all over the world realized the validity of his intent.

As the decades of the twentieth century passed, zoos

grew in size and number. World War II intervened; it was to deter progress. However, it also was to enhance the perception of zoo directors. From the evil of war, a realization was born.

Robert Bendiner, in his excellent book *The Fall of the Wild, the Rise of the Zoo* wrote about it:

> By the mid-1940s many of the zoos from England to Japan had been wrecked or starved out. Zoo people everywhere became acutely aware of what the wisest of them already knew, that populations in the wild were drastically low, and were due to become less and less available to zoos as newly established states in Africa and Asia either slaughtered their wildlife without restriction or began to clamp down on its export. For the first time animal counts were undertaken from the air, along with field studies of breeding habits and animal behavior in the wild, many of them under the aegis of the world's great zoological societies. All of which produced a great ferment among zoo personnel everywhere, and a surge in breeding programs that in turn inspired advances in zoo building, animal grouping, veterinary medicine, ethology, and other scientific research.

Bendiner defined the zoos' obligation to breed animals in terms of three objectives: "to relieve pressure on the wild . . . to raise animals with a view to reintroducing them into the wild . . . to serve as an ultimate haven, the scene of a last-resort effort to save and propagate endangered species as a scientific and aesthetic boon to future man."

Today, there are more than 1,000 zoos in the world, more than 140 in the United States. Zoos exchange information, do research, breed animals, educate the public, and do battle against the forces that endanger species all over the world. Some conduct themselves ethically and effectively; some do not. Some are vulnerable to the criticism of animal rights' activists; some are not. When animals are taken for granted, zoos decay. In our time, most zoos know that many of their sins may be visible, and they guard against them. Their work is costly, but their purpose drives them on.

Lord Zuckerman, the president of the Zoological Society of London, edited the book *Great Zoos of the World*. In his introduction, he wrote:

> Civic pride in a well-run zoo park, however magnificent it may be, is not enough. If those who are responsible for managing zoos do not agree with the minority who are opposed to zoos, they at least have to show that they are just as humane in their attitude toward wild animals. They have to show that they treat their public educational programmes seriously. Their keeper staff has to be properly trained. They should be able to demonstrate—not to the world of amateurs who write about zoos, but to the scientific world—that they are seriously concerned with research of the quality and kind which yields knowledge that is not only relevant to the health and breeding of wild animals, but also to man's own well-being. And finally, they should be able to show that they have a contribution to make to the preservation of species which have either become extinct in the wild or which are now endangered.

The standards that Lord Zuckerman posed test the success of all zoos. The historic course of zoos—jailing animals for the often mocking delight of tourists—has been in transition in the second half of this century. In striving for the profoundly humane, zoos have complicated their mission, and have ennobled it. There will be frustrations ahead for all zoo directors; animals will be in need, and money may be in short supply.

One zoo moving through its transitional period to what its staff hopes will be the best of times is the Lincoln Park Zoo in Chicago.

Its special history began 120 years ago, with two pairs of swans.

In the summer of 1868, New York's Central Park managers, in a small burst of generosity, donated two pairs of mute swans to the developing landscape of Lincoln Park, for display on one of the park's ponds. In time, the swans bred a colony of thirteen. By 1873, in fact, that early animal collection had grown to twenty-seven mammals and forty-eight birds. In 1874, the locals began to refer to the assortment as a zoo, making it one of the first zoos in the United States. (Philadelphia's zoo is the only one disputing the claim of Lincoln Park's to being the first zoo.)

That same year, the zoo made its first purchase, a bear for $10, and became known officially as the Lincoln Park Zoological Gardens, the name it's kept ever since. It continued to spend money to acquire animals; in 1877, it spent $275 for two more bears, two peafowl, a kangaroo, a condor, and a goat.

Three years later, dens were built for wolves and foxes. Buffalo and polar bears were added, and in 1882 a small mammal house was built. Until 1888, the work was done by a group of zoo loyalists; that year, the zoo's first director, Cyrus DeVry, was hired. (He served until 1919.)

As the turn of the century approached, more animals were obtained, more exhibits were built, and more money was spent.

By 1908 the zoo, on ten acres of choice parkland, had 782 birds and mammals, 117 species in all. The lion house, a large classic Victorian building with a great hall, opened in 1912; the first giraffes arrived at the zoo two years later. The early 1920s brought the reptile house. During the depression of the thirties, the animals were fed at night; no one wanted to antagonize those people who were without food. (They were permitted to sleep on the zoo grounds.)

By then, the primate house, another Victorian building, had been built, and Bushman, a lowland gorilla who was to grow to more than 500 pounds and become famous, was in it.

During World War II, Judy, a female Indian elephant, arrived and became a crowd favorite for almost thirty years; she came to the zoo from the Brookfield Zoo in a western suburb. She walked across the city, with police and keepers as escorts. When she died in 1971, she was sixty-eight, and few zoo visitors had not seen her.

In 1945, a new era began, with the arrival of R. Marlin Perkins as director. People all over the country who did not know about the Lincoln Park Zoo did know about Perkins. He hosted the weekly television show "Zoo Parade" for years; he knew that television could serve his cause, and he was right. Thanks to his work, the zoo became famous beyond the borders of Chicago.

During Perkins's reign, other improvements took place. The zoo rookery, a miniwildlife refuge in the heart of the zoo, opened. Perkins acquired four lowland gorillas in Africa. (One of them, Sinbad, was as mammoth as Bushman.)

In 1959, the Lincoln Park Zoological Society was formed; it had seventy-seven founding members—and was to grow to more than thirteen thousand. Within a few years, it had a master plan, and the Chicago Park District, which had supported the zoo, had a supplementary source of funding, a fact that was to generate intensive activity over the years.

In 1960, the children's zoo building was completed, the first year-round children's zoo building in the country. Two years later, Dr. Lester E. Fisher, who had been a consulting veterinarian at the zoo, succeeded Perkins as director. He merged his vision of the zoo with that of the zoo society, and reform and renovation became the bywords of the zoo.

New exhibits were born: the Farm in the Zoo, the sea lion pool, outdoor areas for lions and tigers, a small mammal house. The first baby gorilla was born, the beginning of a program that was to become the world's leader in breeding gorillas in captivity.

In the seventies, funds from the city and the zoo society—a total investment of $23 million—spurred a building campaign designed to produce better, larger habitats for animals, areas set aside for breeding, and better viewing by zoo visitors. The landscape of the zoo was transformed. The Kroc Animal Hospital-Commissary (built with a large donation from the founder of the McDonald's chain), the modernistic great ape house, the climate-controlled flamingo dome, the waterfowl lagoon, the Crown-Field Center (housing the offices of the zoo staff and the zoo society along with education facilities), the penguin-sea-bird house, the antelope-zebra area, and the large mammal habitat were all put in place between 1976 and 1982. The master plan was not completed, however. There was more to be done. A $10 million Landmark Campaign was under-taken to renovate the farm, the children's zoo, the lion house, and the primate house. The funds would support a redesign of the bird house and the creation of a new bird of prey habitat. As 1987 wound down, much of the work was in progress; much of the planning had been done.

The Lincoln Park Zoo today remains a part of the Chi-cago Park District, but almost half of its funds come from the work of the zoo society. Les Fisher continues to be in charge, twenty-five years after he took over.

The zoo is placed on thirty-five acres of choice parkland not far from Lake Michigan. It is one of the few free zoos in the country; visitors don't pay to enter or to view any of the exhibits. It is open every day of the year, from nine to five. Its design is ingenious; thirty-five acres is not a large space, yet in walking along the pathways at the zoo, the visitor never feels cramped, hemmed in by buildings. By comparison, the San Diego Zoo is on 125 acres, New York's Bronx Zoo on 265.

More than 4 million visitors enter the zoo each year; only the National Zoo in Washington, D.C., can match that total, and few zoos in the world are in that league. The visitors come to see the more than 2,000 animals on dis-play. (As habitats grow in size, that number will be re-duced, carefully and selectively, by the zoo staff.) Almost half of them are mammals, a quarter are birds, another quarter are reptiles.

In 1987, $8,603,435 was spent on the zoo by the park district and the zoo society. The money supported more than buildings, services, utilities, and animals. The zoo

staff—including administration, curators, and keepers—
numbered close to 100 (the zoo society staff was 40). In the
zoo's budget estimate for fiscal 1988, some entries revealed
that few employees work at the zoo for profit.

Les Fisher, at the top of the salary scale, earned $74,796.
The assistant director, Dennis Meritt, earned $44,244.
Veterinarian Tom Meehan received a salary of $41,580;
his assistant veterinarian, Peregrine Wolff, was paid
$33,696. For the zoo's five curators, pay ranged from
$32,000 to $33,000, while the upper limit for the full-time
keepers was $21,812. Others on the zoo staff earned less
than that.

It is not surprising that many of the zoo employees
dream about winning the state lottery.

The truth, of course, is that the zoo has little to do with
money, with numbers or dates or even its history. The
zoo's story is about people and animals and how they do or
do not get along. It is about love and disappointment and
the temptations of the anthropomorphic.

There is a steady stream of gossip at the zoo, and the
usual resentments of subordinates against superiors. What
unites them all, and what keeps the gall from rising to do
harm, is the commonly held belief that the fate of the
animals is what matters most.

In that sense, the zoo is a continuing case study in the
relationship of humans to animals. But the effort is not an
easy one. The curators and administrators are inundated by
paperwork, by management decisions, by planning sessions, renovation projects, and frequent staff meetings.
Keepers spend much of their time in the basic labor of
their jobs, the daily drudgery of cleaning cages and feeding
animals. Fortunately, most of them are conscientious. One
factor in that is the presence of women as keepers; before
1972, there were none, then the civil service exam was
opened to women. By 1987 almost half of the keepers were
women. They brought with them qualifications that the
patronage army did not always demonstrate: a college
education and a zeal for caring for animals. Old-guard

male keepers who viewed the job simply as a job were challenged, often successfully, by the women who brought a new perspective to caring for animals.

When all the bureaucratic distractions are swept aside and all the menial tasks accomplished, what remains is that essential measure of a zoo's performance: the well-being of the animals and the devotion of the staff to those animals.

There is much to consider.

In the pages of the journal kept each day at the zoo's main office, a sample of the events that command attention reveals the range of emotions involved:

- A trumpeter swan was sent to the Milwaukee Zoo as a donation. "This bird will be incorporated into the Wisconsin recovery plan for trumpeters and will be released later in 1987."
- A snow leopard was sent, on a breeding loan, to the Oklahoma Zoo.
- A Nicobar pigeon was sent on a breeding loan to the Cleveland Metropark Zoo.
- A baselisk lizard died.
- Three piglets were born at the farm.
- A short-tailed bat died.
- An Arabian oryx was born, a male weighing thirteen pounds.
- Mumbi, a female lowland gorilla, underwent surgery for peritonitis. "Critically ill."
- Another Arabian oryx, a female, was born. She was rejected by her mother and was placed with another nursing female (the mother of the male born earlier). The newborn was "apparently adopted" and "was observed nursing from the surrogate."
- A giraffe was born: "normal birth, seen nursing from female." It was the first viable giraffe birth in the zoo's history.
- A Burmese python laid sixty eggs.
- Two moustached tamarins were born at the small mammal house. One was killed by the parents; the other was pulled to be hand-reared.

- A Mexican beaded lizard was found dead. "Saved head for Education. Body too decomposed to necropsy."
- A piglet died at the farm.
- There was a minor electrical fire in the great ape house; the building was closed for the day.
- A trumpeter swan egg was hatched at the bird house. It was the first hatching of that species in recent times.

The entries go on and on; the set of journals reaches back for years. A lion fell into the moat. A keeper was injured by a hostile animal. A wolf escaped from its exhibit. The clipped, unemotional entries state a series of interrelated truths about life in the zoo. It can be a joyful place, a sad place, a dangerous place. Always it is a challenging place.

That is what keeps it going. The staff are there (often at night and on weekends as well) not for the money; they could earn more driving a cab or collecting garbage. They are not there for the status, although some positions provide that. Most of them get up early, to arrive before 8 A.M., and bring their concerns home with them at night, because they are fascinated by animals. And because they know that a bonding can take place between them and the animals.

That bonding, that passion, can at times border on obsession. Anthropomorphism does exist at the zoo. Most of the zoo staff know what Bent Jorgensen, director of the Copenhagen Zoo, once said: "A tiger is a tiger and not a human in a tiger skin. It is unfair to treat animals as human beings, it is unfair to animals."

Yet, despite the danger of loving an animal too well, that love thrives. For those who work in a zoo, zoos are the best place for animals in this dehumanizing world.

Jon R. Luoma, in his book *A Crowded Ark*, noted:

A compelling case could be made that, if one considers the best interests of animals as individuals, they are *better off* in zoos than in the wild. Animals in the wild are subject to a Homeric catalogue of parasites and diseases. In good zoos, they receive, from extensively trained staff veterinarians, far better medical care than many of the earth's humans ever will enjoy. They are free from sudden, painful death by predation. They live longer lives, their toenails clipped, cataracts removed, lacerations stitched, boils lanced, bumblefoot salved, and hunger sated with carefully balanced, sometimes vitamin-enriched foods.

Yet, Luoma qualified his verdict: "It is still a box with wild animals living in it rather than where they should be." However, as he pointed out, " 'where they should be' isn't there anymore."

It is a dilemma faced by those who work in a zoo. Most agree that a wild untainted by the presence of humans and their destructive fury would be best for animals. Zoos save animals from that fury, from extinction. Yet zoo workers appreciate what Heini Hediger, the well-known director of the Zurich Zoo, once wrote:

In the zoo, where the animal is protected from surprise attacks by the bars, and where every inmate has ample food provided daily, both of these main activities [avoiding enemies, seeking food] disappear. Thus a vacuum—an occupational blank, as it were—is caused, which may lead in the worst cases to complete boredom . . . a distorted or even morbid manner, resulting in all kinds of stereotyped movements; running to and fro hour after hour; endless walking in circles, or all sorts of silly behavior and grimacing, even self-mutilation.

Finally, there are those who feel that zoos are barbaric denials of the rights of animals. In their book *Zoo Culture*, Bob Mullan and Garry Marvin wrote:

Zoos are institutions established for human pleasure, but it is pleasure that can quite clearly be problematic. For zoos represent the power of human beings to command the presence of living creatures which would normally absent themselves from human gaze. Confined in the zoo in an alien environment, they are 'displaced' creatures, and the human visitor must at some level recognize this, for there is clearly a disjunction between the animal's environment in the zoo and that in which it would live if allowed. In a subtle way, anthropomorphism disguises this fact by humanizing the animal, thus suggesting that it is in its appropriate environment.

The debate has raged on for decades, and will continue to simmer. It is not central to the lives of those who work at the zoo, but most of them know that the ideological struggle persists, and they pursue compromise solutions. They keep their attention on the animals.

Someday the wild may be restored, although that is not likely, and zoos may cease to exist (not likely either). It is more probable that the best zoos will prosper and will continue to be the only contact most people will have with animals. At Lincoln Park, the staff takes that responsibility seriously.

*S*unrise in late spring. The zoo is quiet. The grounds don't open until 8 A.M. The buildings open an hour later. The animals have their privacy. Then the first humans arrive, to bring the place to life. A veterinarian with a sick leopard on her mind. A curator working on a research paper without the accompaniment of a ringing phone. A great ape keeper clutching a baby chimp she is raising at home, to feed it during the night when no one would be at the zoo to feed it there.

In the small mammal house, the creatures of the night—owl monkeys, armadillos, civets, bats, and others—have been awake while others slept. Now they will sleep. The animals who have been kept indoors—the lions, tigers, polar bears—can emerge into the sunlight and rest or play as their spirits move them.

The first joggers pound through the zoo. Businesspeople bearing attaché cases strut deliberately along, choosing to share their early morning time expeditiously with the animals they pass. The first contingents of mothers and children arrive; the day will bring hordes of them.

The sea lions bask motionless atop the rock formation in their pool, expressing a contentment beyond words. Inside the buildings the animals stir, make their sounds, stare at the world.

Lights go on. Piles of food are carried into kitchens. The administrative staff arrives, dressed to stay clean. A photocopier wheezes. Typewriters begin to clatter. Keepers turn on their hoses, chop food for the animals, walk past cages, looking for pleasure—the presence of a newborn—or trouble—the signs of sickness.

In the distance, the hum of traffic deepens.

The city and the zoo have come to life.

2

AMONG THE MAMMALS

Even in the land of the American dream, it is rare for a boyhood wish to become a grown man's occupation. For Mark Rosenthal, the zoo's curator of mammals, it happened.

He was born in 1946 and grew up just a few blocks from the zoo. His mother took him there regularly; it was his favorite outing. When he was ten, he met Marlin Perkins, the zoo director and the host of the TV series "Zoo Parade." "If you want fun, work in a zoo," Perkins told him, oversimplifying the reality to coddle a young boy's fantasy.

At twenty-two, Mark got his bachelor's degree in zoology from Southern Illinois University; during his summers there, he worked at the Lincoln Park Zoo's children's zoo. After graduation, he took the Chicago Park District exam for animal keeper. He finished first.

After a year in the keeper's job, he was named associate curator in 1969—and embarked on a master's in zoology at Northeastern Illinois State University. The year he got that degree, 1975, he was named curator of mammals, at age twenty-nine. He has been curator ever since.

Mark's domain was vast. He governed the large mammal house, the small mammal house, the wolves-bears habitat, the primate house, the lion house, the great ape house, and the antelope-zebra area.

It was the zoo equivalent of being the mayor of New York City. In order to manage it, he had to delegate authority and rely upon the skills of the keepers who reported to him. Fortunately, they had dependable skills.

A tall (6'2"), dark, husky (210 pounds), and bespectacled bachelor, Mark spent more time at the zoo than he did in his nearby apartment.

On a gray, uncharacteristically cool Monday in June, he got to work before 8 A.M. and went to the zoo office in the modern bunker that housed it, the Crown-Field Center. He checked the red daily journal that the staff kept to note events of importance. There wasn't much in it that day. A lizard had been donated to the zoo. A red wallaby was sent on a breeding loan to another zoo.

Mark phoned the keepers who reported to him, to find out who was on duty, who was not—and who was assigned to care for the elephants. He walked over to the small mammal house, where he lingered in the kitchen, sampled a few grapes, and chatted with the senior keeper. The keeper reported a broken window—minor vandalism—in the cage of a springhaas (a rabbit-like rodent). The window needed repair, and the keeper had to file a work order to get it done. Mark walked out into the exhibit area and checked the damage. The glass was cracked but not yet dangerous to animal or visitors.

He resumed his walk along the curved walkway to his cramped office in the large mammal house. On a blackboard outside the door to his office, the keepers had noted, "Maddis, spectacled bear, has a bad right eye. Jocko, Jr., maned wolf, is very sick." He knew that the staff veterinarians would have detailed reports on both later.

One of the daily keeper reports on his desk noted that one of the sea lions wasn't eating.

"Could be pregnant," he murmured. "Or could be sick."

A saki monkey had given birth.

"That's exciting, because it rarely happens in captivity,"
he noted.

His office was packed. Copies of *Wildlife Review*. Files, a
typewriter, a tape recorder, a collection of well-worn pipes
and some tobacco. A "trouble" alarm box and a separate
fire alarm box. A pile of booklets: "Lincoln Park Zoological
Gardens International Studbook for the Spectacled Bear."
The "studbook keeper" was credited: Mark Rosenthal. It
was a kind of pedigree book for the breed of bear that most
intrigued him. The spectacled bear, from South America,
was an endangered species; Mark had assembled a small
collection of them at the zoo, and the breeding program
had been successful. As editor of the studbook, he provided
information on the bears—where they could be found in
captivity, which ones had died, and which ones had been
born—for all those interested in the fate of the species.

A young woman keeper walked into Mark's office to let
him know that one of the vets would be coming over to see
the sick wolf. The phone rang. A keeper was needed at the
lion house; Mark had to shift one from the farm. He was
responsible for half of the keepers at the zoo.

Some of them were happy to work for him; others were
not. His critics found him to be imperious; his loyalists
found him to be concerned. His personality did not reflect
extremes: spontaneous laughter or sudden rage. He remained stoical under pressure, often expressionless in emotionally charged situations. Some keepers assumed he
could not manage everything he had been asked to manage, responsibilities collected over the years. Friendly keepers were pleased to help him manage; critics were not.

He tended to staff the large mammal house, where he
spent time in his office, with docile, uncomplaining keepers. He spent time, as well, at the great ape house, where
the senior keeper, Pat Sass, was an old friend and a fan. He
was literal in dealing with keepers he knew might oppose
him on the most trivial of matters. He did not try to court
them.

His large physical presence and his noncommittal demeanor were taken as a taunt by some, as a comfort by

others. For his part, he did not engage in criticism of the keepers in the company of others. Some of his keepers did not share that sense of tact.

Despite the low-level irritants, Mark worked at managing his realm. There was little time for revolts at the zoo; there was too much work to be done.

Mark sat in his office and contemplated an event that could have brought negative publicity to the zoo—but didn't. The previous Friday, a wolf had escaped, somehow managing to scale a ledge in its outdoor habitat and leap into some bushes on the outside. A visitor had spotted it and had summoned a keeper. The keeper got help; the wolf—not looking for a fight—was cornered. The vets arrived and darted (tranquilized) it. The procedure went smoothly, but when Mark was told about it on Monday, he said, "Anything with teeth can be dangerous. We marshalled our forces, and this time it worked out well. The wolf didn't get hurt. The public didn't get hurt. A keeper didn't get hurt."

Still sitting at his desk, he seemed weary.

"I don't like Mondays," he sighed. "You walk in, and they've got twenty thousand things for you to do." One of those 20,000 things: a DeBrazza's guenon, a monkey, gave birth on Friday night. He would have to take a look at mother and child.

He had walked and talked and conferred, and it was only 9 A.M., with a full day ahead. He grabbed his walkie-talkie and headed out of his office. He strolled along the behind-the-scenes area in the large mammal house. He approached two sea lions in small, separate pools.

"Hi, Rocky!" Mark shouted. The small sea lion came out of the water, obviously recognizing him. Rocky was a one-year-old, raised since birth at the zoo. When it was born, its mother had abandoned it; the keepers had hand-raised it, taught it to live in water (newborn sea lions cannot swim), weaned it to solid food. Now, Rocky was eating fish and was getting used to a variety of people and sounds. Mark had moved one of the nonaggressive females from the main pool, Omega, to be Rocky's neighbor in the holding area. If all went well, both sea lions would join the group in the main pool.

Mark continued his stroll. He passed the giraffes, calm and inquisitive. A rhino lumbered across its holding pen toward him. He reached over the wall and patted it. He visited the marmoset breeding room, a holding area for the tiny monkeys. Roaches had invaded the room; it was a serious problem. Marmosets eat roaches, which contain worms that can kill marmosets. Surgery must be done to remove the parasites.

Down the hall, Bozie—a twelve-year-old female elephant from Sri Lanka—was getting a scrub and a bath from a pair of keepers.

"The keepers are trained in-house to manage the elephants," Mark pointed out. "The elephants are trained, too, to respond to voice commands. It's like training dogs, only we use an ankus, that short pole with the curved hook on the end of it. It's not sharp. It is, really, just an extension of the keeper's arm. It makes a point, but with love. You can't abuse an elephant, because it is very large and could be seriously hostile. It must exist in a controlled situation."

Bozie stared at Mark; the knowing quality of her sleepy eyes begged for anthropomorphic interpretation, but Mark did not volunteer any as he returned the gaze. He did not believe that he could easily read the minds of mammals. As elephant and man looked at each other, one of the keepers handed her keys to the elephant, who grasped them in its trunk.

"Drop them," the keeper instructed.

The elephant dropped the keys.

The second keeper asked Bozie to lift a leg. Bozie obliged.

"We're going to mate Bozie with a male at the Springfield, Missouri, zoo," Mark announced. "We'll get her there in a special elephant truck. Uneventfully, we hope."

As he spoke, Bozie had opened her mouth on command, and was kneeling.

Mark ended his tour of the large mammals; he had other visits to pay.

At the zoo office, he chatted with the registrar, the computer specialist who kept the zoo's animal inventory up to date. Then, he walked to the primate house, where he chatted with the senior keeper, who was preparing food for the animals. Mark sampled a banana. On the wall, a list of foods was posted: apples, celery, grapes, lettuce, spinach, oranges, nuts, sweet potatoes, smelt, eggs, escarole, onions.

As Mark walked behind the scenes—the inner corridor behind the cages—he spotted a female mandrill "soliciting" a male, backing up to him.

"She's pregnant, so it's not sexual. She's being submissive, letting him know that she knows he's the boss," Mark said.

He headed for the antelope-zebra area, to a room filled with video equipment. When the wolf escaped, a summer helper in the education department had a video camera and recorded the incident. Mark popped the cassette into a video recorder and watched.

"A woman ran up and said, 'Mister keeper, there's a fox running around!' I looked and saw the maned wolf. We contained it. We used the emergency procedure for animal capture. The vet darted it, it fell asleep, and we shipped it off to the hospital," the keeper recited.

Mark was satisfied with the keeper's performance, in life and on tape.

He walked briskly back to his own office. He phoned a woman at the Louisville Zoo; she needed his advice about caring for a tamarin. Two keepers, both young women, entered to let him know that the sick maned wolf was not in such great shape. "It's deaf and blind," one of them said. The tentative diagnosis was neurological; the wolf could have a brain tumor.

The hours passed. After a brief lunch at a modest restaurant in the park (but not at the zoo; few zoo workers ate at the zoo concessions), Mark plunged into the pile of paperwork that obscured the surface of his desk: forms, work orders, reports, journals, correspondence, and more.

"I was closer to the animals as a keeper than I am as a curator," he sighed.

At 3 P.M., Mark attended a meeting in a classroom at the Crown-Field Center, a discussion about the redesign of the primate house. Also present were Les Fisher, his second-in-command Dennis Meritt, and Chuck Harris, the zoo society's project manager for building design and renovation.

For two hours, the foursome talked about the preliminary plans for transforming the old-fashioned primate house into a more naturalistic exhibit—fewer animals in larger habitats. One suggestion was raised: simply replace the bars and mesh with glass.

"It'll still look like a jail," Dennis stressed. "It's silly to put in glass with the same old tile cages."

Les liked the notion of building vertical spaces for the monkeys, following the example set in the modernistic great ape house. "In most zoos, the gorillas sit on their asses. When the height potential is there, it generates activity," he said.

"Sight lines are important," Mark added. "But we don't want visitors to see only dangling *tushes*."

"Whatever we do, remember this: we don't have space as a great advantage in this zoo. But we do have intimacy. You can get close to an animal here," Les pointed out.

"It's also very important to hear the animals," Mark said. "That's why we put mikes in the ape house. They're behind glass, sure, but they can be heard."

The conversation rambled and, at 5 P.M., wound down to silence. There would be many other meetings like that one; the changing face of the zoo was a common concern and would continue to be until all the major renovations were done.

Mark dealt with the city bureaucracy by being patient.

He remembered a small mammal exhibit he had worked on. Most of the difficult work was done; all that remained was for a park district crew to return to remove one final load of earth from the exhibit. He asked for that.

Two years later, they showed up.

He remembered, as well, visiting one of the park district executives in his office. The executive opened a large file drawer and pointed to a thick stack of work orders.

"See those? The people who sent them in never called again to find out about them. If they didn't care, why should I? It's one way of finding out what's urgent and what isn't. You people at the zoo keep calling, so we get those jobs done," he said.

Sometimes, Mark thought.

It was useless to be impulsive, to expect work to be done within minutes, Mark knew. He courted the workers—the painters and carpenters and electricians and ironworkers and plumbers—who belonged to the park district force. He hoped that when he declared a situation to be an emergency, they would believe him.

It was important, Mark believed, to remain calm, retain information, and stay in touch with the people who worked for him. It was important, too, to appear to be in charge, even when you weren't. Troops needed a commander, he felt, so it was vital to assume the role, even if you didn't feel like leading at a given moment.

A sensible manager dispensed with trivia, whenever possible, with a minimal expenditure of effort.

A keeper meeting in the large mammal house on a muggy day in June: to work on a clogged drain in the wolf habitat, a woman keeper needed a pair of waders; the only pair around was torn and leaked. Mark knew that there might be a spare pair at the bird house.

"How energetic are you?" he asked the keeper.

She smiled demurely but didn't head for the door.

"We're burning daylight," he said. "Let's move on."

She moved, languorously.

Mark passed her on his way out the door.

He visited the newborn DeBrazza's guenon. He had seen it before, but a visitor had stopped him to call his attention to what she deemed parental neglect on the part of the newborn's mother. Mark notified the senior keeper in the primate house to keep visitors away from the cage. At times, monkeys were disturbed by close-up visitors. When Mark got to the cage, the mother was holding her baby.

"The baby is in the right position," Mark said to the keeper.

"Yes, the baby's doing real good," the keeper agreed. "I don't see anything wrong."

"Sensitize your people to keep an eye on them. Maybe you can get a docent to sit here and keep an eye out, too," Mark suggested. Docents—volunteer teachers—could be employed on such missions (but the keepers objected when docents wanted to play hands-on roles with the animals).

Mark moved along, to the great ape house. He enjoyed observing the apes, and he enjoyed chatting with the senior keeper, Pat Sass, who kept him informed about the animals, their joys and their stresses. Pat had been at the zoo for twenty-five years; she had known Mark since he was a young boy wanting to work at the zoo.

Mark learned that Terra, a twenty-four-year-old female gorilla on loan from the Milwaukee Zoo, was pregnant again. The gorilla breeding program was one of the most productive and most famous in the world; it was one of Les Fisher's continuing passions. An occasional frustration did arise. Terra had been introduced to Otto with breeding in mind. But Otto, a massive and occasionally troublesome gorilla, didn't like her and wouldn't collaborate. Frank, a more cooperative male, welcomed the opportunity. Their unions produced two babies, one alive, one stillborn. This would be Terra's third offspring. But Pat knew that Otto could be mean.

"If Otto bothers her, chases her, we ought to keep her away from him during her last trimester," Pat told Mark. "She gets riled up and doesn't turn the other cheek. He could hurt her."

As they spoke, a female chimp in a nearby cage clutched her baby. She turned around, her back to Mark, and she looked at him over her shoulder. Mark scratched her back, satisfying her wish.

In the main areas of the building, gorillas, chimps, and orangutans (in their separate exhibits) leaped, bellowed, banged against the glass, scampered around noisily.

Mark made his way up a narrow staircase to the top of the building, which opened to the outside area for the gorillas. Most of the building was, in fact, underground, but the gorillas could cavort in the sunlight or simply bask in it.

Frank's troop of lowland gorillas was outside; a small, animated baby rode on its mother's back. A female gorilla sat calmly, munching on grass it plucked delicately from the earth, blade by blade. There were three troops in all, led by males Otto, Frank, and Koundu. In the wild, those males would lead, find food, settle disputes, protect the troop against the dangers of the wild, and breed. At the zoo, their role was less demanding: they governed and they bred.

Pat Sass and her keeper staff kept their eyes on the apes and recorded pertinent observations in their daily keeper reports. Frank was one of their favorite subjects:

"Frank bent out of shape about something today. He did not go up; did not move over into nursery. Charged at girls; knocked Hope over and has been slamming into doors. The ultimate pain in the !*@!*!

"Debbie and Kumba got into a screaming, swiping fight at 4:30 P.M. Frank let them fight for a little while, then ran in between the two of them and pushed them in opposite directions. Could not see any bashes, etc., on either one. No blood dripping from anyone. No one favoring anything. They did not resume fighting after Frank intervened."

Mark appreciated the apes; they were smart, imaginative, responsive. When he went to the great ape house, he could get close to them, inches away, with only wire mesh between him and them. It was a throwback to his time as a keeper. Keepers participated; they were on the front line.

Curators were observers, analysts, supervisors. A curator could be a critic, but usually after the fact, not as an eyewitness; it made some curators uncomfortable, like the parent asked to discipline a child who had been unruly while the parent had been at work. The keepers were the game players, on the field; the curators commented from the press box. There was a difference.

Mark passed a small orangutan, a baby recovering from a broken hand inflicted by an overzealous older animal. It was in a playpen, clutching a small blanket, like one of its counterparts in the world of humans. The keepers realized that it had been injured when she held her hand strangely and whined. In the wild, animals resist expressing pain; it makes them vulnerable to preying adversaries. At the zoo, they were less guarded. In the case of the baby orangutan, surgery had repaired the hand.

Mark reached over into the playpen and gently scratched the orangutan's head. It peered up at him and made a nodding motion.

It was time to move on; the luxury of getting to know an animal was the keepers' reward, not his.

He walked quickly into the antelope-zebra building. The senior keeper told him that all was in order, that the yards had been cleaned early that morning. Two keepers not in sight were walking a camel, he told Mark. Such routine matters were important to Mark; cleaning and feeding were forms of drudgery, but they were essential, and Mark did not take them for granted. Better to be a pest about them, he felt.

When he got back to the large mammal house, the keepers were at their midmorning break, devouring microwaved pizza. Mark grabbed a slice and a can of Pepsi, then retreated into his office. He spent the next ninety minutes shuffling papers at his desk, before driving off to lunch in his 1985 Plymouth Horizon, with the license plate ZOO MAN.

After lunch, as he returned to his office, he noticed the

rows of small children in identical T-shirts. "It must be summer," he said. "The school groups are gone, and the day campers are here."

Inside the building, he could hear music coming from a radio near the indoor giraffe area.

"For years around here, the keepers were told to whisper when they were around the hoofed animals—the gazelles, the zebras, the antelope, the deer, the giraffes, the rhinos. So if there *was* any noise, the animals would go crazy. No more. We want them to get used to sounds. So when a keeper drops a shovel, the elephant will know what it is and won't get excited. It makes sense," he said.

Meetings.

It would be easy to assume, from afar, that a zoo curator sits around petting animals. That is a fallacy.

Mark worked—as manager, supervisor, researcher, and conservationist-educator—but he did not have time to fondle animals. He spent as much time with humans as he did with animals. On another sweltering summer day, he had several meetings to fill the day.

At 8 A.M., he attended a keepers' meeting in the auditorium of the Crown-Field Center. Les Fisher presided.

The room was half-filled with people dressed in the familiar keeper colors, khaki and brown. Stragglers continued to enter after Les had begun.

"Are the others coming by elephant?" he asked. His manner was fatherly, relaxed, folksy. But there was often a message in his wit.

Although the meeting was called a keepers' meeting, it rarely became a vehicle for keeper complaints or disputes; those centered in Les's own office, where grievances could be aired privately. Les opposed open warfare; he preferred to be the zoo's ultimate ombudsman.

He used the keepers' meeting to keep the keeper staff informed, to remind them that they were the core of the zoo family.

As Mark sat in the back row, barely noticed, it was Les's

show. He told the keepers that planning was proceeding on schedule for the changes to be made at the bird, primate, and lion houses. The children's zoo renovation, under construction, would be ready in four months, he hoped. A few snickers in the audience symbolized the cynicism that accompanied all such announcements.

There was a "scary fire in the ape house," he told those who hadn't already heard about it. "We had trouble finding the source of it for a few minutes. Happily, nothing bad happened. A supplementary heater was smoking." He wanted to use that event to make a point: recognize that emergencies can occur and be ready for them.

"Think of the staff and the safety of the public first," he urged. "But know how to save the animals. Keep thinking about how you'd react to a fire. And repair faulty equipment before it causes a tragedy."

Mark had known about the fire; he was grateful that it had not turned into something horrifying. He knew how difficult it would be to lead the apes out of that building to safety. The thought of making such an attempt troubled him.

Les went on. Some topiary figures of animals were being installed in front of the penguin-seabird house. "If we're successful, it'll be fun," he said. "It's just a little thing, of course, but if you see someone abusing them, scare them off."

He pointed out that the selection of a new concessionaire for food at the zoo was still in progress. The winning bidder would improve the quality of food sold at the zoo; it couldn't be worse than it had been. But all that was months away.

He introduced Gene Brimer, a new employee reporting to Mark; Gene was an experienced pest control expert (he disliked the term "exterminator" because he felt that he never truly obliterated the foe). He would take on the roaches, mice, rats, and other creatures attacking the zoo grounds and the animals. There were mice visible, running around cages in the small mammal house, in the bird house, and elsewhere.

"The visitors will see them," Les said, wearily, like a father telling a child how important it was to keep the room clean. "We must make a dent in the problem."

Brimer, a personable, gray-haired veteran of such wars, nodded and smiled, more as a sign of courage than joy in the nature of the fray.

The meeting ended just before 9 A.M. Mark strolled through the building for his next meeting, Les's weekly staff gathering in the conference room.

It opened with Mark in his role as visual-aid producer. With the help of a docent, he had put together a ten-minute slide-and-audio presentation: a guide for keepers on the potential dangers in their work. Its message was blunt:

- Animals protect their space.
- You can't predict their reactions, no matter how well you think you know them.
- Elephants are the most threatening. They can cuddle you to death, just by leaning against you.
- Animals kick, bite, and use their horns and tusks.
- Always carry a tool for self-defense, and always be aware—in advance—of an escape route.
- Don't be casual. A jaguar can kill with one blow of its paw to the head. Even rodents can bite and scratch. A parrot can crack a hard nut with its beak; it can crack a finger just as easily. Talons are designed to tear flesh; they work. An alligator can move at a speed of forty miles per hour. A tiger can be provoked by something as subtle as a keeper's shampoo, a new and strange scent.

The soundtrack recited the unadorned advice, while graphic photos—some from newspapers—made the points.

When Mark finished his presentation, he announced that it was truly a low-budget production. He'd gotten it done for a total expenditure of $50. Now, he hoped, all the keepers would view it and learn from it.

Les again presided at the meeting. He repeated much of what he had told the keepers earlier. He then discussed the results of a recent keeper exam conducted by the park district. Approximately six hundred people took the test, and only thirty passed it. Most of those who passed were existing keepers who wanted to turn their temporary status into permanent status—and many of them didn't do too well on the test. In other words, as Les explained, the test may have been unrealistically tough—but there was nothing to be done about that. At least new keepers to be added to the permanent roster would be those already on the job.

Les paused, sighed, and mentioned some papers that had been on his desk when he left the night before and were gone when he got to work in the morning.

"It's part of the never-ending silliness at the zoo," he said, with a pained smile on his face.

An animal rights zealot had contacted him, he said, wanting to know how many animals had died, and why they had died, in the past twenty years. "There are no secrets at the zoo," he said, but he added that information from the precomputer age might take months to collect.

The group around the conference table—Mark and the other curators, the assistant director (Dennis Meritt), the veterinarians, and a representative from the zoo society staff—squirmed almost in unison. Few of them wanted to oppose the good intentions of the animal rights legions; few of them wanted to be obedient to them either.

The meeting lapsed into small talk about troublesome employees. Given the bureaucratic red tape, it wasn't easy to fire anyone; serious infractions had to be documented carefully and that often took months. One example: an alcoholic who had agreed to accept treatment was slated to be back at work after a prolonged absence. There was concern about his ability to function. Another employee had pleaded for a promotion that couldn't be granted; no vacancy existed. A third, formerly at the zoo, had left the zoo business for another field. The consensus of those present was that the move elevated the quality of the zoo profession.

The meeting ended an hour after it began, but for Mark, who sat impassively through most of the staff meeting, jotting notes on a ruled pad, it was simply time to attend another meeting. That one was in Les's office, with Clarence Wright, curator of reptiles, and representatives from the zoo staff and the zoo society.

The American Association of Zoological Parks and Aquariums was going to hold a regional conference in Chicago in April 1988, and three local institutions—Lincoln Park Zoo, Brookfield Zoo, and the Shedd Aquarium— would host it.

What ideas could Les and his staff contribute to the organization of that conference? What workshops might be useful?

Among the suggestions: a workshop on pest control, another on the use of video to study animal behavior (an activity of importance to Mark), a panel on construction and renovation, others on marketing, fund-raising (for which the zoo society was respected), outreach programs (the zoo was the first in America to set up a traveling zoo), publications, keeper in-service training (like Mark's slide show).

The conversation lagged; the conference wasn't soon enough for those present to be eager and inventive.

"How about a workshop on egg management?" Mark asked.

The others looked at him incredulously.

"You know, what to do with eggs. How to dye them at Easter," he added with a faint giggle.

It brought the meeting to a close, subject to be considered again at a later date.

It was close to lunchtime, and Mark needed a break.

The conference room had been turned into the setting for a party to celebrate Pat Sass's twenty-fifth anniversary at the zoo. Mark could toast Pat and munch on the food available.

He never wore a jacket, but almost always wore a tie. In keeping with a tradition set by Les Fisher, many of his ties were animal prints. For Pat's party, he wore his monkey tie.

After the party, he headed back to the large mammal house and his office. As he entered the modern building, with its wide, winding walkway past spacious exhibits, a woman with a small child in tow stopped him. Her sunglasses had fallen into the moat at the elephant exhibit. Could they be retrieved?

Yes, Mark told her. He asked one of the keepers to do it.

He phoned an electronics supplier to solicit a bid for video equipment to monitor the outdoor area at the great ape house. He called a state agency to request an application for certification for the new staff pest control expert, Gene Brimer. Despite Gene's view of his work, Mark referred to him as "the exterminator."

The he headed to the bear line, behind the scenes.

He noticed that the large wooden stockade doors to the bear line had been left open. So had an inner heavy metal door. A nearby sign read: BEARS AND WOLVES ARE DANGEROUS.

Mark spoke into his walkie-talkie, trying to find the person who hadn't locked the doors. (A large inner door and those on the individual bear dens prevented the bears and wolves from emerging, but for Mark, there was a principle at stake.)

His walkie-talkie crackled; a keeper had responded to his call. He asked her to come to the bear line, and within a few minutes, she did. He showed her the open doors. She took his demonstration to be an accusation and denied that she had left the doors open.

"Well, let's find out who did," he said. "It makes me crazed."

He entered the bear line; it was like entering a prison, with heavy metal doors throughout and long, dark corridors, thick concrete walls, bars, peepholes, large padlocks, closed-circuit TV. He moved past the empty dens; most of the bears were outside, and two wolves inside were sleeping. He looked at the floor, then tugged at his walkie-talkie again. A keeper answered.

"There's mouse crap all over," he said, his voice rising, but stopping short of anger.

He moved on, along the corridor past the bears and wolves. Below a slot on one den, a sign read: DANGER. BEAR CAN REACH PAW OUT! In that slot, a large wet nose protruded, an open mouth displayed spikelike teeth grinding against the bar in the slot, a clawed paw barely visible. Mark stopped. He patted the paw, gingerly. It belonged to one of the spectacled bears he had collected; the zoo had seven of them, with six others out on breeding loan.

He went outdoors, to check the bears' outdoor habitat. A mother bear, Goggles, and her daughter, Annie, were running around the exhibit, which had been designed to duplicate the South American setting that the species knew well: high clifflike walls made of Gunite (a mixture of cement, sand, and water sprayed to specifications and used throughout the zoo to duplicate rock formations), trees, dirt, pools—separated from the public by a deep dry moat.

When Mark leaned toward them at the railing that faced the exhibit, the two bears stopped and looked at him. He made a fluttering sound, imitating their own sound. They paid attention to him.

He smiled. "I do a good monkey imitation, too," he said.

He couldn't linger; he had another meeting to attend. He went to the antelope-zebra house, to the video room, where he met with Pat Sass and a pair of docents. They discussed a chimp behavior study, inspired by Jane Goodall's celebrated research, that would involve docent observers in the great ape house. They would watch the chimps and make notes about their behavior. All the work would, if successful, compare chimps' behavior in captivity to Goodall's findings on chimp behavior in the wild. Some believed that chimps in zoos played to the crowds. The study might confirm that.

Although he hoped to leave early for a relaxing cruise on

Lake Michigan on a cousin's boat, Mark sat through the meeting patiently; he liked those present, and the project intrigued him. But when the meeting did end, he thanked those who attended and headed out of the building toward his car.

All days weren't gratifying. There were days dominated by nagging frustrations.

On such a day, with a searing June sun overhead, he had made plans to record on videotape the behavior of a pair of trumpeter swans. The nesting pair, particularly sensitive in that mode, had attacked several flamingos, killing two of them by breaking one's neck and traumatizing another beyond medical rescue. Nesting swans did indeed protect their turf—their offspring were at stake—but this pair presented a challenge to Mark. He felt that a tape of the swans being aggressive would be instructive.

He informed those whose help would be needed. Several keepers would be present, alongside the waterfowl lagoon. A friend of Mark's—the wife of an orthopedic surgeon who had operated on some of the apes—would operate the video camera. Mark would direct. Kathy Brown, the senior keeper in the bird house, who had been attacked by the swans recently (but not seriously wounded) would be on hand, with a large push broom to protect herself. The swans' wings had long been pinioned, clipped, to prevent them from flying, from escaping.

The swans were about to be transferred to Indian Boundary Zoo, a satellite zoo run by Lincoln Park. The value of videotaping the swans made Mark's decision to proceed an urgent one. He told the participants to be on the site at 1:30 P.M.

At his office that morning, he mediated a dispute between two women elephant keepers in the large mammal house. There weren't specific grievances; it was more a matter of temporary incompatibility. He set up a meeting with one of them, Pat, a middle-aged, calm, experienced keeper. The other, Robin, young and feisty, was not at work that day. Larry, the senior keeper, sat in on Mark's meeting with Pat.

From Mark's viewpoint, it was vital for keepers working together to maintain a sense of détente. There was the safety factor; distracted keepers were vulnerable keepers. Large mammals could be lethal.

They met behind closed doors, and when they emerged, Mark hugged Pat reassuringly. Later, he told her, they'd meet with Robin.

It was time for another test: to put together the two sea lions—Rocky and Omega—being held in the separate pools in the holding area at the large mammal house.

If the two sea lions could overcome their fear or reticence, if they would swim in the same pool, he could put them together in a larger pool, in the hippo yard. If that worked, he could move them to a holding pool in the sea lion pool complex. If they were compatible there, he could open the gate into the main pool.

There were risks. "They're like gorillas, in the sense that there are no social graces among sea lions, if you're new to the troop. We can't predict how it will go," he said.

He peered at the two sea lions from behind the wall that separated them from the behind-the-scenes corridor. The two pools were surrounded by a wide concrete deck, providing plenty of room for the sea lions to move around. A small platform, painted red, offered one the opportunity to perch. There was a small two-step staircase for a similar purpose.

Rocky was in his pool; a keeper was tossing fish to him. Omega was being fed, too. Then one of the young women keepers entered the area and unlocked the gate between the two pool areas. Rocky came out of the water and bounced around the floor toward the open space, then retreated to his own pool. Omega did the same, not crossing the border where the gate had been.

Minutes passed as both sea lions emerged from their pools, approached the midpoint, peered at each other, and retreated. Rocky tentatively crossed over to Omega's side, then quickly waddled back to his own.

Mark watched, impatient; he had other work to do. He asked the keepers to watch the pair and let him know what developed. He returned to his office and began sorting through the papers on his desk: forms, letters, work orders, daily keeper reports from all the mammal houses. As he did, a thunderstorm came to life overhead, and a single streak of lightning triggered a loud thunderclap.

And the power failed in the large mammal house.

It was not the first time that had happened. Mark was not shocked. He used his walkie-talkie to inform the main zoo office of the power failure; he reached Larry, the senior keeper, and urged him to check on the moods of the animals in the large mammal house. A few minutes later, Larry responded: no problems to report.

The park district power house was nearby, and the electricians in it would be at work tracing the source of the failure. The rain, which had been heavy, was lessening. Mark made sure that all the keepers on duty had flashlights. He grabbed a Lincoln Park Zoo rain slicker from a hook and headed out to lunch.

When he returned, the power was still off, but the keepers and the animals were undaunted. He went to visit the sea lions. Several keepers and a docent were monitoring matters, but there was little to monitor. Rocky was out of the water, attempting to hide behind the small staircase, his head down. Omega was sitting on the red platform, a few feet away from him. They had achieved one objective: they were on the same side of the gate.

Omega had shared Rocky's pool with him, a keeper told Mark, but just briefly. If Mark was disappointed by the minimal progress, he didn't express it to the keepers.

It was time to videotape the trumpeter swans.

The swans—elegant, graceful birds—stood proudly near the pond, where dozens of ducks and geese had gathered. The swans paid little attention to the other birds. They were conversing face-to-face. They trumpeted at each other, lowered their long necks and raised them in unison; the choreography was precise and beautiful.

Mark signaled to Kathy Brown, and Kathy approached the swans, broom ahead of her. The swans' chatter became more animated as Kathy approached, carefully. The birds became agitated and began to flap their wings, not in emulation of flight, but as weapons of self-defense. Mark's camerawoman was ready, camera pointed at the scene, motor running.

Kathy moved closer to the swans, poking the broom at them. The birds retreated, slowly. Kathy continued to move toward them. The swans stopped, ready for a confrontation. One flapped its wings at the broom, then was joined by the second. Kathy backed up. The swans appeared to celebrate with loud trumpeting.

Mark's camera-wielding friend noticed it first: one of the swans had been injured. In flapping its wing against the broom, it had lacerated it and was bleeding. The smudges of blood were evident against the impeccable whiteness of the bird's feathers.

The two swans moved toward the pond and stepped into it, gliding away, trumpeting at each other, a communication no one there could interpret.

"She'll wash it off in the water," Kathy said.

"Keep an eye on her," Mark instructed.

The swans glided off, side by side, toward the middle of the pond. Yes, nesting swans protect their own, Mark knew, and that—as it turned out—was not a fact out of a textbook. Mark had seen it proved in life and had captured it on videotape.

If he regretted the injury to the swan, he didn't articulate it at that moment.

A few days later, the swans were transferred to Indian Boundary, and the flamingos were safe again. But Kathy had second thoughts about the "ugly" role she had played. Had she been tempted to provoke those swans? She considered that possibility for months.

When Mark got to his office the next morning, he was told that Rocky and Omega were not exactly friendly.

Rocky had stopped eating. And when Omega entered his pool, Rocky would leave it. Mark asked the keepers to try another tack: keep the sea lions together during the day and apart at night for a week.

A few minutes later, Mark learned that the sick maned wolf might have distemper; a second maned wolf also was a candidate for the dangerous disease. The keeper who informed Mark was concerned that the wolf might unknowingly transmit the disease to other animals. Peri Wolff, the assistant vet, was consulted; she wasn't sure that was likely, but she was taking the outbreak seriously.

Mark then met with the two disputing keepers, Pat and Robin, and senior keeper Larry. He held the meeting in the context of a discussion about caring for the elephants, the two keepers' main assignment.

Bozie, the female elephant who had been at the zoo for eleven years, since she was one year old, had never been easy to control.

"She's a six-thousand-pound brat," Robin said. "It's a case of an elephant behaving like a twelve-year-old kid. She can't be allowed to get away with her bad behavior. I say, don't be nice to her. Let her know what's OK and what isn't. After all, one of us could get hurt. You can't take for granted what these animals will or won't do. She'll test you, like kids do, to see how far she can go."

Patiently, slowly, Mark steered the conversation to the disagreement between the two keepers. Without blaming either one, he stressed the need for a team effort.

"I want to go beyond the problems and take care of the elephants. If you're emotional out there, you're going to get in trouble," he told them.

Pat responded, "If we could just go to each other instead of leaping at each other, things wouldn't fester. I don't mean to hurt her feelings, but she was upset. Let's try to discuss it."

"We should communicate," Robin declared. "If I have a beef with you, I should talk to you about it."

"Count to ten," Larry suggested.

"I don't want shouting matches," Pat said.

"Sometimes I do things, and I'm not even aware that I did them," Robin offered.

"When you're together, grow together," Mark told the group. "Be professionals. Make that commitment."

The two women began to talk about their differences.

"You were hyper with me. And when you are, I go boom, boom, boom," Pat said.

"When I get pissed, I let you know about it," Robin replied. "I admit when I'm wrong, and then I forget about it."

"We lost control," Larry interjected. "It got out of hand. When you're both hot, we all lose communication."

"I have to walk away from this knowing I've got a team here, and that's not simple," Mark said. "All I can ask is that we have respect for each other."

"Things can be worked out," Robin volunteered. "I'm willing to try. Sometimes it's impossible not to have personal things affect you."

No one asked her to elaborate.

"The day Bozie drops a baby here, no one out there will know how much work we've done here. But *we* will," Mark said, attempting to propel the conversation to a higher level.

The three keepers went off together, toward the elephants.

Mark went back to his desk, slumped in his chair, and glared at the paper on his desk.

What was it that Marlin Perkins had said to him when Mark was a boy? "If you want fun, work at a zoo."

Mark smiled, got up, and went out of the building to the midday sun, the chains of hand-holding children, the loving young couples, and a few small kids who might, someday, want to work at a zoo.

FIRST PERSON: MARK ROSENTHAL

The first time I came to the zoo, I must have been four

years old, five years old. When I was born, my parents lived right across from the zoo. My mother, like all the mothers around, would take her kid and go to the zoo, and that was a day out with the kid. I remember coming to the zoo every day. I mean every day.

When I was in grammar school, I always loved collecting pictures of animals and collecting the old postcards that they sold at the zoo, reading about animals. When I was in grammar school, I remember taking books out of the library, classic texts about zoos and working in zoos and working with animals. I think I always knew somehow that I enjoyed being with animals. It seemed pleasant; it seemed natural. I wanted to work with living animals. I didn't want to work in a museum with dead animals. I thought I wanted to be a vet. When I got to college, I went into pre-vet, and right away it was eighteen hours of work, and I wasn't in the mood to study. I flunked out. So I went into zoology. I went to junior college to build up my grades, and I did excellently. I was ready. When you're ready to study, you do it.

My parents thought it was strange for a Jewish boy to want to work in a zoo, but they always wanted me to be happy and to do what I wanted to do.

The first job I got at the zoo was working summers in the children's zoo. I was still going to college, so it was summer break. Every day I'd go to explore places in the zoo. Every lunchtime I'd go to a different place that I hadn't been to before. The last day I'm working with Debbie, a baby gorilla, and of course Pat, the senior keeper, who knew me before I started here; she knew me when I was a snot-nosed kid. And Debbie bit me, a puncture wound. Something happened, I don't know what; she bit my hand. It wasn't serious, but it was a puncture wound. And I said to myself, I gotta get a tetanus shot. But I was leaving, I was going to school the next day. Well, I'll go the health service, no problem.

So I went down to the health service at school. I knocked at the door, and the nurse came over. "I need a tetanus shot." "Oh, OK, come on in, come on in." She sat me down, asked my name, what year I was in, and the pertinent information. She said, "What bit you?" I said, "A gorilla bit me." So she was thinking, "Another smart-mouthed student." She said, "OK, that's pretty funny. Why don't we start from the beginning. You were bitten by an animal?" I said, "Yes, I was." She said, "What was it?" I said, "It was a gorilla."

I knew she was losing patience quickly, so I said, "Let me tell you what I did during the summer." "That's great," she said, "oh, that's so interesting, and blah blah blah," and then she said, "Would you wait here just a moment?" And I said, "I'm not going anywhere. I'm waiting for my shot." She went out, came back, and there were two doctors and a nurse with her. And one asked, "You were bitten by a gorilla yesterday?" I said yes, and I told my story again. And they put it in my record, so from that day on whenever I'd go to the health service for a scrape, I always had to explain the gorilla bite.

After college, the animal keeper exam came up, the civil service thing. I took it, passed, and was an animal keeper. And then there was another opening. I applied for that, and I got it. A job as a zoologist, a kind of assistant curator. There I was, a young zoologist who was in charge of keepers who had been there thirty years, guys that could have eaten me up and spit me out, because I had no background, no confidence in what I was doing. Academically, I knew more than they did, but that wasn't the test. Luckily for me, a number of senior people took me under their wing and said things like, "Just shut up and listen, and we'll get you through this." And I learned, made mistakes, and hoped that some of them were not bad enough to get me canned. It worked out.

Les Fisher promoted me to curator. His philosophy of management is very open-ended, very flexible. To some people, that's the kiss of death, because they need to know what to do. I'm not perfect, no one is, but that ability to let people be on their own, but be responsible, well, not many directors of zoos would allow you that freedom, especially in your formative years. Even if your actions were correct, there'd be a tighter rein on your responsibilities. Curators do many things on their own at Lincoln Park, not because the director told them they had to. If you deliver the goods, Les is happy. I think that somehow intuitively he knows if you're doing a good job or not doing a good job. Certain things were requested of you; if you followed through on those things, it was pretty obvious that you were responding to directives. And we picked up extra things that we would do and want to do.

I have a great interest in video. Now, that's not defined as my job. Anybody can use the video room. It's not *my* video room; I don't want it to be my video room. All the Marlin Perkins films, we have those kinescopes as part of our archives. No one said to me, your assignment is to work with Marlin and see if you can catalogue them. It was a three-year project. We have two hundred twenty of these films.

The zoo was always a very positive place for me. People always ask me at parties, or if they don't know me, "What do you do?" "I'm Mark Rosenthal, and I'm a curator at Lincoln Park Zoo." Almost always their reaction is, "That must be great, how wonderful, what is a curator?" I always say it's like being a curator of an art museum. You manage a collection. I tell people what I really do, and they ask, "How do you do all that?" I don't know. You learn about certain things. I mean, I work with nutrition. I'm not the nutrition expert of the world. I work with the vets; we do research projects. I deal with all kinds of keepers and personnel. We put exhibits together, we design things. I'm learning a lot more. I'm not a videotape editor. I can do a little of it, and I'm learning, but when we needed to really get it done, I got the services of somebody who knew what was going on. So to me I'm a manager, manager of a collection, and I've been free to expand that a great deal.

If there's any snag in the job, it's that we don't get paid enough money. When I met Marlin Perkins when I was very young, and my mother cornered him in the zoo, she said to him, "Here's my ten-year-old kid, and he always wants to work with animals." Marlin said, "If you want to have fun, that's a great job; if you want to make money, go into something else." In certain ways, he was right. Of course Marlin had it all, so he could talk. On one hand, I think that's one of the problems: we don't get paid enough for what we do. On the other hand, I'm a big enough boy to know that I could go and do something else that paid more, and then I don't have to crab about it. I truly believe that in the next year or so, just being good little soldiers and presenting our side of it, we will get what we feel is the type of salary that a major zoo should be paying its curators, what major zoos in the United States do pay their curators. The keepers deserve everything they get, but they have a union. I don't have a union. I happen to be single. I've often wondered how married people on a keeper level with kids do things. I've been able to make do with my salary, and I can't complain. On the other hand, I know I'm not being paid what I feel I'm worth. I say that not as curator, but for all the curators.

Being a curator and retiring as a curator is certainly not the worst thing in the world one can do. I've thought that maybe being a director gives you that end point of creativity and that it might be an interesting career move. I am not sure I yet have what I consider all the skills to be a director, and that's more of financial management, things that have nothing to do with animals.

I think that you develop relationships with certain animals. God help you if you didn't, because why would you want to be here? When I was a young zoologist at the zoo, the only elephant that had been in Lincoln Park Zoo was Judy. I worked with her a little, and one day we came in, and Judy was down on the ground. I had seen other animals live and die. When the first couple that I was working with died, it left an impact, but it passed, and I went on to do other things. Well, we worked all day on Judy trying to get her up, and she wouldn't get up. There was something wrong. We later found out it was a blood vessel that had burst in the brain, and she'd had a stroke, but at the time we didn't know that. And so many people came in; the repair and construction forces were called in. How do you lift this elephant, how can we have a sling, what can we do? She was obviously trying to respond to commands, but couldn't. We worked all day, brought all kinds of people in, a lot of energy was exerted. And then in the end, that day she died. And that was a very sad time. It was losing an animal friend that I had known, more as a young child growing up, than as one who had directly worked with her, but that day of intense trying to save her was very emotional at the end. As the years go by, you see so many animals die and be born. The joy of seeing my first gazelle born was a special joy, wonderful, but the feeling of the thirty-eighth gazelle is different from the first. And the death of a first animal as opposed to the four hundredth animal that you've lost is different.

When I was a summer volunteer, still a kid, a curator told me, enjoy your time with the animals, because the higher you go in any job, the further away you are from that which brought you there. If you really want to work with animals, then you don't want to be a curator. I do interact with them, but it's not on a daily basis. I'm more removed.

I do get in and work with the elephants; I try to keep up with that every once in a while. That gives me direct feedback. Maybe that's why I like elephants, because you know exactly where you stand. I mean, they're either listening to you, or they're not. You're either in charge of what's going on, or you're not. A relationship is built up. They respect you. You use certain tricks to get them to respect you, because you are little and they are big. Everybody can't go in and work the elephants. You have to pay your dues, and I think that is what makes me accepted by the elephant keepers, because I paid my dues, and they know that. I'm not as good as they are, because they do it every day.

Some animals recognize me, and that's enjoyment. A bat

does not recognize me, but the chimps do, the gorillas recognize me. When Sinbad the gorilla died, that was very sad. I had worked with Sinbad. I mean I'd been a keeper hosing out the cages, and he had thrown stuff at me, and I knew him. There are not many personalities in a zoo. They all may have house names, or the majority may be known to their own individual keepers, but when Sinbad died, it was in the newspapers, the headlines. It won't be when Mark goes, but when Sinbad died, it was. Certain animals have that individual personality that the public likes. And usually it's mammals. That's not to say disparaging things about birds or reptiles, but . . .

Of course, we do have our critics. Someone says to me, "You know that giraffe that you have, he's not free."

Where is he free?

"What do you mean, where is he free? Don't be stupid. In the wilds he's free, in Africa."

But he's not free in the wild, he's not free in Africa.

"What do you mean?"

What I mean is, this animal has certain biological needs that are a fact of nature, that keep him or her or it in a certain area. Giraffes don't travel all over Africa, they have territories. They don't deviate from those territories; in fact, they're very regimented within those territories. There are constraints. Whatever those are, be they made by man or be they biological, there are constraints. Why don't I go off and live on an island? If I had a lot of money, maybe that's what I would do. But maybe I wouldn't, because of my family, because of this or that. So when people throw the word *free* around, I try to make them define what free means. I think that wherever we get our animals, from captivity or from the wild, we have an obligation to do the right thing, because they have not chosen to be at Lincoln Park Zoo; we have made a conscious decision to bring them here.

When I hear critics attack the zoo, I think of what British author Gerald Durrell wrote in his book *Beasts in My Belfry*:

It is hard to argue with these people [people who do not like to see animals 'imprisoned']; they live in a euphoric state where they believe that an animal in a zoo suffers as though it were in Dartmoor and an animal in its natural surroundings is living in a 'Garden of Eden' where the lamb can lie down with the lion without starting in friendship and ending up as dinner. It is useless to point out the ceaseless drudgery of finding adequate food supplies each day in the wilds, of the constant strain on the nerves of avoiding enemies, of the battle against disease and parasites, of the fact that in some species there is a more than 50% mortality rate among the young in the first 6 months. 'Ah,' these bemused animal lovers will say when these are pointed out to them 'but they are *free*.' You point out that animals have strict territories that are governed by three things: food, water and sex! Provide all these successfully within a limited area and the animals will stay there.

But the people seem to be obsessed with this word, freedom, particularly when applied to animals. They never seem to worry about the freedom of the bank clerks of Streathem, the miners of Durham, the factory hands of Sheffield, the carpenters of Hartley Wintney, or the head waiters of Soho, yet if a careful survey were conducted on these and other similar species, you would find that they are confined by their jobs and by convention as securely as any zoo inmate.

We have to give our animals the best conditions that we can for them to live in, and that's a very basic thing. I would be the first to admit if someone said, "Ah, but there are bad zoos." That's right, and hopefully through education and through other reforms, some of them through national organizations, you can make those bad zoos be better zoos. If you treat an animal with respect, give it the type of food that the animal needs, give it the proper lodging that it's within your power to do, meet the biological needs that it has as an animal, I think the public will see the animals as representatives of their kind in the wild. Part of a zoo's mission is to give people an appreciation of the animal world around them. Many people live in cities, and it's as strange to an African kid in Nairobi to know what a lion is as it is for a kid here to know about cows and where milk comes from.

A gorilla family living together and interacting one and five-eighths inches away from the public gives the public a greater appreciation of the size, the scope, the speed, the intimacy. Why are zoos around? Well, one reason zoos are around is that people have an affinity for animals. They like being around animals, they like being near animals, they like to know the animals are around. I don't want to say it's some inward genetic quality that is within all of us, but it certainly is something that is learned, however it has evolved. I mean when men were hunters, there was this affinity, there was this need for a relationship with animals. You killed, you revered what you killed. Why? Because the animal gave you life. The Eskimos do it today; that's their philosophy. I think people have a positive feeling about being around animals.

Sure, animals die here as they die in the wild, but on the other hand, as the wild shrinks, I think zoos play an ultimately greater part than they ever have before, and the fact that they realize it makes it even more important, because in certain ways they're just coming to discover their destiny. Zoos will never be the saviors of all the animals in the world. No way; it can't happen. But on the other hand, they can play an integral part in the whole equation. They will play their part.

What is their part? Managing isolated populations for the long-term good. We get information from the wild; we hopefully give it back. More and more zoos will find that niche in the conservation of animals, and they will exploit it in a positive way and be part of that mass of people doing whatever they can to bring their expertise to save living things.

I learn about the animals every day. With the great apes, you have animals that are intelligent, very strong, and in the chimpanzees and gorillas, you have a sense of family. So when you're exhibiting those kinds of animals or you're working with them, you have to consider their strength and their thinking ability and the different personalities of the animals. We have some gorillas, males, that like certain females, and others like other females, and certain females don't get along with other females. So in group composition, that individual personality of the animal has to be considered, just as it would be in the wild.

Apes are smart. For example, we put together this termite mound, which essentially was a device for chimpanzees, who could take pieces of twigs, push the twigs down into a small hole, and come out with a honeylike substance, and they'd get just a little of it. Now, this was imitating something that was seen in the wild by Jane Goodall, where the chimps would use simple tools, and they would stick them into termite mounds, termites would come out at the end of them, they'd eat the termites. We put the mound in, put the ketchup, honey, whatever it was we were using, and then we put the twigs in, and the keeper said, "Shall we put the twigs in the holes?" And I said, "No, just leave them in the cage." Within ten minutes, the chimps had taken the twigs and were using them in the holes to get the food. They'd never seen the device before. I'm sure they smelled a honey substance or odor, I think they knew there was something down there; the question was how did they get it? They took these twigs, and all of a sudden one played around with it and stuck it in and came out with a reward, and that was that.

Yes, they're smart. If there's a whole group of people, and I walk over, they'll come over to me, if it's other people they don't know. They'll give me a greeting. Chimpanzees have a way of greeting one another. Sometimes it'll take the form of a hand held out, waving it. Sometimes it'll take the form of coming up to the bars and presenting them-

selves, submitting, showing you their rear, a form of submission saying, "I submit to you, and you don't have to do
anything more than acknowledge it."

The gorillas and chimps can be very tough, if they're
aggressive. If they run away from you, that's one thing; if
they're running at you, that's another thing. We had a
young gorilla that had taken one of the ropes somehow and
wrapped it around his arm and twisted it so tightly that he
couldn't untwist it, and he was caught and was crying. We
had to move all of the other gorillas out of the exhibit, but
that took time, because they were concerned about their
friend, and they didn't want to leave. We couldn't just go in
until they left. We went up on the top of the exhibit, cut
the rope, so there was no longer any pressure. And then we
had to go in and remove it from the animal. Now he was a
small animal, so it wasn't like we were really worried. On
the other hand, sometimes you have to tranquilize them.
With Donna the chimp, whose baby we took for hand-
raising, the only way we could get that kid away from
Donna was to tranquilize her. It gave us an opportunity to
check her medically. She wasn't about to leave the kid, but
she wasn't about to take care of it either. And we didn't
want her to drag the kid all over and do it some harm.

The newborns keep us busy. Bonding is very important.
When we have zebras born, or any hoofed stock, we try to
keep mom with the kid for at least twenty-four hours
alone, to have that child bond on that particular female,
and make sure it's a strong bond, rather than throw them
out with the herd right away. Then, of course, you also can
monitor the animals, depending on the species. Is it nursing? We've used the closed-circuit time lapse a lot for those
kinds of things with zebras. What's the behavior of the kid
the first couple of hours? That's been very handy for us to
have, and I think very good for keepers to see also.

We have a seventy-two-hour protocol for the great apes
when they have babies, and that's based on when Mary the
gorilla had a baby many years ago. The doctor said it could

go five days without nursing, and then, at the end of those five days, as a maximum, if you had a problem and it wasn't nursing, you had to take it. Well that was OK, you still could bring it back, and it wouldn't be the end of the world. At the end of five days, she wasn't nursing it; we pulled the baby to the nursery, and we lost it. We felt maybe kids can last five days in extreme circumstances, but why should that be a protocol, let's back it up three days. Now we still have some latitude, and then we'll make a decision, so we came up with the seventy-two-hour protocol, and that's been reasonably successful. You have to monitor things very specifically. Certainly with a kid, with first-time mothers.

The sea lions are very active animals; I think that's why the exhibit attracts a lot of people. I think that they're intelligent, curious, and energetic animals. They're doing one of two things, generally: they're sleeping and sunning themselves, or they're in the water, patrolling, moving around. They're very much afraid of things that are new or strange to them. When we have divers go into the pool to clean the bottom, pick up pennies, they'll always stay away from the divers. After an hour or so of someone being in the tank, they'll start coming closer, but it's more inquisitive than it is aggressive. They can be hostile, but that's rare.

If it has teeth, it can bite, and it depends on the situation. Mothers defending their babies can be very aggressive. Big beach masters, big males, defending their harems, can be tough at certain times of the year on dry land. So you'd have to be aware of those and be sensitive to that, and usually you can work around it.

One of the things that we've tried to do with the small mammal house is show the diversity of the small mammals that are in the world. When I walk through the building, what always catches my eye is the African crested porcupine. It really is a very striking animal, not as small as the elephant shrew, but certainly very striking. The other creatures that people like among the small mammals are the smaller primates, the marmosets and the saki monkeys.

If the elephants aren't the smartest, they're among the smartest of all the animals. They show an intelligence; they learn very quickly and respond to dozens of commands, verbal commands, that the keepers through training reinforce. They are not above solving problems and making the keepers think all the time. Anytime you have an animal that thinks and is as big as an elephant, then the keepers always have to be one step ahead. They can never lose their temper or their cool; they have to be thinking all the time.

Elephants will test you. So will chimpanzees and gorillas and other thinking animals. A good example is in the children's zoo. We would have chimpanzees there that we were raising. Pat Sass was keeper then at the children's zoo, and she'd walk in and work with the chimps. She'd tell them, through training, "Sit on your shelf so I can clean," and they'd sit on the shelf. She'd give them a treat. And then when she'd leave, they would go swinging around. Well, whenever anybody else came into the exhibit and was going to clean it, he or she would say the same thing: "Sit on the shelf." Well, the chimps would sit on the shelf, but this was another person, so how far can we push this person? Well, they might stand up on the shelf. And then if the person didn't say anything right away, they would swing a little, and then they'd swing a little more, and if the person didn't perceive it as a problem, they'd just go beyond, beyond, beyond. They knew they didn't have to listen. Pat would walk by, see it, walk through the door and say, "Go sit on the shelf." They were on the shelf. They can differentiate between people they know and people they are going to test.

Camels are stubborn and not very inquisitive. We have traditionally halter-broken the young camels and used them as exhibit animals to be close to people. But as they get older, we don't do that. Camels can be mean; camels can spit. That's when they really get upset.

Giraffes are kind of beautiful, elegant, nondescript animals. I mean, they're there, they're majestic, they're tall, they're fleet of foot, many positive things, but because there are no vocalizations in the giraffe adults and because they're not hyper animals like the seals, jumping and running and so forth—they're stately—they have a very positive regalness, but they don't have much of a personality. Maybe every keeper who works with them would beg to differ with me, and they probably are very responsive to the keepers they know. But that takes time.

In most cases, keepers do achieve some kind of rapport with their animals. It can be as simple as when you open the door to clean the cage, and the animal tends to move to a certain spot. And then you do your cleaning, never interacting with the animal. On the other hand, with small mammals, you might be cleaning an exhibit, and the animal will hop on your shoulder. Never going farther than your shoulder, going back to the exhibit. But it will not bite you. Others are too skittish, or you have to move them into holding areas while you clean their area; you wouldn't want to go in with them because that might bother them too much, and they might try to escape. Not to freedom, but away from your presence and then get into trouble.

Rhinos are another matter—very powerful, in short bursts of energy. They are not too good in the eyesight department; they're much better smellers. They tend to like regularity. You start throwing new things into their routine, and it takes them a while to adjust.

Pygmy hippos are very fast, aggressive animals who are a no-nonsense kind of animal. You leave them alone, they'll leave you alone. You push them, and they'll show their teeth and are not afraid to fight.

Bears are very smart. In circuses, bears pick up tricks right away. Very sharp. So the intelligence is there. And they're very inquisitive; they'll check all the locks and

check all the perimeters of their exhibit and will be me-
thodical about it. The problem with bears always seems to
be that, for some reason, they're very difficult to read.
When your cat's ears go down and its mouth opens up, it's
generally an aggressive kind of thing, a defensive thing,
you have a feel for what's going on. You may not know
exactly what's happening but you kind of have a feel. With
bears, they don't telegraph those feelings as much. And so,
to me, if any animal is going to be really a dangerous
animal in a zoo, a bear would be. Bears are powerful, they
may not be afraid of people, they're potentially dangerous,
they're big, they have teeth, they can be fast. If I were
locked into an open space with a bear or a lion, I'd rather be
in with a lion. I might have more of a chance.

Timber wolves are very social animals, timid at times
but inquisitive. They want to investigate things that are in
their exhibit all the time. They're very defensive about
their territory. We had an unfortunate incident with a
Doberman pinscher last year that ran into the zoo and
somehow got in between the public railing and the edge of
the timber wolf yard. Some keepers tried to catch it, but it
bit one of the keepers. We had to capture the dog because it
might have had rabies. Before we could do that, the dog
jumped into the timber wolf yard to get away from us, and
as it did, all the wolves attacked it immediately and killed it.
It was very quick, very fast. The maned wolves tend to be
different. They're more laid-back; they're not a troop animal or a group animal, just pairs.

Polar bears are smart, too. Remember, they're a major
predator in the area that they live in. They have to be a
thinking animal, to be immensely strong; some of the seals
that they pull up out of the air holes that the seals are in
weigh hundreds of pounds, and the bear does it easily.

In the primate house, I like to watch Admiral; he's a
wanderoo macaque. He's the oldest wanderoo we have.
And he'll jut his chin out. That may be a behavioral greeting to people. Or, on the other hand, sometimes male
primates will constantly flash their teeth and yawn, and

open their mouth to show you what their weapons are. It's a visual signal to let you know, "This is off limits, and these are my weapons." Mandrills will do it a lot; people mistake it for yawning.

I like the marmosets. Small, colorful, squirrel-like, very interesting, very hyper little guys. The family situation: mom, dad, usually two to three kids, and there may be another litter after that, that would be their family troop.

It's an old joke: A lion's walking down the pathway, and he sees this baboon, and he roars out to the baboon, "Who's king of the jungle?" The baboon is not near a tree; none of his troop is around, he's afraid. And he says, "Oh, your majesty, you are, of course." The lion says, "That's right, I'm the king." And he walks a little farther down, and he sees a zebra, and he says to the zebra, "Zebra, who's the king of the jungle?" And the zebra looks at him, and he's not near his herd, and there's no defense, and he's a prey animal, so he says, "Oh, your majesty, you're the king of the beasts." The lion says, "That's right, I certainly am." And he walks farther, and he comes to an elephant. And he roars at the elephant, "Elephant, who's the king of the beasts?" And the elephant looks down at him and picks him up with his trunk and throws him down on the ground and kicks some dirt on him and walks down the road. The lion gets up, brushes himself off, and yells down to the elephant walking away, "Hey, just 'cause you didn't know the answer, you don't have to get upset."

The elephant is the true king of the beasts.

Among the big cats, I find the leopards most interesting, and the tigers more interesting than the lions. Certainly, as a social animal, the lion's more interesting, because it's one of the few that forms a social grouping. When I have talked to trainers of cats, they have often said that a lion can be bullied at times and might have to be dominated, but a tiger needs to be talked to; they're a little more sensitive. You can't just shout them down, because they're going to be upset for a long time. That's similar to elephants: African elephants tend to be a bit more flighty, you can hurt their feelings with a word, where Asian elephants tend to be animals you really have to dominate, and they have to know that you are the person giving the orders.

Keepers can build up a rapport with hoofed stock— antelope, gazelles, members of the herd. It takes a long time, but it's possible for a keeper working every day with animals to build up a rapport. It depends on the keeper. In Europe they do it a lot. Here in the United States, it's more of a remote control thing: animals in, animals out. You're managing them remote control, not hands-on. But it is possible for a keeper to build up associations with the hoofed stock, absolutely. Of course, we tend not to walk among them for a number of reasons. One, we don't want them to flee from us and get hurt, go through barriers because they're excited. The other thing is that the animals, the antelopes and the zebras, unless they're conditioned and unless you visit them on a regular basis and condition them to something, they're not going to be responsive to the keeper. Being familiar with them may put you in dangerous situations. A good example is the guy who every day goes to the paddock where the deer are, and he goes in with the deer and he rakes the yard. Every day he takes a bagel, and he throws it away, and the male deer goes and eats the bagel. So this guy can do his work, he throws him another bagel. Now the guy goes on vacation, and the relief guy comes on. And the regular keeper doesn't bother to communicate to the relief guy that he gives the deer a bagel every day. So the relief guy comes in and starts to work, and the deer comes over, he's expecting his bagel. This guy doesn't know anything because there's been no communication, so he doesn't give him any food. The deer gets upset. I want my bagel. Well, he may do something, be aggressive toward the guy. He has antlers.

Deer, or any bull animal in rut, in a season where he's breeding females, has to be considered dangerous, and you don't just go in with them, because they will have their full array of weapons. So you have to be respectful.

We have many missions. There has been a trend in the last couple of years to have species-survival programs, to use all of the zoos in the United States as pools of animals, to breed animals, rather than one zoo or two zoos doing it exclusively. The pool becomes larger then. We all try to work for a minimum number of animals to be born every year to replace those that die. To continue the genetic diversity, we use all of the zoos in cooperative programs. And I think the majority of zoos have gone along with that. Lincoln Park can't do it all, but to certain animals we want to make long-term commitments. Apes. Bears. Maned wolves. Black rhinoceroses. Pygmy hippos, certain of the lemur species, and tamarin species. A lot of those tend to be listed as endangered. Also, we want to continue to show animals that are not endangered, and we try to maintain breeding programs on some, but not all of them.

You cooperate with other zoos. Before you start, you sign a breeding loan agreement with the other zoo. Everything is very specifically spelled out. If the animal dies while at the other zoo, you don't expect them to accept any kind of responsibility for replacing the animal, and they of course will assure you that they will feed and care for it correctly, and then you work out some division of offspring.

But I don't spend all my time on major projects. Sometimes a ringing phone makes me busy. We once got phone calls from the press asking about a report that a kangaroo had been spotted by two police officers in Chicago. Then, we got calls from all over the city reporting this kangaroo, and the radio stations were picking up on it; it was a good story. People swore that they were seeing kangaroos in their back yards, and we started plotting them on a graph. The kangaroo would have had to have been in a teleport machine to get to some of the places, in a time limit, through the city. It turned out to be a hoax.

We got a call that there was a snakelike animal in the engine block of a car on the South Side. The police called us. They wanted to know if someone who was familiar with snakes could go down to the South Side to this garage and investigate it. The police picked up our reptile curator, and I wanted to go along just for the ride. We zipped down there. Big crowd. Eddie—the curator—fiddled in the engine block for a while, and he actually pulled out, not a snake, but a lizard, a Tegu lizard, a lizard from central South America. And it's a big animal, a foot and a half, two feet, something like that. As Eddie was working on it, he was bending over the engine block, and the crowd of hundreds of people were all around him in a circle, looking, and when he pulled that out of the engine block and held it up, you know, because he's tussling, and he finally gets it up, it was like throwing a stone in a pond and watching the ripples go out. The circle of people was about a hundred feet from him. And we bagged it, and then took it back to the zoo. How it got in the engine God only knows.

Years ago, we got a call that there was this large cat on LaSalle Street, killing pigeons. A big cat. Our veterinarian called me, and we went to investigate. Sure enough, high in a tree, we saw a bobcat. I mean it was distinctive, bigger than a housecat; you could see it, so we called the fire department and said, "There is something up there, and we can tranquilize it or try to snare it, but we need a snorkel." They brought out the snorkel unit with all the firefighters that have to come with it, and it had to be approved by downtown. We had all the capture equipment, and a small crowd was there, mostly firefighters. And we said, "Well, we've got to have somebody go up and shoot it, with the tranquilizer gun, or try to lasso it or do something." The firefighters said, "We'll get you up there, but we won't do anything else. You have to send somebody." So we sent the reptile curator up there. He went up there, and he saw that the shot would be too dangerous, so he put a catch pole on it, and ripped it out of the tree. It was holding on with all its claws, and it was dangling there from the catch pole making choking noises. We got it down; the vet worked on it, revived it, and we put it in a cage, and it went to Indian Boundary Zoo.

That's one way to acquire an animal. There are more conventional ways. We don't deal with private individuals. That's been a general policy. Nor do we sell to the general public; that's been a policy, too. We generally sell through accepted avenues, and we pick up animals through accepted avenues, so we know where they are and where they come from, and get a good health history on them. Many times we get calls from people wanting to know more about exotic pets. We try to dissuade them from having anything exotic. The official zoo advice is not to have exotic pets. We don't recommend it, and indeed we don't recommend it because a lot of times calls that we get from people to donate animals to the zoo are because they took exotic animals as pets, and they didn't really have an idea of what would happen when they grew up, or how much work it would be, or that they're potentially dangerous. So we wind up with them.

When I first came to the zoo, I worked as a keeper on the bear line. We had spectacled bears; they were small, the only bears in South America. There wasn't much known about them, compared to other bears, and it just seemed to me that they were interesting and had a story to tell. One could add to the information about them, one could help out in answering questions about them. We weren't doing much with them.

One of the things that the zoo can do, as opposed to people in the field studying animals, is to add certain things to the literature with the animals that we have at the zoo, in a research-conservation kind of way. And when you get animals that are endangered and you can add to the information, it seems that you should do it. And we can't do it with all, so you tend to pick animals that interest you for whatever reason. The bears? Maybe it's because I had a teddy bear like everybody else. God only knows.

You can't work with creatures day after day and not feel

something for the animals in your care. Obviously, the keeper on the line has that direct contact with the animal every day and would be more emotional or caring than the pathologist who finally dissects the creature and learns what some of the problems are, who's never really worked with it. You do get jaded to certain things. It's not that you're uncaring; it's just that some things become matter-of-fact routines.

My first death had to do with a dehorning of a deer at Indian Boundary. Antlers fall off anyway, and there's a methodology, and you tranquilize the animal. That deer died under the anesthesia we were giving it. And that bothered me. I mean, my first animal, and I administered the stuff, and we had a consulting vet who told us what to do. I was just devastated. When you're dealing with a hundred and fifty bats in an exhibit, and you find one dead, it's still a concern, it still goes to pathology, you still want to learn why it happened, but there is less affinity to one of one hundred fifty bats than there is to one deer. That's the fact.

Animals get out; I guess it's inevitable. A lot of times it's human error which allows that to happen. One night I got a call at midnight from a zoo security guard, and he said, "The lions are out." And I said, "Out where?" The kind of call you really need at midnight. "Out where? Out on the grounds or out in the building, where?" "Out in the building." I said, "Well, then they're contained. I don't know how they got out, but they are contained, and we'll slowly deal with it and find the best solution."

So I ran to the zoo and found the security guard. He had been making rounds in the lion house and had seen some of the lions chewing on a rubber hose. The keeper must have left the rubber hose, the water hose, too close to the door, and the lions had somehow reached out and grabbed it and were biting off pieces of it. He was going to be a good guy, go in the back area, pull the hose away so they couldn't get more of it. The truth of what had happened was the keeper had neglected to lock a lock for some reason; the lions had pushed against the door, gotten out, and grabbed the hose and were bringing it back in. So when he went in the back, he turned a corner and walked straight into a male lion looking at him. They scared each other. The lion ran one way because he was scared, and the guard ran the other way, and that's when he called me.

Of course, it was a police emergency, and I called the director of the zoo right away when I got there, and some other keepers for help to get some backup. Les Fisher's line was busy, so I took care of things at the zoo and got everything squared away. And police started coming in droves. They secured the outside; they weren't allowing reporters in. Les Fisher arrived and said, "Why didn't you call me?" I said, "Well, I tried, but your line was busy." The police had asked for the heavy weapons truck to come to the zoo, and that's monitored by all the TV and radio and so forth, so they called Les Fisher up right away and asked him to comment on lions being loose at the zoo. He didn't know anything, and no one could get through to him because the press was calling. We made sure all the lions who were going back and forth in the back area behind their den returned to their exhibit. Then the guard who originally had called me and I went in. I had a fire extinguisher with me because that makes a lot of noise and has a lot of foam, and it scares a lot of animals. The guard had a gun, a shotgun, and we went in and closed the door and resecured the animals. That was it; there was no big deal. But there was, for about an hour and a half, two hours, a little tension, trying to make sure everything worked out OK.

Another day I was sleeping late and was going to take an hour or so before I got to work. I got a call at eight o'clock in the morning. "You'd better get here right away." "Why?" "Polar bear's out." Well, that's not good. Polar bears, anything that's a predator, like a cat, especially bears, can be very unpredictable. I was at the zoo in three minutes. And indeed one of the polar bears had scaled a light ice ladder that had formed from a hose throwing water. This polar bear female had gotten just the right footing. A keeper had seen her scale the ice, couldn't get her to go down, so he called everybody.

We shut the zoo down and got everybody out. The polar bear was not out in the general public area, but it was in a secondary area, obviously out of its cage, though behind the scenes. We got the capture equipment out. We're all trained to use it in emergencies. I loaded up, shot the bear in the rump with the standard dose that we have for just such an emergency, and the bear started to go to sleep. I put another dart into it, and the bear went to sleep. The keepers then rolled it on a tarp and put her into the den, where she slept it off. But for half an hour it was pretty good excitement there; we had a lot of police, we were trying to direct them, make sure that they didn't get in our way but were around. We wanted to contain the situation and make sure everybody was safe.

We had a heavy weapon in case it was needed, but it turned out it wasn't. The darts always work. It's a question of how fast. If an animal is stressed, that amount of concentrated drug may not work as well as if the animal's in a relaxed state. So you have to take that into consideration. I figured I'd done everything I could do that day. I wasn't ready to just go back to doing paperwork.

When I was videotaping those two trumpeter swans, I knew that what had happened was just a minor injury, one that didn't need the vet to look at it. Of course, we called the vet anyway. Anytime we do filming like that, it has to be opportunistic, and I knew that they were going to be moving those swans to Indian Boundary, and that the birds were probably going to be agitated. So there's always a risk; you try to minimize the risk by doing it the proper way. It was opportunistic to get an animal to respond that may again, down the road, save keepers from being hurt by an aggressive animal or to save an animal from being hurt by a keeper misreading it or not handling it correctly. In that context, everything was OK. We don't want to have any animal hurt, regardless of when we handle it.

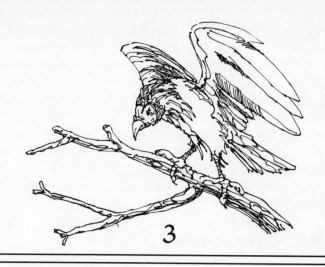

3

FLYING OBJECTS

Kevin Bell went into the family business: birds.

Kevin was born in New York City in 1952, the son of Joseph Bell, distinguished curator of birds (and chairman of the department of ornithology) at New York's Bronx Zoo. Kevin's father, who died in 1986, was more than a curator of birds; he was a woodcarver, a painter, and an author. His text for *Metropolitan Zoo*, a volume of works depicting animals from the collection of the Metropolitan Museum of Art in New York, is a respected commentary on animals and on art.

His father passed along to Kevin a knowledge of birds and a fondness for them. Kevin did not need to choose a career; he knew, from an early age, what it would be.

He got his bachelor's degree in biology from Syracuse University and his master's in zoology from the State University of New York. While he was still in graduate school, he heard about the search for a curator of birds at the Lincoln Park Zoo, and that zoo's director, Les Fisher, heard about Kevin from a mutual friend. Kevin joined the zoo staff in February 1976.

Once depicted on television and in the New York press as "Kevin Bell, the little boy who grew up in the zoo," the adult Kevin was ready to assume command of the bird population at the zoo. Eleven years later, he was firmly in charge.

A slim (150 pounds) six-footer with a brown beard, Kevin's angular frame was often seen in motion around the zoo. As one keeper observed, "If Mark Rosenthal looks like a mammal, Kevin certainly looks like a bird." Kevin spent long hours at the zoo. A bachelor, he also had a social life: for a while he lived with assistant veterinarian Peri Wolff and before that had been known to fraternize with some of the best-looking women keepers.

His social life had to suffer; it was not unusual to find him at the zoo before 6 A.M., in jeans and dress shirt, with sleeves rolled up. He often worked late and on weekends as well. His was a job clogged with paperwork and phone calls.

His neat office in the bird house was lined with the elements of his trade. Two incubators warmed eggs about to hatch. Design plans for the renovation of the bird house abounded. Reference books, a typewriter, and various journals added to the pragmatic decor.

On one cloudy summer day, he arrived at work a few minutes before 6 A.M. The sea lions were resting atop the rocks in their pool area. The lions were stretching, welcoming the day in their outdoor habitat. The monkeys had begun to chatter. Except for a few dedicated joggers, Kevin had little human company.

In his office, he discovered that one of the old incubators had failed; the motor had burned out. Before it could be repaired, a trumpeter swan's egg was lost. One of Kevin's missions was to breed those swans, then release them in the wild of northern Michigan. He couldn't bring back the unhatched swan, but he could attempt to revive the incubator; he phoned for an electrician.

He got up, discouraged, and walked around the vastness of the empty bird house; only the birds' eyes were on him.

He walked past the sterile glass-and-tile cages and the central free-flight area for birds; he deplored the old-fashioned barren confinement for them and looked forward to the redesign, a drastic shift to naturalistic habitats.

In 1983, he had suggested the specifications for that renovation. Outside the bird house, a large complex of cages would house birds of prey. The well-known architectural firm Skidmore, Owings and Merrill would design it. The main cage would be thirty-five feet high, one-hundred feet long, forty feet deep. It would contain a large cliff, a waterfall, a pool, and appropriate plantings. There would be two vulture species in large groups, some storks, and, in smaller cages, eagles, large owls, and hawks—all with access to heated dens and nesting areas on the cliffs (made of Gunite sprayed over a steel frame and contoured by hand to match the look of the wild). It would be ready, he hoped, in the spring of 1988. After that, the bird house itself would be renovated. The birds now in it would be sent to other zoos. Most of them wouldn't be retrieved. The new bird house would have birds suited to the new habitats.

He walked out of the bird house and strolled toward the flamingo dome, where the flamingos wintered. Inside the dome, tiny young ducks—summer transients—quacked and moved rapidly in a holding tub.

"We let them fly away in the fall. We don't need them," he said.

Outside the dome, beside the waterfowl lagoon, the flamingos gathered, a design in pink—tall, stately, ever-watchful. Kevin looked at them.

"Graceful creatures. Ours are Chilean flamingos," he said. "They appear to be very delicate, but their life in the wild was actually rather rugged. They live at high altitudes and can withstand very cold temperatures and very harsh climates. One of the reasons we don't allow them outside in winter isn't because of the temperature, but because the pond freezes. They can get into trouble walking on ice."

A large group of ducks and geese were noisy and busy on

that pond. The waterfowl area was a haven for North American waterfowl; their presence attracted migratory birds. When waterfowl were born at the zoo, they joined those migratory birds in the fall.

"We have only one species of goose, the emperor goose, and one swan species, the trumpeter swan. Plenty of birds pass through here. Warblers pass through in the spring and in the fall. Certain species we see only for a couple of days, and then they're gone; others can be seen for weeks. Some are around all summer. Then they're gone. They'll fly all the way into Central America, the Caribbean, and beyond, even to South America," he said.

The bird house, the penguin-seabird house, the flamingo dome, the waterfowl lagoon, and the zoo rookery—the small nature preserve at the edge of the zoo grounds—composed Kevin's domain. So did the Indian Boundary Zoo, a little zoo in a park on the city's Northwest Side. Once or twice a week, Kevin borrowed a park district pickup truck and drove to that zoo.

On that summer day, with the clouds fading and the sun beginning to bake the city, he made his way through nagging traffic and annoying road repairs to Indian Boundary. As he approached the park, he spotted a nun in her habit, playing tennis on a park court. He smiled.

At the satellite zoo, he made rounds. It didn't take long.

"This is a tough zoo to manage," he said. "There's no nighttime protection for the animals, so we have to bring them in at night."

He passed a pair of yaks; their mood was between relaxed and sluggish. He spotted a pair of trumpeter swans that had been at the main zoo. He greeted them with a wave. The swans trumpeted. One of them had arrived with a small scrape on its wing, a souvenir of an encounter with Mark Rosenthal's videotaping project.

"It's healed," Kevin noted.

A few chubby pheasants shared the pen with the swans. "They won't intimidate the swans," Kevin said. "Nothing scares them."

Nearby, three alpacas were basking in the sun. Next to

them, in their own pen, three reindeer demonstrated their wisdom by splashing in a pool. In a third pen, pygmy goats, some chickens, and a rabbit played out their communal existence.

Inside the small zoo building, Kevin was greeted by two housecats and a temporary keeper filling in for the regular keeper, who had a day off.

"Those yaks are nice animals," the keeper told Kevin. "We should get more of them."

"Talk to your curator," Kevin said, referring to Mark Rosenthal.

"Those swans honk a lot," the keeper told Kevin, waiting for a response. There was none. "But they don't bother us," the keeper went on.

Kevin entered the alpacas' pen; slowly, they moved away from him. So did the reindeer, when he entered their pen.

Kevin conferred briefly with the keeper, walked briskly around, and then, satisfied that there weren't any problems for him to deal with, got into his pickup and drove away.

Overhead, within view, a small, slender bird in shades of green and gray flew by.

"Quaker parakeet," Kevin said, pointing at the bird. "It was probably released into the wild of Chicago by an owner who got tired of it. Most parakeets that you buy in pet stores are expensive, as much as five hundred or even a thousand dollars. But the quaker may go for just forty-nine ninety-five. They're colorful, but what the buyers don't know is that they're not as likely to talk as the more costly ones. They're just noisy. And most of them are adults, not likely to be tamed. A year after it's been bought, the owner gets tired of it and tries to sell it or give it to a zoo. When there aren't any takers, the owner just releases it.

Fortunately, they form groups; there are others out there. I've seen a group at the tennis courts on Fifty-fifth Street. And they survive. They build a stick nest, a community nest. In New York, you'll see them with missing toes. Frostbite. But if there's food, they survive, even in winter.

"We don't take any birds unless we have a need for them

or know a zoo that does. If you do take one, it has to be quarantined for thirty days. That's a bother."

Kevin didn't have much time for city bird-watching. He preferred to see them in Iceland. He had gone there eight times, to observe and capture the baby puffins he'd admired ever since he wrote his master's thesis about them.

The wild seabirds intrigued him. Most of each year, they lived at sea. In summer, they returned to land to raise their young. That's when Kevin wanted to be there. His efforts had been captured in a film, *Arctic Window*, an Emmy-Award–winning documentary familiar to viewers of public television.

Back at the Lincoln Park Zoo a few minutes after he left Indian Boundary, Kevin headed for the penguin-seabird house, one of the new buildings and one of the buildings that existed because of his zeal.

He entered the building, followed the curve of the walkway, and confronted the penguin exhibit, along with a crowd of mothers and small children. Behind the glass, another civilization had been preserved.

The penguins, which can't fly, were romping around their habitat and swimming in their pool. (Penguins can swim at speeds up to thirty miles per hour.) Their chilly exhibit duplicated their home in the wild: ice formations and water. Some of them, the rockhoppers, were collected from the wild (from the island of Tristan da Cunha, in the South Atlantic) and were reproducing at the zoo. Most of the others—including the chinstraps and the macaronis—were on loan from the San Diego Zoo, which had them in abundance. All were subantarctic, from the southern edge of South America, including the Falkland Islands.

The three species of penguins at the zoo—out of the eighteen species in the world—had more in common than they had differences, and that made them compatible in the zoo exhibit. The macaronis were the largest, the rockhoppers the smallest, the chinstraps in between—but all were knee-high to a tall keeper. The macaronis and rockhoppers were easily spotted; they were crested penguins, with gold tufts of feathers on the sides of their heads. The chinstraps were penguins most familiar to viewers who looked for the familiar tuxedo appearance, the dark back and the white front.

The penguins' zoo environment was controlled, with proper lighting defined day and night. The exhibit was cooled to thirty-five degrees; the 18,000-gallon pool was kept at forty degrees. Most of the penguins had been hand-raised in captivity; adjustment to life indoors had not been difficult.

"For the wild ones, it takes a while for them to eat dead fish—which we fortify with vitamins and minerals—instead of catching live ones," Kevin said. "But we do duplicate sunrise and sunset, long and short days as well. Some of these penguins are quite tame, even in the wild. If they haven't been hunted by humans, they don't fear people.

"It's true that wild-caught birds tend to be more stand-offish. If you went into the exhibit and walked up to the birds, the hand-raised birds would probably stand there and let you walk right up to them. They'd probably chew your shoelace or peck at your pants leg. The wild-caught birds would avoid you, even jump into the water if you got close to them. We go in there to trim their nails or their bills. When we grab a hand-raised bird, it usually won't try to bite us. A wild-caught bird might, and it can inflict a fairly severe wound, so you've got to be careful. They can hit you with their flippers, too. After all, they are birds that sort of fly underwater, so those flippers are powerful. A good whack from a flipper can make you black and blue.

"They don't usually breed until they're four or five years old. But when they're ready, they'll do it right in the exhibit. We provide the rocks, and they make rock nests with them."

Kevin was delighted by the antics of the penguins, and so were the children peering in at them. But his pride was the seabird exhibit, which shared the building with the penguins.

He had personally collected all the seabirds in the

glassed-in exhibit. There were dozens of black and white and gray shapes against the eighteen-foot-high indoor cliff and in the 10,000-gallon pool in front of it. The birds—the common murre, the razorbill, and the common puffin—were swimming, diving, strutting, and observing as Kevin approached them.

"We found them all in southwest Iceland, where there are millions of them," he said. "Most of them are collected as chicks, one to three weeks old, and are raised here at the zoo. They're not at all tame, by the way."

A wave machine sent waves across the pool, and filtered the water as well. A misting system, controlled lighting, and a consistent temperature of forty-five to fifty degrees made the environment familiar to the birds.

"We had to modify the exhibit," Kevin pointed out. "We started with a closed system and found out that the water filtration system couldn't deal with the number of birds we had. The amount of fecal material that went into the water was so great that the system couldn't handle it. So we changed the system, to skim a lot of water off the surface and send it out to the sewer system, particularly when we hosed down the exhibit. Now we add fresh water regularly.

"We had a health problem, too, at first. We attributed it to the fish we were feeding them, a common freshwater smelt from Lake Michigan. Researchers told us that there were heavy metals in the fish. Dangerous. So we switched to saltwater fish, and that solved it."

The puffins were his favorites. He had appreciated them in the wild and now could appreciate them in captivity. But once they came to the zoo, they were there to stay.

"Puffins are a very heavy-bodied bird, with small wings," he explained. "In the wild there may not be suffi-cient wind at times, and that means they have a hard time flying. They rely on the sea breeze to get them up into the air, and it takes them a long stretch to gain altitude. We can't achieve that for them here. Fortunately, we won't release them back into the wild. This is their home now."

It was an important conclusion: the birds' lives depended upon Kevin and the conscientious keepers who cared for the exhibit.

He left the penguin-seabird colonies and walked back to the bird house. A few people were strolling around the cavernous building, some of them accompanied by walking birds.

Kevin permitted himself a rare leisurely walk around the building. As he moved along, birds caught his eye and inspired comment.

A pair of Major Mitchell's cockatoos: "That's an old male we've had for years, with a female that's on loan to us from the Cleveland Zoo. What is fascinating is that the two birds look alike to the average person. But if you look at them very closely, the female is the one with the lighter-color eye."

The galah, a cockatoo: "It's very common in Australia. It's even shot there, because of the damage it can do to grain crops. Here it's fairly rare. A pair of these would cost a zoo anywhere from three to four thousand dollars. They can be tamed; most cockatoos can be tamed, especially if they're hand-raised. If they're wild-caught, they're a little more skittish."

Rothschild's mynah: "An endangered species, almost extinct on its native island, Bali. But there is a species survival program, breeding them in captivity for release back on Bali. The first release will be done very soon."

Nicobar pigeons: "They're not endangered, but they are threatened. We started out with six in 1976, and we've produced close to sixty from those six. Fascinating birds. Originally from Nicobar Island in the Bay of Bengal, now found all over the South Pacific. They can be aggressive with each other during the breeding season, especially the males, which chase each other around. They'll nest in the trees, but they like to walk around on the ground, too.

"They're a heavy-bodied pigeon, larger than our domestic pigeon. They have very long hackles, which are long feathers that surround the neck, chest, and upper back. They are colorful, from green to coppery bronze to blue and purple—metallic colors.

"Here at the zoo, most of the Nicobars have two bands around their legs. A metal band with a number on it for identifying the bird in our collection. And a plastic, colored band that allows us, at a distance, to determine which birds are which. To keep track of individuals."

The white-crested laughing thrush: "Asian birds. Popular because they make a very loud sort of laughing sound. We feed them mealworms, crickets, waxworms, some meat, some fruit. There are cricket ranches that sell crickets to us. And places that produce worms—mice, too."

The blue-crowned conure: "One of the parrots. Slim-bodied birds. We don't know a lot about this particular species. We got them when they were confiscated by the government at a port of entry. Someone was trying to bring them in without the proper paperwork. That paperwork never was forthcoming, so now the birds are ours."

The tawny frogmouth: "From Australia. They look like owls, but they're not related to owls at all. They don't have grasping feet, for example; they have perching feet. They have a huge gaping mouth; they can eat small mice or large insects by crushing them with their bills.

"They're nocturnal. Their coloration enables them to blend in with the bark on a tree. During the day, if you walk around here and look for them, it's hard to find them. They are absolutely still and blend in. When it starts to get dark in here, that's when they wake up."

He paused. He could hear a mild commotion between a parent bird and its baby.

"When birds are successful at reproducing, parent birds will chase some of their older chicks out of the area. Aggressively, especially when the parent wants to renest. They'll tolerate a youngster up to a point, but when that youngster gets old enough, they'll chase it out, even roughly. In the wild, they chase out the chicks to head out and colonize a new area."

He resumed his stroll.

"There's a Shama thrush feeding her chick in a log," he observed. The birds were in a small glassed-in cell.

"That spare setting inhibits reproduction. They're helped by more space, more plants. They'll respond better in a naturalistic habitat. There's no depth to these old cages. When the keeper enters to put down some food, the bird flies out of range but can't go very far. It's possible that placid birds, birds that do well in these old cages, we won't want to exhibit in our new setting. Temperamental birds, which may not adapt well, are more fascinating."

He passed a blacksmith plover sitting on an egg.

"Hi, mom!" he hollered. Another plover, nearby, guarding the mother, shrieked an alarm call.

A Jackson's hornbill, from East Africa, was facing the wall at the back of its cage, peering down.

"Looking for a roach to eat," Kevin said.

In the free-flight area in the middle of the building, a Nicobar pigeon, in metallic copper and green, sat surveying the invented landscape: thickly overgrown, with a miniature stream along the outer edges and a waterfall.

"One of the things that goes into planning a free-flight like this is the number of different strata. You have limited ground space, so you have to limit the number of birds who live on the forest floor. Then you have those birds that inhabit the low shrubbery or the water areas. You have to figure out how many birds you can have and then work your way right up to the top of the exhibit," he explained.

Across the room, Sammy—a white cockatoo and a venerable resident of the bird house—called out, "Hello." Sammy had been donated to the zoo more than fifteen years ago by a wealthy woman with a fondness for birds and for zoos. Whenever she returned to visit him, she fed him Godiva chocolates. She died, but the bird survived, and at age thirty it showed few signs of weariness. Old age in birds never surprised Kevin; there was a cockatoo at the San Diego Zoo that was sixty-five, and he knew of a condor that lived to seventy-five.

"It's the only tame bird we have," Kevin said of Sammy. "It'll sit on your arm and take food from you."

When he completed his circle around the bird house, he walked outside, into the summer heat. A common city pigeon flashed by, in a familiar nosedive. Kevin grimaced.

"It's ironic," he said. "There are many pigeons and doves, and some of them are very difficult to keep in captivity. That one adapted. To spread disease and be a nuisance. They're like rats. Dirty. Another dirty urban animal leaving its remains. I get calls from people who want us to kill them. I tell them to call the city's animal control people. Killing animals isn't our business."

By eight o'clock the next morning, Kevin had been at work for two hours. As he often did, he went to the reception desk in the Crown-Field Center to pick up his mail, memos from other staff members, anything that had accumulated in his box. He sat at the desk, alone, sorting out what he'd found, assessing employee time sheets, working in solitude.

The building was quiet, the only time in the day that it would be. As Kevin looked at the pile of paperwork and thought about his schedule for the day, Mark Rosenthal came in.

Mark was concerned.

The previous day, a prominent local orthopedic surgeon (best known for treating valuable and frequently fragile athletes) had operated on Lenore, an eighteen-year-old female gorilla with a wrist infection. Efforts to treat the infection with antibiotics had failed because Lenore wouldn't sit still, literally, to permit insertion of an IV line. Treating animals is not like treating cooperative humans. A plate implanted in her wrist did not thwart the growth of the infection, either. The decision was made—based on consultation with Mark and senior keeper Pat Sass—to amputate Lenore's left hand, wrist, and part of her forearm. It took the surgeon more than an hour to complete the operation.

Mark had just come from visiting Lenore. He talked about it to Kevin.

Lenore was up, alert, and had taken her medicine. Most

important, she hadn't picked at the incision beneath the heavily bandaged arm; it remained intact.

But Mark had unanswered questions. Would Lenore adapt to the loss of her hand once she was returned to the other gorillas? How would the others treat her? Other animals in the zoo, including monkeys, had survived amputations and had thrived. But the riddles of animal behavior did not inspire precise answers.

Kevin was interested, and sympathetic, but the paperwork beckoned; he wanted to get through as much of it as possible before Les Fisher's 9 A.M. staff meeting.

Kevin was curator of birds, but the birds had to get in line for his attention. His administrative responsibilities often devoured hours of his time. He was in charge of many of the items used by the zoo; the inventories were his responsibility. When a broom was needed, he ordered it from the storehouse. He authorized the replacement of missing or broken tools.

All the zoo's purchasing, other than food, was his to govern. He approved all the orders for familiar implements: shovels, rakes, hoses and nozzles, heavy-duty cleaners and disinfectants, chemicals to attack rodents and pests, paper towels by the mile each year, keeper uniforms (Ike jackets, parkas, jumpsuits for the elephant keepers and the vets). The unfamiliar orders were on his agenda, too. An artist's carving tool—an Exacto knife—was used to clean elephants' feet. The timber wolves enjoyed dog rawhide bones. There had to be a supply of Pampers on hand to diaper zoo-raised primates. There was a budget code system to master. He sent purchase orders to the park district; all such requests from zoo staff came to him.

He supervised the timekeeping system. There were daily time sheets and semimonthly summaries to check regularly.

And there were the daily keeper reports waiting for him every morning at the bird house. A sampling:

- "Buffalo weavers definitely doing something, but what?"
- "Terns ate 36 fish."

- "All 3 Blacksmith plover eggs missing. Probably eaten by mice."
- "Male starfinch missing from last cage on west run. Did not look real good yesterday. Maybe died up in the pot hanging from the ceiling. Will check.
- "Went up and checked hanging pot for starfinch, and he was there. Not real sure what he died from. Old age?"
- "School kids today are horrible. Three-quarters of the groups had no supervisors."
- "Have seen only four Inca terns all day. A $1.25 hot dog to anyone who can find the fifth."
- "Flamingo #78-103 attacked by swan, dragged in water west of flamingo nest island. Swan had it by neck and back, submerging it. I threw seaweed at them, and it escaped. Called Dr. Meehan, took it to hospital. No bleeding, but it was shaking and unable to stand.

    "P.S. Died next day."
- "The sunbitterns have taken over the Nicobar nest in rubber tree and thrown the Nicobars out."

The reports informed Kevin, baffled him, amused him. And they contributed to the paper load in his life. He spent as much as six hours a day reviewing the architectural plans for the bird of prey exhibit and the redesign of the bird house. Every meeting on those subjects—and they were frequent—required his comments later. Paper generated paper.

There were reports describing any incidents involving the public, reports of employee accidents, animal inventory forms, updated whenever an animal died, was born, or was sent to another zoo.

His mailbox was filled with literature from zoos of the world, much of it forwarded to him by Les Fisher. There were letters from curators at other zoos. Newsletters, journals, reports on various conservation projects. He consoled himself with a rationalization: all the paper related to one of the zoo's four objectives: conservation, recreation, education, research.

Les Fisher liked to convene his Wednesday 9 A.M. staff meeting on time. He knew that those attending were busy, and so was he. On one hot Wednesday in June, Kevin attended a staff meeting that was to give zoo librarian Joyce Shaw a chance to make a presentation to the curators, the vets, and others in attendance.

Although she had been the librarian for several years, Joyce had not before been asked to report on her activities. Her office was the small, dreary, two-room suite off the north entrance to the sixty-year-old primate house; it had been Les Fisher's office, before the Crown-Field Center was built. As a library, it was a tight fit.

Joyce was thirty-two, tall, blond, bespectacled, an attractive, smart, chain-smoking single parent with a cynical view of the zoo administration. She was underpaid and unhappy about it. She had come to the zoo from a job at the Field Museum (the city's eminent natural history museum) three years ago to bring order to the library. It hadn't been easy.

The library's confined space had to accommodate more than 100 journal-magazine subscriptions, more than 2,000 monographs, English-language zoo publications from England to Australia, a large slide collection, videotapes, and a poster collection.

Joyce's only help was provided by one part-time volunteer. She intended to use her command appearance at the staff meeting to make her case. The library, she reminded all present, was used by the zoo staff, the zoo society staff (she was paid by the zoo society), and a broad range of outsiders. She had to field questions, informed and uniformed, that kept her phone ringing frequently. The air conditioner worked but wheezed; the copying machine was unreliable. Calmly, she seemed to be conveying a message: If the zoo wanted an effective library, it would have to support it. And her.

Les Fisher knew that the zoo could not expand to provide a new building for the library; the park district had prohibited that sort of expansion in the zoo's limited space. But he did not want to clash bluntly with Joyce's ambition for a modern library.

"You know," he said, "a library is a new idea for the zoo. We used to have books scattered around all over the place. And we'd lose them. Our library ought to be service-oriented to the public, but our limitations are there. It's possible that the renovation of the primate house may leave us without a library."

His voice was calm, soft, unthreatening.

Joyce paid attention to him. "We do have a good collection of specialized, unique material that's not duplicated anywhere else in the city," she pointed out. "It's nice to be a research library. It's great to help employees working on research projects."

Les listened, paused, and commented. The others in the room were less attentive; Joyce had her supporters and her critics.

"We just haven't got room in this zoo for everything that needs room," Les sighed. "It may be solved someday. But we may have to assign priorities. Do we want to store more journals than we use? Do we even need a poster collection? I have no personal wisdom on this matter.

"Except this: The keepers shouldn't use the library as the primate house lunchroom. Get rid of that candy that you've got over there. We want to try to keep the place free of vermin."

Joyce lapsed into silence, and the meeting ended.

In the corridor outside of the conference room, she paused and articulated her devotion: "I love libraries, and I love this stupid little zoo library. I feel it strongly. My place is here. I keep seeing its potential. I guess it comes down to this: it's my job to care, even if nobody else gives a damn."

The staff filed out of the room, heading out of the building toward their own work.

One of the staff members who knew Les well turned to another.

"Know what the point of all that was?" he asked.

"No."

"Don't eat lunch in the library."

Kevin walked over to his mail box. He had removed a batch of papers from it early in the morning. It was filled again. He seized the new batch and headed for the door.

FIRST PERSON: KEVIN BELL

When I first heard that I was moving into the Bronx Zoo, I was five years old. I probably wasn't completely aware of what it all meant. It was like being close to a circus all the time. Certainly, after I was there for a period of time, it truly was a remarkable experience. From my earliest memories, it meant getting up as early as I possibly could in the morning. That's probably one of the reasons I get up so early now. I mean it was so exciting to go out and make the rounds with my dad, and go and work with incubators and do the fun stuff of working with the animals before I went to school. And then after school trying to get home as fast as I possibly could. When I was growing up, I probably didn't have as many outside friends as most kids, because after school when a lot of kids were doing things, I always wanted to come home to the zoo right away.

I knew all the keepers as well as I knew my own family. As time went on, and I had a little bit more experience working around the zoo, my role changed from one of sheer enjoyment, of doing things that I liked, to projects that my dad gave me to work on. I actually became involved. When they would get a certain type of bird in from the wild, and they wanted someone to work with it, my dad would just assign it to me. I would work with it in the morning before I went to school, and I'd start working with it again when I came home. It never seemed like work to me; it was always fun. And working alongside my dad added something to the whole experience.

My father was an excellent animal person overall. I wish that someday I become the naturalist that he was, because his knowledge of botany, of natural history, was just fantastic. But his experience dealing with people was different from my experience. I can remember when I left New York, my dad told me, "You're going to work at Lincoln Park, so make sure that you don't allow anybody there to call you by your first name. Remember, you're in charge, and everybody refers to you as Mr. Bell, not as Kevin." Well, of course, at Lincoln Park, there was a very laid-back attitude. The Bronx Zoo was very formal, and he was from the old school; keepers dressed a certain way, the staff members dressed a certain way, and they were addressed properly. He didn't have a work day. He literally worked whenever he needed to, any time of the day or night, just to make sure that whatever he was working on was done in a proper way. Also, living on the grounds meant that he was totally involved in the zoo for twenty-four hours a day. Our phone at home was the nighttime zoo phone, so everybody who had a question about raising birds, or having an opossum in their back yard, would call our number.

My dad openly said that he was not going to direct me into the animal field, but I think there was nothing that made him feel better than when I did enter the animal field. I think he consciously wanted to give me as much experience as he possibly could so that if I did choose that field, I would be as prepared as I possibly could be. I think he knew that I was going to end up in zoos, and end up in birds. He was very strong about my attending graduate school; he was always a little self-conscious about that, because he hadn't done it.

I think deep down inside I always knew that I was going to be involved with zoos. With birds. I think birds are a challenge, maybe more of a challenge in some cases than mammals even. Mammals are very popular; a lot of people know about mammals. There aren't as many people who have experience in birds. There are still birds being discovered, there are still birds, enormous numbers of birds, that have never been worked with, that people know almost nothing about. I think with birds, more than with mammals, reproduction is a good indicator not only of the health of the bird but also of the fact that you've created the proper stimuli in order to get it. You are able to feel you've created that set of circumstances necessary to get birds to reproduce.

Some birds can be very personable, like the penguins; you can almost see that there is a relationship between the keeper and the animals themselves. With birds on the other end of the scale, a lot of the perching birds, unless they're really raised as pet birds or they're hand-raised, they tend not to have the interaction with their keepers and curators that you might see with some of the mammals. But the affection is there. If you talk with the bird keepers, you'll find that they know their individual birds.

Take the Nicobar pigeons. I've got a few people who could identify every one of those birds, of the twenty-five or thirty birds out there, tell you the history of the bird, when it hatched out, how many chicks it's sired. They really know the ins and outs of a bird; whether it tends to be a good mother or tends not to be a good mother. They know the animals; there's a tremendous feeling for the animals. But, again, the animals are not the type that are going to come up and necessarily take food from your hand.

In a lot of cases, that's good, because with birds you don't want an imprinted bird that's more interested in a human than in a bird of its same species. Of course, tame birds sometimes can be better to work with than wild birds. A true wild parrot tends to be so skittish that in a captive situation it never really settles down in the sense that it will reproduce. A tamer bird, provided it isn't totally imprinted, will be willing to overlook a keeper coming into its cage to put the food pan down, to clean up, and then leave. In most cases, if they're in a breeding situation, they're not going to come over and sit on the keeper's shoulder. They're going to tolerate the keeper, but they're also going to be very protective of their nests and stay fairly aloof. It's certainly not like the interaction between a keeper and an elephant or between a gorilla and a gorilla keeper.

There are birds that I happen to like more than others. Species that either I have worked with or I'm fascinated by.

The seabirds, whether the puffins, the murres, the razor-bills, have always been a keen interest of mine. They're colonial nesters, they live in huge numbers, they're not really that well studied. We're really starting to learn more and more about them. Well, to me the most gratifying thing is this: You have a species that maybe hasn't been worked with that much in captivity. But you've gone ahead and you've done all the research on the bird in the wild that you can, in terms of reading all the literature. If you can see them in the wild, that's great, but at least you've covered it in the literature. Then you look around, and you see that in captivity there's no way to duplicate exactly what they have in the wild. You start to look at as many artificial factors that you can put in that closely simulate what they have in the wild, and when you're able to do that and get the bird to successfully reproduce, I think it's a tremendous feeling of accomplishment.

There are incredibly beautiful birds: the whole group of hummingbirds and sunbirds; there are some absolutely breathtaking birds, breathtaking birds of paradise. But there's also a tremendous amount of beauty in some of the common waterfowl that occur in this area. I mean, the mallard duck, as common as it is, is a very beautiful bird. To say one is more beautiful is to say you prefer green or blue or you prefer metallic or flat. There is certainly a beautiful array of colors and shapes in the bird.

Some birds have more intelligence, in terms of learning capabilities. But in general, birds are not a smart group; I guess that's the best way to put it.

The reason that zoos are here, the primary reason, is to do something for the public. If we didn't have any public coming through our gates, zoos would close down. We're not a forest preserve; we're not a wildlife park, although we'd like to be. It would make our job a lot easier if we could just keep animals and do what would be best for them and not necessarily best for the public. But I think our job is to get a message across to the people who are coming in here. Not only show people the variety of birds, but the variety of habitats that the birds live in, and show

how they are specifically adapted to those habitats. That's what we're going to stress in our new bird facility. So that people will get an awareness of environments and an animal's place in the environment, and the need to protect the environment and therefore protect the bird.

Reproduction is crucial because animals are not available from the wild the way they once were. If you don't reproduce, you're not going to have any animals in your zoo, not any birds anyway. Now, fortunately, we're in a situation where animals that are reproduced in zoos will be released back into the wild. That's certainly a very important aspect of our job. There are complications; there are always complications. The habitat is not what it was, and you're trying to take a bird and send it to something that is no longer there.

There's a bird that's not really endangered, called an oil bird, that occurs in Trinidad and lives only in caves. Well, the tourists have come there so much to see the oil birds that the oil birds tended to leave the caves. So you have a situation where the cave is still there, but it's just not usable for the birds. The birds are just diminishing; they're going someplace else, but they're not reproducing if they're not going into the caves. The habitat is very important and has to be maintained, and I think that's why again, we have to teach more about preserving habitats rather than just about birds. Once people learn to protect the land, then the rest will come afterward. If you educate the people here, that's going to help the situation in the wild a little bit. If you establish breeding programs here and somewhere down the road have animals to release into the wild, that's all part of conservation. More and more zoos are becoming actively involved in supporting conservation projects around the world. They're sending people out to study the animals in the wild, to study what the animals need, what their habitats are, the essential parts of their habitat, and why the numbers may be diminishing. Then we have that information that we can relate to the public. It's all really closely tied together.

One of the nice aspects of our zoo, but also a limiting

aspect, is our space. Some of our habitats can't be quite as large as we'd like them to be. There are a lot of birds that will never be exhibited at Lincoln Park. We don't have the open area for ostriches, for rheas, for emus, for cassowaries. There's a certain aspect that we'll be missing because of our limited size. It would be nice to have an area where people could go on a monorail and actually see what the animals would be like if they were out in an open valley. But then one of the nice things about our zoo is the fact that people can come here and in a couple of hours see most of the zoo, experiencing a lot of different aspects of the zoo in a short period of time. At some of the bigger places, they see only part of the zoo, they tire themselves out, and then they go home.

I think there are a number of poor zoo facilities around the country; there's no sense in hiding that fact. There are a number of facilities that for budgetary reasons or whatever don't have adequate conditions for everything. But now our parent organization, the American Association of Zoological Parks and Aquariums (AAZPA), has developed a program of accrediting zoos, so that zoo people themselves go around to each zoo, to each member institution, and look very critically, a lot more critically than anybody else would look at it. If zoos aren't accredited, they have a certain amount of time to correct the conditions that created the nonaccredited status, or they're more or less kept outside the zoo community, and we won't send animals there or deal with them.

Things that would be objectionable would involve having animals in inadequate facilities with inadequate care. For example, if there was no shade for an animal that requires shade, and it was forced to stay out in the sun all the time, maybe was not given free running water, things like that would bother me the most.

In ten years, hopefully, Lincoln Park Zoo's bird collection will have made a complete turnabout from when I got here, which was more than ten years ago. It was an extremely large collection, one of the largest collections around, but very overcrowded and with virtually no reproduction whatsoever. Birds were not kept in any particular order. There was no real management plan for the collection. Our new bird house will put us up there where we will feel good about the collection, in terms of what we're doing, what we're telling the public, our reproductive program, and the information that we'll be able to share with other zoos, based on what we've learned from keeping the birds here.

At this point I really don't have any ambition to be a zoo director. It's a whole different ball game now than it was years ago, and more and more you find people who aren't even animal people who are directors because it's a job of fund-raising, a job of public relations, not a real animal job. I'm still interested in the animal aspect of it. Sure, being a curator is frustrating at times because there is such a tremendous amount of nonanimal work, of paperwork. But most of the paperwork is still related to animals. Some days, from eight to five you're in meetings constantly. As a curator you can still come in at six, or stay until eight at night, and spend that time doing whatever you want. You can walk around the collection, you can think of things that you want to do with the collection, and so the time's there. And, you know, as busy as you are, you can always find the time for the animals.

4

LOOKING FOR MR. WRIGHT

Clarence Wright returned to his post as curator of reptiles from vacation in his hometown, Tulsa, Oklahoma. He knew that he was back at work when, at 7:45 A.M., he confronted a large stack of paperwork that had piled up in his box at the zoo office. The feeling was confirmed when he met with several reptile house keepers a few moments later.

They gathered around him in the vestibule of the old reptile house, not air-conditioned and heated almost unbearably by the morning summer sun. They recited a litany of events that had occurred while Clarence was away.

An alligator had died. Several apes had been born. (Clarence was interested in all zoo animals, not simply reptiles.) The ceiling of the primate house had been damaged— chunks had fallen, but no one had been injured—during the annual lakefront air show. Apparently, the sonic booms from low-flying jets had shaken the old building. It had been closed for repairs; the bird house and the lion house had been closed as well, to be checked.

Over the weekend, vandals had broken into the zoo between 4 and 6 A.M. and had done some damage to one of the gift shops.

That incident triggered a memory. When Clarence had worked at the Tulsa Zoo, vandals had entered the zoo and had released all the chimps. When Clarence drove into the parking lot, seven chimps were there to greet him. One moved toward him, menacingly, its arms outstretched in its attack mode. Clarence knew that he couldn't wrestle it into submission. He glared at the chimp, stretched out his own arms, and moved toward the chimp, emulating the chimp's stance. The chimp looked at Clarence and fled in fright back to its cage, shutting the cage door behind it.

Clarence left his briefing and took a quick tour of the main floor of the reptile house—an oval of glassed-in cages. Two pythons were in a courtship ritual; the male was licking the female. As Clarence walked along the tile floor in the oppressive heat, an oft-felt sense of depression came upon him.

"The building needs new lighting and new temperature controls," he said. "It's too cold in winter and too hot in summer. The humidity can't be properly controlled, and that affects some species, like frogs and toads, whose breeding is ruled by humidity. This building is sixty-five years old."

Clarence was sturdily built: six feet tall and 200 pounds. His blond hair, thinning, was matched by a trimmed moustache. His dress was casual: jeans, simple shirts, ties with animal motifs. Peering through his glasses, he demonstrated a demeanor—reinforced by a faint Oklahoma-southern accent—like that of a kindly neighbor in a Tennessee Williams play. Clarence did not like to shout or lose control. He tried to remain calm. His toughness was not obvious, but it was there.

Two of the keepers who served him were Art, a lively, informed, short, trimly built guy, and Caryn, a tall, tanned brunette with pigtails, long earrings, and dark red nail polish. They treated Clarence with affection, although in his first year on the job, he had initiated reforms in the reptile house that affected the way they had always worked. He was thirty-nine, and they knew that he knew his work and appreciated theirs.

They joked about the dead alligator; there was no mourning for it. Caryn complained about a perpetual problem: low water pressure in the building. She couldn't hose down anything. She did have some good news: a fire-bellied toad and an arrow-poison frog had laid eggs. Within days, they should hatch.

A Gila monster had died.

"I'd like to know what the hell happened to that kid," Art said, as if musing about the death of a friend. He rambled on. "The Cuban boa is not eating, but it's awfully hot out there. And in here."

They talked about repairs needed in the reptile house and the customary wait for park district laborers to show up to make them. "Christ wouldn't have been born if He had to wait for our carpenters to build a creche," Art said.

Clarence and the two keepers walked down a narrow stairway to the gray, decaying basement area, filled with displays for the public, holding areas for the animals, and keeper facilities. In an open plastic jug live crickets fluttered, waiting to serve as food for lizards. A bucket collected a leak from the ceiling; the source of the leak remained a mystery. They paused in front of the alligator exhibit. The seven alligators in it were placid, if not enervated. The exhibit was cramped, unadorned, uninteresting.

"One's got one eye. Another has a cut tail. And a third has a couple of broken legs," Caryn recited. "And there's shit in there that I can't clean without water pressure."

Her comment did not surprise Clarence. The alligator exhibit troubled him; the creatures were crowded into a dark, unadorned space. The one-eyed alligator had lost the eye in a fight with another alligator; the one with the cut tail had lost its battle as well. The alligator with the broken legs would heal itself. It was often easier to allow that to happen; treating an alligator was extremely difficult. And minor wounds did heal in time without intervention by the vets.

Clarence spotted a tortoise egg being fertilized in an incubator.

"Watch the temperature in there," Clarence instructed. "If it fluctuates, you kill the embryo."

A red-legged tarantula ambled toward the front of its case to peer at Clarence. It was common to house spiders in the reptile building; the temperature, humidity, and food served them, too.

Clarence paused in a passageway, looked around, and scowled. Everywhere he looked, it seemed, he saw the potential for change.

"There's so much to be done," he sighed. "We've got to redo our record systems. That's major work. We've got to sex the animals and make sure that our IDs are correct. Some species have been mislabeled in the past. We had a specialist visit us not long ago and take a look at a sign on an exhibit: 'Orinoco Crocodile.' He said, 'No, that's not an Orinoco crocodile. It's an American saltwater croc from Florida.' He was right. It'll take time, a year or two, just to make all the changes I want to make, but it'll get done."

He resumed his walk, passing a large cage that contained a green iguana from Mexico. It was poised on a large branch, motionless. "People buy them in pet stores," he noted. "But they're really very delicate, and few of them make it."

He peeked at the boa who hadn't been eating.

"We fed it three live mice, and it didn't eat them, so we'll switch to dead food. I don't really like to feed them live rats and mice. They can kill snakes. They eat right through to the spine. If this boa isn't eating after three weeks, we'll try mice legs or just open up a mouse to get the odor out and tempt the snake. We can force-feed it if we have to, with special food in a syringe inserted in its mouth; that's a last resort, because you can tear the lining of the throat. But some snakes can go for months without food. Adult pythons have fasted for two years."

He walked over to a small cage and picked up a desert iguana. It did not struggle.

"It's not well. When you know an animal, you know its responses, even if it moves just a little. A snake's eyes may move just a bit, but that's a signal of recognition. If you see an animal every day, you know its subtle behavior, and you can spot sickness early enough to treat it."

He continued his rounds past salamanders, toads, frogs, tortoises, iguanas, and an Asian land turtle, in a cage with the iguanas. "They're both vegetarians," he said. "They get along."

In a nearby cage, a group of Yacare caimans, a crocodile-like creature from South America, moved slowly. "They reproduce well in zoos, but they're difficult to exhibit," he noted. "They need a lot of space, something we don't have right now. We'll have to put these out on loan.

"I've never met a nice caiman. They're vicious. American alligators are more social, not as aggressive, more predictable. You can even feed one by hand. It's an animal that recognizes you."

He moved into a narrow room, where mice were raised as live food. "We're better off buying them instead of raising them, and we can do just that, buying them twice a week to feed the reptiles. Mice are thirty-five cents each, rats ninety-five cents."

Clarence finished his tour and returned to his office on the main floor. It was small, almost claustrophobic. He had a desk, a chair, a file cabinet, a typewriter; there wasn't room for more. But whatever the frustrations he faced almost daily, he was pleased to be at the zoo as a curator. For him, getting there hadn't been easy.

He grew up in Tulsa. During his summers in college, he worked as a laborer at the Tulsa Zoo. He got his degree: a bachelor's in zoology from Oklahoma State University. (Later, he got a teaching certificate as well.) He served as a full-time keeper, as curator of reptiles and amphibians, and as curator of small mammals and primates at the Tulsa Zoo. In 1985, he moved on, to become zoo curator—a complex, administrative job—at the Lowry Park Zoo in Tampa, Florida. In 1986, he headed north, to Chicago and the Lincoln Park Zoo, first as assistant curator, then as curator of reptiles and amphibians.

When Les Fisher offered the job at the zoo, "I took it immediately, no question about it. An honor," Clarence recalled. "I was hired to clean up the reptile house." A bachelor, Clarence felt he had the time—he liked working on weekends, and didn't mind working nights, either—and the energy to do what Les wanted done.

His tiny office was silent, until the phone rang.

The caller confirmed shipment of a batch of tortoises due in from Bermuda. They originated in South America and had been confiscated in Bermuda—their papers were not in order—and had been acquired by the zoo.

"Thirteen? I was expecting six or seven," Clarence bellowed into the phone. He'd have to quarantine the tortoises. If they carried any disease, he didn't want them to spread it to the other animals. And he didn't have space for thirteen tortoises.

He presented the dilemma to Caryn; she was feeding animals in the basement.

"Thirteen!" she shouted. "Where are we going to keep them? And how big do they get? They shit unbelievably every day. We'd better get some Astroturf, so I can clean it. My God, their shit is horrible-smelling. And we'll get roaches."

She was right about the odor, Clarence knew. The foot-long oblong tortoises were vegetarians; in the wild, they were able to consume as much roughage as they needed, creating normal stool. The zoo could not duplicate that diet, despite its best effort. He did better with other reptiles; the stench that troubled Caryn was not a common one.

"If we get rid of some caimans, we can make room for the tortoises," Clarence told her calmly.

The phone in the keeper area clanged. Caryn picked it up, listened, then yelled, "Artie!" Art came up and took the phone from her as she whispered, "How do you identify a caterpillar?"

"Does it have a little horn?" Art said into the phone. "Red or white? On your tomato plant? Is it moving much? Uh huh. Probably tomato hornworms," he said. "They eat leaves and turn into moths that feed on nectar at night. Get a book called *Insect Friends* or something like that." He paused and grinned. "Just look for 'em and pick 'em off. If you want to, bring 'em to Art at the reptile house."

Clarence smiled at the exchange, waved, and walked up the stairs back to his office. A mound of paperwork rested on his desk; he stared at it. He had other things on his mind.

"This is the only building that wasn't scheduled for renovation," he said. He was a man suffering from neglect. "There isn't much interest here in reptiles. Elsewhere there is. The Dallas Zoo collection is world-renowned. An excellent facility. Fort Worth and Houston are, too. St. Louis is the best of the old and the best of the new.

"Here, we're saddled with so many surplus animals. We don't need them, and nobody else wants them either.

"Then, there's that sexing problem. We shipped a male rattlesnake to a zoo that had asked for a female. We shipped an entirely different snake to a zoo that was shocked when it didn't get what it asked for. That's the way it was here.

"Now, we work harder and do better. There are six hundred animals in the reptile house. We can't be ignorant. One keeper used tongs to lift an aggressive lizard. No. Never. You can hurt it. We're learning. I have weekly meetings with the keepers. I hope to conduct actual classes with them, too. To teach. You know, you can't tell how an animal's doing by opening the cage and shutting it. The animal must come first around here.

"It's true that some reptiles shrivel away and die if you don't work at getting them to eat. You force-feed a reptile if you have to, to keep it alive. But it all takes time, and affection.

"At this zoo, the keepers are thought of as generic, interchangeable. They don't have to specialize. Well, they should. They do in other zoos. An ape keeper takes care of apes. I'm used to working with people who have a burning desire to work with reptiles.

"I have to do what's best for the collection. I want to expand its scope, if not its numbers. Here's my ideal. Tortoises on the floor, frogs in the water, massive toads, tree-dwelling snakes—all integrated into a lush tropical setting, including the insects of the region, insects that wouldn't be consumed. That tells a better story than we're telling now. An entire ecosystem.

"I want this to be a research institute, a center for the breeding of reptiles. Breeding is vital. Some snakes breed only at certain times of the year, in season. We have to know what we're doing. For example, we have to introduce the male into the female's territory—her exhibit—at the right time. The first day is the most important if courtship is to be successful. The male will run over her body with his to stimulate her. His penis—actually a double penis—locks into her, and they can copulate like that from hours to several days. The male dominates. We have to know about such things.

"We could get rid of one-third or one-half of the collection, as I see it. I'd like to pull the whole building down and start all over again. But that won't happen. So I'm hoping to do some serious planning for a renovation, and I hope that someone here takes it as seriously as I do. It's my mission."

Clarence had gotten up from his desk chair and was leaning across the desk, gesturing, sweating, imploring an unseen benefactor. But he did not shout.

The next morning, once again, Clarence was roaming the halls of the reptile house, assessing the well-being of the animals. He was an animal person; his view of his work was closer to a keeper's than to a curator's. He believed in a hands-on approach; he didn't mind getting dirty.

The summer heat was unrelenting, but it did not deter

Clarence. He roamed around the basement holding areas; there seemed to be more reptiles stored there than there were on public display.

He spotted a boa who might be sick, a tortoise plagued by parasites, and a lizard who hadn't eaten properly in days. He reached down into the lizard's cage and picked it up gently.

"This is one of those cases in which the creature would be better off in the wild than it is here," he said. "It was wild when it was found and shipped to us, and it's not adjusting well to captivity. Maybe I can arrange for it to be sent back. It'll be happier, and so will I."

He made a mental note to visit the hoofed-stock enclosure; he had sent some radiated tortoises (named for the "wheel" design on their shells), a rare species from Madagascar, to an outdoor pen at the hoofed-stock area. He wanted the tortoises to get some direct sunlight to enhance the breeding process. Sunlight could be duplicated by a special fluorescent light, but the reptile house would have to be rewired for that, so Clarence chose the real thing. By putting them in sunlight in summer, he would help get them through the long, gray midwestern winter. Late summer was the best time for breeding. Later, Clarence would have breeding boxes, filled with soil, built for them; they needed the soil in which to lay their eggs. Without it, they would not lay the eggs and could die of egg impaction.

He walked behind the exhibits on the main floor. He could feel the heat from the sun, and it bothered him.

"This building should be air-conditioned," he lamented to no one in particular. "It's destructive to the animals. That's why the mortality is so high in here."

As he passed the backs of cages holding poisonous snakes—each one marked with a conspicuous red dot—he was aware of the pull cord that ran at eye level across the entire bank of cages. A keeper hadn't been bitten in years (and not fatally then), but if one were, that cord was crucial.

Once bitten, a keeper would have to pull that cord,

similar to those found on big-city buses. It would sound an alarm.

It was important to memorize the rest of the drill. Sit down and relax. The first keeper to respond would take charge and call an ambulance. A snake-bite specialist at a nearby hospital would be alerted. On the back of each cage, a coded letter designated the proper antitoxin to be used. The antitoxins were kept in the reptile house refrigerator. One keeper would bring the antitoxin to the hospital; another would capture the animal.

"The problem isn't easy to predict," Clarence said. He had never been bitten; that was rare for a professional. "A snake can adjust the amount of venom it produces, from none to a lot. With a rattlesnake, within five minutes you can feel an ache and see redness. It's serious. But there are some venoms we simply can't read well. It can take a few hours to work, and then it can kill you. Another complication is that the antitoxin is horse serum, so you have to be tested for sensitivity to it. That's done at the hospital."

As Clarence spoke, a rattlesnake in a cage near him began to rattle.

"He's alerting the predator—me—that's all. But he probably doesn't want to hurt me. Tomorrow is feeding day for him. He's smart enough to know that he's going to get fed." (Unlike many zoo animals, reptiles are not fed daily; they're fed once, twice, or three times a week, depending on the species.)

"In captivity, they rattle from excitement," Clarence continued, looking at the snake. "If they're captive-born, they don't become afraid of you. They feed better, too, when they're hand-raised, and they're less stressed.

"Stress is a perpetual factor at a zoo. Animals can behave neurotically. Take some of the gorillas in captivity. They can have a regurgitation neurosis. They vomit, then eat it. We don't see that here, but you do in some zoos, and the visitors are shocked by it. You don't see that in the wild. In zoos, you see primates masturbating, and you don't see that in the wild either."

He peered at an Asiatic cobra. It was pale gray.

"It's supposed to be a kind of lustrous black, and it was when we got it, but now it's sick. It had a tumor on the side of its hood, and our vet removed it. But then it changed color. I've never seen a snake do that. Maybe some chemical change in its body produced that tumor—and the change in color."

Several mangrove snakes slithered around their cages.

"We have tons of those," he said. "I'm going to have them sexed, then get rid of some of them."

In the next cage, an eastern indigo snake, found in the southeastern United States, rested, all three feet of it. It was a male and was black.

"He's really tame," Clarence said. "He never bites. I can even pick him up. Sadly, the pet industry made these snakes a threatened species. They were sold to people who didn't know how to take care of them, and the snakes died."

A Gila monster glared at Clarence. It was an exception, one of two of the only venomous lizards in the world. (The other is the beaded lizard.) This one had had a long trip from its home in the Southwest (Arizona and New Mexico are the homes of the Gila monster), but it was doing well in captivity. As Clarence returned its stare, the Gila monster closed its eyes.

"Hey, kiddo, wake up," Clarence said to it. It had fallen asleep curled up in its water bowl.

"He's a slow-moving reptile, but a powerful one. They don't have fangs like snakes," Clarence pointed out, "just sharp teeth. The poison runs from ducts in the gums and is chewed into the victim. It's deadly. When a Gila bites, it hangs on. There's swelling, discoloration before death. There's no antitoxin for it, but I don't think about that. It's one of my favorite creatures. And we have eight of them."

On the back of the next exhibit, there was a plastic mask and instructions for the use of emergency eyewash.

"A spitting cobra," Clarence pointed out. "A black-necked cobra from central Africa. Accurate up to twelve feet. I don't like to deal with something that can get you from afar. They aim for the eyes. You just don't open that cage without putting on that mask first. I'd like to get rid of it, frankly, but they're tough snakes to place."

The cobra's venom could damage one's eyesight if the victim didn't wash out the eye immediately. But it was lethal only if it entered an open wound. The cobra's strike was not considered to be an aggressive move; it was the cobra's defense against an attacking animal—to blind it and permit the cobra to escape.

Clarence walked back to his office. As he opened the door, a tiny green lizard skittered across the floor. Clarence waved at it. It was an anole, purchased (thirty-five cents each) as food for a snake. It was an escapee determined to survive, and Clarence was disinclined to deter it from its mission.

His mind was on the snakes.

"A snake doesn't go after an animal it can't consume," he said. "Snakes strike out in self-defense, of course, and they kill for food. That's it. They're remarkable in some ways. Some of them can sense changes in temperature of less than one degree. A snake can analyze the body heat of its victim within 1/10,000th of a degree and conclude how much venom will be needed to kill it. The heat of an animal's footprints can lead a snake to it; the warmer it is, the closer the snake is to it. Remember, the initial bite doesn't kill the prey. The snake must follow it and see it fall. And the snake does just that."

Clarence was restless in his confining office space. He headed out into the warm day, to the hoofed-stock area, where he tracked down the tortoises, in a pen by themselves, eating. One tortoise had almost fallen into a deep pan containing food, but had not stopped eating.

"Pizza pans, that's what we need. Low, flat pizza pans," Clarence mumbled to himself.

He watched the tortoises, who moved very slowly. Some people like them as pets, he noted, but what makes a good pet is not always easy to determine, once you've listed dogs and cats.

"People want wild animals to behave like pets. It doesn't

turn out like that. Animals have temperaments. They can be stressed. When they're irritable, they can attack. And when a wild animal attacks, it's not like getting scratched by a house cat. They can chew an arm off. Or kill. I don't push animals. You can read them, their moods. A good keeper picks up on that."

On his way back to the reptile house, Clarence stopped to visit some friends, human and animal, at the great ape house. His interest in animals didn't end with reptiles; he was a familiar sight to keepers throughout the zoo.

As he strolled around the center core of the exhibit, he spotted Koundu, a large, lively male gorilla bounding around his habitat. Koundu spotted Clarence and, with a carrot in his mouth, came over to where Clarence and a keeper were standing. Koundu stuck the carrot, still in his mouth, through the mesh cage toward the keeper, a young man.

"He's trading. He wants to give me the carrot in exchange for something sweet. He loves raisins, adores peanut butter. If you fake eating the carrot, he'll take it back from you. That's his way of sharing," the keeper said, pretending to munch the carrot.

A second keeper, another young man, joined them.

"Did you hear? Shauri's baby died last night," he said to Clarence.

"No, I hadn't," Clarence sighed. He had known that the likable chimp was pregnant, but hadn't heard about the birth.

"At 5:45 last night, in the zoo hospital. Pneumonia. They took blood from its father and transfused it, but no luck. It was anemic. They tried antibiotics, too, but it probably had a congenital bacterial infection. Nothing would have worked."

There was a pause in the conversation. An unstated sense of mourning silenced the three men.

Clarence headed back to the reptile house. The shipment of tortoises from Bermuda was due to arrive at night, and he would stay late to build two simple pens for them in the basement of the reptile house.

The next morning, Clarence sat in the zoo office conference room, waiting for Les Fisher's weekly staff meeting to begin. He wore a short-sleeved white shirt and tie, his customary corduroy jeans; the short sleeves were his admission that the Chicago summer was affecting him.

Les Fisher convened the meeting on time. Before consulting his notes, the informal agenda he brought to the meetings, he asked Kevin Bell, "Would a loon eat a baby duck? My mother-in-law thought she saw one do it."

"Sure," Kevin answered.

The first item on the agenda: the continuing problem of the few alcoholics on the zoo staff and what to do about them. He urged those present to remember the need to confirm in writing any objectionable behavior.

"If people are impaired, it will show up in their work," Les said. He notified the group that the park district administration was now giving offenders just two incidents of substance abuse before taking significant action.

He moved on.

"Moats. We have stuff growing in the lion house moats," he said. "Eventually, the moat might crack. Weeds. That thistle stuff. The moats at the large mammal area have almost tree-sized things in them. The roots could create a problem. Take a look, please."

Mark Rosenthal made a note on his pad.

For the first time in years, vandals had entered the zoo after hours and had done some damage. They had entered the large mammal house through the outdoor tapir yard. The tapirs may have been unnerved by being awakened, but they had not been harmed, Mark noted, and had not, apparently, harmed the intruders. The vandals either had a key or were gifted at breaking locks; they had gone directly to the gift shop inside the large mammal house and had stolen whatever they could carry.

"There were film packages, hats, and T-shirts littered in the tapir yard. I guess when they saw the animals, they dropped some of their loot and ran," Kevin reported. The discovery of the break-in had been reported to him early in the morning.

"Instant panic," Dennis Meritt observed. As assistant director, he felt responsible for the safety of all the animals. "We're lucky. We could have had some dead giraffes. They're flighty animals, and they panic in the face of the unusual. They've been known to run into walls and kill themselves. Lucky that the people who broke in didn't confront the giraffes."

"I guess this weather's debilitating to both man and beast," Les said, indicating that some keepers had urged him to order T-shirts to replace their khaki uniform shirts. He wanted to help, but there wasn't any money in the budget for T-shirts.

Mark reported that a consultant in elephant training would be in residence all day, training the keepers who worked with the elephants. Don Meyer, the consultant, was based in southern Wisconsin and was a familiar figure at the zoo. He had worked with animals for years, had run a zoo, and had been a zoo curator. He had a positive approach to elephants, to caring for them, that Mark shared. It was Meyer's method to train the keepers to handle the elephants; they, not the animals, were his students. He stressed the importance of keepers talking to each other, the value of standardizing the way the elephants were treated. The elephants had to know—as trained dogs did—what was right and what was wrong. Meyer sought to teach the keepers to avoid confusion, which could lead to trouble. A troubled elephant was a serious threat. The keepers were taught to call the elephants by name, to give them clear commands. The use of the ankus and ropes prodded the elephants without harming them. Good behavior was rewarded, with a food "treat" at first, then words of praise. The system had been invaluable in managing the elephants under Mark's care.

The meeting ended, and Clarence went back to the reptile house. The tortoises had arrived from Bermuda, and they were in their pens. Clarence wanted to take a look at them. On his way, he told Art, busy cleaning cages, to "keep them moist; they dehydrate."

Clarence walked through the basement; he passed a cage

containing a black Tegu lizard. A keeper had attached a homemade sign, THIS ANIMAL NOW BITES. When Clarence passed the cage, the lizard leaped toward the glass, crashed into it, and bounced off, its tongue flicking out wildly.

The Tegu was young, but its behavior mimicked that of an adult. Normally the young were docile, the older ones aggressive. Tegus grew to be more than two feet long from nose to tip of their long tail. A Tegu's black and gold striped appearance kept it concealed in nature. In the wild, it would not chase a larger creature; it would try to get away. Its bite was like a band-saw slash; it gripped the flesh and tore with a sawing motion. This Tegu did not succeed in taunting Clarence, or even in getting his attention. Clarence's mind was elsewhere.

Clarence suspected that the arrival of the tortoises would unnerve the keepers, who felt that they had enough reptiles to care for already.

"We'll have some anxiety attacks. But it doesn't do any good to fret. We have to stay calm. We're overstocked and understaffed. It'll take a year to get rid of our surplus and get properly organized.

"We advertise in the zoo association journal for surplus and wanted animals. Reptile departments keep in touch with each other, too. In due time, everything will be taken care of, but right now those tortoises will inspire some anxiety."

When he got to the two pens, a male tortoise had mounted a female and was clucking happily. He did not dally; his mission was accomplished quickly. Within seconds, a second pair joined them in initiating their new home. Group sex among tortoises. Clarence looked on and smiled; he was pleased to discover that their anxiety level was not high.

It was feeding day. The reptile house was closed when live food—chicks, rabbits, rats, mice—was fed, so children's dreams would not be corrupted.

Clarence passed Art, at work in the basement.

"We're up to the kazoo in rats," Art said.

"Give some extras to the pythons. They'll eat 'em,"

Clarence suggested. "Anyway, I want to cancel the rat shipments and get rid of that rat room. Let's order weekly instead of collecting them down here."

As Clarence and Art chatted, a pair of white rabbits, doomed to be dinner for large snakes, were twitching in a carrier nearby. Large chickens would be on the snake menu as well; the gators and the Gila monsters preferred chicks.

"That rabbit," Art said, pointing to the carrier, "I'll just toss it into the anaconda cage. Believe me, the anaconda will take it. It'll take me, too, if I'm not careful. By the way, Clarence, the puff adder is eating very little. And it defecates just once a month. It's getting fatter and fatter."

Clarence looked at Art with an expression that seemed to say, "That's your problem, Art."

"One of these days, I hope to convert to dead food," Clarence proclaimed. "It's better for the keepers and the animals. A dying rabbit still has the teeth to bite a snake. I've seen it happen."

Again, he had snakes on his mind. He knew all the charges against them. He'd heard that man, the commanding upright presence, has a deeply rooted aversion to any crawling species. It is, some said, biological. He knew, as well, that snakes represent evil in many societies. Nevertheless, he sustained an admiration for them, a respect, and, at times, a profound fear.

"If a king cobra bites an appendage, cut it off. Quickly. That's how dangerous they are. The king cobra has a large venom gland, and when it bites, it holds on and pumps. Don't forget, it's an eighteen-foot snake with a tablespoon of venom in it. If a person gets all that venom, it's terminal. Even newborn snakes have venom, and it's in a concentrated form, which makes it extremely dangerous. What some people don't realize is that even a scratch from a big, or even a small, snake can do harm. It doesn't always take a bite."

He was distracted by the scampering of the black Tegu lizard in its cage.

"We got that one when it was a baby," he said. "That

sucker is going to be mean as shit when he grows up."

He paused in front of the large cage holding the green iguana; as usual, the iguana was reclining along a tree branch, surveying the basement of the reptile house with its fixed glare. Clarence returned the glare, then moved on.

Along the way, he passed cages with snakes and lizards. Occasionally, he would get a phone call from someone who wanted to buy one as a pet. It annoyed him.

"When you think about all the creatures captured in the wild that go to pet shops and on to owners, you ought to know that ninety-nine percent of them die before they've had a chance to live a long, happy life.

"Visit a wild-animal wholesaler, and see a new shipment. Count the dead animals, dead before they can even be sold. The people who ship them in, the worst of them, use the smallest containers to ship them. It's cheaper. When iguanas are packed that way, they trample each other to death, and others die simply because they're so severely stressed. So many die that the price of the survivors goes up. This green one here would cost eighty-nine dollars in a pet store."

When Clarence had lived in Tulsa with his parents, he kept as many as 200 reptiles and amphibians in the house. Some of them remained in that house, cared for by his parents. When Clarence visited home, he visited more than his parents.

"In the old days, when I lived there, they had the run of the house in some cases," he recalled. "I had two iguanas five feet long that certainly did. I guess you could say that they were paper-trained house pets, but I hate to use the word *pet*. I'd rather talk about what I call captive behavior. These creatures aren't pets. They're wild animals that may be able to adjust to their new environment.

"I remember my iguanas crawling up onto my lap, to get my body warmth. They recognized me by my scent. They'd come to me but would stay away from strangers. They can be taught. But within limitations."

He resumed his walk, pausing in front of a cage holding a

leopard gecko, a small, spotted desert lizard from Pakistan.

"If I have to use that word *pet*," he said, "this would be my favorite for kids. It will allow them to hold it. It can be hand-fed. It's very clean, like a cat. It eats live crickets and baby mice, which you can buy. And cleaning its cage is not difficult. If they're used to you, they'll lick your hand. They need some rocks to hide under, some water and some food and a warm room—they like heat—and if you ever need a vet, you can find one who specializes in reptiles. You can buy a gecko for fifty dollars."

Clarence picked up the gecko. It shot feces at him and urinated in his hand.

Clarence looked sternly at the nervous lizard.

"Mine *never* do that," he said.

And then he laughed.

First Person: Clarence Wright

When I was twelve, through a lot of the Walt Disney films, I realized that what I was really interested in was wildlife and animals. As a child I was different from most kids. I never really played with a group. I always was pretty much by myself, doing my own things. Then, when I was twelve, I found a purpose in my life. I started devoting more time to observing wildlife. We lived in a remote area; I think the nearest human was probably about ten miles away, so I was able to do a lot of field observations, and I developed a comfortable feeling with nature. More than I did around people.

I remember buying books; the first book was *Born Free*, which I read two or three times. And then, after I saw Walt Disney's film on otters, I read *Ring of Bright Water*. At that time, I started purchasing small reptiles. I was thirteen when I purchased my first caiman in a pet shop. Like most kids at that age, I knew nothing about it; no one seemed to know anything about it. I lost that first caiman because I didn't know exactly what I was doing. I also was interested

in local wildlife, and I raised a baby coyote. I raised it
successfully to adulthood.

When I was fourteen, my brother was driving past a
nature center—run by Hugh and Zelta Davis—in a little
town called Catoosa, Oklahoma, between Tulsa and Clare-
more. I went out there almost everyday; my brother would
take me out there. He was very understanding. The third
time I went, I was going to pay fifty cents to get in, but
Mrs. Davis said, "No, no, you don't have to worry about it.
You've seen this place more than most people will see it in
their lifetime." She said, "Just come on in and enjoy yourself."

At that time, they had a tremendous collection of reptiles, all kinds of cobras, a large selection of alligators,
about a hundred and fifty alligators, all running loose in a
five-acre fenced-in area.

I was one of these quiet people who would just observe. I
observed body movements, behavior among alligators. I
started learning a lot about the behavior of reptiles. They
also had a very good collection of native mammals, bobcats
and mountain lions and a fantastic prairie dog pound.

I started reading like you wouldn't believe, and the book
collection grew. Today it numbers about thirty thousand
dollars' worth of books. It was a fascination that has not
stopped. Today, it's a pioneering thing for me to learn as
much as I can about natural history. At that time, I decided
that I wanted to either go into wildlife conservation work,
be a game ranger, or be a zoo person.

From the time I was about fourteen, I worked every
summer. I worked at the nature center, and I went out
there on weekends. I spent a lot of time at the Davises'
home, which was just across the street from the nature
center. Their house was like a natural history museum;
they had all kinds of skins, skulls. It was just a real comfortable place for me. I learned a wealth of information
from Mr. Davis. He got me involved in going out and
catching alligators; when I was about sixteen, we went to
Arkansas and collected some alligators down in that area.

So I learned a lot about how to handle animals and about the laws of conservation.

After I was graduated from high school, I was torn whether to go in the zoo business or be in some other kind of business. I worked with my dad for about a year. Hugh Davis, who did not have a degree, told me, "If you're going to make zoos a career, you have to have at least a bachelor's degree." And he said, "As far as I'm concerned, you can take the degree and stick it, but you definitely have to get it." So I decided that I was going to have to. Well, I'm the first in my family to have a bachelor's degree. My parents never felt it was a waste of time, but they just didn't really encourage me to do it.

The money wasn't there; I had to earn it all. But the desire and interest were all there. I started working at the zoo during the summer at college, and those four summers I worked as a laborer, but I worked with animals, too. After that, a keepership at the Tulsa Zoo popped up, right after I was graduated. I worked with reptiles.

I was very green. The zoo was like an open encyclopedia to me because there was so much to learn about the behavior of animals in captivity. And, of course, I read all the literature.

You know, if you get your technique down, you can do it all, cleaning and taking care of the animals. And you learn the animals so well you know when they're going to shit. So you gear your time for it. At that time we had approximately five hundred animals in the collection, lines of three-tier cages, little box cages with full-grown reptiles— western diamondbacks, rattlesnakes, cobras, and on and on.

I was a kind of working curator. That's the reason why I'm really not used to wearing a shirt and a tie. I'm used to filling in for absent keepers and still doing my other work. Most of the paperwork I either did at home or did before or after work. They knew they had someone who was far beyond most keepers. In one of the zoo publications my second summer there, the director mentioned my name and said I was a future zoo director. That got me so much flak from everybody. A lot of them were jealous. I didn't just work hard. I had the abilities and knowledge to look at a new situation and work through it. Common sense. To me, common sense is to look at something and do the best you can with the situation.

That zoo was primitive enough so that every situation that came along I could solve fairly easily. I was comfortable in the whole zoo. It wasn't because of the desire to please somebody; it was the desire to work with the animals and make them comfortable. I was trying to please myself. I still hold to that; I do the best I can with a job, and if it reflects positively, fine. I don't want to say I don't care, it's just that I don't look for recognition for doing a good job.

I was finally promoted to supervisor of reptiles, a curator's job. Within two years in that reptile department, I turned it around. I turned it around to where the animals were being cared for very well, we had reproduction going on, of reptiles that had never before bred in the Tulsa Zoo. We had three endangered species that bred for the first time. I was very excited about the department. And at that time I wanted to switch over to mammals, even though I was comfortable over at reptiles. But I wanted to switch over to mammals because my interest was otters, and I had a big interest in primates. They created a department for me, a primate section and a small mammal section.

I'd been curator of small mammals for about two years, and there was a lot of political stuff going on. They hired a general curator. I thought, "Well, I can live through anything." Well, that wasn't true. I thought I could survive. After all, I was married to the Tulsa Zoo; I mean, I was putting in twelve hours a day, and I'd be there seven days a week, because I loved doing it. I was doing all kinds of research projects. My parents were in Tulsa, and I wanted to stay with my parents. I was still living with my parents, so I tried to weather it for about eight months. The new guy was going in and moving animals around in my department. We didn't get along.

I had a major research project going with Asian small-clawed otters at the Tulsa Zoo. At the American Association of Zoological Parks and Aquariums, they asked me to be the coordinator and studbook keeper for that species. It was the first mammal model species survival plan that the AAZPA ever had, and they said they were probably going to use it as a model for the other mammals. It's a big deal. We had people coming in from other parts of the country to see the program. And when the new guy got on board, he took the whole program lightly, and he told me, "You don't have time for this program anymore," and he threw it out. Just like that, just threw the whole thing out. I gave two weeks' notice. I'd committed almost twelve years of my life to that facility, and the zoo director didn't even talk to me about what happened.

I went back to school and got a teaching certificate. The Tampa Zoo advertised in the AAZPA newsletter. I went down, and the interview with the director went very well. Sure enough, he called me. At that time I was supporting my parents, like I am now, and the salary was nineteen five, which is nothing. And I was to be a zoo curator, which is like a general curator. But I thought, here is a zoo that was an old roadside zoo, bars and stuff like that, that they were going to bulldoze down to build a brand-new zoo. And I thought, "God, here I would be second in charge; I could really design a zoo the way I want it done." Again, I was working seven days a week. I did it because I love doing it. I was working twelve and thirteen hours, seven days a week, and I enjoyed it.

After a year and a half, I needed a salary increase, because nineteen five a year is not very good. I was doing the general curator stuff, all the paperwork, and all the computer stuff. I was supervising the keepers, hiring keepers, doing the curator stuff of getting animals in, getting rid of animals, and we still had a zoo, we still had a temporary zoo I was overseeing. I decided I just had to have more money. Luckily, that's when the job came open at Lincoln Park. I applied for it, and it took them about six months to process it; out of seventy applications they narrowed it down to me.

Otters are my favorite animals. I think it's their outlook on life. It is "Get as much joy out of life as you can." They constantly play; they get so much out of every little thing they have, whether it's a little marble, or whether it's a stone. They take their time and enjoy life.

I had otters from the time I was nineteen, at home. I know otter behavior. Almost by glancing, seeing what they're doing, I can tell you what they are thinking. It's not being anthropomorphic. I interpret it as animal behavior, not human behavior. I literally lived with North American otters in my home, so if they were sleeping at the foot of my bed, I was hearing sounds from them that normal people wouldn't hear by just having them in a zoo and observing them. There were vocalizations that had never been recorded before; I recorded them. Low guttural sounds that meant that otters have nightmares, and they'll start twitching and making little guttural sounds.

Otters that have grown up with me read my face. They look at your face and eyes. My female Millie follows me around; she's always looking up at my face. I can give her a facial signal that I want to play, and she'll jump up and start playing. If I'm in a bad mood, they still may push me. I remember telling Millie not to open the drawers in the highboy. She knew she wasn't supposed to go there, but then I started doing something else, and I actually saw her in the corner of my eye sneak around until she thought she was out of my vision, go to the drawer, and pop that drawer open and crawl in, quickly, quickly.

They are very affectionate. Millie will, if I'm standing, stand up and put her arms around my leg, and then I'll stroke her. And if she wants to be picked up, she'll push her head against my hand while I'm stroking her, and then I'll hold her. They express some affection by grooming. I'll start petting her, and she'll start grooming my neck. Though she's an otter, she realizes that I hand-raised her from a baby. I introduced her to other otters; she knows she's an otter, and she enjoys it and gets along very well with a man.

My main interest, when I first got involved, was to breed

otters. And to understand their behavior. I'm an otter specialist for the International Union for the Conservation of Nature. I do a lot of behavioral observation. I don't have Asian small-clawed otters now; I have North Americans. Vocalization is different between the two species. The Asian small-clawed otters, all they can do is make bird chirps. The North American otters have bird chirps, but they also have a humming sound. You can talk to them that way, and they'll hum back. I think they're even more affectionate than the Asians. Asians are very temperamental; if they're into something and you swat them, they'll turn around and chew your leg off. And North Americans, if you swat them, they walk off. I learned very quickly how to read Asians, because I got bit many times. My otters I kept mainly in the house. Now these three Asians that I had, I did not want to do that. They were tame, but they weren't tame enough.

Asian small-clawed otters run in bands of up to twenty individuals. We're finding out they have extended families, meaning that the sons and daughters stay with the family group for a long time, up to two generations. And they actually help care for the offspring that are born. We're finding out all this new stuff.

Psychologists believe that people feel comfortable around mammals because they are mammals. Also, the fur has a lot to do with the psychological security of a person, who can touch the fur of an animal; it's more soft and gentle to the touch than a scale. Humans feel more comfortable around mammals. Reptiles have gotten a bad rap, because when most people think of reptiles, they automatically think venomous. I don't care if it's a lizard or an amphibian—when I grew up, I was scared of reptiles. When I was twelve years old, before I got to know Hugh Davis, I was scared of reptiles. Somebody showed me a garter snake, and I was unbelievably scared. A lot of the proliferation of the reptiles' image is done by parents, in teaching their kids that all reptiles are bad. Toads give you warts, you know, you don't pick up toads. I was scared of toads. When Hugh

Davis came along and taught me about reptiles, and how to deal with them and their behavior, I realized that it was all bunk.

Do snakes recognize people? If you have a different body odor than other people, they may sense that, but as far as true recognition, no. I don't feel they can recognize an individual: "Gee, this person feeds me, and I want to be good to this person." It doesn't have that kind of intelligence. It doesn't have a sense of remorse; if it bites you, it bites you out of self-defense.

Now, lizards—when you get higher up into some of the lizards—are very aware of people and their shapes and body forms. I think they can recognize a little more than the snake. Supposedly snakes were the last to evolve, so they're the newest type of reptile. Tortoises and crocodilians are the oldest; supposedly that's where snakes and lizards came from. Lizards are more cognizant of their environment. They're more visual than snakes.

You can work with snakes and tame them by just handling them. It's because they get habituated to your handling them. You deal with them every day, you handle them every day, and they know you're not going to do them any harm by repetitive touching. But they're not affectionate.

A lizard may come over and just be curious, and that's the word that I use when they come over to look at you; curious. It's not that they're going to show you affection. I can pretty safely say of all reptiles that there's no affection. They're driven by mating, by courtship, by instincts. You'll hear people say, "Oh, my lizard recognizes me, and he comes over, and he gets up." Well, if they think a little bit, if it's a cool day, the lizard gets up and rests on your body because it's getting body heat from you. And you can calm a reptile down that's cool, that's a little excited, by just putting him on your arm and letting him rest. He'll lie there because he's getting the warmth.

Each reptile has a personality the way all animals do. Even snakes have their own little quirky personalities. You may have one snake that is really curious, when you walk

by, to see if you've got any food. And the other one's just
lying there, couldn't care less about its world. You may put
the food in, and the snake who's curious will grab it and eat
it with no problem; for the other you have to dangle it, and
he doesn't care. Some rattlesnakes will be interested in just
exploring their world. They'll move around and are looking
at it. Others will strike the glass constantly because they're
so nervous and upset. When you get a wild-caught reptile,
you want to try to get a reptile that is the most adaptive to
captivity. There have been reptiles brought in that have
been so nervous about being in captivity they die. They
literally won't eat; they die. With animals like that, if
they're local animals, I'll take them back out and turn them
loose.

There's so little known about reptiles, in behavior, courtship, and reproduction, that it's still an open field. We have
come a long way in ten, fifteen years, on the care of reptiles
and amphibians in captivity. Animals that now are kept so
easily, ten years ago you'd be lucky if you could keep one
alive, because of the lack of knowledge of the care of that
animal. A prime example is green tree pythons, which we
don't have here, but I had in Tulsa. If you kept them alive,
you were lucky. Now, everybody's learned to reproduce
them. Individuals and institutions and research facilities
are doing the pioneering work; that adds to the whole body
of the care of these animals.

As far as crocodilians go, the alligators have the broadest
perspective and broadest personality of all crocodilians.
They are aware of their environment. They're more curious about things. I think curiousness is a sign of intelligence. If an animal's curious enough to go look over and
see what's going on, it tells me that it has enough mental
ability to synthesize. Since I grew up at the nature center
and they had over a hundred alligators, I could see the
behavioral differences in each individual alligator.

We had a female that was a delicate petite alligator who
liked the food a certain way, and if it wasn't a certain way,
she just wouldn't eat it. We had one named Betty, who was

an eight-foot female, very heavy-set. I'll never forget, Zelta Davis was feeding this animal late in the evening, and she had sunglasses on, so she really couldn't see where the mouth was. She would just tap it on the snout, and it would open its mouth, and she'd throw the food in. Well, Betty came lumbering up on the land and was waiting there patiently, and she had her mouth open. And instead of tapping the top part of the snout, Mrs. Davis tapped on the lower part, and of course Betty clamped down and was in the process of pulling her into the water slowly. Betty had her mouth shut and didn't realize what she was pulling on. Mrs. Davis took her hand and said "let go" and slapped Betty. Betty just let go. Like, "What did I do?" and went back in the water. Of course, we had more food, but she wouldn't come up, not for a week after that.

I think tortoises have been given a bad rap as far as being dull and dim-witted. In their own way, they have the ability to be interested in their environment if they are given a chance to have an environment. Unfortunately, when you give them a brick wall, that's not much of an environment. I think a lot of reptiles are that way; if they're kept in small little glass cages, they lose interest, and they look dull. But tortoises are a lot smarter than we give them credit for. First of all, they've survived beyond all the dinosaurs and all the prehistoric mammals, so they've got to have some basic instincts. More than anything, they're majestic in many ways. They seem to have their own purpose in life, they don't care about anything else, they know where they stand.

Some psychologists believe that people are more at ease with objects or animals that are round and really don't have a shape. And tortoises have that round appearance, nonthreatening. There's another point: they're vegetarians, they don't eat meat. Another fascination is that they are a beautiful animal, there are a lot of beautiful colors in them. I'm fascinated by their behavior—courtship behavior has not been well documented in a lot of the tortoises—and reproduction. My fascination with all the reptiles has evolved into trying to set up an enriching environment. The quality of life is super important, for the snake as well as the elephant. Unfortunately reptiles in zoos have been kept in a very limited environment, and I think that's the reason why you get this thing that just lies there and does nothing.

My dream is to develop habitats that pretty much simulate where the animals are from. I know there's no way to totally simulate them, because of our space limitations, but we can give more space and incorporate a very active environment, with flowing water, live plants, soil, and bark chips instead of just gravel, giving them a lot of nooks and crannies they can get involved with and move around in. We can give them all kinds of options that they don't have in a square box. You can incorporate several different species in one exhibit. Some zoos have done it. There's enough known now about reptile care; they won't eat one another.

You can actually feed the animal by hand-feeding or putting the food in a location where the animal in the wild would normally feed. For example, the green iguana lies in the trees and eats fruit off the trees. You have a food dish that is in a bushy area of an exhibit on a log, and you can put out the food pan, and the iguana knows that it can feed there; it doesn't have to go to the ground to eat, which is really not normal. When the dandelions were blooming, I asked the reptile people to feed them to the tortoises. Well, you know, it's extra work, and they don't like doing it. But when you give them a variety of food like that, their whole interest picks up. Gee, this is different, I love it. And they eat it. So their behavior starts developing, they start getting a broader interest. And they can go over, and here's this waterfall coming down, and they can crawl in the pool, or they can crawl underneath the waterfall and get splashed on to get stimulation. If they can do that, they've got some options.

A classic example is our great apes facility; the activity of those gorillas and orangs and chimps is phenomenal. You go to some zoos, and they have the apes set off where the public looks on, and the apes are just sitting there doing nothing. Ours is designed to promote movement, and upward movement, and social connections. They can climb and move and manipulate ropes; I have never seen such an active group of animals.

The major uncertainty I have is what direction this zoo wants the reptile collection to go. Do they want to renovate the building? Do they really understand about giving the animals environmental stimulation? Or do they want just a big box? By having a habitat and environmental stimulation, you can get more activity from your animals and more interest in life. I think our zoo's reptile collection will be equal to others in the United States, probably in two to three years, if we go down the path of renovation and development of new facilities, and taking on the new kind of husbandry that it's going to need to get there. Right now, I feel we are a long way from being on a par with the other great zoos as far as the reptile collection goes.

In five years, I would like to be either a field biologist with a Ph.D., doing field research on otters, or a director of a zoo that is very open and able to contribute to world conservation. My whole purpose in life is world conservation, to develop and help save habitats, to develop habitats if they've been destroyed.

In my life, the animals are number one, whether they're in the wild or in captivity, and I will do all I can in my power, if I have to do it myself, to make sure animals are cared for properly. If it means saving a habitat, I would do all I could to save the habitat. I go by my own drumbeat, and I do what I think is best for the animals. And if that means getting in and scrubbing a cage, I'll do it. When I quit my job in Tulsa, I adopted a philosophy of life: I was going to do the best I could; I was always going to be kind to people, no matter how bad they were to me. And this relates to my whole being. I'm going to always give love, and I think it will always come back.

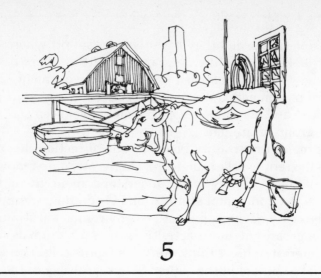

5

FARMER'S DAUGHTER

Picture a typical farmer: a middle-aged man in well-worn overalls, workshirt, weathered boots, and a cap with the emblem of a farm equipment company, surveying vast fields of waving grain.

Then picture the "farmer" who oversees the Farm in the Zoo, five acres of red barns and patches of grass. That farmer was LuAnne Metzger. At age twenty-eight, she was tall (5'8"), trim, athletic; her hair was bronze-colored, her eyes royal blue, her summertime tan calculatedly deep. She wore two pairs of earrings: a pair of small diamond studs and a pair of gold hoops. Her clothing was impeccably fashionable.

LuAnne had come a long way from Carlock, Illinois, a very small town (population less than 500) her family had lived in for generations—and she'd done it in a relatively short time.

She grew up in a house that doubled as the local funeral parlor; when she was born and required a room, she displaced the casket display. Her father was an independent insurance agent who also raised sheep and beef cattle. (He was a minor partner in the funeral home.)

After high school, she went to the University of Illinois, where she majored in agricultural communications; she was graduated in 1980. While she was at college, she spent summers as an intern with the United States Department of Agriculture in Chicago; after graduation, she worked for that department's office of information. A budget cut eliminated her job after five months. She did not mourn.

"They offered me the chance to go to New York to work," she remembered. "But I hated that city. As it turned out, I hated doing everything in triplicate as well."

She got a call from an editor at a new farm newspaper based in Bloomington, Illinois. She was tempted by the combination of journalism and farming.

She had grown up showing sheep and cattle at county and state fairs and had a collection of trophies to prove it. She knew about farming. For the newspaper, she covered fourteen counties. The experience paid off and led to another phone call. That conversation took her to Des Moines, Iowa, to be beef editor of *Wallace's Farmer* ("Iowa's Farm Progress Publication"), founded by Henry Wallace of Progressive Party fame.

For LuAnne, that was an exciting time; she covered crops, too, and was the first woman editor the publication had hired.

"The pay was better. In fact, I could live on it. I could live on my own," she recalled. "Our readers lived and died with *Wallace's Farmer*," she added. "It was a great job. Sure, Iowa was a little hickish compared to Illinois, but I worked with great people, and I had a company car. I even found an Iowa farm boy, who had become a grain trader. But when he decided to take a job in Chicago, I knew I'd have to quit my job.

"I interviewed with public relations firms in Chicago. No fun in them. I came to the conclusion that I wanted to be on a farm again. I didn't want a nine-to-five job. Then I picked up a copy of the University of Illinois newsletter for agriculture grads, and I saw the listing for the farm curator's job at the zoo, so I applied."

She got the job in February 1986 and married the grain trader seven months later.

The Farm in the Zoo was funded by the zoo society, not by the park district. LuAnne worked for the society, but those who reported to her worked for the city bureaucracy. At first, that caused resentment; the keepers wanted to report to a curator who owed allegiance to the park district, not to the zoo society, which some saw as a group of fluttering socialites. No doubt they objected to taking orders from a young new curator, a young new female curator as well.

A year and a half after LuAnne was hired, the situation had calmed down—or gone underground. Keepers griped at times, but LuAnne was in charge.

Her daily commute from a western suburb to her cluttered basement office in the primate house took several hours a day out of her life, but she was often at work before 7 A.M.

"I wound up here by a fluke, but I love it," she said, seated behind her old desk covered with zoo paperwork. "I don't miss the procrastination and pain of meeting deadlines. I like agriculture, and I like the chance to teach urban kids about it."

When she took the job, she was told the Farm in the Zoo would be renovated. The work, in fact, was well under way, and she played a guiding role.

"That encouraged me to take the job. Now I've got a commitment here. I know what I want this farm to be in two years, in five years. I want visitors to see activities and demonstrations, food tastings, folk music, storytellers, and more. I want them to leave here with a basic fact: food doesn't come from a grocery store. I want classes held here and all sorts of things going on. I want this to be a lump of coal that becomes a diamond."

The farm consisted of five red barns: a main exhibit hall and barns for poultry, horses, dairy cattle, and livestock.

The animals she governed included six dairy cows (each producing a calf every year), three to four dairy goats and their kids, a sow and her litter, four sheep and lambs, four beef steers, six horses and ponies, and a collection of chickens. Some stayed on as tenants; others moved on to market.

Every morning, LuAnne would dig into the paperwork in her primate house office, check her box at the zoo center, attend meetings related to the renovation, then head for the farm itself on the southern edge of the zoo.

Early one summer morning, she headed for the farm to make rounds. In the dairy barn, two piglets were nursing with wild abandon on their mammoth sow. "One of the meanest animals—along with the dairy bull—on the farm," LuAnne noted.

Six dairy cows were in an outdoor pen, standing around stoically. A brown-and-white Guernsey calf was in an outdoor pen with two piglets; they seemed oblivious to each other. In another adjoining pen, sheep and goats pranced.

Inside the dairy barn, a sign was posted: "Each day the average cow drinks 25 gallons of water, eats 26 pounds of hay and 20 pounds of grain, to produce 7 gallons of milk." At the zoo's farm, the milking process was for the public's delight; the milk produced by the milking machines, open to view, was used to feed the calves and other young animals.

As LuAnne walked around the dairy barn, she was met by Tom Meehan, the zoo's veterinarian. He was there to visit the mother of the calf in the outdoor pen. The Guernsey was not in good shape.

"After the birth, which was unassisted, she went down," LuAnne said. The expression meant that the animal dropped to the ground and couldn't get up on her own, a serious sign in other animals at the zoo as well.

"We almost lost her. She was close to being euthanized. We put some feed and water in front of her and left for the day. I really thought I'd find a stiff cow in the morning, but she drank the water and ate the feed, and by eight in the morning, she was standing."

Tom was checking the cow's right front hoof for signs of healing; earlier, he'd removed an abscess from it. He unwrapped the hoof, cleaned and treated the area, and bandaged it again. LuAnne watched him work in silence. So did the Guernsey.

A horde of flies had entered the barn. LuAnne swiped at them unsuccessfully, then motioned to one of the keepers on duty: "Please spray for flies. They're biting." The keeper, a middle-aged woman, nodded and disappeared.

LuAnne went outside and entered the pen with the Guernsey calf; she petted it, and it nuzzled her knee. A few yards away, a goat bleated. Two piglets wallowed in a pool of muddy water, a few feet away from the calf; one defecated in the water. A group of morning zoo visitors watched it all with pleasure. In the distance, modern highrise buildings bordered the zoo; the sound of traffic mixed with the sounds of the animals, a living incongruity.

LuAnne resumed her stroll through the farm.

"Imagine. Five acres of farmland. And I don't pay any taxes. Just a few headaches, that's all," she said, as she passed a patch of worn grass that she wanted to turn into a garden. "We'll grow vegetables, soybeans, corn, alfalfa, and wheat, just for city kids to see.

"You know what's funny? I wasn't a zoo person when I was growing up. I didn't watch all those animal shows on public television. I'm even allergic to hay. But now that I'm here, I want to learn. I want to know about the other animals. So when I have time, I go to the bird house. I go to see the great apes. I sit in on staff meetings with my eyes and ears wide open. I'm fascinated by the people who work here. It's quite a gamut. Weird, different people trying to work as a team."

She knew that she was unlike most of them, but she was determined to succeed despite the differences. Most of the others were zealous in protecting their animals; as a child, on a farm, she had learned another lesson. Calves became veal. Pigs became bacon. The zoo got its sow from a farmer when that sow was pregnant, so visitors could see the birth, and the piglets produced. But after the birth, the pigs went back to that farm—and a fate in contradiction to that of the other zoo animals.

The farm raised chickens, too, and the chicks were shipped to the reptile house, to serve as food. That was not recited to visitors, but LuAnne did have to field protests from informed and angry callers.

"I've had calls from people who call me a murderer," she said. "For God's sake, I loved steers. I saved pictures of me with my favorite steers before they went to slaughter. It's either them or us. Everything eats something, and if the reptiles prefer chicks, well, that's how it is. When we raise all these animals here, I watch the docents love them. I know that our steers are sold and slaughtered and our lambs go to market. But I watch the docents loving those animals, and I'm touched by it. I hate to be the bad guy. But I really don't think I am. I think I'm sensible, realistic, not heartless.

"If a cow or a ewe doesn't give birth in a year, we ship it out. On a real farm, you have to keep culling them. That's selective breeding, to breed for the best milk producers, the best meat, the best wool, the best-looking. Here, we want them to look good, and we want them to be well nourished, but we don't have to turn a profit. That's the advantage and the big difference from running a real farm. My profit is in the people who come here and enjoy the exhibits and the animals and go away a little smarter about farms than they were when they got here."

In 1964, when the Farm in the Zoo opened—thanks to the fund-raising mastery of the zoo society—it was part of a major effort to upgrade the entire zoo. The zoo society was just five years old then, developing its fiscal muscles, and LuAnne was six. By the time LuAnne arrived at the zoo, it had grown, the society had raised millions of dollars to support that growth, and the farm had achieved a level of popularity that made it a common stop for two million visitors annually.

They came to see the cows milked, as they were on real

dairy farms. They came to see poultry, horses, and live-stock—and exhibits that explained farm life to street-smart city dwellers.

For LuAnne, the farm functioned, but it wasn't easy to compete with the more exotic collections in the rest of the zoo. Cows weren't wild animals. And LuAnne, new to the business of zoos, was uneasy at first.

"I felt lost," she recalled. "I knew how things got done at newspapers and magazines, but I wasn't a zoo professional. I didn't know how you got office supplies at the zoo. The staff welcomed me; they were friendly. But the keepers were another matter. I felt an icy stare between them and me.

"By the time I arrived, it seemed to me that the farm was being ignored. I was the first full-time curator at the farm. Early on, I met a guy who was supposed to be helping me. He hated women, Jews, blacks, you name it. It was a chilling time.

"As I saw it, the farm had become the zoo's Siberia. If you messed up, that's where you were sent. A zoo professional with knowledge of mammals probably wouldn't have wanted to work at the farm. Fortunately, I didn't know any better.

"It was survival of the fittest. I stuck it out. There were some rough times. I found ways to get along with the keepers. Some of the old-timers, who weren't going to change, retired. I never expected them to change. But I was ready to change.

"It took a while for me to learn about the place. I'm still learning. It's funny, but I've always been the young kid on every job I've ever had. I've had to get used to working with seasoned professionals. One way was to learn how important it was to say, 'I don't know. I'll find out and let you know.' In other words, I didn't want to fake knowledge."

She sat on a bench in the small grassy area in the center of the farm, surrounded by the barns. She knew her weaknesses and how they played into the hands of her critics. She had pride, and she knew her strengths.

She knew farm animals. She knew the six major breeds of dairy cattle: Ayrshire, Guernsey, Jersey, Holstein, Milking Shorthorn, and Brown Swiss. She knew that most dairy cows are artificially inseminated and that a cow would calve once a year. She knew, too, that most older dairy cows were sold to make hamburger, although a few might live to be fifteen years old.

She was a mobile reservoir of farm facts; she enjoyed providing useful information to neophytes. She had written a guide for the docents, so when they lectured at the farm, what they said would be correct:

"Pigs are young swine of either sex, under six months old. Hogs are swine older than six months or of greater than two hundred pounds. When mature, females (sows), may weigh up to four hundred pounds, boars up to six hundred pounds."

Sows at the zoo farm—and at real ones—delivered about a dozen piglets. They were the delight of young visitors. For LuAnne, pigs of any size or shape were transients.

"We only have pigs for a month at a time. But that's long enough to know that the maternal instinct makes a sow nasty. Pick up one of the piglets and watch out. The real challenge is to keep all the piglets alive. The sow will lie down on one, and that piglet will scream. We'll pound on the sow, but if we get her real mad, it's even worse."

Goats were another matter. Their history extended back into prehistoric times. LuAnne pointed to a rambunctious goat in a pen nearby.

"The poor man's cow, that's what they're called," she said. They require less feed than cows, which makes them valuable in underdeveloped countries.

One of the goats in the pen was attempting to chew the fence imprisoning it.

"Goats eat walls," she said, with the hint of a laugh denting her customary low-key demeanor.

"They'll eat fiberglass. It takes a lot to kill a goat. They're the delinquents of the farm. They're cute, and people love them, but if you watch them regularly, it's another matter. I saw a kid lose his plastic Cubs helmet in the goat pen, and the goat even tried to chew that."

In the next pen, several sheep moved stolidly, side by side. For the docents, LuAnne had written some guidelines, distinguishing among "sheep raised for mutton (mature meat), for wool, for fur (Karakul) and for hair (Barbados). All breeds produce lamb (young meat), and most produce wool."

While she was charmed by their appearance, LuAnne was convinced that "sheep are dumb farm animals. They flock together. They're skittish. Trying to catch one is hard. Also, they have sensitive digestive systems. They live or they die. A sickly looking sheep is bad news waiting to happen."

She got up and walked toward the poultry barn; the sound of chickens filled the air. She stopped at the entrance and listened to the noise.

"They're no problem. They have a short life here, thanks to the appetite of the reptiles. When they lay eggs, the keepers eat the eggs for lunch. We keep those chickens that lay eggs; we don't sell them or their eggs. When we're done with them, off they go the reptile house. I guess you could call us the terminal market."

The horse barn was being renovated; the horses had been sent to barns in the area until it was completed. LuAnne felt ambivalent about horses. They were beautiful animals; they were dumb animals.

"They are just not as smart as some would have us believe," she said. She conceded that some had splendid memories. The zoo had been home to a Clydesdale, one of the massive brewery horses, who had been patient with petting children. When the barn was ready to be opened again, LuAnne planned to stock it with several well-known breeds.

"We used to have sorry horses, with bad feet and legs,

who were given to the zoo. Now, some are donated and some I've bought. I'm the one who decides what we'll be willing to accept," she noted, implying the difference between the farm's past and present.

She turned toward the barn for beef cattle. The names were familiar: Angus, Hereford, Shorthorn. They can weight up to 2,500 pounds, so LuAnne did not think of them as playful animals. For most of them, the future held a quality grade: prime and choice were familiar to supermarket shoppers.

She spoke of the animals the way a farm manager might speak of them. She never succumbed to anthropomorphic fantasies. Being farm curator was a job—and she liked the job. She wasn't in the business of preserving endangered species, but she could educate the uneducated masses. That, for her, was enough. She had been a farm girl and now was in the big city. She wanted to combine the best of the two lifestyles.

As she got into an electric cart to drive across the zoo to the zoo office, she waved at two keepers—a man and a woman—standing in the doorway to the dairy barn. She drove off, disappearing over the bridge that spanned the lagoon beside the farm.

"She doesn't like to get her hands dirty," one of the keepers said.

"She doesn't have to," the other replied. "She's smart."

FIRST PERSON: LUANNE METZGER

I grew up in a small town. Sheltered, very sheltered. Things were a lot simpler than they are in the city. Everything revolved around the family and the work that we did on the farm. In little towns everyone knows what you're doing, sometimes before you're doing it. You always kept an eye on what others thought about, what other people would think of you.

It was a town of three hundred people, two churches.

You either went to one church or the other, and a lot of people were related to each other.

I grew up with farm animals, living on a farm. It seemed natural that I wanted to join FFA, Future Farmers of America, and take ag classes. I was always in 4-H as I was growing up, boys' 4-H. Girls' 4-H at the time was sewing, cooking, baby-sitting, things like that. I didn't do that. I grew up working on the farm and being with the animals, and that just seemed the natural place for me. When I went to high school, I wanted to join FFA and take ag classes, and I was the first girl to do so at our chapter, and our chapter was a large one—one hundred twenty, one hundred thirty boys. I think the instructor and adviser truly believed that I joined just so I could be with lots of boys. And as I began taking tests and doing well, he found out that I truly had an interest and aptitude for it.

When I became an officer of the chapter, it was always standard policy that the officers, when they were seniors, got to go to Kansas City for the national convention. There was a little bit of a furor, because I was the only girl—who would chaperon me? They'd have to take another girl to share a room with me; I couldn't bunk in with the guys. They tried to tell me I couldn't go, when I'd earned the right, because I was a girl. Well, I ended up going; they took another girl.

I think it was the way I was raised. I wasn't pampered because I was a girl. My sister and I were on the farm, and there was work to be done. We did it equally. When we went to the fairs in the summer, it was pull your equal weight, take care of your own livestock, do your work.

I remember being around animals from the earliest time. There are pictures of us as young children with my brother's prize ram, and it'd be my brother and my sister and me standing there. The house was always filled with trophies and animal awards that my brother and sister earned at fairs and shows. I had an affection for the farm animals that we worked with and showed. You spend every day taking care of them. But I always had that sense of realism, that these animals were going to a terminal market, that that's what we were raising them for.

I still have a problem with people who say we murder animals, because they look at it with such tunnel vision. I try to let them know that no one cares for their animals more than a farmer. Even though they may be marketing them and in the end slaughtering them, no one cares more for them because that is their livelihood. A healthy, happy animal is a good productive animal.

Wild animals—the other zoo animals—have their place. It's important that we understand them and try to learn how we can cohabit with them and quit pushing them out of their habitats. But to become so attached to them, and almost give them human characteristics and feelings, I think is wrong. Of course, I think I'm still in the learning stage about what a zoo should do and should be to the public and to the animals. I came here ignorant about zoos and wild animals, and I'll be the first to admit it. People would stop me at the zoo and ask me if we had some sort of animal, and the first few weeks I had to say I didn't know. I'm still formulating my view. I think there's a purpose and a need for zoos.

Two years ago, I never thought I'd be here. I was a journalism major, and I thought I would always be writing or photographing or something along that line. Now, after being here almost two years, I can't see myself leaving for a while. I've set some goals.

The farm was basically nothing; it sat here for twenty, twenty-five years. It was nice, it was pleasant, some cute little farm animals, but there was nothing happening. It was very static. With the renovation, we've given ourselves some new, updated facilities without structurally changing too much. We're going to be a lot more consumer-oriented. Not only do I want people to come here and enjoy the animals, I want them to understand the purpose of these animals, why they're here, that milk does not come from the corner grocery store; milk comes from a cow, and that's why we do milking demonstrations. I want them to understand why we raise beef cattle, why the dairy calf is taken off of its mother. I want them to at least learn one piece of something, so that maybe when they see a sheep covered with wool they'll realize that that's where a sweater came from.

There are different levels of information that we may want to set up: something very basic for the six-, seven-, ten-year-olds, and then a higher level of information. We'll do market buys, where we tell what are the best buys at the supermarket that week, whether it's that sweet corn is cheap now, or hamburger or beef is cheap—so stock up if you can—or how to buy a chicken.

My father thinks a zoo's a dumb place for a farm, but I think they're impressed at what I'm trying to do here. But they come from a small town where a farm doesn't look like what our farm does here. We brought my grandmother up here once. She was more impressed with meeting the elephants. She was very interested in seeing what I was doing; she grew up in a totally different time, when almost everybody was a farmer, and she can't imagine that people don't know what a cow is, or what it does. But my job is to explain farm animals to people who've never seen a farm.

I start with the pigs, swine, hogs, whatever you want to call them. They're my favorite, because they're the one thing we didn't have on our farm. We had a horse and a pony, we had chickens running loose, we had beef cattle, we had sheep. Dairy cattle were too much work; I didn't want to be around those. But I was always interested in pigs. My mother had shown pigs as a young girl in 4-H. I'd always wanted to show one. I finally got that wish four or five years ago at the state fair; a hog producer gave me one of his animals to show, and that was one of the highlights of my life. I think pigs are intelligent animals, highly intelligent. More intelligent than dogs and cats. They're easily trained, very easily. When I was growing up, we had puppies, and I remember how hard they were to paper-train. We had a baby pig that was donated to the farm last September. We took it home one weekend, and it was amazing: within a couple of hours, once she'd checked out our whole apartment, she was using the paper. We called her Freckles; she was red with little dark freckles. My husband worked on a hog farm when he was growing up, with ten thousand of these things, and we'd been married one week when I told him I wanted to bring home a piglet. He said, "Don't do this to me." But once I got it home, it was like a boy and his pig; they would walk down to get the mail. We took her to a party that night at a friend's apartment. People thought it was a dog; it minded better than our neighbor's poodle.

They're just highly intelligent, the only farm animal that won't overeat, despite the bad connotations, you know: don't eat like a pig. Or your room looks like a pig sty. Pigs, if they're given enough space in their pen, will have zones. They'll have their bedding area, they'll have their eating area, and then where they defecate. And those last two, if they have enough space, will not meet. I think they've gotten a very bad rap, that pigs stink and wallow in the mud. The only reason they wallow in the mud is they have sweat glands only around their nose area, and they're hot. There's nothing better than cool mud. They're very much like humans in their digestive system, in their heart-respiratory system. Heart valves from pigs have been used in humans. They're used to do health studies, because they'll eat the same type of things we do. They eat corn and soybean meal, in a different form, but it's the same type of products that we eat.

We've got two piglets on the farm now, and they've not been worked with that much, but they've been imprinted on a little bit. They hear you coming, and they're standing, trying to crawl up the gate and snorting at you that they want out. They want to come see you. Pigs don't like to be picked up; they squeal like crazy. But they like to be rubbed behind the ears. They'll start snorting and stretch out, and then they'll roll over and let you rub their bellies. They'll go to sleep and let kids pet them.

As lovable and friendly as Freckles was, however, she

had a mind-set that if she didn't want to go that way, she wouldn't. Pigs also have sweet tooths; they like fruit and blueberry muffins. There are even pigs that race for Oreo cookies.

Beef cattle are smart animals, not super intelligent but not dumb, either. They don't relate to humans as individuals, and I think part of that is that you don't work with them. Beef cattle are raised on the range or in a lot; it's not one-on-one, handler-animal contact. But I know how intelligent some of our own beef cows were. They would have their calves out in the woods, and sometimes we wouldn't see their calves for weeks. We had some cows that would walk one way, and you'd follow them, thinking, "I'm gonna find this calf," and you know darn well that their calf was lying the other way, and they weren't going to go back to their calf, they were protecting it. They may be domesticated animals, but they still have some wild left in them that they protect their young. They're trainable enough that you can break them to lead, you can break them to stand for you. People who truly work with their animals and show them can put a halter on them, drop the halter, walk all the way around it, brush the animal, set its feet, come back, and the animal hasn't moved. It's a matter of personality. There are other ones that we've worked with for a whole summer and never quite got them to mind us and work well.

Dairy cattle can be very docile, and that's because you work with them. They're milked twice a day; they have people walking around. They are intelligent. They may be in a barn with five hundred stalls in it, stanchions for each of the dairy cows. They're released to go out into the drydock to be milked, and when a cow walks back in, she'll walk to her own stanchion. It's hard to get a cow to go into a stanchion that isn't hers, so there must be some level of intelligence there. But not much affection. With beef cattle and dairy cattle, if they're tame, you can brush them, and they enjoy it and they'll stand for you, but I don't see much affection from them. Maybe in a young calf. Ours at the zoo have been worked with. If a calf has been raised out on a farm somewhere where it wasn't handled, it wasn't worked, more than likely if it heard you say something, it would run the other way. One of ours has been imprinted on; we take it out and lead it, we talk to it as we give it its bucket of milk, and we call it by name, so we can work on it.

When I was ten, twelve, thirteen, somewhere around there, I saw my sister get kicked in the face by one of our horses, one that was very tame. She came up behind it, and it got scared and hit her in the face with both rear hooves. So I've always had a healthy respect for horses. I stay away from them, and I honestly don't know much about them. I'm probably somewhat scared of them. Horses are not smart animals. They're one of our least intelligent, but the advantage that horses have is they're able to retain about ninety percent of what they learn. They have a memory. If you keep working with them, it sort of gets ingrained in them; they remember. There are horses that are more highly trained, but horses are, as a group, somewhat dim-witted. That's why they are so good for riding, because they've got the memory retention, and they're dumb enough to let you tell them where to go and what to do.

Sheep are sweet, but they're dumb animals. One sheep walks off one way, and they all follow. It could be down a ditch, and they'll just keep going. Trying to round up sheep is like a circus. They all run, and then they split off and run around. They're so dumb, and they're scared of you. As we were growing up, we'd have dog attacks on our sheep every so often. The ones that were not even touched by a dog would stand in a corner of a barn shaking for two to three weeks. We lost some sheep after that just because they wouldn't eat, they wouldn't drink; they were so scared, you would have to carry the water and the feed back to them. They're very skittish, scared animals.

Chickens are just feathered fowl. They're destined to lay eggs and then go to chicken soup. We raised chickens on our farm just because my father enjoyed them. I have no fond memories of chickens. I never got brave enough to reach underneath a hen and grab the eggs out from underneath her. Even though she doesn't hurt much, I didn't like to get pecked. I remember trying to chase them around with an old wire chicken catcher to catch the young roosters for dinner. Not a good memory.

All the memories may not be perfect, but I never forget where I came from. I want nice things, but my house is filled with antiques, country things that I enjoy telling people about. If anyone asks me, I tell where I'm from. I think people need to know about it. I think that's part of the problem that agriculture has today—city folks are ignorant about agriculture, and they don't want to know. And I know that farmers are ignorant about city people, and they don't want to know about them—their customers. I see myself as a bridge between the two. I work with ag groups, and I want to get them involved at the farm, because I think they should be here. With millions of visitors a year, and the consumers of tomorrow coming through, they need to be here.

I always know where I came from, and it's always going to be part of me. I don't think I could live in the city itself. I prefer the suburbs. But I don't think I could live on a farm, either. I've gotten used to all the conveniences; I've gotten used to going to a museum and enjoying it, running over to the mall if I need something. I can ride my bike to the grocery store, and it's a supermarket, not the little grocery that I grew up near, which was wonderful but didn't have all the options. I like the choices. I can do anything on a weekend. And I also like the fact that I'm not tied to a farm. When I was growing up, we didn't have vacations; the fairs were our family vacations. I don't want to go back to that. But I don't want to leave it totally. I'm walking a line.

6

TEACHER'S PETS

For most of the key employees at the zoo, working with animals had roots in a childhood yearning. That wasn't the case for Judy Kolar, the curator of education.

As a child, she didn't have a pet; her mother had been bitten by a dog and had no fondness for animals. In fact, Judy had never contemplated a career at the zoo until she came to work there in 1977.

What she had been preparing for was a career in education. A native Chicagoan, she had both a bachelor's degree and a master's degree in education from the National College of Education in Evanston, Illinois. She had been a teacher in a north suburban school, a program coordinator for the Chicago public school system, and chairman of the special education department—dealing with the needs of students with learning disabilities—at a city high school.

When she accepted Les Fisher's offer to be curator of education, she easily made the transition to providing knowledge about animals to those in search of that knowledge, from students and teachers to casual zoo visitors.

A tall (5'9"), trim, chic divorcée, Judy was based in a small, neat office in the Crown-Field Center. At forty-seven, with hazel eyes and brown hair flecked with gray, she was a stunning figure; her cool manner enhanced the overall impression that she was in charge.

She ran an education department staffed by seven persons, several of them supported by the zoo society, the rest on the park district payroll. The department produced a wide array of activities, an assortment that had expanded dramatically under her direction.

Among them were zoo classes for school children, from toddlers to high school students. They ranged from films to observation of the animals to supervised hands-on contact with live animals.

For students in all grades, there were forty-five-minute tours of the zoo, introducing the zoo and its commitment to the conservation of wildlife. There was a hands-on zoo for blind and partially sighted students, and a zoology class taught by the zoo staff for high school students.

For the general public, Judy and her staff provided workshops for students, families, and adults interested in in-depth studies of wildlife. Films, slide and video presentations brought visitors an awareness of the lives of animals in the wild and the behind-the-scenes workings of the zoo itself.

The department provided the movable carts often seen at the zoo in good weather, informally teaching visitors using touchable items, such as feathers, eggs, and snakeskins.

The zoo's outreach program included the traveling zoo, which brought the zoo to those who couldn't get to it (during the spring and summer); two vans transported animals and instructors to Chicago's parks, hospitals, nursing homes, senior citizen centers, day camps, and libraries. During the school year, the Zoo-to-You program used the vans to bring the zoo to fourth- and fifth-grade classrooms in city schools, with live animals—small mammals, birds, and reptiles.

The education department was active in the graphic

design of zoo exhibits, educational concepts for the children's zoo, and various publications.

For more than fifteen years, the bulk of the teaching effort had been conducted by docents, the zoo society's corps of unpaid teachers. There were 200 of them, out of a total volunteer group of 400. The docents went through a fifteen-week course in vertebrate biology, teaching techniques, and animal handling, followed by a written exam and on-the-job training. They made a commitment to the zoo—four hours on one day a week, for at least one hundred hours a year—and that enabled them to serve Judy and her staff with zeal and wisdom on a continuing basis.

Finally, Judy worked closely with the zoo society in obtaining grants, such as the $45,000 it received from the Joyce Foundation to expand the Zoo-to-You program and $100,000 from Citicorp to fund a learning center in the renovated children's zoo.

All of these responsibilities made for clogged days in Judy's life. She did not clean cages or chop food or worry about sick animals, but she was usually at work by 8 A.M. Meetings filled her days. Planning provided the main thrust of her career.

"We don't invite people to the zoo simply to have them stare or sit," she said. "The zoo is a unique resource." She planned ways to keep them alert, to keep them thinking about the zoo and its animals.

There were programs and events to offer: an introduction to animals for "tiny tots"; "Animal Talk," a three-year-old's guide to what animals say; "Zookeepers and Their Animal Friends," a presentation by Pat Sass, senior keeper at the great ape house; "Zoo Photography," for families with children eight and up. The zoo lecture series offered evenings with Les Fisher, curator of mammals Mark Rosenthal, great ape keeper Peter Clay, and others.

For Judy, all the hours of preparation paid off.

"It's fun. It's recreation. But it's more than that," she said. "It's the conservation of captive populations. It's the breeding of endangered species. This place is special, for it's staff and what they're involved in.

"My office used to be in the great ape house. A wonderful place to work. It took me no time to learn that the animals were the focus of the zoo. I swear to God those apes were talking to me. I'd look up and see a chimp staring at me through a slot in the wall. I was almost in the exhibit.

"But what matters to me most is not just watching the animals. The education I've gotten here, that's what matters. The openness of the staff, the keepers. They want to tell their stories, to share them. They told them to me. Biology. Ecology. And I learned.

"Respect for animals—you develop that here. Those apes peeking into my office. You need that one-on-one to have that respect. You know, animals are up-front with you. There's no bullshit, no manipulation. I've learned a lot about nature, the most orderly of societies. You know what it's capable of. Animals have a role in life, and you know what it is. If we could relate to each other that way, maybe our disturbances would go away."

For Judy, there had to be quiet time to study animals. It was observation with a purpose.

"Looking at an ape or an armadillo, I ask, 'What's your hidden secret that the world should know about you? What was your life like in the wild?' I'm not talking about being anthropomorphic now. It's that one-on-one feeling that enables you to achieve some understanding of them. Each animal has special features. Why claws? Why a shell? To help us anticipate the questions that the public brings to us, to help us interpret animals for them, that's what those quiet times mean to me."

While Judy sat behind her desk, two docents were on the move, rushing past her doorway to a Zoo-to-You appointment.

Mary Patton was a new docent. She was a grandmother and a retired lawyer, a feisty blonde with time to spare and a conspicuous sense of determination. But she was nervous. It was her first Zoo-to-You mission, bringing small animals—and a lecture about them—to the fourth and fifth grades at a parochial school.

Fortunately, Mary had help. Accompanying her was Charlene Ehlscheid, a docent with fourteen years of service, a registered nurse whose docent time was a needed change of pace. A cheerful redhead with dangling giraffe earrings, she was not nervous; she'd done it before, and she assured Mary that it would go well.

The cast of animal characters they were taking along included Blossom, an opossum; a rabbit named Butch; a ball python; and a kestral (a gray-beige sparrow hawk) named Jasper. Each one was in a carrying case, and the entire group of animals and docents were driven to St. Henry's School by driver Art Cotton in the colorfully painted traveling zoo van.

Along the way, Charlene remembered a Zoo-to-You visit she had made to a ghetto elementary school.

"I asked the class, 'Why does a snake have so many babies?' " she recalled.

A small boy waved his hand.

"Powerful sperm," he proclaimed.

As the van moved through traffic, the two docents chatted.

"The opossum is my favorite," Mary volunteered. "She is so beautiful. I love her."

When they arrived at the school, they were directed to the fifth-grade class. The students were well behaved, sitting on their small chairs behind their small desks. The room was filled with their artwork. On the blackboard, the teacher had written, "No recess if not quiet."

The class was a United Nations assortment of ethnic origins, unified in the girls' white blouses and plaid skirts and the boys' yellow shirts and brown slacks.

"Your mouths are sealed, and you're going to listen," the teacher said sternly.

"We like children and we like animals," Charlene began. She told them that the zoo was free, that it belonged to them, and that they should care for it. The zoo is the place, she said, where they can learn about animals and have fun learning.

Charlene posed questions for the class to answer. They were eager.

"Why do birds go south?"

"For food."

She took the kestral from its cage, and it sat on her gloved left hand. It defecated, and the children giggled.

"He has to eliminate, just as you do," she said, with a serene smile. She did not explain the nature of stress in animals.

She walked around the room with the bird on her hand; the children's faces brightened. The bird had a damaged wing and could not be released into the wild, she pointed out; she assured the students that the bird would be cared for in the zoo.

Mary took over, to talk about mammals.

"We're the brightest of all the mammals," she said. "But which one is the biggest? The tallest?"

The children knew: the elephant, the giraffe.

She carefully extracted the opossum from its traveling case. Blossom, a tidy gray bundle of fur with a long, pink-tipped nose, seemed less than eager to participate, but Mary grasped it firmly. She allowed the children to pet it. They squealed.

She returned Blossom to its case, as Charlene cradled the ball python in her arms.

"We brought a snake today," Mary announced. The children exhaled loudly, in mock or real fear. "Don't worry," Mary comforted them. "It's harmless to us. It kills by squeezing its prey, and we're too big."

The ball python remained coiled in Charlene's arms, its tongue flicking out.

One chubby Hispanic boy cheered the snake. Others moved away when Charlene approached.

"If you don't choose to pet it, that's fine, but don't create a scene," the teacher said firmly.

"Its forked tongue helps it taste and smell," Mary instructed. "And it's deaf."

After an hour, it was time to move on to the fourth grade.

Mary and Charlene introduced the class to the relationship between an animal's habitat and its food supply.

"What if we all ate nothing but hamburger?" Mary asked.

"We'd get sick," a small blond boy snapped.

"True," Mary said. "And there wouldn't be any food left."

"You can read animals like books," she added. "Look at their eyes, ears, nose, teeth, legs, tail, and you find out how they live and how they eat.

She plucked the opossum from its carrier gingerly. The class sighed.

"She's got a big nose—better than her eyes or ears—so she can smell her food. And with her fifty teeth, she can eat almost anything. Even your garbage. She's what we call an opportunistic omnivore. She likes to live in the hollows of trees. And you wouldn't even notice her there," Mary said.

She encouraged the children to pet the opossum.

"When you pet a wild animal, never pet its head," she advised.

Blossom began to quiver.

"She's shivering because she's scared," Mary said, sensing that the animal was stressed. "So we'll put her back in her case." Mary seemed relieved to deposit Blossom inside the case.

Charlene introduced the rabbit to the class. Again, the class sighed in unison. Butch—gray and white and soft and furry—behaved properly. When Charlene placed it on a long table, it made no effort to move. The children rushed up and petted Butch; the rabbit did not resist.

Then it was time to pack up and leave.

The two docents urged the children to go to their library and study about animals—and to go to the zoo whenever they could. The message was well received. The children applauded.

Back in the van, the two women relaxed as Art—an experienced driver accustomed to hearing the sounds of animals in the back of the van—drove slowly back to the zoo. For Charlene, it had been another in a series of gratifying trips. For Mary, it had been the first, and it had worked out well. For both, there would be many more to come.

In her office, Judy was alone, checking plans for the graphics for the lion house once it had been renovated. Joan Friedman, the assistant curator, stopped by, and the conversation led Judy to comment on the use of graphics at the zoo.

"Our graphics aren't an encyclopedia of information," she said. "We know that the average visitor spends a minute or less in front of a graphic. That's OK. We set our own limitations, and we don't go beyond them. Short, succinct, accurate information to motivate them to study. At least we give them some basic understanding of the animal and the meaning of that animal to the environment.

"If an exhibit changes, the graphics must change. Animals come, animals go. We can use temporary signs for new animals. Sometimes we have to; a permanent sign can cost five thousand dollars.

"I've been heavily into all this for five years, and I'll be involved with it for another five. It's a ten-year campaign, the renovation of the zoo, and it's changing the face of the zoo."

Later that day, she met with three members of her staff: Joan; Sue, a full-time teacher on the staff; and Vanessa, a recent college graduate serving a one-year internship in the education department. They discussed a series of portable displays they hoped to have in the learning center at the renovated children's zoo.

Special boxes were being designed to display learning materials about animal diets. Other exhibits would show the beaks and feet of birds, the eggs of birds, and reptiles.

Such displays could cause problems.

"Will the children wonder, when they see beaks and feet, if we're chopping up animals?" one of the women asked.

"Should we use the entire stuffed animal instead?" another proposed.

"Let's go for real parts," Judy decided.

She liked to get children to sit down with her, on the grass, so that she could show them such exhibits, to see what questions they might ask.

"Did you kill the animals?" was one question heard.

Judy was prepared: "No, they died of natural causes, like people do. We save their bodies to teach you about them."

But she knew that there could be a reaction when you took a child who had just seen a live animal and showed it a dead one.

"If the kids' questions persist, there is fear to deal with, or a fascination with death," Joan noted. "If you address their questions, they accept your answers. You can remind them about a dog that died. Or a grandparent."

"In truth, sometimes you lie," Sue said. "When they ask you what happens to the chicks on the farm, you don't tell them that they're fed to the reptiles."

After the meeting ended, Judy went back to her office. At times, she liked to tie all the pieces together—to link the graphics to the displays to the needs of visitors and more. The more closely they all meshed, the better the thrust of the efforts made by the education department.

"We're trying to create an awareness and respect for wildlife," she said. "That's the foundation. Not just the wildlife here in the zoo, either, but the wildlife in its own environment. What does it mean for an animal not to be? Extinction. Some people say, 'So what?' But to me, it matters. Education at the zoo has a bias: conservation. But we don't rush to convert the unconverted. We give facts. We urge consideration. We never tell people that they're wrong if they think that zoos are bad. We give them options to think about."

Perpetual self-scrutiny went with the territory.

"I think we've been successful, but we evaluate our programs all the time," she said. "We survey our audiences. Did you learn something you didn't know before? Based on this program, are you more involved? Did you take action, on any level? Did you pick up a magazine and read about animals?

"What's encouraging is that eighty to ninety-five percent of our people have told us that we did provoke them to action. We want that; we want them to have open minds, to want to investigate. That's for the adults. Children are another matter. They're sponges. They have fewer fears, fewer predetermined attitudes. And there's that conditioning that predisposes them to animals."

She sat back in her chair and glanced at her collection of giraffe figurines on a nearby shelf.

"They're tall, and so am I," she said softly. "Maybe that's why I like them." Outside the building, a line of giggling children was entering the building to see a film. Judy could see them through her office window. They were evidence that she was succeeding in her job, and as she watched them, she smiled.

FIRST PERSON: JUDY KOLAR

I remember my mother not wanting animals in the house. And it stemmed from when she was fourteen years old; there was a dog in the apartment house, and all of a sudden it turned on her and bit her. I think that shook her up. I don't remember exactly how she communicated it to me, but I remember I found a kitten when I was a kid, a stray little baby kitten, and I brought it home and wanted it. She told me, "Oh no, we can't have it." I remember having goldfish and a turtle for a while.

I grew up in the city, on the west side of Chicago. I've always lived in apartments. And I never had kids. If I didn't live in Chicago, I'd have a dog. I absolutely would. I have had tortoises from the zoo in my apartment.

I've always loved kids. It's not that I went through school, grammar school, high school, saying I wanted to be a teacher. I didn't do that. I think my parents certainly made the suggestion along the way. I was in high school in the fifties, and there just wasn't as much exploration of your life then. I truly believe that.

I wanted to do things with people, people in need. That's what led me to look into occupational therapy, and then special education. I liked occupational therapy because it meant working with people and helping them to get functional. I was interested in learning disabilities. I decided this was another direction that I wanted to expand into. Special education is a broad category. In those years, it was called "the exceptional child"; that was the label. They've gone through ten thousand labels. Special education means anything from those who are learning disabled for whatever reason, physically, perceptually, to the gifted. The gifted were separated out, and special ed meant those that were visually impaired, hearing impaired, mentally handicapped. I came into learning disabilities when it was gaining momentum and focus and attention. I went back to school full-time, and I got very involved with diagnosis and evaluation, trying to really pinpoint what the problems were, giving diagnostic tests, and recommending remedial treatment.

In the early seventies, the Chicago public schools were going ahead with special ed. What we did was test kids in the elementary schools and set up resource rooms of kids with learning disabilities. We worked out remedial programs for them and worked with parents. Then I was asked to set up a program at the high school level. It was a self-contained classroom, and they came to me for the whole day. You can help them if you feel for the kids. Through testing, you see the results.

I was there for about five years, and we got the program

going. But in my life, two things were happening. I was starting to think, "What else is there in life?" At the same time, Chicago public schools were going through grave problems. They were going to be denied federal money because of the segregation within the schools. So I put together my résumé, I started talking to people. I was open to do anything. I was at a dinner party one night. I was sitting next to a businessman, blah blah blah blah blah blah. And he said, "You know, something's happening at the zoo." "Something's happening," he said, "but I really don't know what it is. Call Les Fisher." I said, "The zoo?" I was in gear; I followed up anything. So I called, made an appointment, and went in and talked to him. There was a fifty-thousand-dollar grant, and someone was needed to put together a program on environmental education for teachers and students.

I'm an educator, I thought, and they need me as an interpreter. I had felt very bad at the thought of leaving my profession. The zoo staff all felt strongly that the people should know; they felt strongly about education. It was always a dream of Les Fisher's to have an education department here. The commitment was strong on the part of the animal management staff. They'd take people behind the scenes and explain animal behavior. They'd do this of their own accord. They went out on the traveling zoo; they were the zoologists who gave presentations to the public. And the keepers are always in there wanting to talk to the public. So you've got a collective staff that is behind education, wanting it to happen.

I'm a Chicagoan. I grew up in the parks. I mean, that was my childhood. I did have a feel for the city, the communities, and the diverse kinds of people. That combined with teaching. We reached out to so many different audiences.

I was able to put together a program that teachers conducted in their classrooms. It's a multimedia kit. It's an approach to how to utilize the zoo. I had certain feelings on how to utilize the zoo when kids come here. They don't have to come here to do what they do in the classroom.

And that set the format for what we did later on in education.

We know we're succeeding when people come back. We know we're succeeding by evaluations we do in the workshops and the classes. We know we're succeeding nationally and internationally when people come to us for direction, and guidance, and new programs.

There was kind of a hiatus in the last couple of years. We were doing the programming, but we needed more staff to go to the next level. We had reached a plateau, and it was at that time I asked for funding for an assistant curator of education. That's when I started asking for more money for programming through the zoo society. There was no way to go on to more levels without more staff and without more support, all the way around. And so, we expanded, and now we can start reaching for another plateau.

We developed the training manual for docents, a textbook but done in a way for them to relate to better. It's stripped down to the bare essentials that they need; it's an introduction. We tell the trainees, "This is the beginning of your learning. This is a basic foundation and introduction." We have supplementary handouts; we also have some reading assignments that are in other textbooks. If the curator lectures are in the morning, then the docents do the afternoon part in taking people out to the exhibits and doing the general kind of introduction to the exhibits and the animals, and that supports the lecture.

I think there are all kinds of different levels to build on. Let's take one example: adult programs. The zoo lecture series has been terrific, it's been very successful, it's another one we won an education award for, and that's been fine. It had certain objectives. But I also know that other levels of adult programs are needed here. One thing I would like to start investigating is to have higher seminars, that go more in depth. There are a lot of people out there who want more. Seminars. Hook-ups with universities. Selected people on this staff and a university staff, giving academic credit for it. Video would be great. We're going to put video in the lion house, and we're going to have video in the learning center of the children's zoo. The video in the lion house will let us show them what they can't see there, and that's animals in the wild.

I think we're here to tell our story. We're here to give the basic facts as we know them and that we can substantiate. The animal rights people certainly come and listen, I hope with an open mind, and we tell them how we feel. We're not necessarily telling anybody else they're wrong.

I have been involved in things that I never in my life thought I'd be doing. I wrote a filmstrip. I worked with the sound people. I loved it, just loved it. The graphics element, the writing, the programming. I've put everything that I ever learned of the learning process into the materials. It's been a phenomenal opportunity and it's phenomenal because we had a small staff and I was forced to do it. I've had great satisfaction.

We're reaching the general public. We're doing what we think is best, and they're absolutely hooked up to what animal management is doing and to the direction of conservation efforts. If we place a person by the great apes, we put that person there because that's part of our programming in conservation, to help impart that knowledge. If in the amphitheatre we bring out a little European ferret, we talk about it, and it's fun, but there's a hook to everything. "By the way, this guy's kissing cousin, the black-footed ferret, is dying off." There is a thread that goes through everything that hooks up to conservation internationally, conservation that's specific to the philosophy of the zoo. And that ferret is not the only creature that's endangered; there are plenty of other ones around.

Zoo education has such potential to support conservation efforts worldwide. Zoos started out as the showcase of animals, the stamp collection. Then we got into conservation programs. In the sixties, there were the Rachel Carsons and the environmental awareness, and some zoos were realizing they are perfect places to help in that environmental education. There were some major zoos with bigger budgets, that had the staff that could do it. But many zoos didn't have budgets for education. In most zoos, volunteers really started education, because you needed unpaid staff. Many of those volunteers are highly educated people, but there's still a difference between a full-time staff on board with consistent coordination, organization, development, and a volunteer staff. So, all of a sudden, you had professional staffs getting into zoo education, and that paralleled the first endangered-species acts in the late seventies. So this momentum really started in the sixties and grew.

The European zoos have had professional education staffs for years, so there are major international conservation efforts. The U.S. zoo educators are hooking into that; we're starting to look at our programming to help support that. We're telling visitors to help conserve, help this, help that. How do you tell a kid in a starving country that he shouldn't kill an animal for food? How do you tell that to those people who have to clear land for farms because they have to grow crops? There's a big conservation education movement, and I feel part and parcel of it, because I've been very involved with international programs for eight years. What can we do to work with Third World countries? What can we do to pull together Europe, the Americas, the Third World? How can we start approaching it together?

Today, we're trying to talk about alternatives. Are there other options for the land? Are there other ways to achieve what we want to achieve without killing off the plant life that is specific for the food needs of that animal? We're looking to save species from extinction. That's the bottom line. If educators can just enlighten people, by addressing the issues, the alternatives, the options, we're addressing global conservation through education.

I think we'll win. It'll take years and years and years, but if we do our job thoroughly, with great thought and sensitivity to all concerned, I think we can achieve a thinking population of people. Which will mean it's not humans against the animals, but humans with the animals.

7

A TOUCH OF GINGER

It was 8:30 A.M. on a midsummer Wednesday. A handful of early risers were at the zoo. Some jogged through the zoo. Others marched briskly to work past the awakening animals. Small children cavorted under their parents' watchful eyes.

The sea lions were bellowing in their pool, asserting their pleasure by making great sweeping arcs in the water or sunbathing atop the rock formation. They were the endearing comedians of the zoo, and a semicircle of their fans stood at the rail, waving affectionately at them. In the distance, the sound of chattering monkeys filled the air. The lions and tigers, in their outdoor habitat, reclined lazily, warmed by the sun.

Ginger Alexander was there, too. Ginger was a docent, one of those zoo loyalists who volunteered four hours a week to teach, to escort people to various parts of the zoo, and to enlighten them about the nature of the creatures they'd see. Ginger had been donating her time for twelve years; few docents knew the zoo any better.

Ginger was a 5'5" grandmother with a blond pageboy hairdo, glasses, and a serious fondness for animals. She was wearing her khaki safari suit, looking like Miss Marple based in Kenya, wearing a badge that read: "Lincoln Park Zoo Docent/Guide, Ginger Alexander."

She was a native Chicagoan, educated in parochial schools. She was married for the second time; her first husband died, and she met her second husband at a gathering of widows and widowers. She was the mother of three daughters (one of her own, two of her current husband's), who had provided her with five grandchildren. Over the years she had been determined to get her college degree; when she was just past fifty, she got it. She'd traveled; she and her husband had lived in Italy, and they had visited the Galapagos Islands and Africa (to see the animals, of course).

Her favorite animals were the lions, the tigers, the majestic big cats. As the sun grew hotter and the zoo more crowded, she moved off briskly toward their outdoor habitat.

Behind her, a familiar dialogue was heard:

"Erwin, take him to the bathroom. Take him *now*."

"Shirley, you take him."

"He's a boy, Erwin. Take him to the men's room."

Erwin and son disappeared into the lion house. Ginger stopped in front of one of the large windows that bordered the ends of the cats' habitat. A Bengal tiger spotted Ginger at the window and approached to look at her, then began to pace back and forth, staring at her constantly.

"I don't know if she recognizes me, or if she just knows that I'm a docent," Ginger said. "She may be responding to this uniform."

She noted that the Siberians were the largest cats; they had more fur as well, for their northern clime. A second Bengal—the two were sisters—was basking in the background.

"They don't always get along," Ginger said. "See the vertical stripes. That's camouflage in tall grass. Don't

forget that they're predators. See their eyes, always looking straight ahead. Their nostrils and ears pick up the signs
ahead. They're not easily seen. The ideal hunter. Another
fact to know: tigers are solitary creatures in the wild, but
lions are not."

The Bengal had continued to pace pack and forth on its
side of the window, without taking its eyes off of Ginger.

"Some people think that they pace like that because they
are stir-crazy. Not so, not so. They're just exercising. In
the wild, they hunt, eat, sleep, and mate. That's it. They
need exercise. Pacing is exercise," she said. She did not
accept the notion that caged animals paced out of stress.

She went into the lion house.

"Do you realize that a leopard can carry its prey, even a
gazelle, into a tree?" she asked, summoning images out of a
TV nature program.

"Did you know that black leopards have spots? It's a
recessive gene, a genetic exception," she explained. "But
that's not as rare as a white tiger or a white lion." A young
couple standing next to her looked at the black leopard,
couldn't see the spots, but took her word for the fact that
they were there. Ginger spoke with authority.

She moved along, continuing her running commentary:
the jaguar is the largest cat in our hemisphere. The big cats
at the zoo are cats that roar; only the little ones purr. Lions
are the only cats with a social order; the females hunt, the
males eat first.

She paused in her monologue to collect additional facts.

"I wouldn't pet a lion," she declared. "If you touch them,
they're likely to bite. Of course, some keepers can touch
some animals. A nursery-raised animal may allow the
keeper to come close. If animals know and like the keeper,
they'll let the keeper pet them. But these aren't tame
animals. They're not pets."

She told a story: A lion cub had been raised in the zoo
nursery with some tiger cubs. When they were old enough
and were released, they were separated, lions to lions,

tigers to tigers. The lion cub wailed at the loss of its friends, the tigers. It took a female lion to calm it down, to persuade it that it wasn't a tiger.

Ginger strolled out of the lion house and into the reptile house, across the way.

A very small boy was staring at a very large snake.

"Yech!" he screamed.

Reptiles had gotten a bad name, Ginger agreed. "Since the Garden of Eden," she said primly.

She walked around the hall filled with reptiles in their glassed-in cages.

"Reptiles know what to do the moment they're hatched. They're adults even when they're small. When a poisonous snake is born, it already has its venom, and it will kill with it. But that's not the only way snakes kill. They can kill by constriction—actually suffocating the prey. Or just by swallowing it.

"Sure, snakes have gotten bad press. They're always the bad guys. People look at them and think that snakes don't respond to us the way other animals do. But people who have snakes as pets they've raised, say they *do* respond. It's not like having a dog, of course. But they'll stay on your lap or approach you to be held. We've had some boas here who would cling to your waist, a living belt. I've done that. After all, snakes kill only to eat or when threatened—and I'm not threatening."

Nevertheless, she added, "I wouldn't put one around my neck."

She went from one windowed cage to another. A puff adder, from Africa. A rhinoceros viper, from Africa. An Asiatic cobra peered at her from behind a rock. A black-necked cobra, which blinds by spitting venom twelve feet, seemed to be bored. Perhaps a case of dry mouth and inactivity, Ginger theorized.

"When they feed it, they wear a mask," Ginger reported. "And before they put the food in, you can be sure they know where the snake is."

A Gila monster glared at her. Ginger pointed out that they grab, bite, hang on, and chew. And they don't let go until there's nothing left to devour.

"If it gets you, I'm told, you have to cut off its head to get it off. Or cut off your own hand, if that's what it bit. We're talking about a poisonous reptile."

An iguana sat on a tree limb, motionless, passing for weary. It looked like the ugliest of prehistoric monsters, and Ginger mentioned that it had been used as the model for them in many science fiction films.

An alligator snapping turtle was underwater munching on a small herring. It munched, rose to the waterline, stuck its nose above water, took a long, deep breath, and returned to the herring.

A ball python, from western Africa, seemed oblivious to anything but its wish to rest. "When it's attacked," Ginger explained, "it coils into a ball with its head buried, to prevent being swallowed."

The African dwarf crocodile, between four and five feet in length, seemed tired, too.

"He's very old," Ginger said. "In fact, he's the oldest animal in the zoo. We've had him since 1940, and we don't know how old he was then." As if in corroboration, the crocodile reclined in its sedentary state. It revealed nothing.

"What's *that*?" a little girl shrieked.

"An anaconda," her mother told her.

"One of the two longest snakes in the world," Ginger volunteered. "The other is the reticulated python." The anaconda was underwater (they drown their prey); it was more than twenty feet long.

"They're deaf," Ginger continued. "But they feel vibrations. Heat sensors warn them, as well, of approaching creatures. And they smell with their tongues, which transmit messages to their brains."

The reticulated python in a nearby cage was massive. It was coiled underwater, with only its neck and head out of the water, pressed tightly against the glass. It appeared to be looking up, showing off its neck.

"Never try to outstare a snake," Ginger said. "You'll lose."

She headed into the sunlight again; reptiles didn't move her as the big cats did.

She paused at the waterfowl lagoon, home for some birds and stopover for others on their migratory way. A few swans and some ducks were among the permanent residents; they had their wings pinioned (trimmed) to prevent flight, Ginger noted.

"Geese can be used as guard animals," Ginger declared. "They peck, they make noise."

The zoo was getting crowded; Ginger passed the lagoon, its sidewalk clogged with families, with kids eating popcorn. Mothers pushed strollers. The sun was hot.

Ginger marched to the farm. In the bordering neighborhood, apartment buildings dominated the skyline, and yuppie restaurants and boutiques thrived. At the zoo, however, the farm represented other values.

"You know, many city kids have never seen a cow or a pig," Ginger said. "Some of them don't know where milk comes from." At the farm, those kids could get answers.

A goat was being milked by two docents. A week-old calf was resting in a small pen. A month-old Ayrshire calf was in another pen; a sign noted its name, McHale. (There was a Boston Celtics' fan at the zoo.)

"City kids ask me, 'Are all the milk cows female, or are some male?' " Ginger said.

Nearby, a massive sow nursed six piglets; the piglets were brown and white and eager for the nourishment their mother provided.

"Pigs are the smartest of farm animals," Ginger noted. "Some people say they're even smarter than dogs or cats. And they're clean, despite what is said about them. They wallow in mud only to cool off, because they don't have sweat glands, and when the mud evaporates, it cools them.

They don't have much hair, so the sun can trouble them."

Outside the dairy barn, small children clustered to talk to the goats and sheep in their pens. "We don't tell them that some animals go back to the farmers who lent them to us. We don't tell them that they then go to market," Ginger said softly.

She headed briskly toward the primate house. It was a noisy building, with acoustics that magnified all the monkey sounds. The giddy screams of children turned into wide-ranging echoes. A wanderoo macaque, seduced by the attention from visitors, performed. When a docent he knew approached, if the docent stuck out her chin in mock defiance, so did the macaque. It had the face of a wise old Oriental man, with a gray beard. The keepers had named it the Admiral.

Back into the heat of the day, Ginger continued her walk, to the building that housed the penguins and the seabirds. For both, environments had been created that were designed to duplicate their own environments in the wild. The building was air-conditioned; one pass through it was a respite from the summer air.

Ginger emerged and headed along the path that bordered the outdoor exhibits for large mammals. Two rhinos were butting each other, like Sumo wrestlers. They seemed oblivious to the heat and to almost everything else.

"They are very nearsighted," Ginger said. "They charge first and ask questions later. If you see one charging, climb a tree or stand behind it, if the tree's fat and you're thin."

The polar bears were swimming, visible through tall windows at underwater level. "Their hair isn't white," Ginger said. "It's colorless. The light reflecting off it makes it seem white. Polar bears have black skin, and the fur funnels heat to it."

Two elephants were idling, their trunks stretched out to pluck the leaves off the trees beyond their habitat.

"Elephants must be trained. Not to do tricks, but to be managed by their keepers, to be examined. Every day there's a drill to make them respond to commands," Ginger noted.

Bozie, an elephant from Sri Lanka, appeared to be dancing, moving one foot at a time. Suti, an orphan found starving in Africa, was saved by being given a home at the zoo. She seemed to be studying Bozie.

A few yards away, several giraffes moved languorously and munched food from containers at their mouth level. A pair of giraffes were head to head, their tongues intertwined. Ginger wasn't certain if one could term that "kissing."

Her last stop was at the bird house. A tawny frogmouth from Australia peered at her from its glassed-in cage; it looked like an owl, but was more like a nighthawk. It stared in its frozen stance as she passed it. In the free-flight area, birds flew unencumbered.

"They're safe in here," Ginger said, anticipating a question she'd heard from many visitors. "Most birds won't fly out of light into darkness."

She surveyed the vast hall, with its flashes of color and its high-pitched calls.

"Parrots and parakeets like to be touched," she said, "but most birds don't. When birds are sitting in a row, they leave space between them." Next to her, a pair of Major Mitchell's cockatoos were violating the rule; they were side by side on a branch, touching, but with their heads turned away from each other. Predicting animal behavior had its risks, Ginger admitted.

It was time for Ginger to leave. She had enjoyed her stroll through the zoo, a stroll she did often, beyond her work as a docent.

"You know, there's so much personal satisfaction for me here," she said. "The friendships. I've made so many in these years at the zoo. We have a marvelous staff. I can talk to the curators and the keepers and have access to all sorts of information.

"I can touch some of the animals. I think that my biggest

thrill was when I got to play with the lion cubs at the nursery. It was pure enjoyment."

FIRST PERSON: GINGER ALEXANDER

I remember coming to Lincoln Park Zoo when I was little. I remember the lions roaring before they would get fed, and it seemed like they used to roar a lot more than they do now. Maybe it's just a child's perception. But I used to love the lion house at feeding time. I also remember the pony rides they used to have. And I loved to be able to ride the ponies. I think in those days that was about the only chance you ever had to touch an animal at the zoo.

I used to love to come here with my family. We used to have picnics in the park, and we'd always wander over to the zoo. We used to come and spend the whole day here, and of course the two things we always did were come to the zoo and ride the boats in the lagoon. Then, as I got older, we often used to come and ride horses through Lincoln Park, which you used to be able to do. Many times after we would ride, we'd have something to eat and come back. In those days the zoo was not locked with gates at night as it is now. You could walk through the zoo.

My favorites were always the lions. I admire them for the same reason I admire the housecats: the way they move. They have a very graceful way of moving. I don't think of them as slinky, as sneaky, like some people do. I think they're stealthy. They're just doing what comes natural to them when they hunt, but I love the way they look. For example, they'll see something moving, and they will freeze, or they will stalk it. I'm also very impressed with their self-composure. They are the one animal that is not afraid of anything. They are there, and that's their land. And you can see why they're called the king of the beasts, even though they are not the strongest or the biggest.

I've always liked the zoo; I've always liked animals. In 1975, I was looking for something to do. I had worked

before I was married, and when I was widowed I had
worked in offices and done stenographic work in research
libraries, and things like that. But then I stayed home after
I married John. When he started his own business, then I
did all the books and all the accounting. I was the office
worker, of course. I was still doing that, but when the
children were all grown up, the last one was at the university, I was looking for something to do apart from my home
and my husband and office, so I decided I would work with
either animals or children. And just about that time, there
was an ad in the paper saying the zoo was looking for
volunteers, so I volunteered, and I've been here ever since.

The old philosophy of zoos was to have as many different animals as you could have, because people came to see
animals. Basically, zoos were started for entertainment.
The first zoos were only for royalty or for the wealthy
people, and they only existed in the palaces or in big cities.
By the middle 1800s, there were only twenty-nine zoos
worldwide that were open to the public. There are now
over nine hundred worldwide. But we started in 1868 with
a pair of swans. Central Park had a lagoon with lots of
swans. And someone there decided to give Chicago a pair,
so we got the swans. They were so popular that other
people started donating other animals, and we got deer and
more birds, and some antelope, until five years later we
had seventy-five different specimens.

The early zoos were built with what you now see in the
lion house: the typical cages, which were small, easily
cleaned, and made it easy to see the animals. They had tile
walls, tile floors. But we have to remember that in those
days we did not have antibiotics, we did not have a lot of
the medications we now have, so that, if one animal got
sick, any animal with it would also get sick, and there was
nothing they could do about it. So they kept one animal in
each cage. It was the logical thing to do. There were still a
lot of animals in the wild. As ideas changed, it was better
for the animals to be in more natural settings, so they not
only removed the bars, they enlarged the animal area.
They made the animal areas much more naturalistic, much

more like the place the animal came from. We now have antibiotics and other ways of treating animals, so we can keep them in family groups. We have them in larger, more naturalistic settings, and we try to not have bars between them; either we have moats, or, in the case of apes, we have glass.

We're going to redo our lion house. The north side we already have redone with moats, that was done in the seventies. On the south side we have thirteen cages inside and thirteen outside, with bars. We are going to have five outside and five inside, so you can see they're going to be much larger, more than twice the width. They will also be higher and deeper. And between the indoor and outdoor cages, there will be denning areas so that the mothers will have privacy when they have their cubs. But on that side of the building, we will not have lions and tigers, which you can put behind moats; we will have probably snow leopards and possibly Afghanistan leopards and jaguars. Leopards and jaguars can jump across some moats. And they are much smaller animals, so if you had them behind a moat that would be sufficient to keep them from getting out, you would not easily be able to see them.

As I said, in the early times zoos were mainly for recreation and to satisfy people's curiosity. But now that animals are becoming endangered in almost the whole world, zoos have changed their purpose. They are still here for recreation, because it's a lot of fun to come to the zoo. But we also are very much involved in conservation, to preserve the animals that are endangered. Some animals are extinct in the wild and exist only in zoos. Tied in with this is the research that the keepers and the zoo people have to do— not experimental research like you do in laboratories, but studying the animals and their needs, because if we are to get them to reproduce, we have to know each individual species' needs, whether it's space or light or temperature or food. We have to try to duplicate their natural environment.

For example, in the penguin-seabird house, we have a

changing day length, which is exactly the way it is in the place they come from, and this is done automatically by computer. You see, their reproduction cycle is triggered by the changing day length, but you have to know this if you're going to do it. This is why the zoo people have to study the animals. And another reason for zoos is to educate the people, so that they know more about zoos.

Judy was the elephant we bought from Brookfield Zoo. And when they went to put her on the truck, she wouldn't get on the truck. They tried all day, I mean they coaxed her, they used a winch, they finally got her up on the truck, and she immediately broke the sides and got off. So they then decided that they'd make her walk. So she walked, from Brookfield to Lincoln Park Zoo. Miles. She left there at 7:30 in the evening, and she arrived here about 2:30 in the morning. She was accompanied by keepers and armed guards and a police escort. And, of course, as she started out, the children started following when they saw her. As it got to the wee hours of the morning, she surprised a lot of people who were getting out of taverns at that hour, seeing an elephant walking down the street. She only stopped twice. She stopped at a gas station to drink about six gallons of water, and then she stopped at one of the other parks and consumed two hundred pounds of hay. And then she finished walking. I think they stopped for the keepers to rest, too, because they also were walking. She was one of our most popular animals.

As far as escapes in recent years, of course, Otto the gorilla got out. I think it was in '83 or '84, in the outdoor exhibit on the south side of the ape house. They have the concrete wall, and then there's glass above it. There are electrical wires with a mild current through them at the top, and we thought the animals could not get out. Otto was out there. Now, he may have gotten upset for some reason. Usually when the gorillas were out there, keepers left the door open, so the gorillas could come in or out. They were moving some other gorillas, and they closed the door, and maybe Otto got upset because of that. Otto is quite big; he's very impressive. Anyway, a short time later the keeper in the primate house was fixing food in the kitchen. She looked up, and outside the screen door was the gorilla. Outside. In public. She called one of the other keepers. But Otto just kept moving, and he walked along the east side of the primate house and around that. Then he walked along the south side of the lion house, looking at the animals. Out in the open. There weren't a lot of people in the zoo, but a staff member announced over the loud-speakers that everyone should go in the nearest building and stay there.

Otto was looking at the animals. I mean, he had never seen them before. And he was very interested. So he walked the length of the lion house on the south side, then he walked back. Then he walked around and was watching the tigers. He was just leaning on the rail like a person would, just watching the tigers. At that point the head keeper from the ape house came along and walked up to him and said, "Come on, Otto," and Otto took his hand. They weren't sure he'd go back in the building, because he had never seen the outside of the ape house. He had a good rapport with the keeper, but he had never been loose before, and they weren't sure, so they decided the best thing to do was to tranquilize him with a dart gun.

Otto stayed there, with the keeper; they're very gentle animals, really. The vet came with the dart gun to shoot a tranquilizing dart. When the car drove up with the vet in it, and the vet got out, Otto didn't like the vet, because he didn't like shots, which he had gotten in the past. So he then broke away from the keeper and started up the ramp of the Crown-Field Center. They darted him, and he collapsed there. It took six or eight people to lift him onto the stretcher to carry him back to the great ape house. They have since added five feet to the wall on the outside of the great ape house. We still don't know how he managed to get out. But he did.

The high points for me are always handling the animals, helping people to understand the animals. We had a barn owl, Barney, who was an unusual bird. He was just fantastic. Very little ever fazed him. You could take him anywhere, and he didn't get upset. Most birds would get very upset with many people up close, but not Barney. He just looked at everybody. When we took Barney to schools, he knew how he was impressing the children because he'd look at all the children, and he'd stretch one wing, and the children would go aaaaaaahhhhhhh. He'd look around a little more, and then he'd stretch the other wing, and he'd wait. You just knew that somehow he was having an influence on those children. Barney the barn owl.

I handled him from the time I became a docent until he died last summer. He had been at the zoo before I came, so he probably was around fifteen when he died. And he died doing what he liked to do most, he died being handled at an exhibit. One of the docents was handling him, and all of a sudden he seemed to kind of collapse. I mean, he just seemed very weak, and she wasn't sure, you know, he wasn't sitting up right, he started to collapse, so she just took him right away over to the hospital. We don't know what he died of, but it probably was just old age. I had a very special relationship with Barney.

Years ago, when I first became a docent, the majority of weekend docents were young, single working girls who worked Monday through Friday and would volunteer on Saturday or Sunday. And the Monday through Friday docents were mainly married women who did not have outside jobs, who had some children at home or whose children were grown, and they were looking for something worthwhile to do. Now it has changed quite a bit, so that more and more professional people are becoming docents. And many of the weekday docents do have jobs. We have women who are nurses, who are doctors, who are teachers, who are real estate agents or interior decorators, flight attendants, in many different professions. And they find that docenting is the best recreation they can get.

When we advertise for docents, we have an orientation day to which we invite all the people who think they want to be docents. We tell them what it is to be a docent, what they would do, that they would be conducting tours, giving information, taking animals out. We show them a film that describes many of the docent activities, and we tell them what the requirements would be. First of all, they have to be eighteen years of age, high school graduates, and we expect them to give one day a week, four hours a day, from ten to two, every week of the year. Now, with vacations and illness and things, no one's going to be here fifty-two weeks. There is a minimum requirement of one hundred hours a year, which you must fulfill if you want to stay. Most of the docents do much more than that. We tell them they will have a training program; they have to pass a final examination. Each curator has one day with the new docents, when the curator talks about his or her animal group.

It's a very technical course. If you're going to talk about the animals, you have to know about them, so we do learn actually more than we need to know, in the sense that we learn all the taxonomy and things like that which you don't use for the average tour person. But it's a background that helps you to understand. Many drop out after orientation because they didn't realize that it would require that much training. It's not easy to become a docent.

The main thing that zoo docents do is give tours to school groups. We have tours by topics: People want all African animals or all South American animals, or they might want nocturnal animals or a tour of endangered animals. Or they might request a primate tour. We also have tours for younger children, what we call an introduction to the zoo, where we take them to one of the bird areas, one of the mammal areas, and one reptile area, so they get a touch of all three, and then we try to have one animal that they can see up close and touch.

Our direction comes from the education department. They have the professionals and have had the training in this type of thing. They develop all the classes that are taught, and they have done a lot to develop the training.

Before we had the education department, the training was done completely by docents. It is much better now; it has improved every year since we've had the education department.

Basically, we're teachers. We teach them about the zoo, and we try to show them the importance of animal life, why we have to conserve animals, besides teaching them about individual animals. For example, people want to know where animals live and what they eat, but we try to get them to understand and to care about the animals and to realize why they're important in the world.

Everything is interdependent. If you destroy all the animals, you destroy a part of our life, because we are actually tied up with the animals. Trees are important because they supply oxygen, they clean the air, besides providing homes for many things. Animals serve, too, because everything is in balance in nature. For example, in some parts of this country where we once had coyotes and wolves, people have practically eliminated all the wolves and are eliminating a lot of the coyotes. They now have an overabundance of rodents, rabbits, and other animals, which those animals used to keep limited in number. Now the rodents and the rabbits and many other smaller animals are destroying crops.

Don't mess with nature.

8

THE MERITT SYSTEM

Dennis Meritt, the assistant director of the zoo, occupied the office opposite Les Fisher's. It was a jungle of vines, hanging plants, potted plants, a pair of parakeets from Australia in a cage, two bubbling fish tanks, a pith helmet, animal carvings, photos, and paintings of animals. A computer lent the only urban touch to the setting.

However comfortable Dennis was in that jungle, or in a real one, he was, at forty-seven, a decidedly sophisticated man. As the nameplate on his desk indicated, he had a doctorate in zoology (from the University of Illinois, Chicago) acquired in 1987. He had spent the last twenty years of his life at the zoo.

He was born and raised in Rochester, New York.

"I always went to school part-time, never full-time," he remembered. The oldest of four sons, he always needed money; after high school, he went to work. He married at an early age and had to work to support his wife and two daughters.

After holding a number of research and laboratory jobs

at hospitals in Rochester, he wound up in Chicago. (Over the years, when time permitted, he completed work on his bachelor's and master's degrees in zoology.)

"I came to Chicago by default," he said. "I was interested in animals, but I didn't know about the job at the Lincoln Park Zoo. A friend of mine, the director of the zoo in Rochester, told me that a job was open at the zoo in Chicago. I followed up and got it." That job was a zoologist's. He was promoted to curator of mammals shortly after joining the zoo staff, and became assistant director in 1976.

His presence was a commanding one. Fit and tan, with dark brown hair and a dark brown, neatly trimmed beard, he spoke with a deep, resonant voice and an intense, decisive, almost theatrical manner.

His style was thoughtful and assured. Many of his associates commended him for his sense of fairness. Even his critics were left with a modest charge; as one of them said, "He tells you what he thinks you want to hear." Despite that accusation, he was successful in confronting disputes.

As he made his way through the thicket of responsibilities he had accumulated, he was comforted by the way that his fate had contradicted the prediction of his high school counselor: "Don't waste your parents' money. You'll never amount to anything."

Much of Dennis's time was spent behind his desk, but he made time for the animals. On one hot summer morning, he left his air-conditioned office and walked over to the large mammal area. Two rhinos—a male and a female— had been placed together in an outdoor habitat, in an attempt at matchmaking. They engaged in a kind of lumbering frolic. They banged horns, bounced around, raced across the habitat, with the female chasing the male, a sexist's delight. The performance, as Dennis evaluated it, was encouraging. In such attempts at mating, other emotions—fear, panic, or outright hostility—might have prevailed.

"Considering how few of these there are in the world, or

even in captivity, every introduction is important," he said to a keeper watching the rhinos with him.

He remembered the first time he had seen the massive creatures in the wild.

"I was in Africa, my first trip there, and we were in an open-sided International Harvester vehicle. I spotted a rhino in the bush. In nature, what fascinates you first is their massiveness, their latent power. Well, while I watched that rhino, he watched us. Suddenly, he rushed out of the bush and literally lifted the truck off the ground. I've never forgotten that feeling, of both danger and exhilaration. The truck bounced upright and we got away, but as I stared at that rhino, I thought that it was essentially unchanged from prehistory. Think about that."

There was little time to reflect. It was 9 A.M., time for the weekly staff meeting. Les Fisher, wearing a navy tie emblazoned with giraffes, presided.

Les had made rounds that morning and had reported the reptile house water-pressure problem to some plumbers at work in another part of the zoo. He urged Clarence Wright to camp on the plumbing foreman's door if the pressure didn't improve.

He had seen some overgrown patches of lawn.

"It looks like a little jungle here and there. Needs doing," he said.

He reported that "a guy called me to report that he was confronted by an escaped wolf. He said his wife and son had to flee into the large mammal house." It was true: The maned wolf who had escaped a few weeks earlier had done it again. As in the previous episode, the wolf had been darted with a tranquilizer and returned to its habitat.

Mark Rosenthal reminded Les that there was "a weakness in the habitat, a slight incline in the rockwork on one wall, enabling the wolf to jump down and out of the exhibit from an overhanging ledge. The wolf wasn't supposed to be in that area at all, but in another one he couldn't get out of."

The wolf was one of several that had been suffering from distemper.

"He must be fine now," Dennis noted, sarcastically. "He seems to be fully coordinated."

Les was not cheered. "Some other wolf might get out," he said. "We need a barrier, a modification. I'll call the guy who called me about it, and I'll explain it all to him," he added, with visible weariness.

One of the alcoholics on the zoo staff would be on probation for six months, Les advised. "He'll come back to work, and we'll have to monitor him. If there's a problem, we can let him go without cause during the probation period."

A woman employee had let Les know that she had been physically abused by a male worker. "It's one person's word against the other's," he said.

He reminded those present—curators, vets, and representatives of the zoo society—that the zoo functioned on a rigid budget. "Money will be tight, so be totally cost-efficient. Funding is getting tougher, not better. We must be lean, mean, hard. When we spend money, we ought to ask ourselves, how does it enhance the public's view of the zoo? What does the visitor *see* after we've spent the money? That's how to evaluate what we spend."

The meeting ended at 10 A.M., and Dennis returned to his office. He had to phone an old friend, the director of the San Antonio Zoo, to discuss a project few at the zoo knew about, but all would eventually celebrate.

He had to push twenty-six buttons on his Touch-Tone phone in order to reach the number in Texas. "The park district is economizing," he sighed. "Try that on a rotary phone, and you'll have a unique orthopedic problem."

He was phoning his friend to get him to participate in a venture that would bring the koala bear, the irresistible Australian marsupial (it was *not* a bear) to the zoo. They weren't strikingly rare in Australia, but they were seldom seen in zoos. The koalas were available from the San Diego

Zoo, which had had great success in breeding them. It was easier to get them from San Diego than directly from Australia, which imposed restrictions on exports of koalas.

Getting the koalas wasn't difficult; feeding them was. Koalas eat only eucalyptus. It could be grown in California, Puerto Rico, Trinidad, and Hawaii, Dennis had discovered. But he'd found a grower in Florida who could supply the food in large quantities, regularly. Dennis would need enough to feed three to five koalas, and for a sum not exceeding $38,000 a year, he could get the food delivered twice a week, with the air transportation funded, he hoped, by a donation from a major airline. He had the zoo society's support already; koalas would inspire more visitors to come to the zoo. Dennis hoped to get the San Antonio Zoo involved, to share expenses. The discussions would continue.

Dennis hoped to arrange a backup food supply, to be grown in one of the park district's own conservatories. If all went well, the koalas would be in residence in a habitat atop the Crown-Field Center by the spring of 1988.

After he finished his chat with his friend in San Antonio, Dennis looked up and saw Kathy Brown, the senior keeper at the bird house, standing in his doorway. Kathy walked in, bearing good news.

Over the weekend, she told Dennis, a family had come to the zoo to deposit some creatures it had collected and now wanted to get rid of; it was a common occurrence at the zoo. People who became disenchanted with their pets brought them to the zoo.

This family had delivered six ringed-neck doves and a turtle. One of the doves seemed sickly, Kathy reported, but the rest were in good condition. She brought the news to Dennis because he collected ring-necked doves. With the new arrivals, he would have thirty-two of them, in a large, walk-in cage he had put up at home three years ago.

"I've still got one with an amputated wing," he reminded Kathy. "It was hit by a car, but it's still alive and well. It climbs up a bush with its one wing." He assured Kathy that once the new doves were examined and declared to be in good health, he'd take them home.

There were risks, of course. Dennis lived in a northern suburb, and there were wild raccoons around, as there were in the city itself—and in the zoo, for that matter. He had trapped two raccoons and a neighbor's cat trying to pull doves through the mesh of the enclosure.

"A raccoon can pull a dove through a one-inch-by-one-inch opening in the wire," he told Kathy. "All that remains is a cluster of feathers on the wire."

The doves would be the latest additions to Dennis's small menagerie. He owned an "alley dog," part terrier and part beagle, that he'd cared for since 1974, when the puppy had been tossed out of a moving car near the zoo. He had a dozen tortoises. He had two large Oscars, "huge fish with definite personalities," in a large tank. He got them when he received a call at the zoo declaring, "If you don't take this fish, I'm going to flush it down the toilet." He took one, then got another call from the same person, and took the second fish. In addition, he had a Colombian rainbow boa, "just a little guy," and a dozen marine toads.

As Kathy went on her way, Dennis's phone rang.

The University of California had rescued a sea lion. But it was an epileptic and was on dilantin. No thanks, Dennis told the caller, who indicated that if Dennis didn't want the sea lion, Sea Lion Rescue International would take it.

Another call: A woman who had been calling regularly with the same message reiterated it. Every evening when she parked her car, between 2 and 4 A.M., her car was attacked by a giant anteater. It was destroying the finish on the car, she insisted.

"We'd love to have the anteater," Dennis told her. "Just let us know where it is." He put down the phone and gasped, "A lunatic!"

The phone rang again: A woman wanted to donate a one-winged great horned owl to the zoo. Again, no thanks.

He walked away from the clanging phone to the bird house, to pick up some birdseed for his doves and see the newly arrived doves, who appeared to be in good condition. A keeper told him, "Someone brought in a seagull with its feet cut off. Can you believe that? It was one of the sickest things I've ever seen." Dennis grimaced. The bird had been euthanized by one of the zoo vets.

In a nearby cage, he spotted a small gray bird, a nighthawk. It had been brought in by a family that had found it and thought it needed help.

They thought the bird was sick. It wasn't. It was just young, and its mother hadn't been around when they found the bird. Dennis examined it.

"It needs weight," Dennis told the keeper. "Wait a week. Let it eat. Then flip it out in the late afternoon. They're nocturnal. A city bird. Sleeps all day. It shouldn't have been picked up in the first place. It would have done fine out there."

Dennis's days were filled with decisions, large and small. He managed the animal collection—and the curators as well. The ongoing renovations were his concern, too. They were designed to bring the zoo and its exhibits into the twenty-first century. Some animals would be moved out on loan, some would be moved out permanently, and the entire collection would be improved as it was reduced. All of it existed as paperwork, before the construction crews ever appeared. Dennis had mastered the skill of reading blueprints and architects' renderings of the new buildings and the altered old ones. Finally, Dennis filled in for Les when the director was away, and handled any work that Les chose to pass his way.

There were rumors that Les might retire in a few years. Several of the current curators hoped to be knighted, but it was possible that a new director might come from another zoo. For most of the staff, however, Dennis appeared to be the logical heir. It was not something he thought about, at least not much, he insisted.

"I'd be happy if ten years from now, Les was still sitting there. He doesn't have to retire; it's not mandatory. But when he does, there's no question that his is a plum job.

There will be competition for it, within and without the zoo. But I haven't spent my twenty years here just waiting for his job to open up."

He changed the subject. He talked about the nature of the people who became keepers.

"There was a time when we had a huge group of old-timers who hated educated people. Some of them couldn't write their own names. Then, in the seventies, young people applied, and some of the older ones retired or died. Women came on board. They were eager to learn. They moved on, to some degree, after working here—to other jobs, to school.

"Enter the activists. They wanted answers, and if they didn't get the ones they liked, they engaged in provocation. Now, all the generations are represented here, but most of the old ones are biding their time until they retire. As it's all changed, keepers have become more professional, more visible, more accountable. There's a reason for that. It used to be that recreation was the only reason for a zoo to exist. That's gone. Now keepers must know more about animals than feeding them and cleaning their cages."

In the best of worlds, there would be a keeper perfectly suited to care for specific animals. Dennis did not anticipate perfection.

"What we want to do," he said, "is match the person, the skills, the personality, and our need. It's impossible at times. In God's master plan, there is an ideal person for every slot. But not here."

The tribulations of coexisting with a diverse assortment of personalities were only part of Dennis's routine. He worried about the animals as well.

Every week, he chaired the animal management meeting, a discussion of problems and progress related to the animal collection. On one summer afternoon, he found an empty table and convened the group in a Crown-Field corridor.

Curators Mark Rosenthal and Clarence Wright were there, along with vet Tom Meehan and assistant vet Peri

Wolff; curator Kevin Bell would have been there, but he was at another meeting, with the planners of the renovated bird house.

Dennis shared with those present some of the phone calls he'd gotten: the one hoping to donate the one-winged owl and the other offering the epileptic sea lion. There were snickers around the table, and unanimous approval of Dennis's rejection of both offers.

Dennis confirmed with Mark that Bozie the elephant was set to be shipped to the zoo in Springfield, Missouri, in three months, for a stay that could last eighteen months. It was a variation on the breeding loan process. But first Bozie would have to be tested for parasites and tuberculosis. Mark would accompany the animal, along with one of the elephant keepers.

"Should her slot be taken by another elephant?" Dennis asked.

"It's a good idea," Mark replied. "For companionship, and for our keepers' professional growth. We'd take any elephant except a wild, rampaging male."

"We can test her for TB, but we have no way of knowing if that test is worth anything," Tom said. "The problem is more a matter of false positives than false negatives. But we don't have to rely on the test alone; we can do a gastric lavage."

Dennis moved on to the subject of other animals slated to leave the zoo.

"We need to move out about four to six of the Arabian oryxes by the end of the year. They're going back to the wild. In Oman."

Tom reminded Dennis of the red tape involved in shipping animals directly from the zoo to a foreign country.

"Don't worry. We'll send them to another zoo first, in preparation for the shipment overseas," Dennis said. "Oman will pay all the transportation, vet, and crating costs."

Mark told the others that the newly matched pair of

rhinos were doing fine. So was Lenore, the gorilla whose hand had to be amputated.

"She gets around," Tom added.

"Now she ought to be in a one-on-one situation, then one-on-two," Mark replied.

"I want to see if she can use her elbow to climb," Tom said.

"By the way, I've put in a work order to fix the maned wolf habitat, and we're going to relocate that wolf who got out of it," Mark said.

Tom remained concerned with the distemper that afflicted that wolf and several others. He wasn't concerned that other animals would get it, however.

"If they were going to get it, they'd have it by now," he said. "But I can't guarantee that someone won't take the virus home to a dog. There's no danger if the keepers change their shoes and use the footbath before they leave work," he added.

"But we don't have to worry about a distemper epidemic that will last ten years?" Mark asked.

"No," Tom said, smiling.

"Well, let's define that magical date when all's clear," Dennis said. "And we'll be OK. Let's do it as early as possible. And Mark, have that work order put through on an emergency basis."

"By the way, one of those wolves has a bad leg," Tom noted. "A very bad leg."

"If it can't be repaired to give that animal a normal life, we'll have to euthanize it. No choice. We can replace it," Dennis said. He was often consulted by the vets and the curators before an animal was euthanized.

"A professor in Oklahoma wants six of our king snakes. Not a loan. He wants to keep them," Clarence said.

Dennis smiled. The zoo had a surplus of king snakes.

"God love him," he said to Clarence. "Send them as a donation, and we'll pay the freight."

Tom was concerned with a problem affecting the rattlesnakes. Their spines would fuse, causing paralysis. It was a mystery and had been adding to Clarence's anxiety about plagues in the reptile house.

"We'll find out what it is," Tom assured Clarence. "Do they have a history of eating live prey?"

"Yes," Clarence said. "I've thought that whatever it is might be transmitted by mice."

"By rodent teeth. That's my guess," Tom said. "When a snake isn't hungry, it doesn't eat the mouse immediately. Then, the mouse bites the snake."

"That kind of bite could happen, and you'd never even see it," Dennis commented.

Peri had been summoned to the penguin-seabird house earlier that day by a concerned keeper who thought she had a dead penguin on her hands. The penguin had been in the pool and had appeared to be lifeless. But when Peri arrived and picked it up, it moved.

"The penguin was in poor feather condition," she said. "The insulation wasn't there. The penguin went cold. It burned up its energy, and for some reason it got stuck in the pool in a weakened state and was stressed. It may have inhaled some water. So we took it to the hospital. After a while, it started to heat up, so we took it back to penguin-seabird. It's on antibiotics now, to prevent pneumonia, and it's not in that pool now."

"Odd how animals behave," Dennis said. "I once had a dead tortoise, and I put it in a large plastic bag and tossed it into the garbage. Four hours later, I heard a scratching sound. It taught me something. Always give a reptile twenty-four hours to die."

When tamarins, small monkeys, eat roaches, as is common in the zoo, they develop parasites. Earlier that day, Peri had operated on two of them and had removed dozens of the worms from their intestines. The operation was a last resort, if antibiotics failed.

"We're doing well with our roach control in the hospital," Tom said. "But the tamarins come to us from small mammal, and over there they're loaded with roaches. Roaches are going to decimate our collection. We've got to hit them with an insecticide. If the roaches eat that and the animals eat the roaches, it's a smaller risk than the one we've got now."

Gene Brimer, the exterminator Mark had hired, would be spending time in the hospital, working on the problem, Mark said.

It was 4:30 P.M. when the discussion ended. Dennis needed some fresh air.

He went outside and stood at the railing in front of the lions' outdoor habitat. He knew that few of the majestic animals—perhaps no more than fifty—survived in captivity, and not more than two hundred were present in the only forest in India that still supported them.

A female lion was in heat. The scent she gave off could be detected by the male several miles away in the wild. In the zoo, she had tempted a male a few yards away. But she wanted to sleep, not mate.

The male approached her and attempted to nudge her out of her tranquility. She lifted her head slowly, turned it to him, and growled. He paused. She tried to return to sleep. The male approached her from behind and began to lick her genitalia. She endured the advance. He mounted her and proceeded rapidly to achieve his objective. As he did, he growled. Then, he left for a moment, paced, and returned for another episode.

She got up to avoid him. She turned her back against the cliff wall at the back of the habitat. The male was restless, pacing, growling. Then, acquiring a sense of patience that had not been evident, he crouched beside her. She did not respond. He waited for a signal. She did not acknowledge his presence.

Along the rail next to Dennis, a father held his young daughter.

"What were they doing?" the child asked.

"It's time to go," the father said.

"Yes," his wife joined in. "Let's go."

Dennis smiled.

"Usually they say, 'You don't want to watch that. They're fighting,' " he said. "Accompanied by a hooked arm around the kid who asked the question."

He moved on, passing the habitat occupied by the two Bengal tigers, the sisters. One of them was dozing in the sun. The second was propped against a cool wall at the back of the habitat. Her expression was sleepy, peaceful.

Suddenly, the sleepy tiger—in a manner familiar to owners of house cats—sat up. Her gaze fixed on something beyond the moat that separated the animals from the public. She arose and stalked toward the moat, moving slowly, deliberately, never diverting that gaze. She got to the edge of the moat and sat up, unblinking. There were people beyond the moat, floating balloons, vendors. The tiger stared for several minutes, a portrait of the predator in readiness, then turned its head, moved away from the moat, and went back to the back wall.

Something had tantalized the tiger, something had urged her on.

But Dennis did not attempt to read the minds of animals.

Only the tiger knew what had sent her on that brief dramatic prowl. For Dennis, every such mysterious moment was a part of the continuing fascination that made his job so gratifying. It was comforting for him to know that humans could know a great deal about animals. But not everything.

First Person: Dennis Meritt

As a teenager, I had an intense interest in animals and an intense interest in the outdoors. I had a love of nature and a love of walking across the landscape. I didn't share my family's interest in hunting, but I shared their interest in being in wild places and in seeing things and in flipping rocks and collecting squirmy, slimy things.

I had an interest in science, in pure science. Then, at age

twenty-six, I reassessed where I was and what I was doing and what I was really interested in. By that time I was intensely involved in animal things. I thought to myself, "Why not explore the possibilities of being paid for that interest?" I sought out other people who had similar interests, and those people all funneled in a zoo direction. Then I became very close with the local zoo director, actually began to spend some time as a volunteer at the zoo, began to explore what opportunities were within the zoo profession. I began a search, and the search lasted about a year and a half.

When I arrived here, I was shy, introverted, not self-assured at all. I think I compensated for all of those deficiencies with an intense desire to learn, to experience firsthand. The day that I walked into this place, and Les Fisher said, "You know what your job is, do it," and there were no constraints on it, I think that began the evolution of the person. The opportunities that I had here are largely responsible for who I am.

I had a high level of book learning, formal education. I had all of the theory, all of the principles, but I had very little real or practical experience, and that came on the job. I ate it up. As it came to me, I welcomed it. I was very much like Don Quixote; the windmills were different, but I just waded into situations here, particularly animal situations, always with the animals' best interests at heart, always knowing that we could do something more for these animals.

The first weekend that I was on—for the first twelve or fourteen years at Lincoln Park, I worked every other weekend—I was here alone. I'd probably been on the job three or four days. A camel was born. Now, I had seen a baby camel, I'd seen a mother camel, but I had never been in a position to make some kind of judgment about whether mother and baby were doing fine. And as soon as the mother started to kick the baby, I realized that all was not well. And I remember calling the then assistant director and saying, "Listen, I need some help on this, because I think I ought to pull this baby." And he said, "Don't ever call me on a day off again. Do whatever you're going to do, but make sure that you make the right decision, because if you don't, you'll pay for it on Monday morning."

So with those guidelines, I waded in to pull a baby camel, which basically meant running in and grabbing this ninety-eight-pound infant away from its mother, and running for my life. Now, what I didn't know about camels but now fully understand, and have put into my mental dictionary, is that the mother had mastitis, and it was very painful every time the baby tried to nurse, and that's why she was kicking it. She had all of the maternal instincts for that infant. Even though she didn't want it near her, she certainly didn't want me to take it away from her. And I can remember, panting, I mean panting, exhausted, running out of that field pen, with that baby camel, with mom real close to my tail. It was one of those experiences in life that you don't forget.

It actually was a very good learning experience for me, because no baby camel had ever been hand-raised here before. I went to the books, I went to other people in the zoo community and said, "How do you raise a baby camel?" We successfully raised it by hand, and it turned out to be a magnificent animal.

I believe that there is a very high level of interaction between some of the animals and some of the people at the zoo. There's no question about that. During my early years here, my office was in the lion house. There was no question in my mind that those animals responded to my presence every day, to my comings and goings, and that we could play games—hide and seek—and jump around, and that they would respond to me and I would respond to them, as I walked through that building. It was eye-to-eye contact; it was one of those mental things that happen. It clearly happens with other kinds of animals.

Take the breeding male chimp that was here for so many years, Sam. He and most of the females that formed that group came to us as juveniles. I was the person who used to check on the animals and see how they were doing and make dietary adjustments. And when they became sexually mature, I was the one who went to those females to make some judgment about how the babies were doing: Are they going to be OK? Are they strong enough? Are they big enough? Are they too small? What do we have to do? I had a very good personal relationship with the females. A lot of it came with handing out bananas or handing out peppermints. But that male, Sam, didn't like that interaction. Sam, in his mature years in the great ape house, treated me exactly like a competing male.

Jane Goodall was here, and Jane and I had known each other for a number of years. I said to her, "I want you to assess for me what happens when I walk into this building." I said, "I'm not going to say a word. You're the field biologist; you just tell me what happens." As we walked through the building, Sam took one look at me and began his hair fluffing and his foot stomping and his hooting and his swinging. And as I moved to the glass barrier, he would swing down and pound the glass and then go charging off. And she smiled and said, "Well, you're just like a competing male. If you were in nature, what you should now do, to reassure him that you have no intentions on his females, is to go in and groom him. This is the scenario that should happen, but I wouldn't advise it."

If I enjoy an interaction with an animal today, it's probably with the elephants. The elephants treat me as a neutral object. I'm not someone who trains them; I'm not someone who works them. On the other hand, I'm not a stranger, not someone to be either leery of or suspicious of or afraid of. When I'm there with the elephants, it's always under positive circumstances. That forces on me a certain responsibility, because I realize that those animals are potentially dangerous, are thinking, knowing, reasoning, testing creatures all the time. So, while I enjoy the relationship very much, and I enjoy the kind of mutual contact that we have, I have to be real careful, because I have a tendency to become too close to them in terms of trusting. And that is a real bad frame of mind to be in with any wild animal, particularly one that you're directly involved with.

The big cats still fascinate me. I think it has to do with body form, with size, and with knowing that these are predators, essentially killing machines, that they have all of the muscle and bone and form they need to carry out that task and to survive under very difficult circumstances. We know about their speed, and we know about their stealth. From my perspective, it's respect for that, and also realizing that those animals are essentially unchanged. There is very little if any difference between lions and tigers and leopards and snow leopards and cheetahs in a captive situation, as compared to nature. All of the instincts, all of the capabilities are there.

You think that an animal's changed because of a captive environment. We had a particular pair of snow leopards on the outside of the lion house. They were fed this prepared zoo mix, which looks like raw hamburger served in a sausage shape. And these two animals religiously would leave a small portion of that food, and would catnap within reaching distance of that pile, and would let starlings and pigeons come into the cage to feed off of it. And every once in a while, they would pick off a starling or pick off a pigeon. It was to me a living demonstration that that animal still has all of those instincts it was born with.

You can spot an emotional range in animals. Absolutely. It's measured in a number of things. In the higher forms of animal, here at the zoo—whether it be bird, mammal, or reptile—usually it has something to do with either body position or ear position or eyes or where the tail hangs or the way a wing is. Sometimes it's in vocalization. It's all there. After you've been here a while, you know what the usual or the normal posture or activity or appearance of an animal is, of any given species. And then without consciously knowing it, you go by or you look and you recognize, sometimes not being able to define it, that there's something different. It may be the way it's sitting or lying. It may be the luster in its eye or the lack of it. It may be the way its coat is. It may be the way the feathers lie. It's more a sixth sense than it is definable or describable.

A number of my colleagues here and elsewhere across the world see zoos as a last refuge—not a last refuge in terms of we are going to save every single animal or every endangered species in the world, but a last refuge in terms of a gene bank. If a species disappears in the wild, there will be some that survive in zoos. They will survive, not for visitor enjoyment, not for visitor viewing, but simply from a genetic standpoint, meaning that we have the potential to propagate almost anything that we set our minds to. We have the technology, we have the experience, we have the intellectual powers to be able to propagate any given species, given enough time, given enough money, given adequate facilities. So I see zoos as the last reservoir.

I also see zoos as an ambassador of wild places. Zoos are places where people can come, not only to see animals, but to learn about animals, to experience them firsthand, in a three-dimensional living, breathing, smelly, vocalizing way.

Modern zoos like Lincoln Park and others across the country have known for a number of years that they needed to change facilities to put animals into more aesthetically pleasing surroundings that allow interpretation about the animal and where it lives and how it naturally behaves. We've known that for years, but zoos have until fairly recently been poorly supported in terms of dollars. We have had the architectural skills, we've had the technological skills, we've had the interpretive skills, we've had the exhibit design skills to do it. It's just a question of money. So those things are changing. With regard to diet, you have an obligation to provide an animal with nutritionally sound, wholesome, appealing food. The only way to do that, particularly in a northern zoo on a twelve-month basis, is to substitute natural foods—foods that the animal would normally eat in nature—with other foods. In the case of carnivores, critics of zoos would have more to be critical of if we regularly released goats or sheep or gazelles into carnivore cages to provide them a meal. A small example of that is feeding day in the reptile house. We close the building, so that we do not offend anybody.

We have made a conscious attempt to reduce the number of species here in the collection—bird, mammal, and reptile, across the board. We're trying to cut down the number of kinds of animal that we have, to match species to facilities, and to show those species that we exhibit, in terms of visitor interest and international conservation, with those two priorities in mind.

If they're found in nature as a colony, they should be a colony here. If they're found as a herd, they should be a herd. If it's a family group, it should be a family group. This movement had already started twenty years ago. Fifteen years ago it really became a major emphasis. We don't show singletons. And if we show a single animal, it's because we have been unable to find a suitable mate or companion for it. For the last fifteen years, we haven't willy-nilly taken animals into this collection. I think the renovation and the reconstruction and the rebuilding here will allow us to reach that final phase of matching animals and facilities exactly. And that's what we're doing. In the lion house renovation, twenty-six cages are being reduced to ten habitats. We will show five species, and we'll show them well. We'll have backups, areas behind the scenes for sick animals, for pregnant animals, for animal introductions, for the adequate maintenance of any offspring that are produced here. In the lion house, we'll have indoor and outdoor facilities for the Afghanistan leopard and for the snow leopard, showing our long-range commitment to the international propagation programs for those animals.

We have four ways to disperse animals. One is with an outright gift. We have an animal that is surplus that someone else needs; we make some assessment of what that facility is, what their capabilities are, what their physical plant and what their staff are like, and sometimes just simply give the animal to them, because they have a need for it. We sometimes sell animals outright—this'll cost you a dollar and a half, this'll cost you ten thousand dollars, whatever the case may be; the dollar value is unimportant. But the same formula is plugged in: Who is it? What facilities do they have? What is their expertise? What are the long-range prospects for the survival of this animal? And then we have breeding loans, which also fall under the same conditions. Breeding loans are made usually because we have been so successful with an animal species that we need to move some of the animals out of here, but we still want to retain ownership of those animals and some of their offspring for our long-range propagation needs. That's basically what a breeding loan allows you to do: to choose what the satellite propagation facilities are going to be. The usual terms of a breeding loan are if we send a pair of animals out of here, we retain ownership of the adults, and we split any offspring produced equally. The fourth method is a trade—we're one of the few professions left in the world where barter still works. You trade an animal to another institution for some ballpark kind of dollar figure, or to have credit established at the other institution. We may send a particular animal to an institution that either doesn't have the finances to pay for it or wants to do it on a trade basis, and say to them, "Fine, take this. You have a need. You have a perfect match for it in terms of a mate and match in terms of facilities. We will sometime in the future get something from you of comparable value." And we don't worry about what the value is, knowing that the animal is going into a good situation.

I can't remember the last time that we went to a dealer because we needed an animal. We would always go to other zoos first, whether they be here in the States or whether they be international. The same is true for anything that is declared surplus, whether that is a sale, a trade, a gift, or a loan. The zoo community always has first refusal. And then we disperse to licensed accredited dealers. Dealers have become intermediaries or brokers. If we should be unable to find a direct institution-to-institution affiliation for the placement of an animal, there are dealers around who play that role. Basically what happens is that they act as our agent or somebody else's agent for relocating, transportation, and the actual negotiations for the relocation of the animals.

Some of the zoos I admire may surprise you. I very much enjoy going to Milwaukee. They've created a parklike setting, so that you have at least the illusion that you're in nature; lots of trees, lots of landscaping, which contribute significantly to it. In terms of surprises and a very good overall effect, particularly setting and a specific collection, go to Madison, Wisconsin, to Henry Vilas Zoo. It is a little jewel, sitting there alongside the lake, really a place to be savored. It's a retreat, in a very real sense, from city life. It's an opportunity to kind of slide into nature. One institution that has changed its image is the zoo in Pittsburgh, Pennsylvania. That zoo has undergone a tremendous evolution in the last few years; it is a very, very pleasant and enjoyable experience. San Diego has a lot of admirers. I think it isn't the San Diego Zoo at all; I think it's Southern California, the laid-back lifestyle, and the people in that community. I know its staff as well as I know my own family. And they themselves are at a loss to explain why San Diego has the image that it has. They don't care; they want it to continue. From a professional standpoint, a purely analytical devil's advocate kind of position, there are some real stinky things at San Diego that they are busily trying to take care of. There are some ancient, decrepit, outmoded facilities there. We kid our colleagues in San Diego that if they didn't have the climate, and if they didn't have the vegetation that they have at the zoo, that they would be nothing more than a concrete jungle. And that is absolutely true. That semitropical climate allows you, with planting material, on a twelve-month basis, to cover up a host of construction errors. Of course, the wild animal park that is located outside of San Diego, that very much is a model facility. But when people talk about San Diego, they aren't talking about the wild animal park, they're talking about the zoo in Balboa. And I don't know where that mystique came from.

The two zoos that people name as zoos that they want to go to, I mean that they really are impressed by, are the ones in San Diego and the Bronx. Bronx has worked very hard at its image. The Bronx has a long history of tradition. It goes back to the days of all of those wonderful early naturalists, hunters, environmentalists, whatever the right description might be. And they have built on that, and there is no question in my mind, both personally and professionally, that in terms of zoo technology, architecture, exhibit design, interpretation, the Bronx is the finest in the country. They have spent untold amounts of money to accomplish the grand illusion. They have, particularly from the standpoint of exhibit design, duplicated in a captive environment, in a northern zoo, as close as one can come to a natural environment, and have done it extremely well. They've done it not only from the visitors' standpoint, and from a maintenance standpoint, but they also have done it from the animals' standpoint, which is critical.

National in Washington is the nation's zoo. What it should mean, what it should have meant for the last twenty-five or thirty years, is that it should have been the model for all zoos within the country, let alone internationally. It isn't. It's reaching that point, but it isn't, because it didn't have the financial support it needed from the Congress and from its governing institution. It has within the last five years done some major and significant updates to bring it into the twenty-first century. They are busy making changes.

Going away and looking at other facilities energizes me, gives me a renewed sense that this is what we need to do, so let's do it. In a real sense, it's a battery charge. And there's always something to do. Twenty-plus years ago when I walked in here, it was for me a learning experience. And it still is. I learn something every day. Every time that I think that I know all there is to know, the animals show me something different. And as long as it continues to be that for me, I can't think of any better place to be.

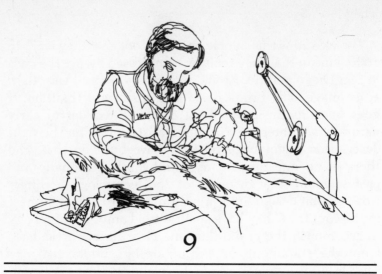

9

HOUSE CALLS

If animals could verbalize their hostility, Tom Meehan would be the most hated human at the zoo. As the zoo veterinarian, he was the one who disturbed their peace, brought pain and fright into their world, even as he saved their lives. He was not an unfeeling, sadistic man at all, but his role did not bring him gratitude from the animals whose peace he had disturbed, any more than a pediatrician won admiration from the infants he introduced to pain and fright.

When Tom approached, many animals displayed their anger and their fear openly. Fortunately, Tom accepted that reaction and did his job.

It was a job he had been prepared to do. At thirty-five, he had a bachelor's degree in animal husbandry and a D.V.M. from the University of Missouri. Born in St. Louis, he had been interested in zoos and in animals as a boy. He decided to be a vet when he was in high school and sold balloons and hot dogs at the St. Louis Zoo.

He served as a keeper at that zoo and worked there part-time while in college. He was a vet at an animal hospital in Indiana and a resident vet at the St. Louis Zoo before joining the Lincoln Park Zoo staff in 1981.

Tom lived in the northwest part of Chicago with his wife (who had been a keeper at the St. Louis Zoo), two young daughters, a dog, six doves, and two cockatiels. His work brought him to the modern bunker that housed the hospital and the commissary every weekday before 8 A.M. and often on weekends. In a dark brown, dark blue, or bright green jumpsuit, with dangling keys and a walkie-talkie attached to his belt, he was a case study in perpetual motion. At 5'9" and 185 pounds, with a full beard and thick brown hair, he had the appearance and energy of a rugged running back.

He spent most of his time treating animals, but he was in charge of the commissary as well; it had been created with a large donation from Joan and Ray Kroc, of McDonald's hamburger fame. From the commissary, food was distributed to the kitchens in the various animal houses. The quantities of food consumed were diverse and massive. Each week, the large mammals ate 200 pounds of hydroponic grass (produced at the zoo itself, it was a quick-growing oat seed grass). Birds devoured 7,500 meal worms and 850 wax worms weekly. The hoofed stock consumed 1,470 pounds of alfalfa and 1,680 pounds of timothy hay each week. The monkeys consumed 36 pounds of grapes per week and 63 pounds of sweet potatoes. The big cats dined on more than 500 pounds of horsemeat fortified with vitamins and minerals, plus 50 pounds of horse knuckles and 50 pounds of horse tails. Bananas were popular with animals in almost every house.

The commissary's keeper staff kept track of food; the keepers ordered it, and the keepers delivered it. Tom maintained control. He felt that feeding the animals properly was a part of his mission to maintain their good health.

"I had an interest in nutrition," he said. "I had contacts in the field. What I don't have now is time. Our diets have to be revamped from top to bottom. We need to bring in some zoo nutrition consultants with their computers. But when we requested that in our budget, we were turned down. So we feed the animals the same old things and handle problems as they arise. We'll shoot for those consultants in the next budget."

Time was the commodity in short supply in Tom's life.

The hospital itself was not identifiable from the zoo walk that passed above it. It was concealed from the view of passersby in its bunker reached from a metal stairway. It was not an architectural wonder. Rather, it was a utilitarian design. A long corridor from front to back doors was lined with offices, a lab, a dining area, an examining room, an operating room, an area to perform necropsies, and various holding areas for animals being held for diagnoses, animals awaiting treatment, and animals recovering from treatment. (Most animals were returned to their houses after treatment.) It was all brightly lit, immaculate. The three keepers assigned to the hospital kept the place clean and the animals cared for.

It was a quiet place, but rarely an uneventful one.

On a hot summer morning, Tom sat behind his desk, confronting a tall stack of mail, forms, and memos.

"The mornings here are always crazy," he said. "There's so much to do. There may be animals to be euthanized. Certainly there are always animals to see, to examine. We have rounds daily; we meet in my office and go over each case. We catch everyone up on what's going on, including Peri [Peregrine Wolff, the assistant vet] and Joel Pond, our lab technician. We don't specialize here. Peri doesn't just do birds, and I don't just do mammals. One of us may be away at times, so the vet on duty is *it*. Last weekend, I got eight calls on Sunday at home, and I wasn't feeling well. Fortunately, I didn't have to come in. It was my first weekend at home in months."

One of the hospital keepers, a woman, entered to interrupt Tom.

"We've got two seagulls. One may have been shot, the

other seems to have flown into a fence. Someone brought
them in," she told Tom.

She reported, as well, that Lenore, the gorilla whose
hand had been amputated in surgery, was showing signs of
recovery. "She isn't crabby," the keeper said.

"Our lemur baby is cold, and the mother threw it out of
their box," the keeper went on. The hospital was doubling
as the zoo nursery while the children's zoo, where it was
normally housed, was being renovated. The lemur mother
had arrived from the Milwaukee Zoo, in transit to another
zoo, and had been pregnant. Tom had not been warned.

"Watch it," Tom said. "Is it moving?"

"Yes."

"Keep an eye on it for a couple of hours. If I grab it and
do a blood sample, I might upset it."

"Can't we just warm it up?"

"Let's put some supplemental heat in there. One of those
infrared heaters. We're going to have to rethink all this.
Call the primate house and find someone who knows about
baby lemurs. We have to keep the mother from rejecting
that baby, if we can."

The incident inspired Tom to be reflective.

"You just never know about wild animals. There's a story
about a lion at the Milwaukee Zoo. It was lethargic, and the
keepers were concerned. Well, they knew that lions are
predatory, and they wanted to do something to stimulate
that inclination. So they tossed a rabbit in with it. What
happened? They became pals."

It was time for staff rounds, which included reports
from a short, boyish fourth-year vet student from Iowa
State University named Jeff, and a recent Michigan State
University vet technician graduate, a tall blond woman
named Sandy. Both were externs, putting in time at the
zoo in exchange for valuable experience and a token salary.
They brought up several cases for Tom to assess.

A baby chimp was upset at night and didn't eat properly.
But it was fine during the day.

"Don't worry about it," Tom said. "That's common."

He told the two externs about the baby lemur.

"There's an eighty percent chance we'll have to pull that baby. My guess is that it ought to go to the primate house."

Several maned wolves had distemper. It had become a nagging problem for Tom. Distemper was a risk for all animals; it was the major killer of dogs. For dogs, there was a vaccine. But the live virus vaccine available for use on wild animals gave some animals the disease itself, instead of protecting them against it. Vaccines of lesser risk were also less effective. Zoo vets were not in agreement about which vaccines to use with various species. There were riddles in the practice of veterinary medicine. Absolute answers were not always available to Tom. The wolves presented a challenge.

One of the wolves might have gotten the disease from a wild raccoon frequenting the zoo and passed it along to the other wolves. A vaccine Tom had tried had failed.

"That's not unusual. Distemper is a virus—as mysterious in some ways as the common cold or the flu in humans. We can provide supportive care, but we can't do miracles. Still, I think that these three should make it."

The two seagulls had to be examined. "If they're not releasable, and they're hopeless, we euthanize them. If they're of value, we'll keep them or send them on to a wildlife refuge. But a bird that isn't fully flighted is in trouble. Let's find out."

He led the two externs to the treatment room, a few paces down the hall from his office. Tom opened the make-shift carrier, a large cardboard box marked "Blue Mountain Apples," and lifted one of the birds out, clutching it in one hand, examining it with the other.

"Bummed up," he muttered.

He examined the second bird.

"An old injury that's gotten debilitating. He's real skinny. Can't keep up with the other birds."

Tom made up his mind. Carefully, he sprayed alcohol on a small area where the bird's wing met its body, then injected a euthanizing solution into the bird. Its fluttering stopped instantly. The second bird took longer to die, a few seconds longer.

Tom put the dead birds back into the apple box and led the externs into an adjoining room. He snapped an x-ray onto a light box. It was a film of gorilla Lenore's wrist. Minor surgery had been attempted to cure an infection in that wrist, after antibiotics had failed, but the infection got worse. It was not possible to give a gorilla a flow of antibiotics via an IV line, so the decision was made to remove the infected bone.

"A mess," Tom said. "We tried to save the hand, but we couldn't. We had to amputate. Everybody says, how could you do that? Well, the infection would have gone systemic, and she would have died. We had to try."

He left the hospital and headed to the bear line, where the sick wolves were kept. Jeff, the extern, tagged along.

"Here's a primitive neurological exam," Tom said to Jeff. He poked a long broomstick into the wolf's cell. The wolf had appeared to be blinded by distemper.

"I think he can see," Tom commented. He moved closer to the cage. The wolf did not appear to see him.

"Maybe he can't," he said.

He visited the second wolf. The wolf's bark, normally piercing, was barely audible.

"The distemper gave him laryngitis. It's a disease that shows up everywhere, in the skin, in the respiratory system, in the nervous system. You can't tell where it will be manifested. As many as half of its victims may die. The young are particularly vulnerable."

With Jeff beside him, Tom left the bear line, got into the hospital's yellow park district van and drove over to the great ape house.

Tom looked at a chimp, Shauri, with a long history of illness, from lung infection to diabetes. She had a weight gain that needed interpretation. Tom went toward her small holding cage. She gazed at him and moved her extended lips toward his. She was one of the few animals to show friendship to him; most of them caused a commotion when he appeared.

He looked at Lenore, too, in another holding area.

One of the keepers told him, "She used her arm as she used to use it. She looks at the stump, but she hasn't been biting it."

"She *knows* it's not there," Tom said. "When you reach for something and you don't feel it, you know."

Tom stared at Lenore.

"She has a distinct individual memory of me. She doesn't like me. Even in street clothes, she'd know me. They all know me. I'm not popular."

"Are you going to knock her down again?" the keeper asked, wondering if Tom would tranquilize the gorilla.

"Not now," he answered. "But in the next three weeks, we probably will, to take care of the problems with her teeth." Lenore's troubles hadn't ended.

"I'm more and more amazed at what we can do for these apes," he said to the keeper as he moved toward the door. "They're tough, tough animals."

A gorilla nearby, behind glass, clapped loudly, cupping its hands on its vast chest. Another, nearby, stuck out a finger through the bars of its holding cage; Tom touched it briskly with one of his.

As he walked out of the great ape house, he stopped to survey a group of gorillas behind the thick glass that separated them from the public. One of the gorillas recognized him and came rushing toward the glass, leaping into it noisily in Tom's direction. Tom flinched slightly.

"Sometimes we forget just how strong that glass is," he said, smiling.

Outside, the sun was heating the zoo. Tom wiped his brow. It was summer; he'd barely noticed.

The next morning, Tom had just arrived at his desk when the phone rang. It was a keeper at the great ape house, letting him know that Shauri, the chimp, had given birth. Normally, any evidence of healthy breeding in the ape colony would have been good news, but in this case it was more than that—it was a shock.

There was little reason to believe that Shauri, a twenty-three-year-old (middle-aged for a chimp), was pregnant. It was not a planned event, and Tom did not conceal his sense of surprise. Shauri had been sickly for years.

"Given her size, you couldn't tell by looking," Tom said. "She weighs two hundred and twenty-nine pounds, and the child probably didn't weigh more than four pounds. A pregnant chimp doesn't look the way my wife did."

At one point, in trying to diagnose one of her symptoms, Shauri had been given a pregnancy test; the result had been inconclusive.

"Well, that explains her breast enlargement," Tom sighed.

At rounds in his office, Tom was joined by the two externs. He told them about Shauri.

"She's a tough animal. She was hand-reared at the zoo. And she's very intelligent. She greets us with a kind of chant-hoot, something the chimps do to each other. One day she bit my arm, then gave me a big hug. Chimps use hugs and kisses to defuse aggression. When they anticipate aggression, interpersonal contact escalates and prevents that aggression. They are demonstrative animals. They don't do anything quietly. They like to make noise. Give them sticks to throw, boxes to tear up and toss around, and they probably won't bother to attack each other.

"Shauri loves to eat. She'll even drink her own milk, instead of giving it to her child. She's lost several babies in recent years. Whatever the reason, the babies just fade out. So we might have to pull this baby. Shauri isn't well, and I didn't want her to be pregnant. The pregnancy could have exacerbated her diabetes problem. Some zoos would put her to sleep if she didn't breed. Not here. After all, she could be a kind of aunt. And we have another newborn chimp in addition to hers. It's easier to raise two of them by hand than just one. They bond."

The phone rang. A large alligator had died during the

night in the alligator exhibit in the basement of the reptile house. The keeper who called didn't seem distressed about it, and Tom wasn't either. An alligator wasn't a potential pet, even to one prone to the anthropomorphic.

Tom told Jeff and Sandy that it would take five or six people, a large tarp, and a pickup truck to move the dead alligator to the hospital.

Other animals were competing for his time. Later in the day, he told the externs, he'd have to check on one of the Major Mitchell's cockatoos in the bird house; it had sinusitis and needed medication. He alerted Jeff to help him treat the bird.

He had to find time during the day to inoculate the alpacas against tetanus. They were going to be sheared soon, and he didn't want them to get tetanus from the minor nicks and cuts involved in the shearing process.

He got up, picked up a coil of strong rope, and led Jeff and Sandy into the van for the trip to the reptile house. When he pulled up in front of it and got out, a jaguar in an outdoor cage facing the reptile house recognized him and went into a pacing frenzy, staring tensely at Tom until he disappeared into the reptile house.

"I upset that jaguar just by showing up," he said. "He remembers me."

On the door to the reptile house, one of the keepers had posted a crudely lettered sign: BUILDING CLOSED FOR REPAIRS. They wanted to get to the alligator exhibit before any visiting children did.

In the exhibit, which had been drained of the warm water usually there, a group of seven alligators rested lethargically on the concrete floor. In the middle of the group, a large belly-up alligator was clearly dead, legs in the air, its pale, lifeless skin peeling off.

"He was alive last night and dead this morning," a woman keeper told Tom. Sometimes it happened that way.

One of the keepers opened a small metal door at the rear of the exhibit, and seven people entered: four keepers, the two externs, and Tom. With long sticks, two keepers

herded the alligators away from their dead companion. Tom
jumped down into the exhibit and roped the dead animal.
With help from the others, he dragged it out of the exhibit
and onto the tarp. It took all seven to carry it up a flight of
stairs.

As they pulled and grunted, the slightly anxious sound
of a keeper's voice was heard.

"Did someone close the exhibit door?"

There was silence. Then, a soft voice said, "Yes." Finally,
all seven laughed.

Four members of the group lifted the alligator, now
wrapped in the tarp, into the back of the pickup truck.
"Cover him up," Tom said. People were walking through
the zoo in the early morning, and all zoo personnel knew
that it was wise to conceal the deaths of animals from the
public.

The cadaver was giving off a foul, rotting odor.

"We need to think this over before we cut this sucker
open," Tom said.

A convention of flies was attracted to the dead alligator
as soon as the truck pulled into the hospital driveway.

"They flew in from four states when they heard about
this one," Tom said.

With help from his keepers and externs, Tom dragged
the alligator into a freezer locker.

Tom had some choices. He could call the Field Museum
of Natural History, and it would have a crew come out to
pick up the alligator for its collection of skeletons. He could
call the dead animal pickup of the sanitation department,
and it would get rid of the alligator. Or he could ask that
the zoo incinerator be fired up to burn the corpse. In any
case, he might want to do a necropsy, because he always
wanted answers to death, even when the creature involved,
like the alligator, had become so singularly unattractive.
But he didn't have time to decide immediately. He had to
move on.

He took a medical kit and drove over to the hoofed-stock
enclosure. Walking through the barn area, he passed a stall

with a sable antelope in it. The antelope glared at him, a hard, antagonistic glare.

"Mean shit," Tom hissed at it.

He had come to the hoofed-stock area to take a look at a baby Arabian oryx, an antelope-like animal with long, straight horns. At first, he could see only the mother, her white body twitching to repel flies. Then, he spotted the baby—a small, awkward, beige oryx with barely developed horns. He had to get a blood sample from the baby; it hadn't been eating properly.

He conferred with two keepers whose help he would need. Sliding doors separated the stalls, and if the keepers were deft enough, they could tempt the mother out and leave the baby alone for Tom to assess.

Their deftness prevailed. They opened a door. The mother sauntered out into an adjoining stall. They closed the door behind her, and Tom and Jeff had the baby oryx to themselves. Before they entered the stall, Tom told Jeff, "The jugular on these guys is a piece of cake."

Tom grabbed the oryx, and Jeff took the blood sample, while the oryx squirmed and bleated. It was over in a few seconds, and the baby was quickly reunited with its mother.

"Maybe it's not a bad problem," Tom theorized. "The baby looks healthy. It's standing well. We noticed that its stool was yellow, but when you think about that, we see that in all nursing mammals at times. My gut feeling is that it won't develop into a problem."

The mother oryx glared at Tom again; the baby hid behind her.

"I just went in there and beat up her baby," Tom told Jeff. "That mother will remember me."

Tom headed on to the great ape house.

He picked up a supply of sliced oranges and shredded wheat and passed them out to several gorillas as he walked past their cages.

"A pretty transparent attempt at friendship," he muttered.

He stopped to visit a baby chimp in an incubator. The

setting was familiar; there were toys and small blankets in the incubator, and the tiny, appealing, vulnerable chimp was hugging its favorite blanket. Pat Sass, the senior keeper at the ape house, had worked with apes for most of her twenty-five years at the zoo. This baby chimp was one she had been taking home with her every night. She'd continue to do so until it no longer required night feedings. When it slept through the night, she'd bring it back to the zoo to stay.

Tom touched the chimp gently. It yawned widely and fingered its blanket.

Pat escorted Tom into the holding area where Shauri and her baby were resting. According to a keeper, Shauri had bred with her own son to create the child; it happened in the wild, but not often in captivity.

Vet and keeper discussed the baby chimp's fate. They could leave it with Shauri, who treated it awkwardly at best, and offer it supplementary nourishment. Or they could pull it and hand-raise it.

Close attention for forty-eight to seventy-two hours might provide some clues. Pat was closer to the apes than anyone at the zoo. Her long experience had made her an astute observer, a good judge of ape behavior. Tom would confer with her frequently; in this case, he would also confer with Mark Rosenthal, curator of mammals, and Dennis Meritt, the zoo's assistant director.

"We're talking about long-range planning," he said. "Not just what to do this week or next. That baby chimp could live for fifty years. It's important to know that when they're hand-reared, they don't make good mothers. You just perpetuate that neglect and create another inadequate mother.

"It's a big decision to pull a female chimp. If we leave the baby with Shauri, it may not make it. If we pull it, it'll survive, but for eventual breeding purposes the baby ought to learn from Shauri how to be a mother. It's a tough one."

He couldn't linger. It was time to head to the bird house, to medicate the Major Mitchell's cockatoo.

First, he weighed the bird, to determine how much

medication would be appropriate for a bird of its size. A keeper had wrapped the elegant pink and white parrot in a towel, so it wouldn't squirm, flap, bite, or hurt itself. After weighing it, Tom held it gently with one hand and gave it an injection of an antibiotic with the other. The keeper watching the procedure put the bird back in its cage, and Tom returned to the hospital.

Behind his desk, Tom shuffled through the white sheets—requests for medical services—that determined much of his schedule. When a sick animal was cured, the white sheet was discarded; the job was done. But some problems were old, chronic. Thick records—Shauri's dossier was book-length—defined sickly animals.

Tom hoped to have a sitdown lunch at one of the modest restaurants near the zoo. When he phoned the main zoo office to let the staff know that he'd be at lunch, he was told that he was needed, because most of the management team was off that day.

It didn't matter to him. He did have animals to see. A cow at the farm had an abscess on its left hock (near the heel). A rock elephant shrew had an external ear infection. A woodchuck and a porcupine were in the hospital with parasites to conquer. The last time he had treated a porcupine, the animal buried 100 of its quills in the thick glove he wore; it took plenty of time to pull them out. He hoped to return to the great ape house, to see Shauri again. If he didn't get there by day's end, he would see mother and daughter again early in the morning.

Les Fisher's weekly 9 A.M. staff meeting began without Tom, who was occupied visiting Shauri and her baby.

"We'll probably pull the baby," Dennis Meritt told the staff. "Shauri's history of neglect is crucial. As is her habit of consuming her own milk."

Les described a "vexing, troublesome, and real" problem—substance abuse among several people working at the zoo.

Another continuing issue: Some of the keepers opposed the use of volunteers in keeper areas, especially those the keepers deemed to be inadequately trained. The issue was an old one; the keepers, at times, expressed resentment about the presence of volunteers in their lives.

"It never ends," Les sighed.

The water pressure at the reptile house was "yuck," as Les put it. It was fixed, then went out again. "I have to assume that some lines got clogged with sediment," he said, wearily.

Tom arrived, to announce that he was changing the name of the great ape house to "fertility hill." Several births—two gorillas and two chimps—had occurred during the past two weeks. The breeding of apes had become a zoo specialty, for which it was widely known in the zoo world, and the current crop would enhance that reputation.

Mark Rosenthal suggested that he could locate an incubator, if Tom agreed that Shauri's baby should be pulled.

Dennis said, "Let's just do it."

Tom was not quite convinced. "We can leave it there for forty-eight hours. The baby doesn't look that bad," he said.

"We can set up a place for it today and pull it tomorrow," Mark said.

"OK," Tom agreed.

Shauri and her baby remained in Tom's mind as he conducted rounds with the externs. He told them about his visit to the chimps that morning.

"Shauri was a pain in the ass. She was covering the baby, and she wouldn't budge. We offered her a peach to get her to roll off the baby. Eventually, when she felt like it, she got up.

"The baby is long and skinny. The vocalization is less than I'd like. It hollers, but not much. The baby isn't nursing enough to get robust. It'll get weak at forty-eight hours. If we knock out the mother, the baby might get a big blast of milk. But it really does look like we'll have to pull it. I'll be happy when the new children's zoo is ready and our nursery there is back in action. We'll be able to care for all of our babies there again."

He went through his agenda:

A female black lemur, Xenobia, had a history of lumpy

legs, lesions, swelling in ankles, wrists, and elbows. "We did tests, the whole nine yards of them, and came up with nothing," Tom told the two externs.

"Then we took it to a bone radiologist at Northwestern Hospital. Nobody could figure it out. We did identify some cancerous breast tumors, but we shot down twenty or thirty diagnoses. Then, an expert came up with one—a rare, hereditary bone disease. We checked. The Toronto Zoo had put its mother to sleep; she had the same signs. Toronto may have radiographs for us to look at. I'll call them. Any hereditary disease in an endangered species is of some import.

"Suti, the elephant, has been having irregular cycles," he told the externs. "In elephants it's a three-month period, a twenty-two month gestation. We've documented that she's cycling, but we're going to take blood and send it to a lab in Oregon that specializes in elephants. The vet there knows all about elephant blood. She can't be pregnant, unless it's immaculate conception, because she hasn't been with a male in five years."

After the meeting, Tom went to the primate house to examine a newborn black and white ruffed lemur. The four-day-old monkey fit into the palm of his hand. As he held it, it urinated in his hand and passed some yellow stool. A keeper expressed his concern to Tom.

"That's what you get from an animal consuming only milk," Tom told the keeper, as he placed the tiny lemur back into its plastic box, atop a pile of towels and small blankets.

"A neat little guy," Tom said. "They're friendly to me. I guess they're too young or too stupid to know who I am."

Behind the scenes at the primate house, in a holding area, Tom found Xenobia, the sick lemur.

She bounded stiffly around the cage as Tom stared at her and contemplated her fate.

"I don't want to put her to sleep," he said, as if in response to an unpleasant suggestion from an invisible associate. "She gets around."

Early the next morning, a plea from a keeper at the hoofed-stock barn brought a number of zoo personnel on the run. Tom, assistant vet Peri Wolff, and Mark Rosenthal were all on hand before 8 A.M.

A sable antelope was giving birth. The baby's nose and forelimbs appeared first, between 7:00 A.M. and 7:40 A.M., then the process stopped. Tom and Peri, joined by the two externs, observed.

By 8:10 A.M., part of its head emerged, then the process stopped again.

The mother, a large, dark brown antelope with gracefully curved horns, was on the barn floor, on a bed of straw, rocking, rubbing against the straw, standing, reclining.

The observers were a floor above the stall, looking down from a large window designed to give visitors a clear look at the animals in the barn. A young woman keeper, watching anxiously, said, "When I see new babies, I don't want to get attached to them. They may not make it, and I don't want to suffer."

The antelope continued to strain. The baby's head and the two front legs emerged.

Peri mentioned that animals differed in the ways in which they gave birth. When a giraffe had delivered not long ago, it stood up—and the baby fell out. Then the mother urinated on it and didn't even acknowledge its presence for several minutes.

"This is a *long* birth," the keeper lamented.

By 8:34 A.M., the baby's entire head was out, just below the mother's tail. It was breathing. The mother was still, munching on the straw. Within minutes, the delivery was completed; what had been a sluggish process gathered momentum. The newborn antelope rested beside its mother.

"If the kid looks good and nurses, we'll just watch it," Tom said. "Tomorrow we'll weigh it and give it some shots that we give the newborn.

"Nature made us expendable. That's the best way. It

would have been risky to knock her down. We were ready to wait two hours before doing that. Once you intervene, you don't know what'll happen. She had it in an hour and forty-five minutes. Very good luck."

By 9 A.M., Tom was back at the hospital, collecting the equipment he'd need to tranquilize Shauri and bring her to the hospital for tests. He would pull the baby; an incubator was ready at the great ape house, and a consulting pediatrician (who treated humans, but was interested in animals as well) would drop in to look at the baby. Tom planned a series of tests for Shauri: an EKG, chest x-ray, blood analysis, urine test, and more. But first he had to hit her with a dart, from a handheld tool that resembled a grease gun attached to a foot pump. At four feet tall and 229 pounds, she was not puny, but Tom trusted her friendly manner and the effectiveness of the dart gun.

At the great ape house, Mark Rosenthal, Peri Wolff, and several keepers were ready in the kitchen area, next to Shauri's small, confining holding cell. Tom attached a long barrel to the dart gun, inserted the darted syringe, and turned to Mark.

"Mark, want a nap?"

Mark smiled.

Tom turned toward Shauri, crouched in the back of the dark cell.

"It's me, the bad guy," he said to the chimp.

Then he fired the gun. The dart struck Shauri, and she wailed once, then weakened. Tom and Pat Sass crept into the cell, and Pat picked up the baby chimp, which began to scream. She handed it to Peri, who placed it in a towel and held it on her shoulder. The baby stopped screaming. One of the externs took a blood sample from a vein in the back of the tiny chimp's leg. Peri whispered to the baby, "Oh, I know, I know. Life is so rough."

A pair of keepers, Tom and Jeff, collaborated to move Shauri onto a wheeled, metal litter for the trip to the hospital. She was numbed, on the edge of sleep, and didn't resist.

The baby, who weighed in at two pounds, fourteen ounces, remained in the ape house. Peri handed it to Pat. The baby did not cry. "Let's travel," Peri shouted, and the procession pushed the litter to the van.

In the hospital operating room, Peri placed her stethoscope on Shauri's chest. "She sounds good," Peri said, "but she smells bad."

On the table, Shauri stirred; Jeff gave her an injection to assure that she remained asleep. A keeper from the ape house held Shauri's hand. Shauri began to snore.

Tom, Peri, and Jeff hovered over Shauri. They examined her vaginal area, drew blood from her arm, attached the EKG electrodes, put an IV line in her left forearm. Peri wanted to extract urine with a catheter, but none emerged.

"Dry as a bone," she complained.

Shauri continued to snore; her lower jaw trembled from time to time, but nothing else moved.

"You know what? Think of this," Tom said. "If this were a human, all of this would be done, easily, in the doctor's office. Of course, you can't do any of this to an animal that's awake."

The ape keeper stroked Shauri's chin slowly and affectionately.

The pediatrician entered, a young, short, dark-haired woman in a proper gray suit.

"Shauri's baby looks healthy, but it's an underdeveloped, runty little baby," she said, then paused and asked, "What about her depression?"

"What depression?" Peri asked.

"Shauri's. From having her baby pulled."

"No problem," Tom said.

"She'll be a little depressed," the keeper said.

"We'll get in with her and comfort her. She's friendly. And remember, she's not that attentive a mother," Tom told the pediatrician.

Peri turned to Shauri, petted her head, and said, "You're being very, very nice about all of this."

By 11:00 A.M., Shauri was ready to be returned to the

great ape house. Tom patted her back. "Let's take her home," Peri said. By 11:12 A.M., Shauri was home. Her baby was in its incubator, in Pat Sass's care.

Down the path from the great ape house, in the hoofed-stock barn, the sable antelope baby—almost forgotten—was next to its mother.

Four hours had elapsed while Tom and associates had dealt with the two cases.

Milk extracted from Shauri's breast was mixed with formula for her baby. Assured of that, Tom left to visit the antelope. In front of the window from which he had witnessed the birth, he saw a docent assigned to keep watch. She sat in a chair, looking through the window at the mother and child below.

"She's fed, she's nursed, and she's been walking around," the docent, a middle-aged woman in familiar khaki garb, told Tom.

"Great," he said, looking down to the barn floor, where the two antelopes reclined on straw, facing each other.

It was self-indulgent to linger. Tom had other problems to deal with.

The Arabian oryx baby he'd checked the day before was being taunted, prodded by the adults in the group. There may be too many animals in that group, Tom thought; he might have to separate the baby from the aggressive older ones.

The day passed; Tom rarely glanced at his wristwatch. In late afternoon, he phoned the great ape house to find out how Shauri was doing. She was awake, eating, and moving around, he was told. Good.

Then he went to the large mammal house to take a blood sample from Suti, the elephant with the irregular menstrual cycle. When he arrived, Suti and Bozie, the other elephant, were outside with a keeper bearing an ankus and a very firm manner. She used both to lead the elephants indoors for Tom and his externs to look at Suti.

On command, both elephants knelt. Tom approached Suti, held her left ear in his hand, and showed the extern, Jeff, the network of veins visible on the back of the ear. He washed the ear, then poked the syringe into the vein.

Suti jerked.

"Steady," the keeper said.

"Good girl," Tom added.

"Steady," the keeper repeated, to be sure that Suti obeyed. An unruly elephant was a troublesome one, and a belligerent elephant was a dangerous one. There was a reason why elephants in the wild didn't have enemies except for humans.

Tom stepped in front of the elephant and patted her; she touched his shoulder delicately with the tip of her trunk.

"She doesn't trust me when she can't see me," he told the keeper. "Now she can see me."

First Person: Tom Meehan

I get to put my hands on animals more than just about anybody else in this place, even the keepers to a large degree. I get to interact closely with animals. I call myself the most general of general practitioners, because it's not only every system and every disease, but every species. There's a breadth and depth to it that doesn't exist anywhere else. It can be somewhat frustrating. The main thing is you do the best you can, you try to keep up, you try not to be too hard on yourself, and if you have enough self-confidence and you do an adequate job of keeping yourself up, then you say, "I can do this as well as anybody."

Overall, I'm as good as anybody out there at doing zoo medicine. I'm better than a lot of them at some things, like the gorillas. The big trick is that it's not a big club, it's a relatively small group, of zoo veterinarians. Around sixty in North America, period. So being where I am in zoo medicine, I know most of them, and I know the ones who have a lot of elephants, I know the ones that do all birds, so I can get on the phone and call somebody who might be able to give me a hand.

We're always finding out things. Everything is kind of

204 ──────────────────────────────────── Zoo

out there on the edge. It's very hard. You never want to get to where you can rationalize things with yourself and explain them away. Sometimes you really did screw up, if that turns out to be the case. You should never be able to explain it away to yourself. At the very least, you ought to know that you screwed up, and make efforts to do otherwise. People who do that soul-searching and know when they make a mistake and when they don't, stand a very great risk of getting burned out because, damn, that animal had pneumonia, and if I would have known that, I could have fixed it.

It behooves animals, wild animals, to look good when they're sick. Sick animals get preyed upon or get left behind. One of the comments off the necropsy table is not why did it die, but why was it still alive? There's so much wrong inside this animal, why was it still up and around? They can have major illnesses, and you may not see them.

I had an animal one time that we immobilized, we went to bleed it. We made a stick into the carotid. It's not anything that should cause any problems, it's done all the time, single stick. The animal bled out from that stick and strangled to death, literally. Its neck filled up with blood, like a soccer ball, and it literally strangled the animal, from within. What I didn't know was the animal had a clotting disorder. I didn't know. There's no way I could have known, so you can't hold that against yourself.

If you keep looking at yourself in hindsight and saying I should have done this or I should have done that, you'll go nuts, you'll wind up leaving the field, as a lot of people have. I tell people who have been through here under me, it's OK to get down on yourself for things that you should have known better. If there was some clue that told you that this was happening and you ignored it or missed it, you screwed up, and you should make your corrections. But if there's no way you could have known, and it's just based on the fact that that's a difference between zoo animals and other animals, you can't afford to let yourself get down on yourself.

If people look sick, they don't get eaten. People do truly amazing things when they think that their life is on the line. For animals, their life is a little different. There are certain things that the animals bring with them that don't change, even after generations in captivity.

Zoo medicine is really not that old. Zoo medicine as a bona fide specialty where you could really do some good has paralleled precisely the development of anesthetics and delivery systems that allowed us to shoot them into an animal, and immobilize them, and have them wake up alive. Until vets could do that, they really couldn't do much. They weren't able to do nearly as much diagnostic work; they had to do it all over the fence.

We still do a lot of that. I sit down with the vet students when they get ready to leave here. One of them said something very interesting. She said, "I learned something here that I didn't learn in school and that I think I can use very well to my advantage on any kind of animals. I learned how to stand back and look at an animal, from a distance. Without laying my hands and feeling and listening to the lung, I learned how to stand back and look and see the whole picture, what the animal looks like, how it moves, how it breathes, how it does it." We learn how to do that because we're forced to.

Of course, we rely very heavily on the keepers. Animals react to me, to what I do. The keepers will call and say, "Oh, he's sick, he's lying on the bottom of the cage," and I go over there and the animal's bouncing off the walls. He's changed in my presence, and I can't tell. One, I don't know how the animal looks day in and day out because I don't spend that time with him, and two, he's different when I'm there than when I'm not there. So we rely heavily on the keepers.

We even go to the point of doing little tricks. For instance, in the morning we give all the marmosets a marshmallow. It helps to get their blood glucose up. That helps boost them up in the morning. But the main thing is, if they don't come up and grab that marshmallow, they're

206 ─────────────────────────────────── Zoo

sick, and you know it. They're not normal if they don't jump on that. The most common thing is somebody calls and says, "The animal's offbeat, it's not looking good, or it's limping." Ninety-nine percent of what we get comes from the keepers, and it comes from them being observant and knowing their animals, just knowing the real subtle stuff. And we see a lot of subtle stuff.

I'm always concerned about epidemics of diseases here. The scariest one by far, because of the value of the collection and the depth of our collection, was that thing that went through our great ape house. We are pretty sure it was a respiratory virus that caused flulike symptoms in people. Great apes can get what humans can get and vice versa. A keeper brought that in, that's one of the reasons we separate all the primates from the public: basically to protect them from the public because that's where disease is likely to come from. A keeper evidently brought this disease in, and, early on, before the keeper felt sick, it had been exposed to the apes. Well, the chimps started it. It started with a cough and a severe mucous nasal discharge. You could just see it march right around the building; it left only three animals unaffected in the entire building. We lost two animals, one baby we're pretty sure died of pneumonia that was probably associated with that. The adult male chimp, Sam, who died, had pneumonia. It didn't look bad enough to kill him. He didn't have anything that looked bad enough to kill him, but he was still dead.

There's nothing you can do when you've got that sort of viral disease. We used a lot of antibiotics, to help prevent secondary bacterial infections; we drew blood samples, we did some diagnostic work and some treatment. But based on the way the thing moved around, fairly early on we thought that it was most likely to be some sort of a viral disease, for which you don't do anything but supportive care. And supportive care is often very hard to give. Peri spent an awful lot of time in there, got sick herself—she got the same thing back—and one of the other keepers became ill. Everybody had the same signs: the cough, the chest cold.

With the wolves, distemper was on the list of differential diagnoses, but not very high up. And Peri talked with probably the premier animal neurologist in the country, one of her old professors. They had it pretty well pinned down to either a brain tumor or some sort of a vascular accident. A week later, another one goes down with the same thing, and all that goes out the window. You don't have brain tumors or strokes that one animal catches from another, so then distemper moved right up to the top of the list. A few tests confirmed that.

Horse births and cattle, sheep, goats, other hoofed-stock births, are very difficult. Horses have a very quick, almost violent, birth process. If the foal hasn't been born in half an hour, it's in deep trouble. So you don't have any time on your hands. It's difficult in a zebra, too. They're like a horse in the way they give birth. The foal winds up in trouble relatively quickly if the horse hasn't given birth. The birth is violent.

One common thing in a horse is what they call a third-degree peritoneal laceration. The mother squeezes so hard that the foal puts a hoof out of the vagina and into the rectum, and when the mother gives birth, the foal tears it open, all the way to the outside. They're a real bitch to fix back up. But they happen.

Well, I got a call at home: a zebra's giving birth. The very first thing that comes to mind is that's neat, that's really neat. But by the time I get in here, it's still not out. That immediately brings you down to a certain level, because it has been more than half an hour. She's potentially in trouble, so there isn't any waiting. We got our stuff together and immobilized her. It took another fifteen minutes or so for that to take effect and for me to get all my stuff over there. Then we tried to deliver the foal. I don't even know at that point what exactly was binding everything up, but we worked. Physically, it was the most difficult thing we've ever done, because we literally dragged the zebra around for ten or fifteen minutes by the foal, because we were trying to get it out, and it was stuck.

The foal was dead by that point, and it's tremendously

exhausting to be in there all the way up to your shoulders, and fighting and trying to turn it and pulling things. Another doctor was here as well, and she and I alternated fighting. I'd just have to stop and sit down for a while and catch my breath. She'd work and I'd work and she'd work and I'd work, and we tried. We tried cutting up the animal inside the mother to bring it out in pieces, as a way of avoiding doing a C-section. We got most of the baby out, lost the rest, couldn't avoid the C-section, rolled her up, prepped her. And the surgery is a whole different thing because horses are pretty prone to infection, and we had to be relatively sterile. So it's change it into a sterile room, clean ourselves all up, go in, do the C-section, get her all sewed up. And as we were putting the last few stitches in the skin, she died.

We went from there to a necropsy, where we just took the mother and chopped her all up. The progression from being called that morning and expecting a birth, to disposing of the mother's carcass in a period of five or six hours, was certainly the most difficult time that I can recall.

You know, they say animals don't know one guy from another; people are people, they don't know who we are. The hell with that. They know who I am, and not just the great apes, not just the ones that are the sharpest. Some animals that aren't given a lot of credit for having a lot of brains, they know who the hell I am. And they know me in street clothes, and they know me when I'm with a crowd of people; they know who I am.

The first time it struck me about that drawback to zoo veterinary medicine, I was working at the St. Louis Zoo, and they were opening a section of the zoo, and they were having a big dedication. The trainer was walking up to the dedication with a little chimp in hand. The chimp was walking along, happy as a clam, holding hands with this trainer, and up walks the zoo vet. And he takes the chimp by the hand, and they're walking along and the chimp is walking between the two of them holding hands, and then he looked up and saw who it was that had come along and grabbed his hand. All the hair went up on his back, he started screaming and slapping his legs, trying to bite him and it was all the trainer could do to keep him from tearing into this veterinarian. And I realized, damn, he really hates that guy. But I've gotten used to that. You try to establish a relationship with the special animals like Shauri or animals that instead of displaying and pounding the glass will come over and let me feed them or play little games with me.

Chimps are a lot like people, in that they can be very explosive, very emotional. They have a pretty short attention span, but they're very demonstrative. They're a little bit too much for my taste. But there's no doubt that they're a very sharp animal. The gorillas, I like their attitude more. It changes a lot more. It's easier for me to see the personalities, to know the differences between them. For example, Koundu is such a character, trying to offer me a treat of some urine-soaked piece of straw off the floor, in hopes that I'm going to grab it with such relish that he's going to be able to get hold of my hand and do harm to me. But it's the kind of harm you laugh at on "The Three Stooges," typical juvenile mischief. It's kind of a crude practical joke.

Orangutans are real sharp. They're deep thinkers, and they're very manipulative. They take things apart. They'll watch you. You hear all kinds of stories about them. There was an orang at Omaha that got out repeatedly, a number of times over a relatively short span. There were a lot of keepers in danger of losing their jobs over who screwed up and left the lock open, that sort of thing. The director finally wound up spending most of a night on a level above, watching the animal, and the orang was fiddling around in his mouth, and then started working the lock. And what he had was a big long piece of wire that he kept in his lip that he would pick the lock with; you know, it was one of these old skeleton-key-type locks. He's got nothing but time, so he'd just use it as a key and work it until it came open and he could get out.

I've only felt in danger once. Shortly after we had a new arrival of an African elephant who was about three years old, weighing a thousand, eleven hundred pounds. A small elephant but a big elephant. This was a wild elephant, not trained. And we had an elephant trainer come in to train that elephant, and also to train our keepers in how to take care of it. But the elephant was not far from being very wild. She was held during this period on chains. This was, as I recall, about two or three months into this process, and she had made remarkable progress in terms of being well-behaved. I worked with the animal almost daily at that point in her training here, because it was something new to all of us, bringing an animal in from the wild at that age.

I went over there one Saturday, and something had happened, we don't to this day know what it was, but something happened to her that upset her a great deal, or just changed her, or she just decided she was going to be different that day. One of the things that she was doing was using her trunk to hit and push, things that were ill mannered, things that she wasn't supposed to do. Trunk down, back and forth, kind of pushing and shoving. She found that I had stepped away from the doorway out of this habitat, that I had my back against a wall, literally. And so she just stepped forward, wrapped her trunk around my arm and hoisted me up and slid me into a corner. She tried to pick my arm up and put it in her mouth with her trunk and bite it. I was able to keep my arm down, but she was able to pick me up and down, six inches or so off the ground. It didn't accomplish what she wanted. So she stopped that rather quickly, dropped her head, put it in my chest and started shoving me into the corner, with a big wooden beam in my back, and she was trying to smash me. You know, there are lots of ways that elephants kill people. One of the more popular ones is just pushing them into something, whether it's pushing them into the dirt, pushing them up against something.

There was one other person around, a keeper. You'd never go in with an animal without the keeper. Two keepers had been there; one had gone in to go to the bathroom. So there was one keeper there, and he had the ankus. He was flailing away at her with the ankus, trying to get her back. I think the only thing that saved me was the fact that she had a long chain on her front leg, and, in turning around, she had stretched that to its full extent and didn't have enough motion, enough freedom, to really shove me up into the wall. But she had her head right in my chest. The first time I recall feeling like I was in deep shit was when I tried to scream for the keeper but no noise came out, and I realized that she'd compressed my chest enough that I couldn't vocalize. That's when I was scared. Fortunately, when the two keepers got there, they both flailed away at her. Eventually she just turned around and quit, and I walked away.

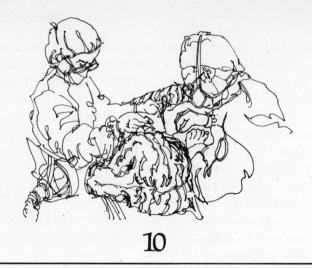

10

HOUSE CALLS II:

Young veterinarian Peregrine Wolff, known to her associates as Peri, succinctly summarized her work: "Animals get sick. They get well. They love you. They hate you. It's the people who give you problems."

At twenty-eight, she had made her way to a major zoo from Middlebury, Vermont, where she was born. Before retiring, her father had been an economics professor at Middlebury College; her mother had been a physician's assistant.

Peri attended Middlebury College for a year, then spent two and a half years at the University of Vermont, where she majored in animal science. During her final semester, she worked at a zoo on the isle of Jersey, off the coast of England.

In 1984, she got her D.V.M. from Cornell University (a four-year program) and headed to Chicago. During her junior year at the University of Vermont, she served as an extern at the Lincoln Park Zoo; after she became a vet, she returned to that zoo for a year as an intern. When funding became available, she was hired as a full-time vet to work for Tom Meehan.

Peri lived in an apartment across the street from the zoo, with a dog named Bear—a shepherd-collie cross.

Her life at the zoo was an active one; she arrived at work long before most of the keepers got there. It was not unusual for her to be dashing around the zoo at 6 A.M.

In her green jumpsuit and white sneakers, she was a familiar sight. Tall (5'8") and slim, with an Ivory soap complexion and a blond ponytail, a gold chain around her neck, small earrings, and a gold bracelet on her wrist, she was a combination of the hard-working professional and the liberated woman.

One day in late summer, when the heat had faded and a cool breeze served as an indication of a less desirable season to come, she headed for the hoofed-stock area. With her in the yellow zoo van were a curly-haired young blond extern from England named David, and Joel Pond, the young, sturdy, mustached animal health technician, who ran the hospital lab.

They headed into the hoofed-stock barn. Peri had to vaccinate three zebras that were being readied for shipment to another zoo. They were being given boosters; shipment made them vulnerable, due to the stress involved. First, Peri had to tranquilize them; she would knock them down, and David would return later to give the vaccinations. She did the job quickly, pointing the long-barreled dart gun at each zebra and firing the dart with the foot pump that triggered it. The zebras twitched when hit.

By 9:15 A.M., Peri and her crew were in the lion house. Chandra, an old female lion, was down, literally; the senior keeper at the lion house had reported that the animal couldn't seem to get up.

Peri found Chandra in a holding cage. The lion spotted her and began to growl sluggishly.

"She's old, but she looks older than she is," Peri said. "She looks like hell."

"She's real shaky," the senior keeper noted.

Peri stared at the lion for several minutes, then told the senior keeper to keep the lion in the cage, give her water, obtain a urine sample if possible, and give her aspirin.

"To treat joint pain, if that's what it is," Peri explained.

"She's sore in back and in her front leg, too. She's not putting any weight on it. We may have to immobilize her," Peri said. She knew that cats were sensitive to many drugs tolerated by other animals; even aspirin had to be prescribed with care.

She wanted to assess the condition of a sickly black leopard before she returned to the hospital. The leopard—on the verge of kidney failure—was in an outside cage, sitting motionless with a glazed stare. It did not respond to Peri's presence, an indication in itself, since many animals reacted to Peri and Tom with instant rage.

Peri watched the animal for several minutes in silence.

"Why let him die this way?" she asked no one in particular. "That seems cruel to me." To euthanize the leopard, however, she would first confer with assistant zoo director Dennis Meritt and curator Mark Rosenthal.

By 9:45 A.M., she was back at the hospital to conduct rounds, an assessment of pending cases, with David, the extern, and Joel, the lab technician. Tom Meehan was out of town, so the rounds belonged to Peri.

Before the meeting could begin, the phone rang. Peri answered it.

"Butch? Walking funny? What does that mean? Dangling? No. Does he go outside? OK. I'll go look at him. Wake up? I can't. I'm tired."

Butch was one of the maned wolves; she'd check on him after rounds.

Among the cases discussed:

Two female lions, Sheila and Shelley, awaiting shipment to another zoo because of the renovation of the lion house, needed fecal and blood tests before they could be shipped out. Zoos did not seek to ship or receive sick animals.

A lame pacarana—an animal from South America that

resembled a huge rat—wasn't doing well, but it wasn't an emergency. "Her liver looks big," Peri noted.

"Who knows what a pacarana's liver is supposed to look like?" Joel asked, smiling.

"True," Peri admitted.

A group of capybaras—also large rodent-like animals—had had diarrhea for months.

Otto, a well-known gorilla, had a toe that had been gnawed by an angry female gorilla, but it was improving.

Peri was leaning toward euthanizing the black leopard; she wanted to resolve that matter promptly.

A crow with a damaged wing needed repair.

A pigeon had to be euthanized.

At 10:05, Peri stopped at the bear line to see Butch. The maned wolf was in an indoor cage and wouldn't move when Peri entered the area.

"He thinks I'm going to knock him down," Peri sighed.

The keeper opened a gate and allowed the wolf to go outside, where Peri could get a better look at him.

The wolf limped out, its left foreleg clearly damaged. It stopped and turned toward Peri.

"He sniffs vet," Peri said.

The wolf had broken its leg seven years ago and had been treated for troubles related to it ever since.

"Lock him up tonight," Peri told a keeper. "We'll do him at eight in the morning." She would arrange for an orthopedic surgeon to consult on the case, but first x-rays would have to be taken of that troublesome leg.

The morning passed quickly, as Peri moved from case to case. At lunchtime, she returned to the hospital, where she made a lunch of boiled hot dogs, a chunk of Swiss cheese, and a Diet Coke. She read her mail, which included a gift her mother had sent. It energized her for what she had to do after lunch: operate on Sam Gamgee (a name out of Tolkien), a nine-year-old cottontop tamarin, a tiny monkey plagued by worms in its intestines.

The tamarins were among Peri's favorite animals: small,

agile, animated, hardy. They came from South American rain forests, where they rarely came down to the ground, choosing to thrive in the upper reaches of the forest. Amazingly, some adjusted to the drastically different environment of the zoo.

In the wild, tamarins had a low level of parasite invasion. In captivity, where roaches thrived, the rate seemed to increase.

"They poop. The roaches eat the poop, which has parasite eggs in it. The tamarins eat the roaches. The eggs turn into adult worms in the tamarins and burrow into the wall of the gut. They make holes, causing peritonitis, which kills primates. The only way for us to fight it—if antibiotics don't work—is surgery. We've cleaned up a bunch of them. In just one procedure, we got sixty-six worms out of an animal that weighed less than a pound," Peri said.

The tamarin awaited its fate inside an animal carrier in the hospital examining room. It flicked its tongue rapidly.

"I wish I could do that," Peri said, smiling.

She put on a pair of heavy-duty gloves, leather and canvas, and grabbed the tamarin. It shrieked and tried to elude her grasp. She won. After David gave it an injection of an antibiotic, Peri put it in a weighing basket—which looked like a perforated pot with a lid—and carried it into the operating room.

The tamarin continued to shriek.

"I haven't done anything yet," Peri said to it.

In the operating room, Joel was serving as anesthetist. He placed the basket, with the tamarin in it, in a large plastic bag and piped gas (isofluorane) into it.

Joel and Peri waited; the sound of small claws against the inside of the metal basket was the only sound in the room.

Peri put on a cap and mask and whistled Brahms' "Lullaby." The tamarin slept; its little brown and white body was still. As Joel put aside the basket and used a cup on the tamarin's face, Peri shaved its belly for the incision she would make and the electrodes she would attach for the heart monitor. As she worked her way through the preliminaries, the tamarin twitched in its sleep.

"God was having an artistic day when He created these," she said, looking affectionately at the tamarin. "They look like punk rockers."

She draped the animal and gently made an incision. Suddenly, the tamarin thrashed violently, displacing the drape. It had to be replaced, and so did Peri's gloves.

Again, Peri went to work on the incision. Again, the tamarin moved.

"My God, your guts are hanging out," she shouted.

"I'm giving him twice as much gas as he might need," Joel said. He couldn't explain the tough little monkey's resistance to modern science.

"Let's tape down his legs," Peri said to David, who did the job. But the tamarin continued to jerk. Peri did not stop working; she had extracted his intestines through the incision and was examining them for parasites.

"Is there gonna be some lawsuit from this patient?" Peri said. "His gut is spastic, tight. This isn't turning out at all like I wanted it to."

She spotted several nodules and extracted three worms; she had expected to find more.

"Well, we've had them die from as few as one," Joel said, reassuringly.

Peri sutured the intestinal wall and closed the original outer incision.

"This is the most difficult one we've done, out of twenty-nine procedures," she said. "And the hardest part is getting the gut back in the hole you got it out of, especially with a nervous guy like this one."

As Peri completed her work on the tamarin, the hospital secretary, Debbie, entered unexpectedly.

"A marmoset just came walking down the hall," she said calmly. "I put it in Tom's office."

Peri and Joel stared at her, then at each other.

"Are you going to make something of that?" Joel asked Peri.

"Yes, I'm going to make something of that," Peri answered.

One of her continuing grievances was directed at keepers who were less attentive than she thought they ought to be.

She found the keeper on duty at the hospital.

"I thought I had the door locked," he appealed. "But I didn't."

The marmoset—another small, lively South American monkey—was screeching in Tom Meehan's office. The keeper grabbed a small net on a handle and entered the office.

The chase was on. It took several minutes, but man triumphed over animal. The keeper put the marmoset back in the cage in the examining room, from which it had escaped. He locked the cage.

Peri watched it all. After the marmoset had been returned to its cage, she turned to the keeper.

"They are crafty animals," she said.

The keeper did not respond.

The next morning, Peri got to work at 6:30 A.M. In a powder blue polo shirt, jeans, and sneakers, she sat at her desk before the problems of the day seized her time, and dealt with the paperwork that was inevitable in her job.

By 8 A.M., in her blue jumpsuit, she was ready for action. On the phone with curator Mark Rosenthal, she told him that if the black leopard, named Satan, after testing and examination, was found to be terminal, she felt it ought to be euthanized.

"We're going to give it a rabbit, and if it doesn't eat it, well, that means it won't go for anything," she told Mark.

She called Dennis Meritt for his view of the situation.

"He looks terrible," she told Dennis. "They're going to offer him a rabbit. We'll see." Dennis agreed with her; euthanizing the cat might be the best move.

Down the hall from her office, Sam, the cottontop tamarin she had operated on the day before, was in an incubator. He was recuperating impressively, dashing around the incubator, making beeping sounds. Peri went in to examine him; she put her gloved hand into the incubator. Sam went wild, but she managed to grasp him. David, the extern, gave him an injection of an antibiotic, and Peri placed Sam back in the incubator. He glared at her.

By 9 A.M., Peri was off on various missions around the zoo. At the bird house holding area, she examined a crow suffering from parasites. She and David collaborated; he held the bird, and she dropped liquid medication into its mouth.

"Crows are easy," she said to David. "You can see their larynx, so you make a point of missing it. Anywhere else you drop it, they swallow it."

At the reptile house, she visited a small salamander that, according to the woman keeper, was "losing weight and looking ratty." It was eight years old, old for a salamander, and it ate two crickets a day only if it was hand-fed.

"It could be dying of old age," Peri suggested, holding it in her hand and stroking it gently.

"Can we give it antibiotics?" the keeper asked.

"I can't use antibiotics if I don't know what I'm treating it for," Peri said.

The keeper was discouraged. "Do you know that there are mouse droppings in every cage in this place?" she asked.

Peri knew and didn't respond.

Clarence Wright, the curator of reptiles, was busy elsewhere in the room. And he was troubled. He reminded Peri of a memo he had sent to everyone working at the zoo, a memo titled "Disappearance of Mangrove Snake Eggs." It read:

A keeper reported the disappearance of eight Mangrove Snake Eggs that were incubating in the 'hot run' of the basement of the reptile house. The plastic shoe box that the eggs were kept in was secured with tape to hold the lid in place. The tape was removed and the eggs taken and the tape was then resecured to the box.

These eggs each measured one inch in diameter and if hatched would produce an animal that is rear-fanged and venomous. Anti-venin is NOT PRODUCED for this animal.

Eggs should be returned, with no questions asked, or the eggs should be destroyed.

According to Clarence, if the eggs were shaken, the three-week-old embryos would perish. But if the person who stole them knew enough, in three months the eggs would hatch, and the young snakes could attack. In Clarence's view, it must have been an "inside job." No locks were tampered with in getting to the eggs.

Peri noted his concern. She had to move on, however, to the great ape house. It was time to visit Otto, the burly gorilla who had attacked a female named Terra and was biting her neck when Terra decided to retaliate. Terra took a large chunk out of his toe.

Peri picked up a banana in the kitchen and, with senior keeper Pat Sass, went to visit Otto. She found him in a cage in an upstairs holding area.

"He looks healthier," she said to Pat. "How's his attitude?"

"Well, he's not chasing girls around anymore," Pat said.

"Let's keep him on antibiotics," Peri said, moving toward the door.

Back in the hospital, Peri noticed that one of the keepers was defrosting a rabbit in the microwave of the keeper dining area, for Satan, the leopard.

It was time for Peri and David to check on Butch, the lame maned wolf. At the bear line, Butch awaited them, but not eagerly. When Peri arrived at his indoor den, Butch looked right at her, snarled, and turned away.

Peri aimed her long-barreled tranquilizer dart gun at Butch. The first try didn't work; the dart didn't seem to penetrate far enough into the wolf's reddish-brown fur. Peri shot a second dart. Again, no success. Each time, she retrieved the dart with a long pole poked through the bars separating her from the wolf. The third try seemed unsuccessful as well, and Peri was baffled. But Butch began to buckle, slowly.

"I've never seen that happen before," she told the male keeper who was helping her. "And I have no idea why I wasn't getting the right force."

Finally, Butch fell. Peri and David lifted him onto a litter. Butch had his eyes open, his ears up, his tongue dangling out of the side of his mouth. His body was motionless, but he was breathing heavily. They transported him to the x-ray table in the hospital operating room. Butch reclined like a large, resting dog. He was giving off a strong, foul odor. He had defecated on the x-ray table.

While Joel cleaned the table, Peri did a conjunctiva scraping from the wolf's eyelid membrane, for a distemper test. Several of the wolves had distemper; two of them, including Butch, had been testing positive. Peri hoped that the test would now be negative. She and Tom had not been able to cure the disease; somehow the wolves had improved on their own.

Joel posted an old x-ray of Butch's bad leg; it showed a steel plate and assorted screws, the work of an orthopedic surgeon who had worked on Butch in the zoo hospital. Then Joel arranged the wolf on the x-ray table and shot several x-rays of the leg.

The wolf made a faint sound.

"I think he's snoring," Peri said. "Not growling."

When Joel was done, Peri and David moved Butch back to his den on the bear line. Peri headed for lunch.

After lunch, she went to the lion house to obtain blood samples from the two female lions being readied for shipment to another zoo. She knew that both lions disliked vets on sight.

Shelley was asleep in a holding cage when Peri arrived, with David and a keeper to help her. It was a squeeze cage, designed with a moving back wall of bars that could be brought forward to trap the animal in a narrow space, preventing it from moving, so the vet could examine and treat it. The keeper turned a wheel on the outside of the cage to bring the back wall forward.

When Peri entered, Shelley came to life in a frenzy. She

growled loudly, ran around the small cage, tried to reach through the bars to get at Peri. The second lion, Sheila, who had been in a tunnel behind the cages, entered an adjoining cage, saw Peri, and stood up on her hind feet, growling loudly.

Peri took a look at Sheila and spotted an abscess on her foot.

"I suppose no one has noticed that," she snapped at the keeper. He had a calm manner and didn't respond. Both lions continued to growl.

The keeper began to turn the wheel to trap one of the lions. As he did, the lion in the next cage tried to get at him through the bars. He flinched.

The rear bars moved forward, trapping Shelley. Peri grabbed her tail, pulled it out of the cage, and drew a blood sample from it. The keeper turned the wheel again, and the bars moved back, enabling Shelley to get out. She did, rapidly, heading for an empty cage out of reach.

The keeper moved one of the sliding panels that sealed off cages; it opened, and Sheila dashed into the squeeze cage. Soon, she was tightly encased. Peri and David repeated the procedure, adding an injection of an antibiotic for the abscess—and an instruction to the keeper to "keep her inside, so that can heal."

Sheila growled mightily.

"Be a big girl," Peri said to her. "A good kitty. Just a little blood from your tail, that's all. A good kitty."

The lion growled again, a deep, resonant roar.

Peri packed up her gear, her blood samples, and walked back to the hospital. She was exhausted. The sound of an angry lion was intimidating, even if she knew that the cat could not reach her. Once again, she was reminded that her work could not be appreciated by the animals she treated. If she were to achieve satisfaction, she would have to generate it herself.

Tomorrow, she knew, she faced another troubling test. She planned to immobilize Satan, the sick leopard, and determine whether he should live or die.

The next morning, Peri studied the x-rays of Butch's leg. The bone that had been broken in the past had not been broken again, but the plate inserted by the surgeon might be loosening. It was possible that the wolf had contracted a soft-tissue infection, and she could attack that with an antibiotic. Results of the distemper test wouldn't be ready for a week; she was hopeful that Butch would recover.

At 8:15 A.M., she phoned the lion house; she wanted to know if Satan had eaten the rabbit. He had not. The prognosis was not good. Satan had come to the zoo eighteen years ago; he was an old cat and a failing one. In a month, his weight had dropped from eighty-six pounds to sixty-eight pounds.

She was unhappy that the lion house keepers had not informed her more rapidly about the leopard's loss of appetite. If she had known earlier, she could have done a kidney function test, at least. Now, if Satan had gone into kidney failure, she would have no choice but to euthanize him.

Joel, the lab technician, would be the one to administer the fatal injection, if it came to that. It would be a lethal dose of an anesthetic, a barbiturate or T-61, literally a euthanasia solution. It was known as "blue juice," for the color added to it to prevent it from being given accidentally.

Peri, Joel, and David made their way in the van to the lion house. It was not yet open to the public. The leopard was in an indoor cage in the cavernous hall. At the front of the cage, the uneaten rabbit was a clump of flaccid white matter.

"Yech. Even if I didn't have renal disease, I wouldn't eat that," Peri commented.

Satan was prone, his head resting on his front paws, his yellow-green eyes fixed straight ahead. Peri assembled the dart gun; she had determined that what failed when she used it on Butch was the barrel. She had attached the wrong one, which permitted air to leak out around the dart.

Satan remained with his head on the floor of the cage, until he saw Peri holding the gun. He snarled at her weakly, more a hiss than a roar, and raised his head.

A lion keeper prodded Satan with a long pole to entice him to the front of the cage, giving Peri a clear shot. Satan grabbed the pole with his front paws, as if in play, and the keeper tugged, pulling the animal to the front of the cage.

Peri's dart hit Satan on his right side, and he fell. His tongue moved slowly, in and out of his mouth. He vomited. Peri guessed that was because he was toxic, in renal failure, or from the tranquilizer, probably the former.

In the next cage, a slowly pacing jaguar observed.

Within minutes, Satan was unconscious, on a metal litter on his way to the hospital.

On the table in the examining room, Satan breathed slowly, almost imperceptibly.

"Are you sure he's breathing?" Peri asked Joel.

"Yes, I'm sure. Slowly, but breathing," Joel replied.

In his incubator a few feet away, Sam, the tamarin, peered at the scene in front of him. He sat still and watched, then, seemingly in agitation, moved rapidly around the incubator.

Peri went to the phone and called Dennis Meritt.

"We have this pathetic black leopard on the table now. He is skin and bones, and his skin is dehydrated. You can pull it up and it stays there," she told Dennis. "I don't know the point of saving this animal. It's time to call it quits. It's a sad scene."

Dennis agreed with her.

Mark Rosenthal showed up, looked at Satan, patted him gently.

"We're euthanizing him," Peri told him. "It's cruel and unusual punishment to keep him alive."

"Sure," Mark said.

In his incubator, Sam pressed his face against the glass and watched in silence.

Joel injected a large syringe filled with T-61. He looked at Satan as he did. The leopard's black hair was flecked with white. His eyes were open, his teeth bared. Already tranquilized, he took a few minutes to die.

Suddenly, Sam became agitated, making a frantic, high-pitched beeping sound.

Peri, Mark, and Joel looked at the tamarin. The unspoken thought: did the tamarin understand?

No one knew, or even theorized.

"Don't worry, Sam," Peri said. "You're not next. Never."

She turned to Satan and murmured, "Poor kitty."

David and Joel carried the leopard off to the necropsy table in the back of the hospital, where two pathologists from the University of Chicago would do their work on it.

Joel returned and washed the examining table, slowly, methodically, with more dedication than was required.

"You never get used to doing that," he said, softly. "Never a pleasant thing, no matter what the circumstances are."

Behind him, Sam was seated in a corner of the incubator, silently staring out into the room.

When Joel went home to his wife and two young children that night, he would have a story to tell.

He went off to chat with the pathologists, who had just arrived. One of them looked at the leopard and said, "He looks like an old man."

Peri and David returned to the van; there was no time to consider Satan's fate. Two calves needed their attention in the dairy barn at the farm.

Peg, a brown and white Guernsey calf they had dehorned earlier in the week, needed to have a fifth teat removed. It was an "extra" teat that served no purpose and could get infected. Peri would crush it, and it would simply fall off.

Max, a black and white Holstein calf, needed to be castrated; it would end up as beef, not for breeding.

Both procedures were done with a Burdizzo, an Italian-made clamp. On the Holstein, it would crush the cord supplying blood to the testicles, which would then atrophy.

They began on the Guernsey. The Burdizzo severed the teat, instead of merely compressing it. It fell off. No harm done, Peri declared. Both animals had been given a local anesthetic. The Holstein suffered less gracefully, struggling, but eventually conceding defeat.

On the wall nearby, three signs were posted for the edification of city kids:

Heifer: female cattle that have not yet had calves.

Cow: female cattle that have had calves.

Calf: cattle under 1 year of age.

Peri and David paused to check the abscess on the hoof of the Holstein calf's mother. Peri medicated it again, and David wrapped the hoof. The massive animal, its black coat gleaming, offered no resistance.

As they walked out of the barn, Peri paused and returned to the Guernsey calf in its small pen. The calf came to the edge of the pen and stuck its face toward Peri's. She kissed it. It mooed.

On the way back to the hospital, Peri stopped at the bear line, to ask how Butch was doing. The keeper told her that Butch seemed OK, but that another maned wolf, Jocko, was limping. Peri looked at Jocko in its outdoor habitat and watched it walk. There was a visible limp, but not a serious one. She told the keeper that she would wait and see, and headed back to her office in the hospital.

She had intended to go out to lunch, to cash her paycheck at a local supermarket. When she sat behind her desk, however, she noticed a brown bag on it. She opened it. A friend had bought lunch for her, a Reuben sandwich, one of her favorites.

She smiled, exhaled loudly and sat back in her chair. She did not know what the rest of the day would bring.

FIRST PERSON: PEREGRINE WOLFF

My parents wanted unisex names, so that they wouldn't have to think up two names for the kids before they were born. My sister's name is Ashley, which goes either way. And they wanted to name me Peri, they liked that name, but they wanted something longer, so that it would be shortened to Peri. There was a very eccentric naturalist friend of my parents who was a mythology professor. And he said, "Well, why don't you call her Peregrine?" And they couldn't think of any reason why not to, so that's what they settled on.

I was talking on the phone to the head of the Chicago Veterinary Medical Association, and he asked who this was, and I said, "Well, this is Peregrine Wolff." He said, "I'd seen that name, and I saw that it was at Lincoln Park Zoo, and we thought it was a big joke. I didn't know you actually existed."

I think I can definitely attribute any animal likings to my father, because he's always been a kind person, always very gentle. We always had a dog, and we always had some birds, and things like that, nothing fanatical. But I always had an appreciation for wildlife, birds in particular. My parents sort of instilled that.

We spent fifteen months in Europe when my dad was on sabbatical when I was eight. In Germany mostly, between Berlin and Munich, and then we spent three months in Norwich, England, for the last three months of the time we were there. Mom and my sister would go shopping, and Dad and I would always go to the zoo. He liked to go, and I always wanted to see the animals. I think it was at the Berlin Zoo and the Munich Zoo, they had a great ape collection, a lot of orangutans, and I remember really being infatuated to the point of telling my parents that when I grew up, I was going to marry an orangutan. Which I think they thought was fine, you know, a nice redhead in the family. I had a little book; I would cut all the animal pictures out from the guidebooks and paste them in this book. I think it was when we were in Europe that I really got hooked on zoo animals.

I remember when I was in fifth grade, there was a veterinarian who lived just down the hill from us, and I'd go down on weekends and work with the kennel woman, and we'd clean cages. I was doing that in fifth and sixth grade. And then I was baby-sitting for a veterinarian, and he said, "Well, you can come ride on calls with us," so I started doing that. Dad once asked me how to spell rhinoceros, and I was being defeatist about it. And he said, "You can't be a veterinarian unless you know how to spell rhinoceros." So he sort of was cluing me in at that point. By the time I was in college, I pretty much knew that I wanted to be a veterinarian.

We'd traveled to England on vacation; we went to the zoo on the isle of Jersey, and we just asked, "Do you ever take students?" "Only British students," they said. When I was getting ready to apply to vet school, everybody had good grades, everybody had animal experience, everybody wanted to get in because it was right during the James Herriot craze, which really affected vet school entrance a lot. I was moaning around the house, and my mother said, "Why don't you write to them? All they can say is no." So I did. And they sent me back an application, and I applied and got accepted.

It was great. I had a wonderful time. It started out as a four-month training program where you were basically an assistant keeper. And then you did a research project. I lived with an English family, rented a room from them. Jersey is only seven miles long and two and a half miles wide, and the coastline goes from beautiful beaches to real rocky rugged coast, where they have puffins and all sorts of shore birds. They have fields and fields of irises and daffodils.

The zoo was set up as a trust by Gerald Durrell, who was an animal collector in the fifties. It's very conservation-oriented. It's about the same size as ours, about thirty-five acres.

I met Durrell. He's an absolutely charming man, overweight, old, married to a fairly glamorous young American woman. He has the most enchanting blue eyes, and if you've ever read his books, he talks the same way he writes.

I learned there, as I have here, a lot about the animals and learned much more about the different personalities, the people who were there. I stayed on for two extra months as a keeper, because I had been wait-listed for vet school, and I was going out with one of the keepers there. If I hadn't gotten into vet school, I don't know what would have happened. It was hard to leave because I was leaving not only good friends but this person that I was really fond of.

I did return home, to vet school at Cornell. I think if I could have gone back and just said, "I don't want to have anything to do with men for the whole time I'm here," it would have been a much better experience. But I did reasonably well and had a lot of fun. However, my senior year was not a good year for me emotionally. I really wanted to be in a zoo, but I didn't feel that I was brilliant enough to be in that position. I had spent the summer of my junior year as an extern at Lincoln Park. Then, during my senior year, Tom Meehan told me that there was an internship being offered. Tom knew that he could get along with me, we had worked together OK. I was an easygoing person, knew the bullshit that goes on here, and could probably handle it, although sometimes I don't think I can. He said, "I know you're not the most qualified person in the world," because I wasn't, I was fresh out of vet school. I didn't have that much experience, there were other people. But as Tom said, he didn't really want to hire somebody who was smarter than he was. So I got the job. After my first year was up, he asked the zoo society to fund the position for a second year, which it did. And then the park district said, "OK, the money's in for a second veterinarian." You really can't do this place with just one person.

I grew up with some very close friends in high school, and I just naturally assumed that all these people would be going to college. Then, when I came back, I found out that half of these people who were considered really groovy in high school were married and had two kids and never left Middlebury, Vermont. It just never occurred to me that everybody wasn't going to go the same road I was taking. I don't think there's anything wrong if you want to stay home and have children; that's fine, if that's what you want to do. But if you want to aspire to something else, then I think you should do it. I think all my views were instilled in me as a child. I've never really sat down and thought about it that much. I've never really had a desire to sit down and read *Ms.* magazine or anything like that.

I think I intimidate a lot of people. People have told me that they think that I come off differently than I think I come off. People think that I tend to exude much more confidence than I think I do, more than I personally feel. I know that I've spent time feeling incompetent. And I never think of myself as possibly threatening men, and yet I'm sure that I do. Maybe I'm just an ornery Vermonter. I'm definitely much more New England than I am midwestern. That's one of the big problems I have here. There's nobody here who I really have that much in common with, even though we all work in the same place. That was a problem at vet school, too. I don't really have any close female friends at all. Which is kind of annoying.

My favorite animals? The marmosets and tamarins, I really like them. A lot of that goes back to Jersey; the guy that I was dating at the time was the marmoset and tamarin keeper. I really enjoyed working with them. You could open the cage door and clean out the enclosure while they were in it. They would just move away, and then they'd come up and look at you. I'd wash the glass on the inside, and they'd come down and play with the soapsuds. I think they're very intelligent, even though they're really high-strung and very piercing, which I usually don't like. I don't like hyper dogs or anything like that. But they don't have diarrhea all over the place; they're not always covered in shit like mandrils. They're just fascinating little animals. I'd like to see them in a really nice environment. It would be great to have a huge aviary full of plants with marmosets running around in it.

I really do enjoy the gorillas, especially appreciating each one's individual personality. I mean, they're so individual in the way they look, and they are so civilized in the way they behave.

I've had a special relationship with just one animal. The only animal that I actually got upset about when it died was a sloth that used to be here, that was hand-raised in the children's zoo, and her name was Woolly Bully. The animal was off, just not eating and was getting bloated, and she turned out to have an infection in her chest—pus in her chest—and ended up having other problems. We brought her to the hospital, and we worked with her. She was here for months, and we were doing all sorts of tests. She was just neat. The way she used to eat oranges, or eat grapes, she'd take them with her claws and put them in her mouth, and then she'd keep poking her toenail in her mouth to eat them. And she'd kind of hang upside down and look at you with those strange little eyes that they have. I was way down at the pathology meeting the night she died. That really upset me. That was probably the only animal that I've really cried over when it died. I really liked her.

You know when the animal is sick. Unless I pick it up myself, the keepers are the first line. They're excellent judges; they know the animals. It's like the owners of dogs. You can tell when an animal's in pain. One particular incident really emphasized it to me. It was a marmoset that was sick; we'd done surgery on it. This was one that did live, even though it was sick. We gave it the usual anesthesia, and I'd just opened its belly, and I thought, "This animal's in a lot of pain." Because it was lying there all curled up, in the fetal position. So we gave it a pain-killer— after the anesthesia—and half an hour later, it was stretched out on its side asleep. The only thing I'd given it was this painkiller, and we saw such a difference between the animal before and, you know, the animal sleeping quietly. And now, since we've started using painkillers, they'll stay asleep for an hour or two after surgery. And I've done surgery without giving a painkiller, and they wake right up.

I've seen some animals that act totally normal and are dead the next day, and you open them up, and they've had pathology that's been going on for weeks. Breeding on

Friday, off food and a little bit lethargic on Saturday, dead on Sunday. You couldn't know, unless you were spending all day watching the animal, and that would be impractical. We've had marmosets die that have been totally infected, worms everywhere; you open their stomach, and the worms are out of their intestines crawling around. And you know that didn't happen last night; that's taken at least a couple of days to happen. And they were apparently fairly normal.

Parasites are a problem in all animals; they're in people, too. A lot of people in America are carrying around worms, and a lot of people in Third World countries are infested with them. But these animals are constantly rein-fecting themselves. If we clean to get rid of some of the parasites the polar bears have and the lions have, we would have to either dig up a foot of dirt in their outside exhibit and change it, or else flame-throw their whole inside exhibit and kill the eggs. That's how resistant parasites are to water and soap and ammonia and all that stuff. The eggs are passed in the feces, and then they progress to a third stage, infective larvae. And then when the cat or whatever is licking the floor and licks up the infective third-stage larvae that have settled down from the feces, it reinfects itself. A lot of these animals come in from the wild with worms. And sometimes you don't get rid of the worms because sometimes they may not be passing eggs that day, so then you get a negative fecal, and well, fine, the animals go into the collection. Worms aren't necessarily lethal, because it's not really advantageous for the parasite to kill the host. Then they'd have to find a new host. But in captivity we see deaths that closely follow some sort of stress. Some animals will have been moved to a different cage, or just been weaned, or the keepers will have caught them up and done something to them, and then a week later, we'll start seeing a couple of deaths. With some parasites, the host builds up sort of an immunity, so the host kind of keeps the parasite at a dull roar rather than a raging infection, but a lot of young animals that are naive to these parasites will be overcome. They'll get so many in their intestines that the parasites starve them out basically.

Other diseases cut across this place, too. Bacterial infections. A lot of the viruses are very host-specific, like the canine distemper, which is going to hit the dogs and some of the ferrets and that sort of thing. But you're not going to have the primates dying of canine distemper. So really the only major threat is the bacterial infections that can hit a whole different realm of hosts. We had an outbreak go through our marmoset colony. If the parasites don't kill you, the bacteria will. We had animals in the basement of the primate house; it's closed down now, a horrible place. We were starting to lose animals, and I'd walk through with the keeper, Pam Dunn, and she'd say, "Well, this one's doing fine and that one's OK," and invariably one of those two would be dead the next morning. Some sort of primary stress was causing the host to be weakened, and a secondary bacteria was lurking to kill them within twelve hours. We would aspirate some blood out of the heart, and it would be loaded with bacteria.

Many diseases go back and forth between humans and animals. I've got a textbook in my office on just that subject. Parasites can be passed from animals to people. Animals donated to the zoo can bring rabies with them. It's rare, but when it occurs, it's bad news. People bring TB to primates, and the reverse can happen as well. Many animals are vulnerable, especially the great apes. They get colds, the flu from keepers, and then they give those back to us.

Apes get most of the things that humans do, and we had a very big problem with that. I think this came directly from Pat Sass, who was sick, because it started in the chimps. From a sick head keeper who happens to love chimps. It just marched right around the whole great ape building in a matter of a week. We think it was a virus, a flu type of thing, just snotty noses, coughs, lethargy. We ended up losing an adult male chimp, just bang, dead, from one day to the next. I put them on antibiotics, but whether that was helpful or not is conjecture. I think most of them cured themselves. But it was scary, because there was nothing I could do. We were getting sick, too. I got sick, a keeper got sick. I got sick because Tanga spit in my face a number of times, and she was sick. It was frightening.

Sometimes, I experience a really high level of frustration. What Tom and I tend to do a lot of is fire engine work. For zoo animals, if you're sick, someone's going to eat you, or you're going to get left behind. In the wild, that's what's going to happen, so you try to look as normal as possible, because if you look abnormal, then you're automatically picked out by something else as fair game. I think that zoo animals really hide it; that's something instinctual that is left over from the wild. So you often tend to get animals that are beyond help, that are too far gone. Like the leopard we euthanized: If that leopard had been a domestic cat, he would have been under treatment a long time ago. But what do you do if you can't give him fluids, you can't give him an IV? You know you're basically treating the symptoms, and it's not always that practical, because you can't treat the cat if he's well enough to kill you, but if he's so sick that he can't hurt you, you can help him. But then as soon as he gets better, the first thing he's going to try to do is kill you even though he may need more help.

Sometimes, I feel a sense of risk. Once, Lenore woke up ahead of schedule just outside her holding area at the great ape house. I felt that definitely there was a big risk, but it was overridden by the fact that there was a risk to the animal, who was shrieking and thrashing, surrounded by us, by people. She had an IV in her so that we might have had to knock her down again just to get it out. If she pulled out the tubing that goes to the bag, well, then she's got a perfectly open line that's dripping blood—not that she's going to bleed to death in five minutes, but it could have had potential complications. The first thing that goes through my mind in a lot of these situations is that I'm not as worried about myself getting hurt as I am about somebody else getting hurt, because we're directly responsible if anyone else gets hurt, in my opinion. We're the ones who are calling the shots. If I'm out with a vet student, I'm in control of the situation, the one who should be making the judgment call as to whether this is not a safe procedure.

With Lenore that day, Tom grabbed her, or grabbed a leg or an arm or something, was trying to turn her around so that she'd go straight up instead of out into the kitchen where people were scattering. But he said Lenore eventually did what she intended to do all along, which was to stay inside, away from the people. You can't manipulate any of the great apes. With Lenore, I didn't feel as much in danger of my life; I felt in danger of having her get out or bite somebody else. I don't think I really have ever felt in danger. I had a tapir fall on me, which was an unpleasant experience, but it happened so fast, I didn't really have time to think about it. That was the only time I've ever been really hurt here.

Many of the animals here don't want to attack. However, I think that if a lion got out, it would kill you. I think that the big cats would. I think that you could almost intimidate everybody else. The pygmy hippos are supposed to be really nasty, if you walk into their territory. I think if they were off their own turf, that they might run. Run away from you. A polar bear would probably kill you. The only other animal that I feel has the potential to do the most harm, and almost killed Tom, are the elephants. We tend to treat them like big dogs, but a lot of people have been killed by elephants. There've been more people killed by elephants than any other zoo animal. I think I have a fairly good relationship with them, but if they wanted to, it would be over so fast that I couldn't do anything about it.

I think that animals in zoos have the right to the best possible care that we can give them, and I don't think that in a lot of situations we're doing the best job possible. We can't even keep some of the animals we have here alive; I'm not even talking about breeding or doing well, I'm talking about keeping them alive. That's wrong. There are some animals that do not do well in captivity. And those are the species that are heading for extinction. There are some lemur species in Madagascar that they just can't keep alive in captivity; they live a week, they live two weeks, and then they croak. They just can't do it with today's technology. And with those animals that have probably reached such critically low population levels and are so difficult to keep, it may be better, instead of spending millions to save them, just to divide that up for species that we might be able to save.

I went up to Iceland earlier this year, and we did some necropsies on some birds up there, versus the necropsies I've done on our young birds that are only a year old, birds that are living here. They were comparable weights, but the ones from Iceland are muscle, and the ones here are fat. The animals here are flabby; they don't get a lot of exercise, they just kind of roam around and do nothing. That's not killing animals, but every animal has its territory, and we keep them in twenty-five square feet rather than two and a half square miles of territory. I think that a large part of an animal's beauty is its motion. And that's the same with people. I think that's why people like horses, because they're beautiful when they move, and like seeing giraffes. Seeing a giraffe gallop is an incredible sight; so is seeing monkeys run around.

The whole zoo population is changing now, because the percentage of animals that were born in the wild is reducing, and the percentage of animals that are born in captivity is increasing. Those animals born in captivity probably will not suffer any psychological damage, as long as certain conditions are met in captivity. That may be one reason why we have a lot of success with our great apes, because if they don't want to be looked at, they don't have to be looked at. They can go upstairs and pick their noses if they want. I think as long as they can get away and not feel threatened by the public or by whatever they feel threatened by, then that can help keep them psychologically fit.

This is probably a lot of anthropomorphism, but I'm not sure about living inside your whole life. Never having exposure to the sun. Never having exposure to anything but your own world, the smell of your own urine or feces or whatever cleansing agent the keepers are using. And to me, I can't help but think, when I see animals that are just lying outside sunbathing, or just hanging out, they seem like they're appreciating the outdoors. My dog does, so why should he have any more sense of feelings than the animals in the zoo? To live inside your whole life, that bothers me the most. That's one thing I don't like about northern zoos. And why I think that a lot of the southern zoos might have healthier animals or happier animals; at least they get out and get some sunshine.

I like San Diego's wild animal park, because it allows for natural manipulations, the herding instinct, a male standing in one spot and guarding his territory, and the females moving in and out of it. You see the same stuff out there that you see in Africa, and you don't realize that until you go to Africa and see it.

We can offer that for some animals, the smaller species that you can put in a relatively large space, so that they still can carry out a lot of their activities. But for some of the larger animals, you don't see it. I'm not sure how much the big cats suffer, but they sure look like they suffer a lot in those old cages.

The best keepers in the zoo have a lot of common sense. If I ask one to do something, she will not say, "Oh, I can't, the animal won't do it." She will say, "OK, I will figure out a way to do it," and she usually gets it done. A good keeper will call me on an animal and be able to tell me what happened the day before. She'll give me her impression of it, what she thinks, if it's normal behavior, if it's not normal behavior. I like the traits of someone who will spend extra time reading about the animal, someone I can communicate with, someone who will initiate some things on her own, someone who is keeping her eyes open.

Then there's the I-don't-give-a-damn school. I've seen animals suffer because of them, which really angers me. They suffer from neglect, pure and simple. Say an animal hasn't eaten its food for days. Now, granted, I probably should have been checking up on it, but the keeper should have come to us before that animal looked like hell. The keeper should have said, "Goddamn it, you veterinarians better get over here because this animal looks awful." I would rather have a keeper call me up ten times a day and say, "When are you going to get over here? The animal looks sick," rather than not do it. I tell a lot of people, "I'm not that organized. I tend to forget a lot of things, I'll get distracted by something else. If you want it done, call me up and bug me. I'll never hold it against you if you call me up five times and say, "Don't forget to do this tomorrow," or, "Can we do this today?" I've told a lot of people that, and they'll do it, and it helps me get things done. But, please do that rather than just assuming that you know more. And another attitude that I really don't like is that of the people who imply that they know more than I do, that I'm just a stupid veterinarian. They don't tend to think on the scientific side of things. Which is one of Tom's big bugaboos about this place; he's always trying to inject a little science into everything, rather than black magic.

I don't like holistic medicine in animals. I mean it's fine, a lot of people's problems are psychological, and I think you can believe a lot of your illnesses and problems away. Well, are you going to convince a black leopard that if he only has positive thoughts and believes that this raspberry leaf tea is going to help him, it's going to work? Give them a break.

I think that there were definitely some animals here that have died because it's our fault. There are some animals that they forgot to bring in that froze to death at night, things like that. There was one little agouti, one of those South American rodents that got left out last year. No one really thought that it might be getting cold all alone. I mean, it lived outside, but you know when it's below zero and an animal is all by itself and is from South America. His core temperature was seventy-six degrees when he came in, and four days later his little toes all turned black and fell off. He lived, but he went through a lot of pain and suffering.

We lost a bunch of saki monkeys. The reason might have been that they were getting bacterial infections from the meat. If the meat was being improperly handled and being chopped up, and then grapes and the salad were chopped up on the same cutting board with the same knife, there could be a problem. If you eat meat your whole life, that's fine; if—like sakis—you tend to eat vegetable matter and then get exposed to these horrendous bacteria that are in meat, you could get wiped out. Maybe that's how those saki monkeys died. If it was, that was our mistake, I mean that was the zoo's mistake.

I think that my next move I will make for location. Like if somebody offered me a job at the Lincoln, Nebraska, zoo as head veterinarian, I don't think I'd take it. I'd like to be a head veterinarian somewhere; I'd like a little bit more responsibility, a little bit more control. But then I know there's a lot of headaches, too. Tom does an awful lot of paperwork, and that frustrates him. I know I'll never give up exotic animals. If I had to choose today between being a small animal veterinarian and never practicing another day of veterinary medicine in my life, I'd choose the latter. If I could do field work somewhere, go off and work on some exotic animal conservation project somewhere, I would stay in the conservation field and give up the veterinary medicine field. How long I stay here, I don't know. I guess it depends on whether something better comes along. It also depends on my out-of-work life. If I'm happy, really happy in that, then this is a good job.

Tom and I have our ups and downs, but we get along. I still feel that slowly but surely we are hammering away at some of these really hard-to-change problems—getting diets settled, things like that, trying to make everything better for the animals here. And making the zoo a better place, educating the keepers. This is a good job; the place has a lot to offer. At my age and for my number of years out of school, you really couldn't ask for anything better.

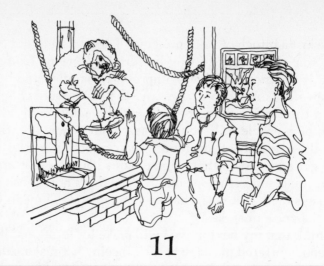

11

MONKEYS' BUSINESS

When asked if she and her husband had children, primate house keeper Pam Dunn smiled and said, "No, with a capital *N* and six or seven exclamation points."

There was an intended irony in her declaration. During one three-month period in her recent past, she spent only three weeks without transporting a newborn primate between work and home.

She did it with pleasure.

"I've been doing what I want to do for as long as I can remember," she said. A powerful affection for animals had characterized her life.

Pam was born in 1952, in a Chicago suburb; she lived most of her life in Chicago. She attended the University of Illinois at Chicago and acquired a bachelor's degree in anthropology.

As a teenager, she began to volunteer her time at the zoo. She did that for ten years, then won a keeper's job. She served as a keeper, with particular interest in primates, for another ten years.

On a cool day in late summer, Pam emerged from her car carrying a familiar parcel, an animal. She wore a pink T-shirt and jeans. Her round, cheerful face was framed by curly blond hair. Her plumpness seemed less characteristic of her than her obvious energy.

The animal she carried was a DeBrazza's guenon, a small West African monkey. At birth, the monkey—which Pam had named Max (for Max Headroom)—had been neglected by his mother. A quick decision had been made in an effort to save the baby's life; the baby was pulled. That night, Pam took him home. Seventeen days later, she was still transporting him back and forth, feeding him by hand, stroking him, keeping him warm, buying toys for him. After more than two weeks, he still weighed less than one pound.

He was a tiny, squeaking creature, with a small fearful face and a delicate, spindly body. As Pam entered the primate house kitchen to begin her day, she placed Max, in his carrier, on a table in a warm corner of the room. Inside the carrier, Max was clutching a manufactured replica of himself, a stuffed monkey.

Across the room, a sign read: "Danger. No Unauthorized Personnel. Chimps Can Grab. Be Aware."

Pam had spent the previous evening worrying about Max. His early efforts to survive had been flawed. He seemed to be in teething pain. His legs seemed weak. He did not eat sufficiently.

Motivated by that concern, and affection, Pam carried Max to the zoo hospital, where vet Tom Meehan looked at him. When Tom picked him up, his squeaks became high-pitched screams. Tom extended two fingers, and the monkey grabbed them. He stroked the monkey's legs, gently.

"The legs look OK," he said. Max urinated on the examining table.

"He won't eat voluntarily," Pam told Tom. "Last night he seemed to perk up, but I had to swaddle him to get the bottle in."

"Keep an eye on him," Tom said. "Encourage him to

move around. Try to get him to climb, to cling, what he'd do if he were still with his mother. He doesn't have much coordination."

Pam picked up Max to return to the primate house; she had other work to do. The monkey, wrapped in a small blanket, went silent; only his little face was visible, wide-eyed, staring up at Pam.

It was early morning, and the zoo was quiet except for the occasional sound of an animal. Pam walked along, holding Max.

Several wolves in their outdoor habitat howled. Yards away, a dog barked, as if in response. The wolves howled again. The dog, a rust-colored Irish terrier named Rosie, had climbed up into a tree on the outer side of the zoo fence, to see the wolves. Howls and barks were exchanged, then Rosie's master coaxed her out of the tree, and the wolves returned to their relaxed state.

Pam did not notice. She held Max and walked back to the primate house. She was feeling reflective.

"You know what? I think of what I do as an honor," she said. "Especially when I get to care for an endangered species, like this one. I gear my lifestyle around raising these little guys. Fortunately, I have Chris, the best husband in the world. We go to a party, and we have to leave early because I have to feed Max. It's like having a kid, but you can't get a baby-sitter who'll take care of this kind of kid."

Pam had taken home bush babies, tiny creatures who weighed less than three ounces at birth; Pam had remained awake for twenty-four hours on several occasions, just to keep them alive. There had been tamarins, marmosets, lemurs as well. It was the part of her job that sustained her passion for the animals and her understanding of them.

Much of her job, as it was for all keepers, was routine, repetitious, drudgery. She kept the cages clean and the animals fed. She hosed down the cages. She fed the monkeys early in the morning: monkey chow, which they weren't eager to devour, and a canned primate diet (both

were nutritionally complete) that they ate with enthusiasm. After that "breakfast," they were served a meal of
fruits and vegetables later in the day.

With Max back in his carrier, Pam cut up celery in the
kitchen. A clatter arose in the cage nearest the kitchen. It
was occupied by a pair of chimps, Patsy, the female, and
Keo, the male, both in their early thirties. When the great
ape house had been opened in 1976, they were brought to
it, but they didn't tolerate the move well. They were older
than most of the other chimps and were hostile to them.
They were returned to the primate house, where they
shared a double cage just outside of the kitchen.

Keo, at times, would demonstrate his power, pound on
the steel door at the rear of the cage, cup his hands against
his chest, display his strength. He was at it again, and Pam
knew it without looking.

"He can still make plenty of noise," she said, without
looking up from the celery. "When someone out front
teases him, he takes it out on Patsy. Sometimes even when
he's not being teased. There are certain physical types that
urge him on. A guy who looks like a construction worker.
A machismo persona. A weirdo drug addict or a drunk.
They set him off, even if they're not provoking him.
There's something out there, whatever it is, that gets him
into a mood.

"Patsy used to be like that, too. She used to set you up.
She'd put her hand through an opening in the cage, in the
back, and offer a keeper a string bean. When you reached
to take it from her, she'd grab your arm and hang on.
Sneaky. But now they're both like people when they get
older. They've mellowed out."

The chimps were in a class by themselves. The other
inhabitants of the primate house fell under the broad desig-
nation of monkeys. The names were exotic: mandrills,
black and white ruffed lemurs, Celebes black apes (actually
macaques, small monkeys, not apes), black howler monkeys, squirrel monkeys, black lemurs, black and white
colobus monkeys, DeBrazza's guenons, pale-faced sakis,

wanderoo macaques, red and black ruffed lemurs, and lion-tailed macaques.

Pam hacked away at sweet potatoes and bananas. Hard-boiled eggs she sliced in half, with the shell intact; the monkeys would peel it away carefully. She chopped apples, tore lettuce, and seasoned much of it with vitamin powder.

The phone rang; it was her husband, asking how Max was doing. Pam peeked at the monkey, who was asleep, clutching the furry chest of the stuffed monkey. Pam told Chris that Max was as well as could be expected.

Pam returned to her ritual. It was part of her job to make certain that the monkeys ate a sound, satisfying diet. But she knew that her worth as a keeper went beyond being deft with a kitchen knife.

The primate house, built in 1927, was old now and slated for renovation. The renovation plan was splendid, but Pam knew it would not be completed on schedule. For her, you did what you could with what you were given.

"This is an old, crappy building," she said. "Because it's old and crappy, you try to do as much as you can to stimulate the animals, without turning into one of those animals-are-my-good-friends types. I never forget that the animals in here are capable of doing a lot of damage. Most of them can't kill you, unless you let them kill you, but I've seen lemurs in a fight, ganging up on one of them. They bite. One of them once needed two hundred stitches after-ward. But sometimes you have to let them fight, to work out their disputes. They are social animals. But there's a line. I monitor it carefully, but I don't necessarily rush to intervene."

At 10 A.M., it was time to "feed the kid." She warmed a small bottle of formula—one of the same brands used to feed human babies. She carried Max to the library, housed in the primate house, a quiet place to read or to feed a monkey.

She wrapped Max in a small blanket and sat in a chair. The monkey stared at her. She placed the nipple in its mouth; the monkey retained it but didn't suck on it. The formula dribbled into his mouth, and he swallowed. Suddenly, but without much force, it began to suck on the nipple, continuing to stare at Pam. It was a moment begging for anthropomorphic interpretation. Pam abstained.

For her, Max's survival was the main matter. It would be important to get him back with his family, even with a mother that had been less than supportive.

"At first, I'd want to sit with him in front of his family group, so he won't be frightened when we put him back in with his mother," she said. "But that's seven months to a year away—after he's on solid food. That's the time to try to reunite them."

A few minutes later, she checked the level of formula in the bottle. Some of it had been consumed. She carried Max back to the kitchen, to his carrier, to his stuffed monkey. He grabbed the monkey and curled up against it.

Pam stood at the window, looking out at the people strolling through the zoo.

"When I was a zoo volunteer years ago, they'd ask me all sorts of questions. But there was no doubt about what was the most popular question, by far," she said.

"It was, 'Where is the bathroom?' "

Late that day, when Pam was ready to take Max home, she heard that a baby saki monkey named Morgan would need her, too. The saki's mother had died suddenly in the small mammal house, but had nursed the baby for two months, and someone would have to substitute for the mother. Pam volunteered.

The next morning, Pam arrived at work with two animal carriers.

Morgan had consumed some formula at Pam's apartment, had eaten a little bit of banana, but had vomited. Pam was concerned; Tom Meehan would have to see the saki.

In the primate house kitchen, Max squeaked in his carrier and wrestled with his stuffed monkey. The saki seemed lethargic in its carrier, and as Pam looked at it, she was unhappy.

"Sakis are laid-back at best," she said. "They can even be morose in captivity. Is this one depressed, or is its behavior merely a characteristic of the species? They're rarely hyper, so it's a matter of degree."

Morgan issued a high-pitched whistle, then a howl; Max continued to play with his stuffed animal. Pam was concerned about Max, too; he had what appeared to be a blister on one leg. Tom Meehan might have to "pop it."

Last night at home, she had kept Max at one end of the apartment and Morgan at the other, running back and forth, stopping to wash her hands. Morgan might have the disease that killed its mother; she didn't want Max to become infected.

By 8:20 A. M., she had changed into her keeper uniform: dark brown slacks and khaki shirt. She filled a bowl with warm water and mild soap. She opened Max's carrier and said, "Hey, tiger, hey, tiger, come here."

She reached in and grabbed Max, who urinated. She held him in one hand easily, and gently rubbed the soapy water on him with the other. He responded with an occasional peep.

"I know, I know, life's tough," she murmured.

She washed only his bottom and his legs; he sat in the water, clutching her shirt. She dried him with paper towels and a dish towel, as he ran through a repertoire of protest sounds, stopping only to glare intently at her face.

Gene Brimer, the recently hired pest control technician, dropped in to take an inventory of the pesticides in the primate house.

Pam asked him if he'd ever conquer the pests at the zoo.

"We'll make a dent," he said. "The truth is that we'll never eliminate the problems. We don't really exterminate, although that word is still used to describe what I'm trying to do. What we do is try to control the infestation."

Pam was well aware of the problem. Roaches eaten by monkeys implanted a potentially fatal parasite. Marmosets had been particularly vulnerable, and she was fond of marmosets.

Gene was likable; his gray hair belied the presence of a youthful energy. But Pam didn't have time to chat; she had to go to the hospital to get a heating pad to warm Morgan's carrier.

On the way, she met curator of mammals Mark Rosenthal, who mentioned that a female lion had fallen into the moat that separated the lions from the public. She wasn't injured, Mark said.

A stop at the lions' outdoor habitat revealed the lioness sitting calmly at the bottom of the moat, looking up at another lioness peering down at her. An open door in the moat awaited the lioness, who chose not to enter it and make her way into the building, where the keepers could take charge.

Les Fisher had been notified and was taking in the scene.

"Over the years, maybe ten or twelve lions or tigers have fallen in, and only one even cracked a bone," he said. "Eventually, she'll come in, if only because she'll be hungry."

Pam got the heating pad from the hospital and returned to the primate house. Morgan seemed sluggish, a weariness that resembled depression in humans.

Tom Meehan called. His test on the dead saki mother revealed that she died of bacterial pneumonia, common and contagious; the baby might be in jeopardy, he told Pam. The little saki had vomited again, and Pam was concerned.

"Nothing much I can do," she sighed.

She went out into the main hall, where the public circulated, and walked along the row in front of one bank of cages. In one cage, she spotted Molly, a colobus monkey with a white face, and Puddles, a male DeBrazza's guenon, a brownish-green monkey with a white beard. Molly's mother didn't nurse her, Pam recalled, so she was pulled, and Tom Meehan took her home. Puddles was thought to be sickly at birth and was covered with sores; his mother had been urinating on him. When an attempt was made to reunite mother and son, the mother wouldn't pick him up, and he was retrieved again.

"We weren't sure that Molly would make it," she remembered. "Colobuses need a special diet, with higher greens content. She had thrush, and she had seizures. But there she is, just fine.

"Puddles was a weird cookie. He'd rock and beat his head against the wall. At first, Molly didn't like him. But slowly they got along. He likes her now, but she's more independent. Gradually, once we put them together, they grew confident in each other's company. Now, they've been OK for two weeks, so we've broken down our contact with them. We're planning to reintroduce each to its own species."

In the next cage, four colobus monkeys raced to the front of the cage when Pam appeared.

"With these monkeys—and they're all females in this group—the females are like aunts. It's called 'aunting' behavior. They take care of another's baby. It's a highly social thing. They'll go so far as to play tug-of-war with a baby, which can get scary.

"For me, they look as different as people. I know them as individuals," she said. The four colobus monkeys looked almost identical.

"Actually, all four of these will go, with Molly, to a zoo in Little Rock, Arkansas, where there's a male waiting to breed with them. Their progeny will come back here. It's a good situation."

Stopping in front of the next cage, Pam hollered, "Gracie, come in."

From the outdoor cage—connected to the indoor cage by a short tunnel and a door the keepers could open by lever— a Celebese black ape—looking like a dwarf ape but actually a monkey—entered, bared her teeth and made a lip-smacking sound. Her daughter, named Patience, followed her to the front of the cage where Pam was standing.

"When Patience sees me paying attention to her mother, she objects," Pam said. "She'll reach through the cage and try to pinch my arm. Hard."

Patience did reach, and Pam dodged her grip.

Down the row, a group of five black and white ruffed lemurs—"laid-back animals" Pam called them—were asleep. When they heard Pam's voice, they woke up.

"Sorry," she said.

A group of mandrills seemed to be waiting for Pam to visit them. The mandrills, regal members of the baboon family, had grooved facial markings that surrounded their red noses; the markings were deep enough to go all the way into their skulls. The mother of the group, called Jonesie, was, according to Pam, "bizarre, schizzy, hyper. She plucks her own hair until she looks like she's been shaved. I'd expect that of a neurotic animal low in the pecking order, but she's subordinate only to the male. She's a tense animal, a high-energy animal, but it's not all positive energy, unfortunately."

Jonesie turned her butt toward Pam.

"That's a submissive gesture," Pam said. "She's showing submissiveness to me, too."

Pam made her way back to the kitchen. She called Tom Meehan, who told her that a second saki had died, but not of the same infection that had caused the previous saki death. It was confusing, he told Pam. He would come over to see the saki baby, Morgan.

She peeked in to look at Max, still asleep beside his stuffed monkey, his slender arms around it.

"It's not that the stuffed animal is a monkey to Max," Pam said. "They have a clinging instinct. Little marmosets will clutch a stocking cap. They don't care if it looks like a monkey or not. I don't think that this little guy looked at the toy and said, 'My God, it's one of my own.' "

She had grown used to her role as a surrogate mother. She preferred to think that it made her a better keeper, rather than a woman with an anthropomorphic fixation. When nature failed, she had to be there.

"You never know if a mother knows something when she neglects her baby," she said. "First-time mothers will reject babies because the situation is stressful and they don't know what to do. That's especially true when the mother was hand-raised herself and doesn't have experience as a mother. In marmosets, the males are the ones who carry the newborn, not the mothers. And if they don't do it well, or if there's more than one baby, the mother may not be able to cope."

Tom Meehan arrived, reached into the carrier, and extracted the saki. The monkey arched its back; its eyes rolled from side to side. Tom studied it for several minutes.

"He may be hypoglycemic. We can medicate it for that," he said.

He wanted to change the formula Pam had been feeding it, in search of one it would tolerate. He wanted to give it glucose via an IV line, but, he said, "I'll have a helluva time getting an IV line in." He was prepared to insert a stomach tube, to assure that nutrition got to the saki.

Pam wrapped the saki in a dish towel and attempted to give it some Pedialyte, an oral electrolyte maintenance solution. The weary saki wasn't getting much of it, and Tom was attentive to the lack of success.

"I'll have to try to get that IV line in. The oral stuff just isn't as good. And I want to warm him up. I'll take him to the hospital," Tom told Pam.

Before Tom left, Pam wanted him to look at the blister on Max's leg. She had mentioned it to Tom earlier, but he had forgotten.

"I guess it wasn't high on my priority list today," he said, commenting on his own clogged schedule. He washed his hands and plucked Max from his carrier. Max urinated and tried to clutch his stuffed monkey. Tom ducked the flow of urine and separated real monkey from toy monkey.

Delicately holding a syringe, Tom removed fluid from the blister for the lab technician to analyze. As Tom prepared to leave, Les Fisher walked in; he had heard about the plight of the sakis, the dead and the living.

He told Pam he knew how frail sakis could be. She agreed.

"I've seen a keeper just open a cage and have a saki faint before the keeper could even grab it," she said.

Les and Tom went on their way, and Pam was alone in

the kitchen. She had chores to do. One of the primate keepers walked in and sat down. A young woman, she appreciated how seriously Pam took her job. They talked about the sick saki and the job of the involved keeper.

"Sure, after all these years, I know that this isn't Disneyland," Pam said. "An epidemic can race through here. I've seen it happen. I know when an animal can't make it. That's when I say to myself, 'I don't need this.' But then I just keep going. When they survive, and you know when they have, you're so drained that you don't feel much of anything. But the days pass and you recover, too.

"After all, it's my choice, to do what I do. And when an animal gets better, I feel proud."

Early the next morning, Pam learned that Morgan had died. The sad little saki had died in the zoo hospital shortly after arriving there the previous afternoon. Its depressed state had been a sign of things to come. Tom Meehan concluded that Morgan, like the two older sakis who had died within days of each other, had succumbed to strep pneumonia. Morgan's body was sent to the University of Chicago pathology lab for detailed analysis. The infection that had decimated the saki colony had left only one male alive; Tom was medicating it in the hope of saving it.

For Pam, the bad news only compounded her mood. Max, the DeBrazza's guenon baby, was less alert than he had been on the previous day. She was still concerned that it wasn't eating voluntarily and that its clutching instinct wasn't fully developed. Last night, she had washed its stuffed monkey but had forgotten to put it back in the carrier.

In that carrier, back in the primate house kitchen, Max seemed edgy and was scratching the back wall of the carrier in what seemed to be a display of nervous energy. Pam realized that she'd left the stuffed monkey at home and set out to replace it. She found a dish towel and rolled it into a ball as a replacement.

As Pam talked to Max, a young woman keeper prepared a potion for Patsy, the old chimp.

It contained one birth control pill—the same used by

women all over the world—which the keeper had pulverized and had stirred into a paper cup filled with Tang. To pacify Keo, the ill-mannered male chimp, another paper cup with Tang alone was readied. Patsy had given birth to seven children over the years, then had given birth to an eighth and had neglected it. The decision had been made to pull the baby and put Patsy on the Pill.

Pam went to the outside cages to check the locks; they were intact. It was part of her routine. Then she went into the back run and pulled the levers that opened the outside cages to the monkeys inside. She yelled, "Good morning!" and the monkeys, screeching excitedly, bounded down the runways into the sunlight.

Inside, Pam paced past the glass-enclosed cages, looking at each animal as she passed. She knew what to look for: any sign of blood, diarrhea, bloody urine—either a sign of a cycling female or a sign of trouble—the posture of the animals, a tool left in a cage.

"I see them every day," she said. "I ought to know if anything's changed."

The most obvious, and potentially most threatening, sign was a monkey sitting silently in a corner.

"A nonmobile primate is an indication of a serious problem," she said.

She proceeded to hose down each cage thoroughly, a job that the keepers did daily. The monkeys scrambled for a place away from the stream of water and watched her work.

As she passed each cage, she commented about her relationship with the animals in it.

Seven red and black ruffed lemurs struck a family pose to greet her, as if a photographer had given them instructions. They all leaped upon a long branch in the cage, in a perfect row. One of them leaned forward toward her.

"For a lemur, that one's aggressive," she said. "When you feed him, he tries to nail you."

She moved along, then cried out. "Gaylord!"

Gaylord, a black male howler monkey, lumbered toward

the front of the cage. The lemurs she had passed made a loud racket, a territorial call.

"They're telling me, 'This is my territory, and I'm letting you know it is,' " she interpreted.

Gaylord peered at her. She imitated his howl, hoping to get him to respond. He didn't. Instead, he turned and gnawed some bark off a branch in his cage.

"He's responsive, interactive with people, but it's not friendly," she said. "That's a distinction that's important to make. You have to know that when he solicits attention, he may appear to be 'cute,' but he may not be friendly. It's not an invitation to play with him."

In the next cage, a group of wanderoo macaques cavorted. One of the males, Jacob, was a misogynist. He coexisted only with one female, Gertrude. All the others were in danger in his presence.

"He attacks them," Pam said. "We had to send one out of here, to the Baltimore Zoo. And another one had to have a leg amputated, thanks to him. He pulled her leg through the bars and bit her so badly the leg couldn't be saved. She survived, however. What's a little odd is that she was his daughter. Now, even though she's got only one leg, she's very aggressive, like her father."

In the cage holding the DeBrazza's guenons, Max's father sat proudly; he was a large monkey with a serious demeanor. When Max had to be pulled, his mother, Jenny, was walking along with Max on her hip. Pam had to reach in to get him. She held Jenny's tail with one hand and grabbed Max with the other. Jenny remained calm, fortunately.

In another cage, a family group of DeBrazza's guenons sat around: Lucas, the father; Olive, the mother; Mark, a son; and Kathy, a two-month-old. Pam looked at them.

"Olive rocks back and forth. Abnormal," Pam noted. "She's not very friendly, either, but she's a good mother. She's had many children. Some of them are adults now. In fact, she's a grandmother. There's some nice, loving stuff going on between brother Mark and the new little sister, too. It wasn't like that in the beginning, when she was born, but they've worked it out. Or he has."

Pam continued her stroll, out of the building to the row of outdoor cages.

"And here's my favorite animal in the entire house," she announced. It was Admiral, a male wanderoo macaque who had been caught in the wild years ago; he was now in his midtwenties. He was black with a light gray full "beard," and the hair on his head emulated a widow's peak that made him seem to be wearing an old-fashioned admiral's hat.

Pam went back to the kitchen to get Admiral his reward, a few fresh, sweet, green grapes.

"He responds to women very well," she said. "Not just to me, but to all the women keepers." She held out a grape, and Admiral reached through the bars and took it gently, put it into his mouth, but did not chew it.

He held Pam's hand, lifted his face toward hers, and opened his mouth. His teeth looked in need of repair.

"He's had a lot of dental work. Fillings. Root canals. We've got a dentist for humans who comes in and does the work," she said.

Pam continued to hand Admiral the grapes, and he kept her hand in his.

"In ten years, he's never attacked me," she said.

"You've got the worst-looking teeth," she said to him, "But you're still handsome."

Admiral offered a gesture closely resembling a salute. Then he began to chew on the grapes, which he had held in his cheek pouch.

"You're the best boy in the whole place," she said. "Yes, you are."

She invited him to reach out, beyond the bars, to hold her hand again.

"If I stuck my hand inside the bars, he probably wouldn't bite me, but why take the chance? How would I explain that in an accident report?" she asked herself.

She took a quick tour of the isolation room, where animals were held for a variety of reasons. Some were awaiting shipment to other zoos. Some were awaiting medical treatment. Single animals awaited mates or simply another of their species to serve as company.

Two red and black ruffed lemurs were in cages side by side.

"They're both males," Pam said. "We want them to hear each other, see each other, smell each other, for companionship. An all-male group can live in peace, and sometimes breeding isn't a consideration. We have enough."

When it was time for her midmorning break, Pam grabbed a Coke from the food locker in the kitchen and went to the library. She sat at a small table with the librarian, Joyce Shaw. She thought about the last twenty-four hours and the death of the saki. For several minutes, she was quiet. Then she spoke.

"I was tired and disheartened yesterday. A few weeks ago, I had a black and white ruffed lemur baby die on me, of pneumonia. The mother rejected that one, so I took it. In Morgan's case, the mother died. For that reason, until we knew why she died, I had to be cautious. Could other animals get what killed her? Could I get it? We had to find out. So when I had both babies at home, I had one in the front of the apartment and one in the back, and I was running, front to back, stopping to wash my hands in Betadine.

"What's strange is that I didn't think there was anything seriously wrong with the saki. But stress in itself can take its toll on a saki. I thought, 'Well, it never tried to bite me. It nursed.' But the cards were stacked against it, I guess. Sakis are so sensitive. And I'd never before been given an animal whose mother had died. Maybe that meant something, too."

She sipped her Coke. Two other keepers entered the room and stood nearby, listening.

"You know, one minute an animal can be hanging on the

bars. Then, it slips down. Half an hour later, it's dead," she sighed wistfully.

The others nodded.

Then all three went back to work.

FIRST PERSON: PAM DUNN

As far back as I can remember, I've always had an affinity for animals. Even before I had anything to do with the zoo, I had a lot of exotic pets. I was seven or eight years old when my father brought home rabbits for me, and ducks. I had reptiles, mainly turtles, the little dime-store turtles.

We lived in a place where they wouldn't allow dogs or cats. I was about nine years old, and I used to devour *Dog World* magazine. My parents were tolerant, and I kept begging and begging for a dog, so finally they said they'd ask the landlord if I couldn't have some sort of small innocuous dog. The landlord said no. They came back to me, and they couldn't just say the landlord was a jerk, so they said the landlord said that we couldn't have a dog because dogs bark, and they would disturb the neighbors. So I ran into my bedroom and came out with this article on basenjis, which are barkless dogs. My parents were just floored; they didn't know what to do. I sort of trapped them. They came up with some other reason why I couldn't have a dog. But we finally did move to a place where the landlady had two dogs, and I thought I'd died and gone to heaven. And that's when it really started, the animals started pouring in, and that was about the time when I began seriously exploring trying to become a volunteer at the zoo. I went there all the time.

In high school I was a good student, and I was quiet and did my work, and that didn't fit in with the basic high school party scene. By that time, I was a sophomore in high school. From that moment on, I really didn't involve myself in high school things at all; all my spare time, weekends, and during the summer, five to six days a week I was at the zoo as a volunteer.

At that point, I didn't have any interest in specific types of animals. I liked everything. I started working with the reptiles. I always tried to stay with the things that weren't real popular—reptiles and birds of prey. Then I was allowed to graduate to handling the monkeys.

At the University of Illinois, I majored in anthropology, and I was able to specialize in primates. I encountered a wonderful professor there, Dr. Reed, who encouraged me. He's still in my mind. His expectations of everyone were high, and as he got to know me more, his expectations of me got even higher. Through him I was able to realize a lot of my own potential and get a direction, and the primate thing just began to evolve. In the children's zoo, I was able to handle the monkeys. I let everything else fall to the wayside, and I spent most of my time with the monkeys.

I wanted to be a keeper at a zoo before I even went into college, though when I started at the zoo there were no women keepers. If you were female and you were an employee, you were called a zoo leader, not a keeper. I was still in college when it changed. I was beginning to get my career aspirations together once that area did open up and I could become a zoo keeper. On the test I came in number six out of over four hundred people.

I started on January 3, 1978, and it was cold and snowy, miserable, and I didn't drive at that point, so I had to take the bus, and I wanted to be prompt, because my first thing was an interview with Dr. Fisher. I had the job, but I didn't know where I was going to be working, what building, anything. I walked out, and on my way to the bus stop, I slipped on some ice and fell. I had knit slacks on, and I tore a big gaping hole. I was bleeding, but I couldn't go back and change because I was afraid I would be late. So I sat there through the whole interview with my hand over my knee trying to cover this big hole in my pants, the blood dry. It was terrible, but he sat me down and basically told me that I would be going to the primate house.

They knew my background in primates, that it was very heavy. I also had a lot of years in the children's zoo. I could have easily ended up there, and it would have been just as valid. I didn't want the children's zoo through; I was hoping that I'd get the primate house, but back then I was not the type of person who would toot my own horn and speak up. I remember Dr. Fisher stressing the safety aspects, giving me tips on how not to get killed.

So I had to deal with Sinbad, a big male gorilla, who could be nasty. I was the new person, low man on the totem pole, and all of a sudden one day I'm walking down the back run, and things start flying out of his cage. He was throwing everything, feces, food. At me, definitely. He hit me in the leg, and I said, "Oh, my God." He had this huge tractor tire that it took several people to lift if you needed to move it. It was about four feet tall, just immense. And he would take this thing, and I'd be walking down the run, and I could see him out of the corner of my eye, and he would swing it backhand into the back bars of the cage. He wanted to elicit some kind of reaction from me. He didn't care if you screamed at him; if you jumped, all the better. The more you reacted, the better he liked it. Even though it couldn't hit me, it's very hard to not react when you see a tractor tire flying at your head. I got put on that run almost right away. And I'd be cleaning the gutter, sweeping, and inevitably you have to avert your eyes. And as soon as I'd look away, something would come flying and hitting me. I went home and thought, "This animal's going to torment me forever. He's going to live forever, and his whole purpose will be to make my life miserable." Everybody else went through this with him. Some people he never let up on. The senior keeper said, "Just think of him as an old bozo with nothing better to do than to give you a bad time, and just ignore him. He'll get tired of it." So I did, and he did let up on me finally. And then we were able to develop what became a seven-year very good relationship.

I have been singled out in a positive sense, and I have been singled out in a very negative sense. In a positive sense, we had a spider monkey named Sam that I started working with in the children's zoo, and when he got older, he was sent out on breeding loan to another zoo. He was gone for several years, and I never thought I'd see him again, because rarely when you send an animal out does he come back again. This was when I was still in the children's zoo, and one day I was going outside, and they had a huge cage that went up several stories. We'd have spider monkeys, capuchins, and woolly monkeys in there, sort of a mixed group. I was heading out the back door and was a considerable distance away when I saw this black spider monkey hanging on the bars with his arms outstretched, squealing and squealing. I had no idea that Sam had come back.

It sort of reminded me of one of these movies where you see the two people running toward each other. You could almost hear the music. I realized it was Sam, and he came flying down the cage, and I came running across to him, and through the bars we just had this intensive greeting. I knew it was him, once I saw the face, I knew; there was no doubt in my mind it was him. And he had remembered me after two years of separation. Eventually, he graduated to the monkey house, and I stayed in the children's zoo. When I came to the monkey house, there he was, and it was like old home week all over again.

There are cases of bad rapport. We had a marmoset colony in the basement of the monkey house. We had a few animals who were nursery-raised, and you always have a problem with a nursery-raised animal, or any kind of hand-raised animal. They lose that little edge of fear that keeps them from attacking you. I've heard that even lion tamers prefer to work with a totally wild cat than one that's hand-raised, because that little edge is to your advantage. They may hesitate. Marmosets are small animals, but they have the potential to be very aggressive. We had these animals down there that had come from the nursery, and they became so aggressive toward us that it was almost impossible to work around them. You had to wear leather gloves, because even if they couldn't get to you to bite you, they have claws, little squirrel-type claws. So if they get your finger, they can really scratch you up. They reach through the bars, and you're trying to take the water bottle off the front, and they're going after you like crazy. Trying to take the food plate in and out, you'd be wearing your heavy leather gloves, you'd reach in, and they would just grab on. There were two of them, and you could hardly get them off. And the whole time they were just biting and biting and biting.

They alienated one person at a time. One guy bit four different keepers. And sometimes he'd get out and come after you. They're so fast that it's very hard for a human reflex to counteract that.

Marmosets are high-strung animals. They're more sensitive animals, more easily spooked. Some types of marmosets and tamarins seem to be more aggressive. There's one called a red-bellied tamarin, which seems to be exceedingly aggressive, and if you have to go in to a cage to separate out one individual, you go in looking like a snowman. I mean you have your heavy coat on, you have a hat, because the whole family is going to come after you.

Among the primates, there are different personalities. It's very hard to get an accurate measurement on gorillas because they are more introverted. I saw Sinbad over the years do some absolutely amazing things. He was known to be a thrower, so you would not allow him to have things like rocks or sticks. You had to be very selective about the play objects you gave him. So he'd go outside, in his outside cage, and invariably he'd find rocks, little stones, whatever. He'd bring them back in, and I'd be working in the kitchen, and pretty soon I'd hear this tap, tap, tap, tap. And I knew he'd gotten something. So I would go and look, and he'd show me blatantly that he'd gotten this stone. He had been taught early on to trade things. If he had something he wasn't supposed to, he learned that if he'd give it to you, you'd give him some nice treat. So I would go and get a bunch of grapes or a couple of bananas. And he'd hand me this rock. I wouldn't even have to say anything. And you had to be fair, you couldn't say, "Ah ha, you stupid animal, you gave me the rock." You had to give the treat to him;

otherwise you'd blow the whole deal. So I'd go back, and five, six minutes, later, tap, tap, tap. It turned out he had a whole pile, but he was only revealing them one at a time.

Finally I caught on. I came in and had a nice big bunch of grapes. He threw out one rock, and I said, "No, I want them all this time." He was going to snooker me out of everything I had, and we were always trying to keep him on a diet. I would talk to him just like I'd talk to a person. Not that he understood, I have no illusions that he understood everything, but he got the point. Eventually, all of a sudden, he took the back of his hand, his enormous hand, and just shoved everything out, because he knew that this was it, that I was on to his game and he had had his fun with me.

The chimps are probably, up along with the baboons, the most dangerous animals in the building. They're intelligent. They have a lot of time to sit and figure out ways of getting at the keepers, if they want to. The male chimp is very volatile. It doesn't take much to set him off, and when male chimps go into a frenzy, they are not in control. He's not a bad animal, he's not a mean animal, but when he goes into these temper tantrums, he is not in control and becomes very dangerous until it blows over. Sometimes you can almost literally see him just sit down and get it back together again.

Patsy the female chimp, on the other hand, is more of a sneak. She sets you up; she will offer you things. There's no way to interpret it but offering. She's got something in her hand, and she's holding it out through the bars and waving it at you. If you take it, she will grab your arm. I've never tried to accept the offering, but if you do, what she will do is hold on. If a chimp gets a hold of you, unless it wants to let go, you're stuck. Chimps could break your arm if they wanted to.

The hamadryas baboons, which I worked with, were probably the most volatile animals I've ever been around. I'd rank them above the chimps in terms of being dangerous to work with on a daily basis. By the way, every animal has an inventory number in this zoo. It's an identity; its medical files will have that number, it has a computer sheet. But when you're working in the building daily, giving an animal a name gives it an identity. If the animal has an identity, you're much more likely to be more keenly aware of that animal and what it's doing. And that makes you better able to determine if there is something wrong. When you're dealing with a hundred animals or more at a time, that becomes crucial.

The Celebes are a species of macaque: they're called Celebes apes, but they're not really apes. They're intelligent, they have a bright-looking face, but they are macaques, they're in the same group with the lion tails and the rhesus monkeys. Celebes are a lot of fun to work with. They're a challenge. They are very destructive, so trying to hang rope in the cage becomes the challenge of a lifetime. You can spend two hours in there tying knots that you think no one will get undone, and, sure enough, you come in twenty minutes later, everything's lying on the floor. They're very inquisitive, very aware of their surroundings, very aware of the public, more so than a lot of the other primates. They react. I see them respond to different people. They make a lot of face gestures, and they do lip smacking, which is a greeting.

They're active, but in a different sense than the squirrel monkeys. Squirrel monkeys seem to be running around aimlessly all the time. The Celebes are deliberate. They're always reaching out to check the locks to make sure you've locked them and trying to find some kind of loose screw.

The lemurs are right up there as one of my favorite animals. When I first started, I thought that my interest was going to be the great apes. Now, as much as I enjoy the great apes, it's the prosimians and the small monkeys like the marmosets that fascinate me, because the diversity is unbelievable. On the one hand, the lemurs are not very bright, so it's not a tremendously challenging, stimulating thing to work with them. But they're fascinating because they're catlike.

We have a lot of lion-tailed macaques. Lion-tails are terribly endangered. I mean, you're dealing with a very fragile captive population that is going to, at some point, be reintroduced to the wild. They've started with the golden lion tamarins, they've started putting those back in, and the lion-tails are one of the animals that are targeted for it. They come from India; the government's been working very hard to stabilize certain areas, to protect them. I was fortunate enough to attend both lion-tailed macaque symposiums, where scientists from all over the world and people from the Indian government, people from zoos, had gathered to talk about strategies for the management in captivity and in the wild.

The premise is that until an area can be stabilized, the best thing that a zoo can do is manage the captive population as best as it can, in terms of developing good blood lines, not in-breeding, trying to retain as much of the natural behavior as possible. Golden lion tamarins were probably the first primate that was reintroduced.

Our role has changed so much over the years. Just the term *keeper* in my mind applies to something from a bygone era. Where you're keeping, you're maintaining. Now it's become sort of a progressive thing where you've gone beyond just maintaining animals and trying to keep them healthy. You're actually working toward long-range plans, and there's a certain amount of decision making and input. Now it's beyond just coming in eight to five and cleaning cages, putting food out. That always will be part of my job, and I want it to be. That's all part of the continuing contact with the animals. If you lose that, you begin to lose your roots.

With zoos in general, there's so much going on that is vital. I want to continue working on a daily basis with the individual animals, but it's become such a critical thing now, with the way the environment is being so poorly managed, you get so frustrated. I belong to a lot of environmental organizations, and aside from sending in my twenty-dollar membership and writing letters, my level of frustration rises tremendously. I often feel that maybe there's more that I could do, in a positive sense, than what I'm doing now. But I wouldn't feel bad staying a keeper for the rest of my life; that wouldn't bother me.

These days, I have animals at work and at home. Pat Sass had just finished raising six tamarins at home all at one time, a tremendous amount of work, and something came along and she needed help. She asked me to help her, and that's how I started.

It's probably the most incredible learning experience I've ever had. Each animal is an individual; each has its own behavioral peculiarities. But it's also a tremendous amount of work. A lot of people say, "Well, it's just like having a kid," but if a woman has a baby, she has certain hormonal instincts that link her to the baby. The job has invaded my home. Before I got married, my husband became aware of what my life is like and that this is the way it is.

The first baby that I raised was a cotton top tamarin and is now a father; in fact, his daughter is here at the zoo. It was like the line is going to go on. But it is a trade-off. I don't want to minimize that fact. It does affect your social life. For example, we were invited to a party last Saturday, and we went but could only stay for two hours, because I had to get back. And the people that I'm friends with have come to accept this. I try to snatch a vacation between babies. Where do I go? Sometimes to other zoos. I've been to many of them.

San Diego impressed me. It's a very large facility. To me, the most impressive thing is the plants. They've done a lot of research work there, they've pioneered a lot of stuff at San Diego. It's probably the premier facility in America.

I was very impressed with the Gladys Porter Zoo in Brownsville, Texas. It's a beautiful facility. They have a lot of little lakes, so they've utilized this area to make a lot of little islands. It's a small zoo with a very nice collection. I saw some tamarins there that I'd never seen before in captivity.

Minnesota State Zoo, outside of Minneapolis is a brand-new state-run facility. They have a beautiful native American animal collection. They have other stuff, too, but it's very impressive what they've done with their North American animals. It's an impressive place to visit.

It's not just the big facilities that are impressive. We went on a tour through the Smokies and found a small zoo that I had never heard of, didn't know existed, a small private zoo called Soco Gardens, in Maggie Valley, North Carolina. This place was marvelous. The keepers were top-notch, enthusiastic. It was the most immaculate place I've ever seen.

Seeing other zoos gives me perspective. It makes it possible for me to evaluate the Lincoln Park Zoo. It's a place that has a tremendous amount of history. It's a place that has been looking forward for a long time now. I've been here long enough to see so much of the renovation and the changes and remember what it was. It used to be a classical menagerie; in the monkey house, you can see the cages were designed to exhibit as many different species in pairs as possible. That whole philosophy has changed. We have our shortcomings in that we're land-restricted, so we have to make some hard decisions about what we're going to keep. I keep saying that I want a Madagascar building, full of as many different kinds of lemurs as we can get our hands on. But the realities are that that won't happen unless I win the lottery. We are still locked in with old buildings, still living with the past, until it's all renovated, updated.

The role of the keeper is changing almost daily. There are more responsibilities, which is good. Responsibility implies competency and trust. We've changed over the years from an all-male staff of keepers and curators to a tremendously large percentage of women. Right now, in many areas, we are world-class. As long as we stay a free zoo and we're in the city environment, we are going to continue to draw tremendous numbers of people. You're going to see more and more educational programs, another thing keepers are participating in.

Sometimes I thank God for feminism. I do. I think women have a very significant role. We're proving it daily. I'm not a rabid feminist. I don't march in protests or anything like that, but I think it would have been a very sad thing indeed if the old stereotypes, that women can't do this and can't do that in terms of zookeeping, hadn't been eradicated. There were people in the field who felt that women should not work with the great apes because when women had menstruation that would agitate the social structure; the males would get bent out of shape. There was no truth to that. Not that any of us had ever known. There were all kinds of reasons why women shouldn't be keepers, and they've all become irrelevant. We've arrived.

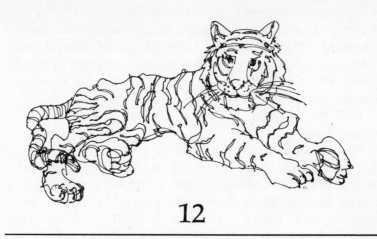

12

The Lions' Den

Many animal keepers developed an infatuation for animals at an early age. Jim Campbell was not one of them. For him, being a lion keeper was a job. He had hoped to be an architect, but that didn't work out. Once he became a keeper instead, he chose to pursue matters of art and philosophy in his own time.

Jim was born in Deerfield, Illinois, in 1945, but his family moved to southern Texas when he was four. He grew up in Texas, then headed west. In 1964, he found himself at the University of California in Berkeley, then the most incendiary campus in the country. It was, as he put it, "during the free-speech movement, as the riots were called." But Jim was neither militant nor scholar.

He flunked out of Berkeley and was drafted into the navy, to serve in "the South China Sea," where he saw some combat.

"It was not active combat," he recalled. "The enemy didn't have a navy to speak of."

After that tour of duty in Vietnam, he returned to

California, where he studied architecture—still in pursuit of an undergraduate degree. After a stint at San Francisco State, he dropped out and went back to southern Texas, where he "scratched around, took more courses." He got a job at a zoo in Brownsville, Texas, but the job didn't pay much, and he got weary of small-town life.

In 1973, he went north to Chicago; he had a brother living there.

"It was a congenial place," he remembered, "and it was better than the West Coast. More important, there were jobs in Chicago. I wanted to study architecture, but not in an academic setting. I wanted to be an apprentice at an architectural firm. I talked to several of them. They weren't interested.

"Then I heard about a test being given for a keeper's job at the zoo, so I signed up."

He got the job, in 1976, and has kept it ever since, serving in the lion house. Over the years, he continued to take courses at various colleges, studied at the C. G. Jung Institute of Chicago, and got his master's in general studies at Roosevelt University. (He passed a test that conceded his bachelor's degree level.)

His master's thesis was on alcoholism.

"I knew about it," he said. "I wanted to know more."

In 1987, he enrolled in the University of Chicago's returning scholar program, as a student in the divinity school, studying "the ethical dimension of alcoholism."

"I don't like to be a regular student," he said. "I'm not a twenty-four-hour-a-day scholar."

He lived in a house he bought a few years ago, a short drive from the zoo. (In good weather, he used his bicycle.) He shared the house with a couple of cats.

Jim resembled an Old Testament prophet. He was tall (6'1") and solidly built (180 pounds). He had a full salt-and-pepper beard and thick brown hair. He wore gold-rimmed granny glasses. He spoke carefully; he rarely slurred a word. His conversation could be simple and direct or turn complex and learned, according to his mood. In matters that related to the welfare of the keepers, he was an activist and had been a spokesman for workers' rights at the zoo.

His day began at 8 A.M., at the lion house, an old dilapidated building scheduled for renovation. In the immense hall, one row of cages faced two glassed-in habitats and the kitchen across the wide tiled floor. Outside, cages lined one side of the building; two habitats—one for lions, one for tigers—bordered the other side.

On one cool summer morning, he arrived, changed into his keeper garb, and strolled past Princess, a lioness being kept in an indoor habitat.

"Hey, old Princess," he called out. He reached between the bars on a door that permitted keepers to enter the habitat, and he patted her nose.

"She's a friendly cat. Nursery-raised," he pointed out. She was twelve years old and had spent her life at the zoo.

Jim knew each animal in the lion house, in biographical detail. The collection included:

- A pair of Bengal tigers, Erica and Denise, sisters, both born at the zoo ten years ago, hand-raised.
- Ajax, a massive Siberian tiger, a male, the largest cat in the lion house.
- An Afghanistan leopard, a young female named Nouri, caught in the wild.
- Two jaguars, both born at the zoo: Jan, a female, and Junior, a male, both ten years old.
- A female black leopard named Lisa; she was between fourteen and fifteen years old. Satan, a sickly male, had been euthanized earlier in the summer.
- Five lions in the larger pride: Bernard, the male, and four females: Sister, Princess, Sheila, and Shelley. The first two were sisters; the last two also were sisters (Sister was their mother).
- In a smaller pride were Anthony, a seventeen-year-old male, and Chandra, a fifteen-year-old female.

Jim made distinctions among the big cats: leopards tend

to be solitary animals, except at breeding time. So are tigers. Lions live in prides, in families; that group atmosphere is gentle, except when the dominant male chooses to make a macho point. Tigers are excellent swimmers. A tiger will kill after a short leap or a quick chase; long pursuits are not its strong suit. The lion is the only cat that can truly roar as it does. And there is no satisfactory evidence to explain whey they do. Two theories await confirmation: roaring is simply a display of exuberance, no more than that, or it is a sound informing the "ownership" of a territory. A leopard's spots are not the same as a jaguar's; a little study reveals the difference. The leopard's are plain rosettes; the jaguar's rosettes have a center spot. The two spotted cats look alike, but the jaguar is larger, with a shorter tail.

Jim had absorbed the hundreds of details that defined the creatures in his care. He did not flaunt that knowledge. Occasionally, he was prepared to be judgmental, however: "Tigers. Leopards. Jaguars. Lions. That's the sequence, going from the most complicated animals on down to the less complicated."

Jim began his day with a stroll through the lion house basement, a dark, dirty, depressing retreat. He snapped on a light switch, and when he did, he illuminated a row of cages and awakened an assortment of owl monkeys in them. The monkeys froze and glared at him with their enormous eyes.

"They breed prolifically," he said, "but they get nervous when they're on display." The monkeys were kept in the lion house basement—there was no room for them elsewhere in the zoo—so assistant director Dennis Meritt could study them; he'd done research on them for years. In a nearby room, there were a number of South American rodents (pacas, pacaranas, and agoutis) of varying sizes, also of interest to Meritt. There were anteaters, armadillos, and sloths as well. Some were there to breed; others were awaiting shipment to other zoos. All of the animals in the basement were cared for by the lion house keepers. If one of them wanted solitude, it did not find any in the basement, where the mingling of odors and sounds was perpetual.

Jim's first chore of the day was to hose down the cages inside the building. As he did, the leopards, the jaguars, and the Siberian tiger all got out of the way.

"They don't like water," Jim pointed out. "Without stressing them or hurting them, we can direct them with a hose if we have to."

He turned around and looked at the inside habitat occupied by the lions, Anthony and Chandra. They were not allowed to join the larger pride outside; the two prides would do battle. So Anthony and Chandra were kept indoors, in a warm exhibit that kept them sluggish, except for those rare times when the larger pride was taken inside, and they were allowed to roam outdoors.

"Discomfort on exhibit," Jim called the arrangement.

He turned pensive as he considered what he had said.

"I'm not in charge here. The senior keeper and the curator make the decisions. I don't always agree, and I don't always have any influence."

When he was done hosing the cages, he retrieved the food that had been delivered for the big cats. In the distance, Ajax, the Siberian tiger, growled.

"Show-off," Jim mumbled.

He carted the food—horsemeat for the cats, and apples, bananas, celery, carrots, and grapes for the monkeys and the rodents—from the main floor entrance to the kitchen.

"Clean up and feed 'em," he chanted, with a faintly mocking tone.

In the kitchen, he kneaded the horsemeat, mixed it with a nutritionally balanced feline food, and put it in buckets. Each cat got fed once a day, from two and a half to ten pounds of meat. (The Siberian tiger could eat more than that, easily, and occasionally was given more than the allotment.) Finicky eaters might get a small supplement later in the day. Twice a week, the cats got bones to gnaw on, actually horse knuckles.

"Their diet used to be more complex," Jim said. "Chicken, liver, kidneys. They liked it, and it was good for them. But it was simplified three years ago. I had very little to say in it, except for the brand of food to buy.

"They were afraid of salmonella in the chickens. What the cats get instead isn't very chewy or very tasty. But they do seem to like the bones."

The offering of food was the device used to lure the lions inside from their outdoor habitat, to clean it or retrieve a lion that had fallen into the moat. When that happened, the lions above were lured inside, so another lion wouldn't be tempted to jump into the moat, and the stranded lion below was then coaxed in as well.

"Actually, they get a little lonely down there and want to know where the others are," Jim said.

At 9:20 A.M., he released Anthony and Chandra from their indoor exhibit into cages in the isolation area—it required a knowledge of the complex of tunnels and interlocking cages in the building—where he fed them, tossing the meat mixture through a narrow opening in the bars.

Chandra slopped it across the floor, trying to chew it.

"She doesn't have many teeth," Jim noted.

Anthony did better, crouching in front of the meat and licking the mound with his tongue, directing it into his mouth. While they ate, Jim hosed down their habitat. A mouse scurried away from the stream of water. Occasionally, a stray mouse had a confrontation with a lion; the lions played with mice, stomped them, but rarely killed them. Outdoors, the lions preferred pigeons, who underestimated the lions' speed of movement.

In the second indoor habitat, Princess sat at the door and peered through the bars at Jim, working in the other habitat. He spotted her looking at him.

"She's in heat, so we brought her inside to give her a chance to eat without interference from Bernard. He wouldn't permit her to go in to eat. He wouldn't let her go anywhere. Just separating them gives her a chance to eat," he said.

Princess sat in front of a pile of yesterday's food, turned rancid overnight; Jim washed it away. She was among his favorite cats, one of those who might tempt him to extend his friendship. But he wouldn't enter her habitat when she was in it.

"I don't think I'd ever play with her," he said. "I mean, really go in and play with her. She's too strong for me. Even if she were friendly, she'd be too strong a friend."

Princess was sitting against the barred door, with the tip of her nose poking through the bars. Her eyes were on Jim.

"She's waiting for something to happen. Maybe she wants to go back outside with the others. She knows that something will happen, but she doesn't know when."

He enticed her out of the habitat, into a cage area between the indoor and outdoor habitats, by calling her name and clapping. He wanted to clean her habitat; she could exit to the outdoors through a door he opened with a lever.

"You want to get their attention, but you don't want to frighten them. They get used to people's voices, what you might call the form of address. Sometimes, I even make lion noises," he said.

In the main hall, several sparrows raced and chirped in the rafters. It was 10 A.M., and the visitors had begun to arrive in numbers. The young woman who ran the lion house gift shop was counting her money before opening for the day. Outside, the lions and the tigers demonstrated one of their differences. There was a pool of water in each habitat; the lions drank the water in theirs, the tigers bathed in theirs.

For Jim, it was time to clean the outdoor cages.

While hosing down the Siberian tiger's cage, Jim heard a voice behind him. A man was leaning on the rail.

"That's a beautiful tiger," the man said to Jim.

"I have to agree with you," Jim responded.

As Jim moved down the row of cages, the animals retreated, hid, peeked at him, went indoors, as he turned the hose on their cages. Lisa, the leopard, moved her sleek black frame toward the back of the cage. When Jim finished washing it, she moved forward, sat down, and licked the wet floor.

A pair of German tourists paused, then the husband took a photo of the leopard. Lisa opened her mouth without growling; instead, she hissed.

"She's just vaguely bothered," Jim said. "If she were pushed enough, she'd growl."

At his feet, Jim discovered a penny someone had tossed at one of the cats. He picked it up and put it in his pocket. The keepers kept a collection of found coins, and with the money they bought catnip, which delighted the big cats as much as it did house cats.

The day moved along, as Jim's rituals filled the time. He finished all of the cleaning. He opened a door to entice the lions in from outside to feed them. They entered slowly, at their own pace, on their own initiative. Bernard, the male of the pride, was first, and he was hungry. He ate noisily, rapidly, and thoroughly, then relaxed and growled. In the next cage, Sheila nibbled her meat in a more delicate way, slowly. Finally, when all the lions had come in and were secured in their cages, Jim went out to clean the outdoor habitat. He washed the window that enabled the public to get a close-up view of the lions, picked up the gnawed horse bones, and collected feces from those areas the lions had designated for it. They were as determined to mark their territory in captivity as they were in the wild.

When he came in, Jim let the lions line up in the caged runway, then he opened the gate and they raced into the sunlight.

He could hear Anthony banging on the door from his indoor habitat to that runway; he knew where it led.

"He wants to get out there, to be with the females in that pride. Not a chance. Bernard would fight him. And both might lose," Jim said.

Day after day, Jim did much of his work in silence. It was either a kind of channeled brooding or a practiced introspection or a combination of the two. He rarely volunteered to speak, unless he spotted another keeper he knew and liked. When spoken to, he responded with measured replies, editing his own speech before he issued it.

Another keeper stopped him in the main hall, to ask about the death of Satan, the male black leopard who had been euthanized.

"Impaired kidney function," Jim told him. "He wasn't eating, and when he did eat, the kidneys couldn't process it. We were going to ship him out, but we had to alter that plan. We didn't want to send out a crate with a dead animal in it. It was better for him to die here."

The other keeper asked about Satan's age.

"He'd been here longer than I have," Jim said. "Everything that happened before I got here is ancient history."

When his day's cleaning chores were done, Jim went to the basement; he passed a sign that read "Have You Checked Your Locks?" In working with the big cats, safety was a factor always.

"You can make a mistake with an animal you've known well, an animal you think will be friendly," he said. "Beware. They may make a move on you. Especially males," he added. "Animals behave according to their moods, and you can never entirely predict those moods.

"Anthony does what I tell him to do, which is unusual. That's why I think he's one of the smartest. Most of the others don't do what I tell them to do. Some females respond because it's what they want to do, not because it's what I want them to do.

"Anthony wasn't hand-raised, so he doesn't like to be petted. Nevertheless, he responds. Go here. Go there. Stop doing that. He does. When Bernard gets an idea, it's *there*. You can't do anything to stop him except turn the hose on him. Most cats are like that. You can't make them go through an open door.

"Being a keeper is knowing what to do, knowing the routine as well as the animals do. But when they're excited, be careful. There's a lot of control involved in keeper work. I used to get mad when an animal didn't respond. So self-control on my part matters, too. Sometimes I spend two or three hours getting an animal out of a cage. Wait. Go away. Come back. Use the hose.

"At times, there's a reason why the animal won't do what you want it to do. If a male is behaving peculiarly, females won't enter the space that he's in, so you have to isolate him from them. A cat will skip a meal without a qualm if something else strikes it as more important. Sister won't come in to eat if Bernard is roaring.

"The Bengal tigers—at least our pair—were afraid of the dark. They wouldn't come in from outside into that dark back space, unless the lights were on. Finally, we left the door open between outdoors and indoors, so they could explore that space. After that, the darkness didn't matter to them.

"Tigers are more sensitive. They react to smaller things. Noises, subtle changes in the environment. What's normal in a tiger is neurotic in a lion. A lion may notice something, but it won't be upset by it. Not by what would upset a tiger.

"You can't read them by their faces very well either. Most animals have blank stares. Some lions seem to stare right through you, to the horizon. When they're not staring, they're probably sleeping. Cats sleep a lot, which makes it easier for them to be in captivity. Another factor is that most of the cats get used to a routine.

"We once had a leopard who couldn't adjust. She hid between the light fixture and the ceiling in her cage. All you could see was the tip of her tail. She couldn't tolerate people, so she tried to hide from them. She didn't want to be in a cage. We tried her in an outdoor cage. She wedged herself between the downspout and the wall, facing away from the public. You can't reeducate them once that attitude is fixed. A cat that appears mildly neurotic can get better, but that one never did. We sent it to another zoo."

Some of the keepers were upset about the lion that had fallen into the moat. One of them urged opposition to the zoo practice of walking elephants and camels around the zoo. When the cats spotted those large mammals, they grew excited. No one was certain about the link between the walking animals and the confined cats, but the theory persisted in the keeper circle.

Jim Campbell took the theory very seriously.

"That must be a twelve- or fifteen-foot drop," he said. "I've never actually measured it. Once two male cubs pushed their father, Bernard, into the moat. He cracked a tooth, a canine, but otherwise he was OK. Still is.

"Sometimes they just jump in or they fall in while they're chasing pigeons or they just get too close to the edge and slip in. Sure, it's possible that they can be agitated by seeing another animal walked by. The camel does resemble a lion's prey, but the elephant is too large to be prey.

"We had a female lion who fell in after the elephant walked by, but she was an aggressive one, and she might just be bold enough to attack an elephant in the wild. It's not common, but it happens.

"Of course, I remember when the lions used to get worked up when they saw a toy horse pulling a kid's cart. I've even seen them look out there, spot a child, and stalk it."

The days passed, the summer began to fade, relieving the heaviness of the air in the non-air-conditioned lion house. Jim did his job, cleaning, feeding, studying the behavior of the cats.

Late one afternoon, Sister, the female lion, was indoors. Jim approached her cage. Sister turned her massive head toward him; she looked directly at him. She moved close to the bars of the cage and turned her profile to him. He scratched her nose, her ears, her neck as she pressed against the bars, obviously permitting him to give her pleasure.

If she had purred—and lions do not purr—her behavior would have matched that of a house cat with its beloved master.

But the bars were between them, and the similarity, Jim knew, ended there.

FIRST PERSON: JIM CAMPBELL

When I was about four years old, I had an Easter bunny, a

small Easter bunny, a live Easter bunny. I remember looking at it very intently, trying to figure out what was going
on in the Easter bunny's mind. I decided that there was
absolutely nothing going on in the Easter bunny's mind.
And that was my earliest contact with animals. It bothered
me that there was nothing going on in the Easter bunny's
mind. I guess I thought it was a person because people were
treating it like a person. But it wasn't; if I had a tendency to
anthropomorphize, I was disillusioned at a rather early age.

The rootlessness of my childhood was mostly due to my
family's moving a lot. It was usually for economic reasons. I
always thought we were going to better ourselves econom-
ically somehow by making a move. Usually, it didn't work
out that way. So we'd make another one. I didn't feel
particularly rooted in the place that I grew up, which is
southern Texas. I didn't really feel like I belonged there, but
I didn't know where else I belonged. And when I got into
my college years, I think that became part of my quest for
roots, for a sort of self-identity that I didn't feel that I had.
That's probably the reason why—when I didn't do well in
school and discovered I wasn't suited to be a full-time
academic because there was too much competition for
me—I began looking for myself in other ways. Mostly
introspective ways.

About the time that I resigned from the University of
Texas, I started a course of reading on my own. I decided I
would educate myself. At the time I was a very withdrawn
and isolated person. And I knew that that was not normal.
So I spent a lot of time trying to figure out why I wasn't
normal and if it was worthwhile to become normal. I think
I've come to some of the answers, but not all of them. I'm
still searching. I don't think that I'm a career zoo keeper; I
don't think that this is my niche in life.

The military years were a turning point for me. They
provided me with a number of things I had not really
acquired when I was growing up: A sense of the limited
nature of authority or power, of discipline. That there was
a limit to how much I had to do in order to meet the

standards. Before that, I'd always been a perfectionist. The navy taught me simply that there was an objective standard that wasn't one hundred percent, maybe it was only eighty percent. You had to shine your shoes so well to pass inspection, but you didn't have to shine them perfectly.

We were an offshore bombardment unit; we went in and shot at bridges and various troop emplacements on the shore. And we rarely saw anybody, any ships or any enemy troops. I think we were fired at once or twice, from the shore, and we got hit by a shore unit, but it was very minor. We saw that we were engaged in a futile task. There was no way to win that war.

When I got out of active duty after two years, I tried going back to school in California and discovered that it was much more amenable to my temperament to take night courses. And also financially necessary, since I had to find some sort of an income in the daytime. That's when I went back to Texas. I needed to retrace where I'd been and see what that still meant to me and see if there were missed opportunities there that I could pick up on. So I went back.

When I was in California, there was a dog running across the freeway one day, and I managed to clip him, and I was never able to find the dog to find out whether or not I had injured him or whether he'd gotten away or whatever happened. I felt sort of guilty about that for years. And when that would come to my mind, I would think about the fact that I didn't really know anything much about animals at all.

The zoo that was opening in Brownsville was offering a training course for docents; they certified these people to take school groups around and give guided tours. I was working in construction at the time. I finished the course and was certified, about that same time the construction job ended, I didn't have any work, and the zoo was hiring. When I found out they were actually only paying minimum wage, not really enough for me to buy gasoline for my car, then I knew that it was a short-term engagement. But I decided to stay on for the year, get some experience, and at least take that with me when I went where I was going, which by that time I'd pretty much decided would be where I was born, which was the Chicago area. I wanted to go into architecture, but that was frustrating. Then I got the zoo job.

If there's a conflict regarding the management of an animal or a personality conflict here at work, I'll tend to brood about it until I figure out what to do about it. Occasionally, I even dream about the animals. The last dream I had I was in a pickup truck with Bernard the lion, and we were going someplace, and I was saying, "Isn't this a nice treat?" He wasn't talking much, but he seemed to be enjoying it. Other dreams have involved escape routines, where the animals would be out, and I'd have to come and put them back in their cages. I've usually managed to get them back where they're supposed to be. I've never had a dream about being injured by an animal.

There are lots of different dimensions to this type of work. I think you need a basic sensitivity and a willingness to see what the animal is telling you. The animal will usually tell you things through its behavior, which may or may not conform to your ideas about what that animal is like or what that animal is doing or wants to do. I've seen cases in which cats, even cats that are not normally friendly, will come down, approach the front of the cage or the keeper areas, when they are ill. It's not part of their normal routine. They will come down and start hanging around close to the keepers. If the area's inadequate for the animal, the animals begin to show unusual and abnormal behaviors, which may or may not be harmful to the animal. Stereotypically, these behaviors are sometimes called excessive pacing, doing strange things that they wouldn't normally do, hiding in corners all the time.

A cat should have a variety of places to go. If the presence of the public or the routine cleaning procedures didn't adversely affect the cat, and if the cat obviously had and used the various things in its enclosure for climbing, scratching, sleeping, I think that then the cat would probably be well adjusted. Zoos can help animals adjust to confinement.

Zoos can achieve that—and more. Zoos may carry a message to people, that if you like this animal that you see in the zoo and you want to see it continue to exist and flourish, then you'd better get out there and do something to save its habitat, because in the long run, without the habitat, the animal disappears.

Some keepers resist that. They pretend that this animal is like a person, is like a friend. Now, to a certain extent I think it's inevitable. I talk to my animals. I make up little nicknames for them. But I try to leave it here at work. I don't take it home. I don't put pictures of my animals on my wall; I don't regard them as the focus of my life. I think that's a danger. We can develop those sorts of relationships with animals, and they're not healthy emotionally because they interfere with the normal life outside and away from the zoo.

This profession will attract people who have the susceptibility, an emotional void in their lives which they have found that animals can fill. I think it also tends to attract people who have a penchant for collecting things, who like to control, label, classify, keep things in their place. That can be very valuable to a keeper if it means that you double-check your locks every day. People who have a lot of emotional contact with animals, a lot of emotional concern about animals, can use that in a constructive way by being very receptive to the state and condition of an animal, because they can pick up very easily on when an animal is feeling depressed or sick. Point it out to a veterinarian, and maybe something can be done about it.

On the other hand, you can become very callous as a keeper; you can become very controlling and domineering. You can become wrapped up in an illusionistic world, about the animals. And that tends to create a lot of problems. Everybody is supposed to know that we shouldn't project human characteristics onto our animals.

You learn to be a realist. I was nailed once by a black

leopard, soon after I began working the upstairs. I was routinely filling the water bowl on one of the old cages. There was a small protective grill that was supposed to prevent the animal from reaching through while you have the hose close to the water bowl, filling it. And I was trusting, blasé, and just stood there. The cat came down to the water bowl, and I thought, "Oh, well, so what, it can't reach around that thing." Well, the cat reached right around it and put a little hole in my hand. With its claw. I filled out a first aid report, put some iodine on the wound, and a Band-Aid and that was it. It was healed within two or three days. I never put my hand close to a water bowl that way again.

One of our keepers was walking in front of the tiger cage, and the tiger reached out and took her glasses off and left a little scar on her temple. I don't think the tiger was attacking her; the tiger was trying to play with her. There are times the animal will attack whoever is disturbing it. If we're trying to move it or crate it, or do something to it that it doesn't want to do, it will attack. You know in these sorts of situations that most cats will eventually charge.

They don't like to be stared at directly. If they know that they're safe, they know they're behind glass, it doesn't really bother them. But with most of them I've seen, if you come and do that, at least among leopards, they get nervous, particularly if you get something out and start pointing it at them. If they've ever had that experience before—a vet pointing a dart gun at them—they'll react.

The first six months I worked in this building, I was told that there were certain cats that I could pet, and I said, "No thank you," because I wasn't at all comfortable with the idea of petting a lion. Particularly a lion that I didn't know, and in the long run I think that's been justified. Until I know an animal on an individual basis and that animal knows me, I don't even attempt familiarities. There are certain signs. For instance, when a female lion comes in and comes over to the bars, and she rubs against them and turns her back toward me, in that situation she cannot make a move that would potentially hurt me. I know that she's asking to be petted. If she were to come in that same enclosure, stand up on her rear feet and put her front feet up on the bars and open her mouth, I'm not gonna stick my hand inside her nose.

You read their moods by their behavior. When they are feeling affectionate, they will come over and make it known, and if they're just feeling distant, then they are distant, and they walk back and forth. That's when I just do my job and open and close the doors, try not to disturb them, and we get along pretty well that way. I've found that cats really don't like loud, sudden noises. They don't like sudden moves. If you don't do them, on a consistent basis, then the cat recognizes you as somebody who doesn't disturb them. Then after a while you can develop a better relationship with the animal.

Actually, sometimes I think my own reactions are very protective. Protective of the animals. In situations in which I think they're being mistreated or are in potential danger, I get very upset. Which I guess means I have a large degree of emotional identification with some of them. We've had a lot of cats die, and there were cats that have died that I've been fond of, but I can't say that I really felt that as a loss. The only time I would feel much more severely about it is if we're responsible for it. My favorite Siberian tiger was a very nice animal, and she died of cancer, but there was no way that she could have survived. Things like that don't bother me as much as instances of an animal being injured or overly stressed or inadequately fed.

Accidents happen. And I'm not in control of everything that happens in this building. Sometimes curators or other keepers do things that I do not agree with, and sometimes I can make my position prevail and sometimes I can't. I suppose the one I still feel worst about is when the lion named Sister lost her tail. She was anesthetized for a routine operation for putting a birth control implant in. Since it was a routine operation and we were a little short in the building, I didn't stay around all the time when she was coming out of the sedation. She was in a cage that at the time had a rather large crack underneath the door. When they positioned her, unfortunately they positioned her so that her tail was close to that crack. And there was a mistake of putting an old lion, a very aggressive male, on the other side of that door. And that male lion reached through, grabbed her tail, and chewed it off. I had left another keeper there to monitor the situation who wasn't very familiar with the animals, and I was outside doing something else. By the time I got back, the tail was gone.

That is a typical example of how things can go wrong. The people that I left in charge didn't know about the possibility of using a fire extinguisher to drive an animal away. Nobody seemed to know where I was, although I was just a few feet away. They were there, but they couldn't stop it. So I still feel partly responsible for that. And that's the sort of thing that makes me feel very bad.

I've *become* a lion keeper. It was never my obsession as a youth, and it was never my ambition as a keeper. I'm still in the middle of things, I guess. When I first took this job, I took it because I wasn't able to fulfill my architectural ambitions, and this was the best type of job that I figured I was qualified for. So for me it is a job, not a career. But it's a good job. It's a job that I like and that I do well, and that I enjoy doing well. There's a lot of independence involved in being a keeper. Also, it does do some good in the world, maybe not the greatest good possible, but it doesn't do much harm. And it allows me to develop my life outside work, in a number of ways that I've never been able to do before, because it's such a secure and comfortable civil service position. There's a lot less pressure than in private employment, and lot more time off because of our particular system of comp time and working weekends. And that allows me to further my educational goals, which had been pretty well shot for years. During the years that I've been here, I've managed to learn a good deal of elementary music theory and finish a master's degree, and go on beyond that.

This job does provide opportunities, when you're hosing and doing purely routine work, to think about things, other things, in a fashion you might not be able to do with another job that demanded full attention all the time. That's one reason why I do like the job. Another is because it provides a modicum of physical exercise. I need some sort of physical exercise, or I tend to get fat. And it does provide these periods of silence or isolation from other people. If I choose to carry problems around with me, I can brood about them, which I have done, but on the other hand, it also allows me to get clear of them sometimes, just by doing something routine. I find it very, very good that I can make my living doing this sort of simple task.

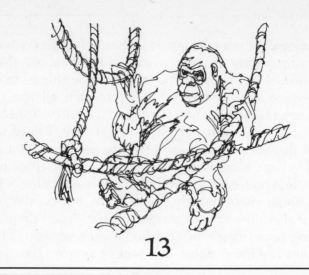

13

HOUSE OF THE APES

When the keepers themselves got around to talking about those among them whose devotion went beyond the call of duty, one name always came up: Pat Sass, the senior keeper in charge of the great ape house.

The forty-five-year-old native Chicagoan genuinely enjoyed the company of animals, at work and at home. She had never married.

"Since I first began to volunteer at the zoo, when I was nineteen, my reputation has gone from that of a promiscuous young girl to that of a lesbian. The truth is that I've never found a man who wanted to compete with the animals for my affection," she said.

The product of a working-class family and the city's public high school system (she went through one year of junior college), Pat had channeled most of her substantial energy to the animals.

She began as a volunteer, working at the children's zoo, in 1961. In 1965, she became a full-time zoo leader, the highest position available for a woman in those days; they were not eligible to work as keepers.

In 1972, a notice of a keeper exam was posted, for men only. It was time for a breakthrough, and Pat was one of the aspirants.

"We had some friendly guys pick up applications for us. We contacted some of the women's lib groups, if we needed them. Then we went down and applied," she recalled.

The bureaucracy at first resisted. A few days later, under pressure, the applications were accepted. When the exam was held, Pat finished near the top of the list. She got the job. She worked at the children's zoo at first, then went on to work in the primate house where, in those days before the great ape house was built, the chimps and the gorillas resided. For eight months, she was in charge of the children's zoo, then abruptly was shifted to the bird house. (At the zoo, keepers could be transferred without appeal.)

"I cried," she remembered.

She was moved again, to the lion house for a year, while the great ape house was being constructed. In June 1976, she joined the apes in occupying it; four years later, she had to face another frustration.

She was given the opportunity to become a senior keeper, but not at the ape house, where a senior keeper was already in residence; she had to return to the children's zoo.

"I've always had a thing for monkeys. I'd dreamed of working in the ape house. But all my friends told me to take the promotion, so I took it. I was lucky. Eventually, the senior keeper spot opened at the ape house, so I was where I wanted to be all along," she said.

By that time, her lifestyle had been established. Unable to find a landlord who shared her love for animals, she bought a house. Her pets would have a comfortable place to live. It was no small matter. Her pets included six cats, two dogs, a lemur, three turtles, a toad, several small rodents, a crow (named Edgar Allan Crow), and an assortment of transient ape babies.

Since that first day as a zoo volunteer, she spent more than twenty-five years at the zoo. She knew curator of

mammals Mark Rosenthal when he was a small boy coming to the zoo to photograph the animals at the children's
zoo.

At five feet tall, she was not a commanding presence.
Her pageboy hairdo had turned to gray. Her eyesight
required her to wear glasses, aviator-style. She did not
wear makeup. She had become somewhat rounded in the
years since she first appeared at the zoo; the word *plump*
applied. But she had not slowed down. Her manner was
pleasant, open, friendly, never overbearing.

On one typical summer day, she arrived at the great ape
house—in a co-worker's car—carrying a small creature
wrapped in a blanket. It was a baby chimp named Susan.
Susan was two months old and weighed less than six
pounds. Pat has assumed control of Susan's life since the
chimp was born. In her office, which contained a pair of
incubators, Pat removed the baby clothes with which she
had dressed the chimp, changed the chimp's Pamper and
put her in one of the incubators. By 8 A.M., the chimp was
on her back, eyes closed, with her arms wrapped around a
stuffed monkey her own size.

"Her mother just doesn't like her children," Pat said.
"She's abusive to them, sends them to day camp on day one.
So we pull them."

After making certain that the chimp was sleeping peace-
fully, Pat turned to her chores for the day. They would keep
her busy. But unlike many keepers, she had the benefit of
working in a modern building.

The great ape house, just beyond its eleventh year, was
largely underground, lit by massive skylights above ground
level. The apes would sleep more in winter and less in
summer, thanks to that natural light. At the center of the
building, within the large glassed-in areas for the apes,
areas fitted with ropes and pillars holding climbing coils,
was the inner service core. Visitors circulated along an
outer circular pathway; the keepers worked at the center.
The animals were in between.

There were three communities of apes. The chimps and

the gorillas had originated in Africa; about half of them had been born at the zoo. The orangutans were from Asia (Sumatra and Borneo).

In the chimp group there were eight animals, including the male, M'Chawi, 9; Donna, 10; June, 22; Kibala, 7; Shauri, 19; Vicki, 16; and two just months old, Akati and Susan.

The twenty-one gorillas existed in three family groups, led by males Otto, 19; Frank, 21; and Koundu, 12. Among the members were females Bassa, 10; Benga, 16; Debbie, 21; Helen, 27; Hope, 4; Makari, a few months old; Kisuma, 11; Kowali, 9; Kumba, 17; Lenore, 18; Mumbi, 24; and Terra, 8. The other males were Bebac, 3; Brooks, 4; Gino, 7; Joe, 1; Joe-Ray-K, 10; and a newborn, Mokolo.

The orangutans comprised a four-animal group: two males, Ray, 7, and Stanton, 13, and two females, Tanga, at 37 the oldest ape in the house, and her daughter, Batu, 1.

From the central kitchen, Pat could, at any moment, spot what most of the apes were doing. It was important to win their cooperation, to work out the rules with them. Male gorillas, for example, preferred women keepers; men were considered competitors. To clean a habitat, the keepers had to tempt the apes to vacate it; that was done with oranges, sweet potatoes, apples. The apes' fondness for sweets could do the trick.

Pat did not underestimate the intelligence of the apes, particularly the chimps. She knew that chimps and humans were 98.4 percent similar in their DNA; the gorillas were almost as similar, the orangutans not far behind.

"Chimps have the average intelligence of a four- to six-year-old kid," Pat noted. "Chimps are the extroverts of the lot."

In one of the holding cages just off the kitchen, Shauri, Pat's favorite chimp, was relaxing. Pat had raised her from infancy. She was a sickly animal, but when it was necessary for the vets to obtain a blood sample from Shauri, they could do it without tranquilizing her. With Pat beside her to comfort her, Shauri permitted the vets to apply a tourniquet and draw the blood. It was not a procedure the vets would even attempt with most of the zoo animals.

"Bring your cup over," Pat shouted at Shauri.

Shauri dropped off the shelf on which she had been sitting, with a plastic container in her hand. She held the container against the bars of her holding area.

Pat poured iced tea into the round plastic container. Shauri drank it, then tapped the cup against the wall of the cage. She wanted more.

Pat filled another container with canned fruit salad, unlocked the barred door and handed it to Shauri. Shauri handed Pat the empty iced tea container and took the fruit salad.

It was a special relationship. Most of the animals were fed with food placed in their habitats; bananas were handed out. The kitchen was filled with boxes of greens, carrots, potatoes, hard-boiled eggs, and more. Some animals, like Shauri, were given treats.

Shauri banged her container on the wall again. The fruit salad was gone. Pat was slicing apples for all the apes; she handed a slice to Shauri.

Everything was proceeding on schedule. Each day the cages were cleaned, hosed down, and the windows washed. Breakfast was served early in the morning, then snacks— including a monkey chow pellet food—at ten. Milk, nonfat enriched milk, was given once a day, and the main meal was served at 3 P.M.

Five keepers worked in the three-story building, including the outdoor habitat. No fewer than two keepers, no more than five, were on duty. Only a night keeper for the zoo checked the building after midnight.

While Pat worked in the kitchen, Shauri gently scratched her forehead and sat in her cage, staring at Pat. Pat cut a large slice of cantaloupe and gave it to the chimp. A few minutes later, Shauri reappeared at the front of the cage; Pat handed her a slice of potato.

"In her mind, she thinks she's getting extra goodies," Pat

said. "All that happens is that I hold it out of her feeding later."

Behind the wire mesh in a habitat on the curve of the core nearby, with a view of the kitchen, a pair of gorillas glared at Pat while she continued to slice and chop.

She smiled at them.

"They get plenty of good food. They don't have to worry about predators. They get the best medical care. Not a bad life," she said.

Caring for apes made demands on even the most zealous keeper.

"It's a bummer when you lose one of them," she said. "Even when you've done all you can." Nine years ago, when Shauri gave birth to a son, Pat had to teach her how to care for it.

"I sat in the cage with her," Pat recalled. "We go back a long way; when she first came here from Africa, she was a year old and weighed ten pounds. When she had her baby, she let me cut the cord, but she wouldn't let me touch the baby. She wasn't hostile, just protective. So we gave her a mild tranquilizer. It just made her yawn a lot. She wasn't being an attentive mother. We knew we could leave the baby with her just up to seventy-two hours, that's the limit, and it was getting close. So I went into the cage with a bottle of formula. I couldn't get it to the baby. Shauri kept reaching for it. My patience was thin. I just wanted to feed the baby, to buy time for Shauri to take charge.

"I didn't think. I just said 'no,' and I hit Shauri. I hit a hundred-and-eighty-five pound chimp. She cried. Then she put out her hand to me, for reassurance. I touched her and gave her that reassurance. It's a matter of mutual respect. In her area, you play by her rules. You let her know what you're doing.

"I picked up the baby and put it on Shauri's nipple. She tried to push the baby away. I said 'no' and held the baby while I pushed its head onto Shauri's nipple. It worked. She raised that baby herself."

In the background, as Pat told the story, Shauri began to make noises, loud, shrill, forceful. She wanted more food.

"No," Pat yelled at her.

Shauri went silent.

"She bit me once," Pat remembered. "Just a nip. I was so upset that I cried. She was upset, too. She went into a corner; I went into another. Then she came across the room to me and put her arms around me and whimpered."

At 10:15 A.M., during the keepers' morning break, Pat poured herself a cup of iced tea and took a small bottle of formula out of the kitchen refrigerator-locker for the baby chimp upstairs. She went up the spiral staircase that connected all the floors of the building.

In the keeper area (her own office adjoined it), she warmed the bottle in a microwave, picked up the chimp, and fed it. The baby clutched one of Pat's fingers in her own long, slender fingers.

"As they get older, the ones I hand-raise keep their relationship with me. They may be feisty with others, but not with me," she said. Hand-raising meant keeping the ape at home every night from as little as two weeks to as long as four months, until the animal slept through the night. At the zoo, that was not possible; there was no one on duty in the building at night.

After the hand-raising was done, however, "you have to be able to let go, and that's not easy," she added. "It makes a better animal, better adjusted. You try to give them the security and love that their mother would have given them. Their mothers cater to their every whim. Some of them are worse than I am in spoiling these kids.

"I know, too, that once they learn what 'no' means, you can discipline them. They do understand. They're very fair. I guess that trust and faith goes both ways."

As Pat sat at a table in the keepers' room, she saw a familiar face peering at her through one of the slots in the wall. On the other side were the gorilla habitats, and Debbie, one of the older gorillas, had used a rope to raise herself to that slot, from which she could peer in and spot some familiar human faces.

Debbie's large hand encircled the bar that kept her from reaching into the room; she tilted her head to get a clear view of the room. Finally, bored by her own eavesdropping, she swung away. At a nearby slot, Kumba, another female, peered in at the keepers and made a sound—smacking her lips to make a cork-popping sound—that gorillas do not make; Kumba had learned it while growing up in the children's zoo. Debbie returned to her slot, and both gorillas became spectators.

Pat had brought treats from home for Shauri: rice cakes, Cran-Raspberry juice, and a sugar-free cherry-flavored drink mix. Shauri enjoyed all of those, and there might be leftovers for a few other favored apes.

"It's all low-cal," Pat said. "Shauri likes them, and we don't have to feel guilty about giving them to her." She had brought vitamin tablets for the chimp as well.

Pat sat beside Cathy and Richard, the other keepers on duty, both young and industrious; the other full-time keeper was on vacation, and a part-time keeper had the day off. The three on duty would work hard; Pat would have to contribute as a keeper as well as the supervisor of all the keepers in the great ape house. But first, there was the usual small talk.

Pat smiled and told the others, "I had a dream last night. I dreamed that a group of young foxes were nipping at my hand until my whole hand came off. The zoo staff said it was my fault, and the staff was coming after me. Weird. Most of us dream about animals coming after us. I dream about the staff coming after us."

A hairy arm was beating at the wall slot, patting the inner wall. The three keepers took no notice; they discussed their assignments for the day, the moving of animals that enabled them to clean the habitats.

Certain apes would have to be tempted out of their habitats. Koundu, a male gorilla, resisted at times, but Pat had the solution.

"He loves the smell of pipe tobacco, so sometimes we go up there and smoke until he comes in. I don't even smoke, but we keep a pipe and tobacco around just for him. He follows the scent, tries to pull the smoke toward him. Nine out of ten times, it works. Maybe it's because he came here from England."

When the meeting ended, Pat checked the baby chimp in her office; it was asleep in its pale blue and yellow pajamas, its head resting on the stuffed monkey, its hands clutching a small blanket.

Then she made her way up to the top level of the building, where hard hats were mandatory to avoid concussions from low-hanging pipes. She went to that level to help Cathy extricate a baby orangutan, Batu, from her mother Tanga's grasp.

Batu hadn't been drinking her milk, seemed enervated, and had diarrhea; the keepers wanted a zoo vet to take a look at her. But Tanga hadn't been cooperative. In a caged tunnel used to divert apes from one location to another, Tanga, a very large, round, rust-colored mass, was determined to protect her daughter.

Within the caged tunnel, there were gates the keepers could open and close, to trap apes inside. Batu was small enough to slip under one of those gates and seemed interested in doing just that. Once under it and out the other side, she would belong to the keepers. As she attempted to slide through the low opening, Tanga grabbed her and pulled her back. Cathy and Pat tried to distract Tanga, who would not be distracted. She hated women and spat at Pat.

Cathy went down to the kitchen and returned with a treat, slices of cantaloupe, to bribe Tanga. She showed the plate of fruit to Tanga, who responded by clutching Batu. Slowly, she reached out and took a piece of the fruit, while guarding Batu at the same time. When the baby got loose momentarily and headed toward the gate, Tanga seized her and pulled her back.

"Some days you're smarter than they are, and some days you're not," Pat said.

Cathy agreed.

"With these guys you may get only one chance," Cathy said. "If you don't take it, the mother knows what you're up to. And what could have taken ten minutes takes four hours. We'll just give her a break and take it as it goes. We could stick her with a dart and send her to sleep for a few minutes, but she's pregnant again, and that might put the fetus at risk.

"Batu will sneak out. She'll know when to try, when her mother is distracted. The truth is that Tanga happens to be a great mom, and you can't punish her for doing just what she should do."

Batu was likely to respond to Pat's urging, eventually. While Tanga had raised her own child, there was a period of time when Pat had been a surrogate. Tanga had bumped the baby's head, causing a skull fracture. After that, as Cathy recalled, "Batu was poking around at the top of the orangutan habitat, and she discovered a small open space near the ceiling. The moment Batu stuck her hand through the opening into the adjoining habitat, one of the chimps grabbed her left arm, bent it backward, and bit Batu just above the wrist." The vet, Tom Meehan, sutured the wounds, but x-rays revealed the fracture of three bones in her arm; it was repaired, and a cast was placed on the arm. Pat had taken care of Batu throughout her recuperation.

Then it was determined that Tanga's milk was not sufficiently nutritious, so the baby had been pulled, and Pat took it home. After that, the mother and daughter were reunited. Batu had gotten to know Pat, so it was possible that Pat could influence her, assuming that Tanga would permit it.

"Most animals that are hand-raised don't do as well as they would have with their mothers. Primates are the exceptions. They like us. We give them an unlimited amount of nutrition. Of course, you don't want them to be obese. But you can give them what they need," Pat said.

Cathy and Pat resumed their effort to trick Tanga. She was not agitated; the large orangutan never lost control. Cathy gave her a cough drop, a treat she loved. While Tanga sucked methodically on the cough drop, Batu edged toward the gate. Tanga was not fooled; she rushed over and retrieved Batu.

The two keepers agreed that it was time for a waiting game. They were confident that they would succeed.

Back in the kitchen, Pat checked on Shauri. She opened the lock on the door to the holding area and entered it. Shauri reached out and gently put several fingers into one of Pat's pant pockets.

"There's nothing there," Pat told her. She proceeded to clean the holding cage, as Shauri watched her. "It's like going into a teenager's room and seeing all that stuff under the bed," she said.

Shauri proceeded to untie Pat's sneaker. Pat let her. Shauri removed the shoe and played with it, relacing it as a small child would. Pat hopped out, locking the gate behind her, to get another shoe; she'd retrieve the original later.

"She has a passion for buttons and zippers, too. Luckily, I don't embarrass easily," Pat said.

She handed Shauri a rice cake; Shauri devoured it.

"All this keeps Shauri from getting bored," Pat said.

Shauri retreated into a corner, holding the sneaker in her left foot while she attempted to lace it. Pat resumed her cleaning. She handed Shauri a small brush dipped in soap-suds. Shauri rubbed it against a dirty wall.

When she finished her other chores, Pat went back into Shauri's cage to get the shoe and some tools that Shauri had been playing with.

One of the tools was a window squeegee on a long handle. Using only her fingers, Shauri had unscrewed the blade of the squeegee and had removed the rubber insert. She had done it in minutes. It did not surprise Pat. Locking Shauri's cage, she looked back in admiration.

"A very sweet animal." she said, "A very special chimp."

Late that afternoon, Cathy and Pat did succeed in distracting Tanga with assorted treats. Then a long strip of burlap dragged across the cage floor tempted Batu to slip under the gate. Tom Meehan obtained a blood sample from the baby orangutan, and Batu was placed in a playpen-cage near the keepers' room, a home she had occupied before when Pat had cared for her.

The next morning when Pat got to work, she plucked Batu from the playpen and put her on her lap. Attired in her Pamper, Batu had her arms around Pat's neck and was sucking vigorously on Pat's chin. Pat pushed her away and offered her a baby bottle filled with Kool-Aid.

"What's better, kid, my chin or the Kool-Aid?" she asked Batu.

Batu looked undecided, moving from one to the other.

Eric, the part-time keeper, commented, "It looks like a miraculous recovery to me."

"I love you," Pat said to Batu, "But enough is enough."

"She's bonding with you now," Richard, the keeper, noted.

Pat extracted a chocolate chip cookie from a new package, and Batu nibbled that as well.

Downstairs, in a holding cage adjoining the kitchen, not far from Shauri's cage, Lenore, the gorilla with an amputated hand and a nasty temperament, could be heard grumbling. It was the day for her dental checkup and an x-ray of the arm. Whenever she had been tranquilized in the past, she had caused a commotion; she inspired unrest among the gorillas in the habitat when they heard her howl. The last time she had expressed her displeasure, some of the gorillas were moved to panic, and one of the young gorillas emerged with a broken arm.

This time, Pat would avoid that sort of misfortune by separating the other gorillas from where Lenore was sure to howl.

In the keepers' room, the other keepers sat around watching Pat care for Batu. Two gorillas, Kumba and Debbie, appeared again at the window slots, clutching ropes and peering in.

"Trying to mooch again," Cathy said. "They know that this is where we eat. They hear us and come up and slap the wall to let us know they're there. At lunchtime, Frank comes up, too, to see what we're eating. We'll give him a rice cake or some shredded wheat. He thinks it's special because he came up here to get it."

Pat got up and attempted to move around the room, but Batu clung to her left leg, creating a limp. She picked up the orang and carried it to her office.

"Tear up the joint. Have a good time," she told Batu, putting a box of toys beside the animal. Batu held her leg with one arm and the bottle of Kool-Aid with the other.

"OK, punk. OK, junior miss princess," Pat said to Batu. "It's time to go into your cage." She carried Batu to the toy-filled playpen-cage. "No yelling and screaming and carrying on?" Pat asked. "Good."

Pat went to the kitchen area to check on Lenore, who was sitting on a shelf in her cage. Pat cautiously opened the door and tossed straw on the floor below the cage. It was to ease Lenore's fall if she fell to the floor when she was darted later. Pat was careful; it was not like her friendship with the chimp Shauri. When she finished dumping the straw, she visited Shauri nearby.

She fed Shauri a few monkey chow pellets, which Shauri munched quickly. Pat tried to be careful in feeding Shauri; the chimp was diabetic, and the vets wanted to regulate her diet. Pat's affection for Shauri was, at times, in conflict with the vets' wishes.

When Shauri finished the pellets, Pat handed her a spoon and a container of yogurt. Shauri placed the spoon in her right hand, dipped it into the yogurt, and slowly ate it.

"You're lucky we like you," Pat said to Shauri. "They don't have yogurt in the jungle."

Tom Meehan called to say that Batu's white blood cell count was slightly elevated; a minor infection might be present. The vet prescribed antibiotics, which at the very least would prevent a secondary infection from developing.

A few minutes later, Tom and Peri and their entourage arrived. Lenore, a veteran of battles with the vets, recognized Tom. She bellowed: a declaration of fear and menace.

Tom's role was to prod Lenore with a long rod, to get her

down from the shelf; once down, she would be darted by Peri.

Tom prodded and Peri aimed. Lenore howled mightily.

Peri fired the dart gun, and the flying syringe hit Lenore in the side. She shrieked loudly, then retreated to a corner of the cage, making belching sounds. Her motions began to slow down.

Lenore had a history of being slow to react to the anesthetic, so she was given a larger than normal dose. After fifteen minutes, while the vets and the keepers stood back and watched, she remained relatively alert. Peri picked up the dart gun again. When Lenore saw it, she ducked and put an arm across her face.

The second dart went into her upper arm. It worked. Lenore went down, unconscious. The vets and two summer externs, helped by two of the keepers, got Lenore onto a litter and out of the kitchen to the hospital van parked outside. A dentist waited for Lenore at the hospital.

At the other side of the kitchen, watching it all, Shauri calmly munched a carrot.

Cleaning Lenore's cage was left to Pat. It was a mess.

"The first thing to go—at least in primates under sudden stress—is their pucker," Pat said, grimacing from the odor in the cage.

"Shit is my life. That'll be the title of my book if I ever write it," she said, laughing. "Without it, I'd be out of a job. The next time they build a building for the apes, I want flush toilets for everybody."

She resumed cleaning, as a mouse dashed across the kitchen floor, scared out of a drain by the activity.

"Every day's a routine day, right? A piece of cake. No problems," she sighed. "It never works like that."

She went upstairs and fed the baby chimp, Susan, who was wearing her pajamas. The chimp's wide-eyed, wrinkled face looked up at Pat; she fondled its thick black hair and large ears, then put a blanket in one of its hands.

"As long as she's got her blanket, she's OK," Pat said. "Take it away, and she's a problem." She carried Susan back

to the incubator in her office. Next it was time to comfort
Batu again.

On the wall in the keepers' room, a happy-first-birthday
card to Batu was on display, signed "Mom Pat."

She opened the playpen, and Batu leaped into her arms
and immediately fastened her mouth to Pat's chin. Her
desire to suck would not be thwarted, and Pat did not
attempt to deny her the pleasure, although Pat's chin had
taken on a bright shade of red. Pat pulled her off, put her
down, and removed her diaper, to discover that the orang
still had diarrhea. She picked Batu up, took her to the
bathroom sink, and washed her bottom, then put a new
Pamper on her. She carried Batu down the stairs to the
kitchen.

Batu quickly resumed sucking Pat's chin. Pat stared at her
with obvious affection. "Whatever you've got, I'm gonna
get," she said. "Do you care?"

Pat's respite with Batu ended abruptly. The vets and their
student externs, along with the dentist, showed up with
Lenore, asleep on a litter. Their work was done, and it was
time to return Lenore to her cage next to the kitchen.
"Where has the time gone?" Pat wondered; several hours
had passed while Pat tended to her work.

The vets and a male keeper slowly slid the litter into the
cage. As they did, Lenore awakened prematurely.

Both vets, the dentist, and the keeper were suddenly
faced with the prospect of dealing with Lenore, who had
started to behave wildly, shrieking and thrashing. A wave
of anxiety passed through the room. Lenore weighed 240
pounds.

Pat, across the kitchen from the tumult, clutched Batu
and froze.

The dentist fled toward an outer door. He spent most of
his time treating humans, not gorillas, and was not curious
about the temperament of gorillas. Peri slipped out of the
cage. So did the keeper. Tom wrestled with Lenore briefly,
then emerged, his face red. Lenore leaped onto her shelf.

She did not want to escape; she simply wanted to be
alone.

The dentist, who had fled into an outer corridor, returned. Pat, holding Batu, sought to change the mood.

"Show the dentist your pretty teeth," she told Batu.

Batu opened her mouth and displayed her teeth.

The crowd in the kitchen laughed, including the dentist. What he didn't know was that by blowing gently on Batu's mouth, Pat got the reaction she wanted from the orang.

In the background, Shauri, unaffected by the noise, was banging her plastic container lightly on the wall of her cage. Cathy took a metal pitcher of water and moved toward the cage. Shauri didn't respond; she gazed blankly at the pitcher. Pat watched, then got a container of Kool-Aid and approached Shauri. Shauri pushed her cup beyond the bars for Pat to fill.

Slowly, the crowd vanished; the keepers went back to their work. Pat held Batu and walked up the stairway to the keepers' room. She sat down with Batu in her arms. As she did, Batu moved forward and put Pat's chin in her mouth. Pat kissed Batu's forehead; they were linked.

First Person: Pat Sass

Like the old cowboys say, I rode on a horse before I could walk. My dad was a pigeon fancier, and he raced and showed homing pigeons. When I was real little, we had a cat, her name was Tabby, a tiger-striped cat. I used to carry her everywhere with me. Back then we didn't know about spaying, so she constantly had kittens. My mother's favorite story is about the time I'm carrying this cat under my arms, and she is ready to have babies any second. I insisted I wouldn't take a nap unless Tabby went with me. Of course, while I was asleep, Tabby proceeded to have her kittens, and Mom got everything all cleaned up. And I woke up and not only was there Tabby, but there were all these little kittens, too. Then when I was about ten we got a dog, named Puddles for the obvious reason.

So I've always been interested in animals. When I was old enough to cross the streets, I used to walk about seven blocks to the veterinarian's, Dr. Higgins, who was real instrumental in getting me into this kind of work. I used to go to Dr. Higgins's animal clinic, and I would just sit in the waiting room. That's all I did. He was wonderful about it.

When I got older, when I was graduated from grammar school, I worked for him as a kennel person, cleaning up the cages where he kept the dogs. When I was in high school, I had graduated a little bit more and was the receptionist. He saw the interest that I had, and he encouraged it. My mom and dad were instrumental too, because I was one of the kids in the neighborhood who always said, "It followed me home; can I keep it?" I didn't know who the neighbors were, I didn't know them by name, but I knew where Sheep lived, and Jackie the dog, and Fluffy the cat. I ate Milk Bone dog biscuits as a kid; I thought they were pretty tasty. That's why I still have strong teeth. Never give an animal anything you wouldn't at least try yourself. That's the kind of person I was. As kids, we would come to the zoo during the summer. I had always been fascinated by monkeys, apes, and I'm sure it was Tarzan movies I used to watch as a kid.

After I graduated from high school, I started at junior college, and it must have been summer and I decided to come to the children's zoo. They had Bambi the deer, and Flower the skunk, Walt Disney–type things. I talked to one of the keepers and asked if there were summer jobs available. And he said, "It's kind of late. They're all taken, but we do have a volunteer program." And he said, "You have to talk to the director of the zoo," who was Marlin Perkins. So I stopped in at the office and made an appointment to see him. He could not have been nicer. I'm nineteen years old, very impressionable, very naive kid I guess, a late bloomer. He asked, "Besides dogs and cats, what animals have you had and what kind of success have you had with them?" He let me come in as a volunteer.

There was a lot of hard work involved. In all the years I've been here, everybody says, "Wow, do you have a nice job. Would I like to do that." Because they come in, espe-

cially in the children's zoo, they see you playing with the
baby chimp or bottle-feeding a baby lion. But they don't
see you at eight o'clock in the morning, when you're cleaning up diarrhea or vomit. Or you have to make up fifty
plates of food, and you have to remember whose plate goes
where.

On my first day in the children's zoo, I walked in, and
this baby gorilla came from nowhere and sat on my foot
and wrapped her arms around my leg. That was my introduction. I was a volunteer for a year, and then I became a
part-time zoo leader. Now, back then a zoo leader was a
woman. It was an hourly position, five days a week, six
hours in summer, and then in winter they worked weekends and holidays. "Zoo leader" was just a term that was
given to the women who worked in the children's zoo,
because back then women did not work in the main part of
the zoo. Between '61 and '72 there was one civil service
exam held for keepers, and one of the qualifications was
that you had to be male. Nobody really protested it then.

I was a part-time zoo leader, then I became a full-time
zoo leader. I worked eight hours a day, had all the benefits
that the keepers had. The keepers and zoo leaders did the
same job at the children's zoo, but we were not getting as
much money. What really got some of us thinking was if a
new keeper, a man, came in, his very first day on the job,
we taught him his job. Yet because he was a keeper and we
were zoo leaders, he was our boss. That didn't make sense.
It wasn't Pat against the system; it was a few of us girls
against the system. I don't think it was the feminist movement. It was the fact that we felt that we could do the same
if not a better job than the men. We didn't feel that just
because you're a man you could do a better job.

In '72 they held another civil service exam. Again, one of
the qualifications was you had to be male. Eight of us filled
out applications, had the picture taken, the whole thing,
and went down en masse. We had contacted a few women's
groups; we were ready to contact radio, television, anyone
we needed. If I can do it the easy way, I will. If we had to do

it the hard way, we were willing to prove a point. After a little stalling, they accepted our applications with no problems. And when I took the exam, I think there were a hundred and eighty people who took it. And out of that, there were eighteen jobs open. Out of all of the people that took it, a woman placed number one. I was number nine, which I thought wasn't bad, and I got my job.

When I look back now, about my life with animals, sometimes I think I get a little carried away and get too involved. People have said, "I'd rather have somebody just come in and do the job than someone who comes in saying, 'I love all the animals.' " Loving all the animals doesn't cut it. You don't always think of what's best for the animal. I contradict myself a little bit because I treat a baby orang just like a person, and I treat the apes like people to a point. But I think it's more like I become one of them, than trying to make them one of me. I become the orang mother, the chimp mother, the gorilla mother, the opossum mother, the pig mother, whatever animal I'm raising at the time. Not necessarily that I'm trying to make them human. I've got scars on my body to prove that even the ones you trust the most, on occasion, will bite you.

To me, a good keeper is someone who cares. Someone who is not a clock watcher. When I worked in the monkey house, it would take me forty-five minutes to get in and scrub one cage, and scrape crap off the shelves, climb up into the runway and get in between the bars; somebody else might take the same time and do fifteen cages. Of course, it sounds good, organization sounds real good. It's a Wednesday, I know there are going to be five people, I'm at home having breakfast and think, "Well, we're going to have five people, so today we're going to hang ropes in the orang cage. We're going to scrub this particular area. We're going to make sure we do this and that." I get into work, right? First the phone rings, and it's "How many people do you have?" "Well, all of us are here today." "Well, fine. The lion house is short; we need you to send somebody over there." "Oh, OK." So we're down to four. Hey, we can still hang ropes, we can do this and that, we'll just have to hustle a little bit more. And then you go upstairs, and the baby orang doesn't look too good. It's nothing we can put our finger on, but she doesn't get up to greet us. She doesn't try to reach for my fingers like she would normally. Her eyes don't look as bright as they should. So you call the vet. This is what's going on. An animal gets sick, has to be knocked down, taken over to the zoo hospital. Again, it isn't something that happens quickly; it takes planning. We've got to try to separate this animal out before the vets come over, because once the vets walk in the building, it gets telegraphed around the entire building, from chimp to gorilla to orang, back to gorilla again, "Hey, the vets are here, we're all in trouble."

We have a chimp mother, Donna, that doesn't like kids. If you leave them with her, and we've tried, she gets abusive with them. She just doesn't want anything to do with them. And we have to raise them. It's either that or within three days you're going to have a dead baby. So with Donna, when she has a baby, we know we have to pull it. With the other ones, we'll give them the benefit of the doubt that they'll take care of them. The ones that we really worry about are the younger mothers, the first-time mothers among the chimps, the gorillas, the orangs. A lot of it is an innate behavior, but a lot of it is learned. Luckily in this building now we can keep them in family groups, so they see creatures being born.

The classic story that I tell is when we had Kumba, who was the first born at the zoo, in 1970. Her mother Mumbi took care of her for thirty-five, thirty-six days. And then she started doing strange things to her. Mom would lie up on the top of the bars and swing the baby. And we're going, "She's gonna drop the kid! We're going to lose the baby!" Now we see them do the same thing, but we've had twenty-some births, and we know that's normal, a piece of cake; don't worry about it, it'll be fine.

There's a story that has been going down probably since zoos began, since Noah. If you give a screwdriver to a group of chimps, or even one chimp, the chimp will throw it around; he'll make noise with it, he'll try to eat it, and then will throw it out of the cage. Put it in with a gorilla, and the gorilla will look at it, examine it, sniff it, maybe taste it, nyaa, doesn't do him any good, throws it out. Give it to the orang; the orang'll look at it, and all of a sudden it'll be gone. You think he threw it out, but five days later he'll be out of his cage, because he's used it to take the cage apart. They're more mechanical.

We say that the chimps, gorillas, and orangs have the average intelligence of a four- to six-year-old kid. They can do what a four- or six-year-old kid'll do. Well, they also can survive a heck of a lot more. I mean you can take a baby chimp out of the wild, away from its mother, put it in our environment, and it grows up. Granted, we're nursing it and taking care of it, but it grows up pretty well. I mean, how many humans can you take, other than Tarzan, and throw them in with a group of apes?

I talk to these animals. I think it has some effect. Years ago, way back when I first started, when I didn't know anything, I was working with the first chimp that I ever really worked with, Wesley. When I first started working with him, he would play with me. He was sent to us from the Los Angeles Zoo. He was mother-raised, and he was taken from his mother, put in a crate, and shipped here. Petrified. I would sit with him and play with him; I was his play object, I would tickle him, but he would not cling to me. I didn't know what to do about it. I was sitting in the cage with him one day, and we're playing. One of the keepers came by and as a joke pounded the side of the cage. Scared me, scared the chimp. The chimp jumped into my arms; our instinct was to just grab one another and hug. I never had any trouble handling him after that. He needed the security. I was his security. That's what I do with these guys, I play mom with them. I'm their mother; they can come to me. I have a fine line drawn—don't cross it, or I'll get mad at you—but if you need security, you need reassurance, you come to me.

I work on their mind because I'm physically not strong enough when they get older to do things with them if they didn't have the respect. With Wesley, I'm cleaning his cage one day, and he's sitting on the shelf. He's not supposed to get off the shelf. When I finally finish washing the walls and the windows, I throw the shavings in and put the straw in, and somebody comes up and starts talking to me. While I'm talking I look around, and ten, twelve feet away are the rags that I had been washing the windows with, and Wesley's still sitting on the shelf. In the same conversation, I say, "Oh, I forgot the rags. Wes, could you pick them up and bring them here?" Wes gets down off the bench, picks up all the rags, walks them over, and hands them to me. That's the first time something like that ever happened. My mouth fell open.

Now, I don't even know why I turned and said that to the chimp. It was just in passing. It wasn't like you say to a dog, "Sit down, heel, stay." Wes knew his name, he knew "rags," "come here," whatever the words he knew, but he was able to put that together, and he got down, picked up the rags, and brought them to me.

Chimps have, they claim, thirty-two different sounds that mean things. Again, you work with them. You teach them, you show them something, you say, "This is a cup, this is a pen or pencil, a rag. The chair, sit in the chair," that type of thing. Having worked with them over the years, I know that if a chimp sees something and he's looking at it and he's going, "Ooo, ooo, ooo," he's inquisitive. If chimps are upset, they have temper tantrums. When she was in the children's zoo, June the chimp had the best temper tantrums I've ever seen. Yet, to show how smart she was, if she started a temper tantrum, you could stop her just by touching her. If you moved your hand, she'd start up right where she left off. If they get what they want, they stop.

Sometimes they will point. Vicki the chimp, if she wanted something, would point to it, and if we missed it, she'd point again. Shauri, when she wants a drink, will take her cup and rattle it on the bars. You learn what the sounds mean, you learn the greeting; because you deal with them, you pick it up.

Gorillas are not as vocal. They cup their hands and beat on their chests. Males and females will do it. I do it better on my belly; I have more of a belly. Some if it is innate behavior, some of it is learned. They see the others do it, they do it. You can yell because you're mad, or you can yell because maybe you just feel good.

I can imitate chimps, I can do a few of the gorillas. The orangs have these real high-pitched sounds I can't imitate. They don't make as much noise. Chimps and gorillas live in communities, in groups. Orangs in the wild usually don't. The males are by themselves, and then they come together and breed. Females will have their offspring, maybe one or two offspring, and then as they get older, they chase them away, so they're just with an infant. Orangs tend to cling a lot more; they play mainly with their mothers, because that's all they have. The little chimps will play with each other, they have their peers, they have their brothers and sisters, their elders, they've got cousins.

When I had the orang at home, I couldn't do anything. Unless she was asleep, I couldn't get up and do anything without having her right with me, or screaming because she wanted to be where I was. Did you ever try to wash dishes when you've got a baby orang? You're trying to vacuum or dust or do anything. Get up to change the TV station, thank God for remote control. An orang is that clingy.

To clean the ape house, we hose everything down through big drains. Then we pull up a basket in each drain. We empty it and then drop it back in.

Cardinal rule number one is, if there is an animal in the habitat, you don't stick your fingers through the mesh. It's just common sense. You try to be aware of that constantly, but some days are better than others. One particular day, my mind was not where it should have been. Frank was in the habitat with the rest of the gorilla group. And, being short, I had to step down into the basket opening, and I didn't want to lose my balance. Without even thinking, I grabbed the side of the mesh on the cage. The next thing I know, I say, "Ouch!" and Frank is there. I'm convinced he could have taken three fingers off and handed them back to me if he wanted to. All he did was apply a little pressure and snicker behind his hand. He used his teeth, but it was just kind of like, "Gotcha! You weren't paying attention, but I was."

We got Shauri the chimp from Africa when she was not quite a year old. She was very, very sick. As a matter of fact, when they took her out of the crate, they thought she was dead. She was malnourished; she had roundworms that were a foot long coming out of her. She had pneumonia. She never really should have lived. And I said, "She's not going to die." I basically nourished her back to health. I had her at home with me. She's one of the nicest animals you'd ever want to meet in your life. As she got a little older, we started doing tea party. We'd bring them out, and they'd sit at the table and chairs and eat. We had anywhere from one to six chimps. This was in the outside section of the children's zoo, and it was summer.

On one particular day, we get the table set up, the dishes are there, the cereal's on the table, we've got kids, because the chimps are all real good. I know if I let the four chimps go ten feet away from the table, they'll all go sit in their chairs. The kids are sitting in a kind of semicircle on the grass. So I let all the chimps go. Three of them run up and jump in their chairs. Shauri doesn't; she goes and sits with the kids, in the grass. And I go, "Hey you!" She turns around to see who I'm talking to; it couldn't be her, you know. I go: "You—the hairy one!" She just flips back, still looking, moving backward, and sits in the second row and kind of crunches down a little. As I've always said, you could do it one of two ways: you can get mad at her, go over, spank her, make her go sit down, but then you might upset the kids. Or you make a joke out of it. And I go, "You, Shauri, we can't do tea party. After all, you're the star of the show. Could you please come up here?" With that, she got up, and she came and sat down.

You have to be emotionally involved to do what I do. The biggest problem is letting go. Batu, the baby orang, is the perfect example. I love that hairy little red kid. She's the second orang that I've worked closely with. I've worked with lots and lots of chimps, quite a few gorillas, but orangs I really hadn't had that much experience with. I know that she's an orang, I know I'm a people, and I know in order for her to be happy, she's got to be an orang. Then we decided to reintroduce her. Emotionally, it's a tough thing. Logically, I can understand that she should be with her mother, she should be an orang, this is the best thing for her. Emotionally, not being able to cling to her little body, have her suck on my chin, I had a difficult time with it. I really wasn't making her human, I was trying to be that orang mother, I was trying to do what orang mothers do.

I try to do the best for them, whatever type of animal they are. Maybe I get a little bit more emotionally involved than I should. I've cried over a lot of chimpanzees, like the first chimp that I ever worked with, Wesley, who was shipped to another place. I got really upset about that. Donna's first baby that I raised, I had at home for eleven days; it lived for three weeks and died at my house. It was real hard to take. I've had a couple of gorillas that we raised, that were doing well, they were about a year, a year and a half old. But they were hit with salmonella, and both of them died. You get upset, you cry. When we first put Batu back, I missed her. I got tears in my eyes, and my voice cracked. The people here are real supportive.

There's always the risk of being attacked. I know there's that remote chance that it will happen. I am not consciously going to do anything stupid. I'm not going to push a two-hundred-pound chimp and say, "Hey, I want you to do it because I'm telling you to." I don't. When I go in there, it's with respect and mutual affection. I don't think anything of it if I go in with Shauri and she throws her arms around me and puts her mouth on me or something. I know that that's a greeting. I will do the same thing to her. I will bite her on the neck like she's biting me. And I feel that I've been around and have read enough and have had enough experience that I know what's going on. When she was real sick, we pushed her a little. Again, her reaction nine out of ten times is to try to get up and walk away from us.

But if you're going to do something, like try to get blood from her without knocking her down, you give her an escape route. You don't stand in front of the door and say, "Well, we're going to do it, or you're going to have to go through me." I mean that's stupid. But you go in and say, "OK, look, this is gonna hurt, but this is what we have to do." I talk to her. Now, I don't know how much she understands, but nine out of ten times I've been able to get across what we want. She's known me all of her life. And there have been times I've been off and they've wanted to take blood pressure or to get blood or to do something, and they have tried, and she will not let them. Yet when I come in and sit with her, and we talk about it, and I explain what we're gonna do, she has let me do it.

When I first started as a zoo leader, I don't know that I ever thought of being a keeper. I saw myself as a ninety-year-old lady with a cane, walking toward the bunny pen: "You want to pet a bunny, little kid?" Now, I've been here half my life. I really think of doing what I'm doing. I enjoy doing what I'm doing. Sometimes people can get to me, the public will at times, but I enjoy it. I can get as much pleasure in raising a baby squirrel, a baby pig, as I can with a chimp or a gorilla. Really—if in my mind I commit to it. I've got animals coming out of my ears at home. I get up at five-thirty, and I do a whole run at home before I come here. The lemur that I've got, I hand-raised him. He was two ounces and nine and a quarter inches from the tip of his nose to the tip of his tail, and now he's full-grown. He's not as big as normal lemurs; he's a runt. But, I'm the only one now who can touch him. He's my commitment. Lemurs can live twenty-some odd years; we've got a few years to go yet.

You commit to things. I'm not married, I don't have children. These are my kids. I really do know I'm a human and that they're animals, but they're my family. I've had problems in relationships with men because they feel threatened by what I do and by my commitment to the animals. I don't know, maybe if I was ever really, as mother would say, truly in love, I would give all this up, but I don't feel I should have to give all this up. I would like to find somebody I could share it with. And I know there are people somewhere out there. But, boy, it sure beats pumping gas in a gas station. I'm dealing with living things that have emotions, that show they care. They're sometimes a lot more honest than people are. Keepers I work with, acquaintances, friends, who are nice to me to my face, as soon as I turn my back, they're talking about me to someone. The animals don't do that. They have their likes and dislikes, and they let you know exactly what those are.

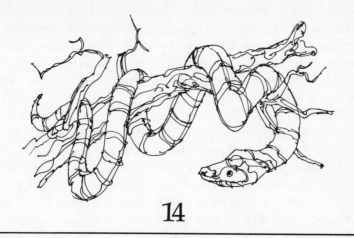

14

THE REPTILE RAP

Art Maraldi liked to talk: "Yeah, we've had people attack animals. We had some Galapagos tortoises in a big fenced-in area. People would climb the fence at night, probably kids with pipes and bricks. They'd smash the shells. . . .

"I remember a woman who was working as a temporary, years ago. There was a small baboon, and she'd carry it on her shoulder. It was kind of tame. Well, the baboon was a male, and he'd have an erection, and he'd stick his erection in her ear. When the director saw it one day, he screamed, 'Get that animal out of here!' . . .

"Gorillas are majestic. It's an aura. There's something about them. In the wild, they don't kill animals, they don't eat meat. Whereas chimps are much like humans; they'll kill a monkey and have a party eating it. . . .

"Elephants are intelligent. Any animal that can live in excess of fifty years has a lot going for it. . . .

"A human you've known for fifteen years, you can't predict what he'll do. How can you predict what a wild animal will do? . . .

"There was a true, authenticated situation where two tigers were mating in India, and they were crossing a stream, and an elephant barred their way. It was during the mating season, remember, so when the elephant wouldn't let them cross, they attacked. One got on its back, the other clawed its eyes. . . .

"Some palsied kids, with helmets on, in wheelchairs, came to the zoo. Their doctor asked if we had any animals the kids could touch. I took Henry, a chimp. We went to one of the kids, who was all excited. Henry went to the kid, hugged the kid, and kissed him on the side of his face. Then he went to the next kid. I cried. He went to all the kids and hugged them and kissed them. I still have tears in my eyes when I think about it."

Art was one of the zoo's amiable eccentrics, one of its amateur historians. He collected lore, firsthand and secondhand, polished it, and passed it on. He could be bluntly realistic, then disgress into matters of cosmic destiny, flights of mysticism, considerations of "auras" and such. Animal behavior always commanded his attention, along with the employment histories and sexual inclinations of the zoo staff.

As a keeper at the reptile house, he was conscientious, informed, and concerned.

Art began his career at the zoo in 1972, when he was thirty-six. He had tried other jobs, various exercises at paper shuffling and administrative drills that he couldn't tolerate. Compared to his years at the zoo, that part of his life seemed empty, boring, wasteful. He had a bachelor's degree in biology (from Northeastern Illinois University) and decided to put it—and his curiosity about animals—to work at the zoo.

Art was a short, 140-pound packet of energy. Whether he was at the zoo or at his modest home, which he shared with his wife, a public school administrator, and his teenage daughter, he kept busy. At home, he collected hobbies: mounting butterflies and moths, building framed insect environments, listening to music (from the Carpenters to

Bach), working with Indian beads, and gourmet cooking.

At the zoo, he spent his time with the reptiles, but he had worked in nearly every section of the zoo during his more than fifteen years there. His interest was intense enough to inspire him to spend ten years doubling as a docent, volunteering his free time to teach zoo visitors about the animals while he was a full-time keeper.

Unlike some keepers, he believed that he had an obligation to learn. He read zoological journals and every other form of information about animal behavior that he could get his hands on. In debates with curators, he had emerged victorious. He had come to grips with the role of the keeper, its rewards and its frustrations. He never thought of changing jobs.

His dark hair was thinning, and his eyesight needed the help of glasses, but his enthusiasm remained. It was not daunted by having to work in the old, decaying reptile house; he took that environment for granted.

Early one day in late September, Art was on duty on "the hot run," the area behind the main-floor exhibits that housed the poisonous snakes. As he unlocked the gate leading to the run, he noticed something.

"Someone left-handed locked the padlock," he mused. On hot run duty, he had to pay close attention; he was aware of the deadly nature of the creatures that inhabited it.

He checked the run, walking slowly from cage to cage, looking for anything that might seem suspicious. He found nothing to disturb him. On a wall, a large sign read, "You Can Be Sure! When You Are Up to Your Ass in Alligators, It Is Hard to Remember That Your Objective Was to Drain the Swamp."

He walked down to the basement of the reptile house, to change into his keeper uniform. He greeted Caryn, another keeper, who was busy feeding tortoises and a batch of doomed chicks which would become meals for reptiles.

Caryn told him that Joel Pond, the lab technician at the

zoo hospital, wanted a stool sample from a snake who had recently been donated to the zoo. Art phoned Joel.

"Another stool sample on that snake? The eastern indigo? You've had two already. Well, he just defecated in his water bowl. You want that stool sample? Yes. OK."

"He's looking for parasites," Art told Caryn. "You know, as long as people explain things to you, you don't mind going out of your way to help them."

He walked up the stairs to the main hall, where visitors would gather later in the day. He blocked the view of the Gila monster cage with a large wooden board; he would be feeding them later, and he didn't want visitors to see him do it.

He stopped to peer at the African rock python.

"He doesn't like rats or chickens," he said. "I'd better find him a rabbit." Other snakes would eat minnows, mice, even dead snakes; a king cobra would eat any kind of snake. The python preferred rabbits.

Art went downstairs again and found a frozen rabbit in a food locker. He carried it to the hot run, to permit it to defrost by the end of the day.

His first order of business was to clean the case that held a puff adder, a potentially dangerous snake in a cage marked in red, HOT.

The adder had defecated, and the newspaper that lined the heavy fiberglass case was dirty and had to be replaced. Art carefully unlocked the two padlocks that held a clear acrylic panel on the front of the case and slid the panel open, exposing the snake to the outside world.

The adder's tongue flicked out rapidly, but the snake did not resist Art's effort. He used a long pole with a metal hook on the end to lift the adder out of its case and into a larger metal container. The adder hissed. It was three feet long, in shades of gray with a flat head, expressionless.

"He's upset. He's very upset," Art said. "He doesn't like being moved. I wouldn't either, if someone came in and moved me out of my house."

He put on a pair of rubber gloves and cleaned the adder's case.

"They don't shit often," he said. "Once every few months. They process a lot; they make maximum use of everything they eat. Eat a little and get the most out of it."

He put the case on the floor and hosed it, then wiped it with a nontoxic antiseptic.

"The big snakes can come off the hook. Using it on some of them is asking for trouble," he said. "But if I use the tongs instead, I have to grab them around the neck, and I could strangle them. No thanks. With the big snakes, you need two people, at least, because you never know what the son of a bitch is going to do."

He put clean newspaper on the floor of the adder's case, slid the acrylic panel into its slot, and moved it across, leaving a small opening. He hooked the adder in its metal cage, lifted it cautiously, and put it into its clean cage.

"He doesn't want to be out here. Now he's in his home. Some snakes are curious when you move them, and they want to get out. When they do, they're actually frightened by me. That's why they may strike out. Snakes will bite the hand that feeds them.

"In general, however, the animal just wants to take things easy, that's all. And I'm the one who has to disturb it. Which means I've got to be up, constantly aware. By the end of the day, I'm the one who's pooped."

The Asiatic cobra, a sleek and lethargic snake, was next on Art's list. There were several of them in a cage that Art had to clean.

"They're slow compared to rattlers," he said. "But they strike all the time. They fling themselves at you. They'll come up high and sway and get you with a face shot. Snakes don't have to be coiled before they strike. That's bullshit."

The cobras, aware of his invasion, began to hiss and make a growling sound. He disregarded their objections and hosed the cage, being careful not to intimidate them with the stream of water.

"They see me as a threat. But they're not sophisticated. Not like a gorilla, which recognizes the keeper. These snakes don't know who I am."

He had to clean an old concrete tank with a hinged wire mesh top. Inside it, three western diamondback rattlesnakes were resting. When he opened the top of the tank, the three created a loud chorus of rattles.

Art chanted to himself, "Be careful, always. Expect the unexpected."

He hosed the tank with the snakes in it, watching them. But a drain in the tank seemed to be blocked. Art attacked it with a plunger, while he continued to keep an eye on the snakes. They rattled loudly. He told them to shut up. They didn't. To work on that drain, he concluded, he had to remove the snakes from the tank and put them into a large, wheeled plastic container. Deftly, he lifted each snake out of the tank with the long hooked pole; when he had them in the plastic bucket, he put a cinder block on top of it to restrain them.

"I have no time to fuck around with you guys," he said. "You know, sometimes I wish I had an easy day. It never happens with reptiles. Something always comes up."

He spoke to the drain: "Come on, you son of a bitch, flush out. It's these minor jobs that take forever. Just a normal day on the hot run. What did you do at the zoo today, Daddy?"

The drain wasn't working, so Art had to trace the line through adjoining tanks; they were devoid of snakes but were filled with odds and ends that other keepers had stored in them. Art pried some of that out, tossed it on the floor, and went to work again with his plunger. In time, he found the point at which the drain system was clogged, and he cleared it.

"Well, at least the rattlers hadn't eaten. If I used a hook then, they'd puke. So would I, if somebody picked me up with a hook after I ate."

He was ready to put the rattlers back into their own tank.

"Here we go, kids. It's Uncle Artie. OK, boys, who wants to be first?"

He hooked one snake, and it slithered off the hook, back into the plastic bucket.

"Better than if it fell on the floor," he said to himself.

"Now, you're going to be really pissed," he said to the snake, after he had hooked it. "Who's next?"

He hooked a second snake. The third one began to crawl out of the container.

"Don't act stupid," Art shouted at it. He hooked it, and all three were back where they began the morning. Art was sweating.

"There's a certain tension in moving a snake you know can kill you," he said. "There is that tension all the time around here. But you can't panic. A rattler on a hook can strike, so you can't let it get out of control. I'm sweating. You sweat when you handle the hot stuff. One thing for sure, it's not like working with a bunch of pissy birds. When I get a little weary, I go out for a walk, a little break. You don't want to get tired and get careless."

He walked over to the case holding the newly acquired eastern indigo snake. It was lively, wriggling swiftly around its case, its head poking against the mesh on the top of the case. It was not a poisonous snake, so Art relaxed a bit, slid open the acrylic panel, and reached in. He held the snake by its neck while he removed its water bowl, with the feces in it.

"A nice snake," he said. "That's why they're endangered." He put the feces in a lab specimen container and gave the snake a bowl of fresh water.

"You never quite get used to it all," he said. "You can't because when you think you know what can happen, something you didn't expect happens. You can watch a gorilla's eyes and know what it's going to do. Or make a good guess. A snake won't tell you anything with its eyes. There is no real warning with them. So you try to think of what might happen. Think the worst and be up for it, all the time."

His nerves were a bit frayed, despite his familiarity with the work he had done. It was time for a therapeutic break.

Art picked up the stool sample and a couple of packages he wanted to deliver. He had made a mock military medal for one of the secretaries in the main zoo office; sewing was another of his hobbies. He had bought a baby gift for a park food vendor, a new father and an old friend. He strolled outdoors, through the coils of visitors clogging the zoo. He delivered the presents. He stopped at the zoo library, to collect some science magazines for his daughter's school class. He dropped off the stool sample at the hospital lab. He scrounged a few grapes at the commissary. And he exchanged mock flirtatious banter with an attractive docent he knew.

He walked back to the reptile house; it was time to feed the Gila monsters. The Gila monsters ate mice.

Art tracked down several large, flat cartons marked LIVE ANIMALS FOR RESEARCH. The cartons contained tiny, live white mice; other cartons contained rats. All could be heard scratching within the cartons.

Art opened a carton and methodically plucked out the mice, one at a time, using metal tongs.

He removed a mouse from the carton, held it at shoulder height, then threw it to the floor. Those that did not die instantly died within seconds. When enough of them were dead, he bagged them and headed for the rear of the Gila monster cage.

He opened the cage and jumped into it, along with the eight Gila monsters—medium-sized lizards and poisonous ones. It was hot in the cage; an overhead sunlamp warmed the sand and the cactus in the cage. The Gila monsters were pink-and-black or yellow-and-black. They did not move to greet Art or to escape from him.

Art began to feed them by hand; with the tongs, he reached into his bag, extracted a mouse, and tried to force it into the Gila monster's mouth. Several of the Gilas were reluctant to eat; Art held them at the neck with one hand and pushed mice into them with the hand holding the tongs.

He wanted them to eat on their own, but he had to be sure that each Gila had its fill—two or three mice each— and he couldn't be sure of that if he simply tossed the dead mice into the cage. So he proceeded from lizard to lizard, pushing mice into their mouths. Several crept through the sand with just long tails protruding from their mouths.

"You've got to wait until the tail goes down before you offer another mouse," he said. "They're not too bright."

Time passed, and Art began to sweat profusely. His glasses began to slip down his nose, and he had to push them back up repeatedly.

"At least they won't come after me," he said, commenting on the Gila monsters' deadly bite. "I'm too big." The Gilas moved sluggishly at best. Art concluded that they had eaten what they wanted to eat; further prodding would be futile. All of the Gilas seemed sleepy.

"At night, they move like greased lightning, believe it or not. They're nocturnal."

Later, he would feed rats to some snakes.

"You don't feed a snake the way you feed a Gila," he said. "Shit, it'll kill you. I just throw the rats to the snakes. Rats, mice, birds, lizards—snakes will eat any of them. We feed them chicks because chicks can't fly. We used to feed them sparrows, but they did fly, and it got out of hand."

He was sweating and tired, and the day was barely half over. It was time for lunch. He liked to cook and occasionally would bring food he had cooked at home, to be heated in the convection oven he kept in the hot run. On this day, however, he was too exhausted to cook. He walked out of the reptile house, over to one of the vending stands, and bought a packet of M&Ms. He sat on one of the benches in front of the reptile house and ate the M&Ms slowly, one at a time.

Clarence Wright, the curator of reptiles, walked by on his way to lunch and waved at Art. Art smiled.

"He's secure in his job," Art said. "And he knows the problems; he's been there. Many zoo administrators I've come in contact with don't know a damned thing. I consider Clarence to be a class act. He's willing to listen to your ideas. He'll explain to you why he wants this done. He lets you vent your frustrations. If you're a good administrator, and he is one, you know it's the keeper, the laborer, who does the work. You shine when they shine."

In his uniform, Art was recognized by visitors. They

brought their questions to him, and he answered them
with courtesy and kindness. He was particularly attentive
to small children.

He watched several of them race in front of the reptile
house and he smiled.

"Zoos are for children," he said. "If you don't love kids,
you shouldn't work in the zoo."

He got up and went off to feed the rats to the snakes.

First Person: Art Maraldi

I've been at the zoo almost sixteen years. Crazy things
have happened. People are interesting. In the early part of
my work at the zoo, we had experiences right outside the
gate and even on the grounds, where people, cultists,
would sacrifice goats, roosters, chickens. These are not
poor people doing this, because poor people would eat the
animal. Then we had two mute swans in the zoo rookery,
and they were pinioned, which means they couldn't fly at
all. Now the male's very aggressive during breeding season, and a big male swan can break your legs with his
wings. They're very dangerous, so you have to be very
careful. Yet someone climbed the fence, probably at night,
and stole both birds. Stole them. Now what I find amazing,
what I think is terrible, is that you have to have a market
for something like that. And the only place you have a
market is someone with a private lake that can accommodate swans. So we're talking about this individual who had
an order for two swans. The guy who bought them is
worse than the guy who took them.

Last year in September, the wolves already had their
winter coats. They were full. But they had very little fur on
their legs. That led me to believe that it's going to be a
windy, cool kind of winter, very little snow. Because
wolves in any storm situation tend to stay outside; they
don't like to come into the den area. They will lie down, but
in doing so they keep their legs under them. So since

they're running animals, if there was going to be a lot of snow, they'd have a lot of fur, but they don't want to overheat. So it turned out last winter we had a lot of wind off the northeast and very little snow. The snow leopards will tell you how the winter's going to be. One year we got a leopard in from Buffalo, New York, for breeding. He came into Lincoln Park in October or November. His coat was twice as thick as on our snow leopards. We had a mild winter, and they had a hell of a winter in Buffalo that year. So he grew his coat based on the assumption that he was going to stay in Buffalo. He had no way of knowing he was going to be transferred. I mean, that poor guy was panting all the time.

Look at the animals. If you see the squirrels burying peanuts in November, it's going to be a terrible winter. If they eat them, it's going to be mild. So this is how you can tell some of the things about animals, what's going on. You can observe them.

You cannot always predict why an animal will do something. The record for an animal jumping in the *Guiness Book of Animal Records* is a tiger jumping eighteen feet to pull a man out of a tree. And tigers are notoriously bad jumpers compared to leopards and jaguars. So you don't know why the animal did it. Maybe the animal had a bad day; maybe it had a bad toothache or something, you just don't know.

They tell you snakes don't by and large swallow their prey headfirst. There were four guys out hunting in Sri Lanka, and a thunderstorm ensued. And they probably weighed about a hundred and twenty, a hundred and forty pounds, short-statured kind of men, and one man ran under a clump of trees, the other three ran under a group of bushes. After the storm abated, the three called the fourth, and he didn't answer. They went over to the trees, and they saw a thirty-one-foot reticulated python with a bulge in him. Their friend's hat was there, and his sandals. They killed the snake, they opened him up, and their friend had been swallowed feetfirst.

They say snakes have to coil before they strike. That's

not true. They can strike many times from any position. I've had cobras throw themselves right off the ground at me. You just can't predict. You don't know what the animal is going to do; that's only in the books. Anything can happen at any time.

There was another situation which just amazed me. It was kind of sad. A young Doberman got loose. This Doberman came running into the zoo, and the people were running after him, trying to capture him. He apparently didn't want to be captured; maybe he was going to be reprimanded, who knows, he's a puppy, you know. He came running in, and he came to the wolf compound, the outdoor area. He apparently smelled wolves, and being a young animal, not understanding the ramifications of adulthood, he thought that was a safe area. He jumped in there. It took the wolves less than a minute and a half to dismember and eat the Doberman. So to a wolf, a dog is not the same thing. With any of these predatory animals, you have to be careful.

Animals have their idiosyncracies. You have an animal who's incarcerated, you've got to help him if you can. You don't give him maid service, but on the other hand, you do what you can if you know he is a nice animal. Take the anaconda, Yolanda. You open her door, she could be hungry, but if you spray a hose on her, she'll move away. On the other hand, the reticulated python, you open his door, he may not be hungry, and he will try to grab you if he can. He'll strike at you if he has the opportunity. So he's not a nice animal. Yolanda's a nice animal. Her motives are strictly food, nothing to do with you. If you're doing something foolish like you get too close, she might just react without knowing. But if you give her an opportunity, she'll know what's going on, she won't try to do anything. That's not to say you're going to go into the cage with her, but on the other hand, the reticulated, you know, from the time you open that door, if he has a chance, he's going to try to grab you. That's what I mean by nice or not nice.

There was a story about Mike the raven. He would talk

all the time. He'd say, "Whaddya say Mike, whaddya say Mike?" One July evening, it had been very hot, and all of a sudden a high-pressure system moved through Chicago; it got very cool, and there was actually fog along the lake. And it dropped to the sixties. The zoo cop that had been here was ill, and they sent a policeman named Michael, his first name was Michael, and it was his first time at the zoo. Mike the raven was in a cage down by the old duck yard. We also had some peacocks in that yard, and it was the mating season, so the males would call, and that call in the middle of the night can scare the hell out of anybody. Well, the cop heard that—he was just walking around, he heard that noise—and he thought it was a woman being attacked. So he ran down toward the area of where he was hearing it, and he had his gun out, and it was foggy, and meanwhile the cocks had seen him and stopped calling. And as he's walking, he goes past Mike the raven's cage, and Mike is right there, and Mike says to him, "Whaddya say Mike?" And the guy nearly had a heart attack on the spot. Nearly blew away the raven. That actually happened, and it was funny as hell.

There was a tragic episode with a German shepherd. A keeper on the bear line, outside, looked behind him and saw a shepherd charging him. So he jumped over the railing. When the dog charged him again, the keeper slammed a gate, so the dog was locked between the guard railing and the bars. Mike the polar bear, who had looked like he was asleep, suddenly came to the front of the cage and stood up with his paws up on the inside of the bars. Now, all these animals know to a thirty-second of an inch how far they can reach beyond their barriers. I don't care if it's a python, a polar bear, or a tiger. They won't make a move until you're within range. The dog spying the bear standing up got real aggressive, growled with his canines bared, and went for the bear. The bear—imagine, you're talking a twelve-hundred-pound bear—can't get much of his paw through there, but with just one deft motion slapped the dog's muzzle, knocked it right off, and it went about eight

feet down the line. The dog went down in shock immediately. The bear then pulled the dog through the bars like
you pull a fat bag of potato chips through a little slit, all at
once, breaking his bones. Then he ate the dog; there wasn't
enough left to block a drain. That was early in the morning.
Then, at two-thirty I guess he ate a big pile of meat and
about twelve big fish. But the tragic thing was this guy
came looking for his dog at eight-thirty, nine o'clock. He
seemed to get a kick out of his dog out biting the hell out of
someone. Well, his dog had never met a polar bear.

A monitor is a carnivorous lizard. The biggest lizard in
the world is the Komodo dragon, a monitor from the island
of Komodo off Sumatra. They can be ten feet long, weigh
three hundred pounds. They use their tail like a whip;
they're very adept at using it, and if you got hit in the face,
you'd have a welt for a couple of weeks. They would take
the tongs right out of your hand with it. And they also have
a dirty bite; that's how Komodo dragons bite, kill their
animals. If they bite a deer, grab a deer by the leg, at dawn,
invariably the deer gets away with lacerations on the leg,
but by dusk it dies of blood poisoning. The condition clears
up once you get a Komodo dragon in captivity, because he's
fed clean meat. They eat a lot of carrion in the wild. I've
read in journals that researchers who've studied the Ko-
modos are deathly afraid of being scratched, that's how
pathogenic they are.

We had this monitor in the back tank, one of those
concrete back tanks, and he would always try to get you—
very aggressive animal, very defensive. So one day I'm
working the cage, and sure enough, he whipped his tail.
And I jumped back, recoiled, but not fast enough, and he
knocked my glasses off my face, and they fell, bounced off
the cage onto the floor and broke. I sent in an incident
report and a request for compensation for frames. The
word came back, the park district doesn't pay for frames. I
said, "It happened on the job, and it was an animal." So this
guy proceeded to tell me that for a dollar and a half I could
get this kind of cord I could put on my glasses that'd keep

my glasses from falling off. I said, "Yeah, but if you're working with an orangutan and he grabs your glasses and they don't come off, he's going to take your head with them." He said, "Oh, I didn't think of that."

We had another male polar bear, it wasn't as big as Mike, its name was Alfie. Alfie was very adept, and he loved squirrels. People used to throw popcorn and peanuts and crap like that, not realizing polar bears will go after sweet things but really they're basically meat eaters. He would lie down in the middle of the cage, with his arms stretched out, and he had his one red eye open. And in the middle where his paws were stretched around, there'd be peanuts and things. The squirrels would come in, and they'd try to go for the peanuts. As they kept coming closer and closer, each time he'd let them get closer and closer, and then all of a sudden he'd take his paw and go gwiisssh. And then he'd pick up the hairy pancake and would eat it. He was really good at it.

Keo, the chimp, had some idiosyncracies, too. One time he caught a pigeon in his cage. He meticulously plucked all the feathers out, then he was running it around like a little windup toy in the cage. While it was alive. He didn't want to kill it, he wanted a little toy.

15

BIRD WATCHING

Kathy Brown was the senior keeper in the bird house; her responsibility extended beyond that building to the waterfowl lagoon, the flamingo dome, and the zoo rookery as well. She cared about birds, understood them, and could not imagine her life without them.

It wasn't always so.

Kathy, at forty-six, looked back on a life that had taken several courses before delivering her to the zoo. She was born in Moline, Illinois, but spent her preschool years living with her family in Nebraska, before returning to Illinois, to Peoria, where she attended school.

Her parents were divorced; there were no funds for her to attend college. She got a clerical job in Chicago with Time Inc. and spent more than ten years with that publishing conglomerate. As she approached thirty, she feared being frozen in her job; she quit and "bummed around for eighteen months." After that, she got a job as a school bus dispatcher, a job she remembered as offering "no money and no future."

She heard about an exam being given for keeper jobs at the zoo. She took it, but she "didn't sit around and wait" for the results. She had never been a zoo volunteer, although she did have a fondness for animals.

"I never thought of working as a zoo keeper. It wasn't my big dream," she recalled. She continued to work as a bus dispatcher. Then she got the word that she had passed the keeper exam, and in 1975 she joined the zoo staff.

She grew to love the work. In 1987, she was promoted to senior keeper. During her twelve years at the zoo, she had spent all but seven months—working at the farm—with birds.

A short (5'1"), chubby, natural blond with blue-green eyes and a calm, reasoned demeanor, Kathy had lived with the man in her life for ten years; they shared their home with three cats. In her spare time, she took college courses at various local schools: English, Russian, art, music.

She drove to the zoo, arriving well before 8 A.M. On one cool fall morning, she began her day by visiting a pair of barn owls obtained from the Cincinnati Zoo. The owls, Alba, a female, and Spartacus, her brother, were in adjoining cages in the basement of the bird house. Kathy looked at them admiringly, but did not speak to them; she was not given to fits of anthropomorphism.

The two birds stared at her intently, moving slightly from side to side. Their feathers were brown and white; their faces were outlined with a brown line, as if drawn by a mask maker. They were members of an endangered species and had been acquired for use by the education department.

They were birds of prey. Kathy's simple definition: "Anything that hunts live food and nothing else." The owls did not look threatening; certainly, Kathy did not fear them. When she was confident that they were untroubled, she moved on.

She had to feed a seventeen-day-old Nicobar pigeon, whose mother had been found dead in the bird house ("bad kidneys," Kathy called it) when the son was only ten days old. She mixed a bowl of Gerber high-protein baby cereal and brought it to a holding area upstairs where the Nicobar, a small iridescent blue-green bird, was caged. She opened the cage, but the bird did not move. Inside the cage, she had placed a small mirror and a doll—an attempt to remind the young bird of its origins.

"The mirror is to help him retain a sense of visual identification, so when he returns to the group, he'll know who he is and who they are," she said.

She fed the bird using a syringe, simulating the way the mother—or father, because fathers feed their young, too—would have fed it. The bird accepted the meal calmly.

"At times, I wish he'd bite me and hate me, so I can be sure he'll adjust when we put him back. I want to lose him. He's not a pet, an imprinted animal. An imprinted animal is not a true member of the species. I don't appreciate having to hand-raise them. Natural parents are so much more efficient. I worry that he's going to lose a piece of his personality to us.

"I want to toss him out on the floor in our free-flight area and hope he reverts. An imprinted animal is an aberration, and it can be abused by the nonimprinted birds, with their pecking order. It has to learn the behavior that will make it compatible with the other birds."

In nearby cages, several American kestrals (also known as sparrow hawks) glared at her. Common in the city, they were federally protected birds of prey. One of them was a one-year-old male, who would be released after being retrained to return to the wild, in an area south of the city. Another, a female, had a damaged wing and would be retained for display by the education department.

It was time for Kathy to walk around the main hall of the bird house before the visitors arrived.

In one of the glass-and-tile cages, she spotted a superb starling, a beautiful blue, white, and rust-colored bird. It moved effortlessly. But it had only one leg.

"That happened eight years ago," Kathy said. "It got tangled in the foliage here and tried to break free. Its legs are fragile, and in its panic, it broke one of them. The vet amputated it. But this bird is highly adapted to flight, and it moves quite well with one leg by flapping its wings."

As Kathy watched, the bird did just that.

It was time for her to serve the insect-eating birds a snack of meal worms. With a metal pie plate filled with the small, squirming worms, she went from cage to cage, unlocking a panel in each and tossing a handful of worms to each group of birds.

"They don't have strong nutritional value, but they're useful in fending off stress. Birds that eat insects like live food. It gets them excited, entertains them. It's an early meal before the main meal," she said.

When she had distributed the worms, Kathy grabbed the long hose that ran the length of one run and began to clean the cages. The birds flew away from the steam of water, not in fright, but to observe from a distance.

"They respond to a routine," she said, "when I hose, when I feed them. Some of them can separate keepers from the public; they know the difference. When they're nesting, they're hostile to the uniform, because we invade their privacy. A few have actually tried to hit me when I encroached on their territory."

She hosed and talked. At the far end of the spacious hall, in a wide, open area, Sammy, a salmon-crested cockatoo—a large white bird with touches of salmon-colored feathers— sat sternly on his high perch, watching her.

"Hello!" she yelled at him.

There was a long pause, then the sound of the cockatoo. "Hello."

"Some of them do get to know you. Me, that is," Kathy said. "But most of them live as they do in the wild. They're not tame. They're not pets."

In one large cage, ten noisy blue-crowned conures— green parrots from South America—flew to the upper corner when Kathy intruded with her hose. They had been seized by federal authorities from an importer caught exceeding the number of birds he was authorized to bring

into the United States. The government allocated the birds
to the zoo temporarily. Kevin Bell, curator of birds, didn't
want them; soon they would be shipped to another zoo
that did want them.

As Kathy moved along the run, the birds flew away from
her and her hose, chirping at her in a language she could
not translate.

"Birds are territorial," she said. "Give them food, companionship, housing, and they don't want to get out. If
they have an appropriate flight space, they are at home."

The conures were making loud noises, summoning
Kathy's attention. She looked at them.

"You can try to train parrots, but I think that they react
reflexively. You can teach a wild bird to perch. But there's
just too much anthropomorphism with parrots. Sure, a
parrot trained to perch will perch. It may also attack the
hell out of you. A wild bird is a wild bird."

As she cleaned the cages, Eddie, one of the park district's
experts on flora and landscaping, entered with two of his
laborers. A short, balding, congenial worker, he was, at
sixty-two, a veteran of many years at the zoo and a long-
time friend of Kathy's. They chatted about a plant to be
removed from the bird house and a few trees to be planted
in the free-flight area. When they were done with their
conversation, Eddie walked over to Sammy, the cockatoo.

Although Sammy preferred the company of women to
men, Eddie was an exception. He petted the bird, who
tolerated the petting.

"I'm one of the few men he likes," Eddie said proudly.

When Eddie and his crew left the building, Kathy walked
over to Sammy.

"When he's feeling nasty, he bluffs and pretends to bite
you. But he doesn't bite down, really bite. He loves attention. He'll scream and yell when he doesn't get it, when he
wants it."

She sprayed him gently with the hose. Sammy moved up
to a higher position on his hanging perch.

"Come down, baby," she urged. He came down slowly,

barely within her reach. She scratched beneath his soft, thick feathers. He stared into space, not acknowledging her affection.

"He's mad at me because I haven't talked to him lately," she said.

"Spoiled is the word for you," she said to Sammy. He shifted his position so that he was hanging upside down. She dug her fingers into his feathers to his skin. The bird remained still.

"You can achieve this kind of familiarity only with a bird that was hand-raised," she said. Sammy had been pampered by a wealthy socialite, who had donated the bird to the zoo.

"I tell people who call us about buying pets to buy a hand-raised bird from a breeder, not a wild bird. It's so much better, even if you do pay more for it," she said.

When she removed her hand from Sammy, it was covered with white powder. "Only cockatoos have this soft white powder," she said. "It's a lubricant to keep their feathers in good condition."

She walked away from Sammy, who made a loud cackling sound.

She went to the keeper area in the basement for her morning coffee and a cigarette. When she was done, she picked up a stack of pie plates with food on them—fruits and vegetables for the most part—and carried them up to the run she had cleaned earlier. Normally, another keeper would have done the feeding, but the staff was short-handed that day, and Kathy wasn't reluctant about filling in.

She put the plates in the cages; some of the birds rushed to eat, but Sammy remained on his perch, while a Nicobar pigeon sampled Sammy's plate of food. Sammy showed no sign of objecting.

"He doesn't relate to other birds," Kathy said. "Just to people."

She finished feeding the birds on one side of the hall; another keeper fed the rest. Kathy walked out into the sunlight and the cool breeze and headed for the waterfowl lagoon, to feed the flamingos, the ducks, the geese, what she called "basic work."

She took a peek into the flamingo dome, the glass bubble next to the waterfowl lagoon; it was empty. The flamingos would not be brought into their heated habitat until the rigors of winter demanded it. In the keeper service area beneath the dome, she filled containers with dry food. Outside, she dropped a trail of food along the lagoon bank and tossed some into the water. A free-for-all ensued, with a few city pigeons, ubiquitous scavengers, joining the ducks and geese.

"Most of these birds will be out here all winter," she said. "They're putting on body fat to keep them warm once winter arrives."

With a hose, she filled three tubs of water for the flamingos and added their food, "Flamingo-Fare." On the bank, away from the ravenous fowl, the tall pink birds poised gracefully on their long legs and glared, but did not acknowledge her presence.

Kathy had worked almost without interruption for four hours. It was time for lunch, for her an expedient rather than a profound pleasure. After having a bacon-cheeseburger at a nearby restaurant, she was back at work. That afternoon, she would instruct a group of docents in bird lore; it was her role in the docents' continuing education, which they would pass along to zoo visitors.

Later in the afternoon, she walked over to one of the zoo's hidden treasures, the zoo rookery. At the north edge of the zoo, bordering on the busy traffic to and from the lakefront, there was a nature preserve, a curving walk past a pond filled with ducks and geese and swans, protected from the sight of high-rise apartment buildings by arching groups of tall trees. It was a small, separate world.

The zoo rookery, built as a W.P.A. project in the 1930s, was—as a sign at its entrance announced—"a place where birds stop to feed and rest during spring and fall migrations. Some may breed, nest and hatch their young chicks in this area."

Actually, a few of the zoo's own bird collection lived in the rookery as well, but most of the birds to be found on the rookery pond were migratory mallards and Canadian geese.

Overcrowding was a problem, to be managed.

"If a bird hatches here, this is its home," Kathy said. "So we collect those eggs and destroy them. It's a form of birth control. If the mallards multiply, the cost of the food we have to provide—and making sure our own birds get some—becomes a problem."

She strolled along, listening to the shouts of small children as they encountered the ducks and the geese and the swans.

"This is one part of the zoo where the public is not discouraged from feeding the animals," she pointed out. A small boy was tossing chunks of bread to the birds.

"The migratory birds are lucky and smart," she said. "They can eat here at the rookery and then head right over to the waterfowl lagoon for more."

The rookery was a place that some keepers used, as well, for a respite in a demanding day. Kathy saw Barbara Katz, a keeper at the penguin-seabird house, pausing to appreciate the behavior of the migratory birds in the pond.

They chatted amiably for a few moments. Barbara was thirty-one, a keeper for seven years, a college graduate with a degree in biology and a special interest in hooded cranes. Short and trim, with dark brown hair cut very short, Barbara was used to being mistaken for a man; it amused her. It did not amuse her to know that any animals were being mistreated. She had a reputation as an activist, zealous in defending the rights of the penguins and the seabirds against all corner-cutting efforts by the bureaucracy. Barbara's methods, sometimes lacking in tact when an issue was at stake, were not Kathy's, but Kathy admired her tenacity, her devotion.

As Barbara saw it, "I'm here to provide the best possible care for the animals I take care of. That's my job. I couldn't live with myself if I let my animals down.

"Captivity is supposed to be the easy life. We are not reproducing natural ecosystems here. Just because an animal faces certain hardships in the wild and survives doesn't mean it's all right for us to supply anything less than luxury accommodations," Barbara said.

"The only higher-ups I'm accountable to are my penguins and seabirds," she added.

There were many reasons for her loyalty to the animals. Among them was one she would not forget. As a teenage volunteer at the children's zoo, she had been trying to conquer her own shyness. An animal had helped her win that struggle.

"I met Nicky, a two-year-old capuchin monkey at the children's zoo," she remembered. "She had been a pet, but was donated to the zoo after she became too unruly. When we first met, she was terrified of her new home, and I was a painfully shy teenager. She hid under her blanket, and I hid within myself. At first, she wouldn't even look at me when I sat in her cage. But I persisted. We sat together for days before she would come over and look at me. After several weeks, she came to trust me and enjoyed going outside to run around on the grass and climb trees.

"Of all the animals I have known and worked with, Nicky remains, to this day, the most special. We were inseparable that summer. We each did a lot of growing up. We helped each other.

"By the end of the summer, each of us was more comfortable in the company of others. I knew that I was drawn to her because of her fear and shyness. I knew that as long as I didn't pressure her, things would be OK. And they were."

It was a touching story, and there was little to comment on. Barbara headed toward the penguin-seabird house, and Kathy lingered in the rookery. She stared at a pair of elegant black swans on the pond, moving effortlessly across the water. Then she made her way slowly through the zoo back to the bird house.

She walked past the polar bears and the spectacled bears and the wolves and the giraffes, without stopping to look at them.

Suddenly she stopped, her eyes fixed on the sky. She had spotted a belted kingfisher, a bird seldom seen in Chicago, zooming overhead. She froze and followed its path, as the gray-blue and white bird headed north, to the rookery and beyond. She was sorry that she hadn't been with a birder, to share the treat.

"They're not as prolific as starlings or robins," she said. "You see just a couple every season."

It was late in the day. There was only time for one look around the bird house before she had to drive home. Still staring up at the sky, she quickened her pace.

FIRST PERSON: KATHY BROWN

I've always liked zoos. If there was a zoo around and I was on vacation, I usually went to the zoo. I liked the animals. I wasn't really motivated by any real desire to understand or relate to them at all. And here I am.

I took the keeper test because it was a lark. It wasn't a priority in my life. I didn't take seriously the fact that I passed or failed. I somehow wasn't surprised at the fact that I passed. I test well. I think at that time my perception of keepers was as a labor force, as opposed to a real profession, which it's evolving into now. It might have been after I started working here that I found out it was the first test given to women. I always have a tendency to fall in; I've done a number of things in my life that in hindsight I really shouldn't have been able to do. I wasn't looking at zoo keeping, it was really coincidental that I was called at a time I was seriously thinking of changing jobs. I simply had nothing to lose. If it didn't work out, if I didn't like it, I could go away.

I was looking for a change in direction. This was back in the very early seventies when pantsuits had just come in. Up until then, I was used to having to get into a girdle; we didn't have panty hose. I didn't like that; I wanted to be comfortable in what I did. So I was prepared; I was looking forward to a challenge.

Getting dirty didn't bother me, animal shit didn't really bother me. I'd been around animals before. I've never been scared of spiders, I've never been scared of snakes, I've never had fears of those things. When I was hired, they asked me questions like "Do you know you're going to have to pick up fifty pounds of grain? Do you know you're going to have to move hay?" I didn't know I was going to have to do that. But I've always had this attitude that I can do what everybody else can do.

I think I was a bit of a feminist before feminism actually got a name and an organization. Keep in mind that the sixties were my twenties. My parents were conservative enough to think that marriage was ultimately what I would do. You know, it wasn't too important if I made a great success of my life, as long as I got married and had children. I had a lot of problems with that. For the first time in my life at thirty I got hit with the idea that the reason I'm not married is I don't want to get married. As soon as I came to that conclusion, then I was really open to taking other directions and to being very independent.

It wasn't that I liked animals. I had no fear of working with the animals. I felt I would be competent enough to do the job, but a good part of it was getting out of that restrictive thing that women, even to this day, are in. The idea of getting up and putting on a dress, having to be immaculate. The birds don't care, you know.

Actually, it wasn't that I chose and stayed with birds. The staff usually determines personnel changes and transfers. My first seven months were on the farm. I'd proved myself there, and I was transferred to the bird house. I didn't ask for the bird house. I came in here totally blank on birds. I knew maybe four species of the common birds of North America, and that was about it. I stayed here for twelve years. I enjoyed it, and there's a tremendous amount of information to be learned here. If I was going to do my job right, I had to learn what was going on, what birds were about. And I set about doing just that, trying to understand what I was looking at, why I was looking at it, what the behavior meant, what this bird eats, what can I do to change a diet for a whole breed. It all became a challenge for me.

I've never been bored. There's just too much to do. If you're bored, there's books up here, there's books at the library, there's animals you can stand and watch. I get a lot of affection from birds by allowing them to do what they want to do. Take the Nicobar pigeons. Kevin Bell and I started about the same time back in 1976 with three pairs. He immediately saw the value and the rarity of these birds. And they were already actively breeding, so it was very important these animals be documented and detailed and records kept. This is a perfect example of spending a lot of time doing observations on what is essentially a wild animal. I got to know them a little bit individually, and their offspring, and how they related to their offspring, and how their offspring related to *their* offspring. As years go on, they peel back these layers; they're living their whole lives in front of you, they're not just hopping from a branch and then going to another branch for five minutes and coming down and eating and going to another branch. There's a pecking order, there's a community, and you see how this guy doesn't fit in well because of this problem, or all of a sudden he displaces this boss and now he's boss for the season.

I don't know what's going through their brains; I'm not a bird. Some people may think I'm a bird brain, but I don't have a bird brain. But we've had communities as large as thirty of these guys at one time, and every bird is known by the others, every bird has its place in that group. You know it's not random. It's a city, it's a village, that they've created out there, and each of them has responsibilities. I get a tremendous emotional reward from watching that.

And there's more. Yesterday was a good case. I came in, and a man was waiting for me. He'd brought in a rail, which is a small marsh bird. I understand that the cliché "thin as a rail" comes from the bird, actually. If you look at them head on, they're very narrow birds, almost like something hit them and crushed them. Anyway, I took the bird out of the bag. I looked at the bird, and I had never seen anything quite like it before. It looked to me like a juvenile sora rail, even though I'd never seen one. It certainly wasn't an adult. Anyway, the bird was perfectly healthy, it had just come down over on Clark Street instead of right here in the park and got confused by the cars and the gangways and everything. So I walked with the man down to our waterfowl area, which is an area typical for rails, and we released it there. And the man was very comfortable in our doing that. The bird ran into the bushes, which is what I expected him to do. So it was a healthy bird. He got back on track, you might say. The whole point of this, though, is that I was not real comfortable with the identification of the bird as a sora rail. So I took the time then, after the man left, to look in my bird book and check it out. Well, it was in fact a yellow rail, which is far more rare. We've only had one brought in here in the twelve years I've been here, and that was a damaged one many years ago that I don't think survived.

The public does bring in wild birds. If they're capable of recovery, even if it takes a few days—assuming we can get them to eat in captivity, which is sometimes a problem— we'll offer them those few days for recovery. We get a lot of head bashes, birds flying into glass windows, into the high rises. If a bird doesn't recover, if it's seriously damaged, it's euthanized. A few of them find their way into our collection.

In captivity, some birds have to make a lot of adjustments, some birds don't. For instance, sometimes we can have a pair of birds in the center aviary, and we can't introduce a third bird. They'll kill it, or it'll interfere with breeding behavior. In other words, their territory in the wild is so vast in terms of their own species, that they must have the whole aviary for their own territory. So then you can only have a pair of those birds. Other birds are more communal, and they might only require fifteen or twenty square feet of space, so maybe you could have two pairs. Maybe one pair will set off at one end, and maybe the other pair will go to the other end of the building, and they'll function quite well under those conditions. The Nicobars are communal and thrive in a large group.

I can think of one instance where unfortunately we were a little slow understanding what was going on. We had a baby Hartlaub's touraco. After many years of trying to breed them, we finally were successful in getting a baby touraco out of them. We had some problems with it, but ultimately they raised the baby themselves fine. And so we had the three birds up there. Well, a year went by, and we just weren't keyed in, but the touracos went back into breeding condition. The baby was a third bird. They don't want a third bird, they want that whole territory for themselves, so they killed their own baby. If we had just sensed that this was happening, we could have removed the baby from the aviary; it would have been no problem. But everything seemed to be going well, you know, mom, dad, and the kid. Under normal circumstances in the wild, that baby would have been long gone from the group, and they would have reestablished their territory. They wanted to breed again, and here's a third bird; they didn't care that it was their kid, if they even were aware that it was still their kid. So they killed him.

Among the most beautiful birds, my favorite is the paradise tanager. The tanager is a small fruit-eating bird probably no more than five inches long. They're kind of a Caribbean, South American bird. And their markings are just incredible. They have brilliant colors on this basic black velvet type of plumage, and their heads are turquoise blue. They have a big patch of turquoise blue, a big patch of orange, a big patch of red, a big patch of yellow, and it's all on this black velvet background. Absolutely beautiful. I don't think I've ever seen anything quite as beautiful as the paradise tanager.

You learn from breeding birds. And what we're doing is breeding birds to be what they are. Imprinting turns an animal into a pet. Dogs are imprinted, cats are imprinted, a couple of the birds here are imprinted. That's fine if you want a pet. But we're not in the pet business. We're in the business of taking a species of animal out of its habitat, which may be mostly gone, keeping it going and alive as a species that you hope down the road, someday, can go back. You've got to let it retain as many of its basic qualities as it can. We don't raise a bird with the intent of imprinting it. I've never taken a bird home with the intent of imprinting it. I've taken it home to keep it alive, because sometimes they're valuable enough that just having that bird alive on earth is more important than risking imprinting it. If it gets imprinted along the way, it's unfortunate, but better to have it alive and imprinted than not alive at all. You run into that situation.

Zoos started out to be displays for the public, and most of these buildings were designed to accommodate people who walked through, and the least amount of space was turned over to the animals. The animals were there to show the people what a lion or a monkey or a chimpanzee looked like. That wasn't good, so zoos began to change to at least give animals a bit more credit. But here we are, in an ecologically disastrous age, we're killing the earth and a lot of the animals with it. And so, all of a sudden, the world has come to determine that a lot of these animals, if they're going to stay alive, there is no alternative institution that's going to keep them alive. Zoos are already set up to do that, even though that's not why they were created.

Now it's my job to breed these damned things, to keep them alive and keep records and that's not something zoos set out to look for. Zoos just kind of woke up one day and said, "Wait a minute, we gotta do this, because we're the only ones around who can do it." I was vaguely aware of that when I came in here, that what I'm dealing with are wild animals.

Sure, it's very difficult to try not to relate to these birds, to try to keep from anthropomorphizing them. If I'm hand-raising a bird, I don't want to imprint him, I don't want to do it. But when I'm doing it, it's very hard. I mean, I'm not going to stand here and say, "Well, the heck with you." It's very hard for me to keep from snuggling, wanting to snuggle with a certain bird. Very hard to keep from going "cootchy cootchy cootchy coo," you know. Very hard. When you're hand-raising them, they're shifting their identification from the parent to you, because you become the parent. What I try to do is prevent that, but it's very hard for me to even draw the line sometimes. I want to just grab that bird and give it ten minutes of very intense affection. That's not good for the bird.

I've had my heart broken many times. A couple of years ago, we were breeding rose-breasted cockatoos. They're fairly common in zoos. One year a pair gave us two fine healthy chicks. The following year they went through the same behavior, but something went wrong. We recovered one chick from the nest box who was virtually starved, emaciated. The mother was not well at the time, and she was trying to starve the chicks out. That's sometimes how birds fledge; parents just stop feeding the chicks. This creates the initiative for the chick to start going out and seeking things. It's a basic pattern among birds. Well, I ended up being the person taking on the responsibility of trying to turn this emaciated baby that had been living in a little black hole, a nest box, which is normal, into some kind of a viable bird. And I didn't really care about imprinting at that point. The whole point was to keep it alive and do whatever was necessary. I named her Rosie, took her home, just to see that she got extra feedings at night, and she was getting better and better. I was going to night school that fall, and she was doing very well. I started leaving her at the zoo overnight. Three or four nights had gone by, and I came in one morning, and she was dead. She had appeared to be doing very well the night before. I thought I was doing the right thing. Her state of deterioration was so bad when she came out of the box that all I did was buy her time. But it was just coming in, knowing I left her in what I thought was good shape the night before, walking upstairs to give her her morning feeding, with a smile on my face, expecting her to respond to me, and I'd been dealing with her now for three or four weeks maybe, and there she was.

If you're dealing with an animal on a day-to-day basis, one on one, regardless of how hard you try not to imprint, there's still an affection that occurs. In many situations, regardless of whether the bird is imprinting on me or not, if I'm trying to nurse it, trying to keep it alive, sometimes by the time two or three days go by, it's too late for me emotionally. Now, if a bird dies within the first day, I can deal with that. But if I've been dealing with it for three or four days or longer, then it becomes very difficult.

Not all stories are sad. This starts with a man and a woman who came from Finland. He was quite a well-known magician in Europe, traveling with his wife as his assistant. They were retired, and how they ended up in Chicago I have no idea. Julius and Nadia, almost every keeper at the zoo knows these people. By the time I came to the bird department, Julius already had an ongoing relationship with Blackie the swan. His passion for that bird! I don't think anybody ever really understood it. I don't even know if Julius really understood it. Blackie was a black swan, actually an Australian black swan. This attachment that Julius had bordered on the obsessive. It was very passionate; the man and his wife would come almost every day. It didn't matter if it was ten degrees or five degrees, they'd put their mufflers on and their coats, and they'd come to the zoo rookery and see him anyway. So there was no way that we could take that bird away from him. Blackie stayed on. Nobody really wanted Blackie. It's not that we didn't like Blackie, but it would have been nice to have put him out with some other swans in another zoo somewhere. But Julius just wouldn't have stood for it. So we kept Blackie for a number of years alone. Nadia was very supportive of her husband, like the swan itself, but her approach was a little bit more logical.

Well, Julius had lung cancer but kept himself in very good health. Julius would bring treats, he'd bring lettuce, he'd buy watermelon out of season because Blackie loved watermelon. Blackie knew him, without a doubt. And Blackie could be aggressive; I mean, he was a male swan. But he knew Julius very well. Julius would sit down, and Blackie would come up and lay his head in Julius's lap, and he'd pet this swan. Blackie would bite the heck out of me, Blackie never liked keepers much, I can tell you that. But he loved Julius. It was my hope that Julius would pass away before Blackie did, and Blackie was not a young bird. I thought that Blackie's death would devastate him, that would be the end of Julius, that's how intense their relationship was. It's hard to say, but unfortunately Julius did die first. He was walking two days before he died.

By then we had a swan called Nadia, which is another little story in itself. I named it Nadia, even though it's a male. This black swan was brought to us by animal control, although actually the bird was very healthy; somebody was taking care of it. I named it Nadia because Julius's wife's name was Nadia. When I brought the bird in not knowing what sex it was, and knowing that this was Blackie's territory, I had three or four keepers standing around prepared to break them apart. I wasn't sure what was going to happen. It was love at first sight. Both are males, but I think they were just happy to be with one of their own kind.

You've taken this animal out of the wild. You've thrown it into this cage, and of course you get a lot of comments from the public about how inhumane this is. But these birds aren't really suffering. Nonetheless, if you're looking at a relatively rare animal that five years ago was in the wild but here it's been living in this cage for five years, it has lost quality of life. But if you've got an animal that's breeding, you've got a happy animal. I mean you're doing something right, because if it's not a happy animal, it's not going to make babies for you. You're allowing it to do something it would be doing in the wild. Maybe it's confined, granted, but you've made that animal at least comfortable within the confines of its life. It has a mate, it's got food, it may have offspring to raise. For me, that type of thing is very much a reward.

When I first took the job, I thought, "Well, I can give it five or ten years." I wasn't that serious about being a zookeeper. "I'll give it five years, then maybe I'll look around and see if there's something else I'd like to do." Well, it's twelve years now. I've learned a lot. It's been a teaching experience that I can carry over into my retired life. I toy around with the idea of getting permits to allow me to sell certain wild animals, maybe continue working with birds that are injured. It's not just a job, you know, it's kind of become a part of what I do, who I am. When I go on a vacation, I take my bird books, I find out what birds I can see while I'm on my travels. Before I worked here, it never would have occurred to me to do anything like that.

16

THE SOCIETY'S GOSPEL

The Chicago Park District owned and maintained the zoo.
The 4 million visitors who came to the zoo each year to see
the more than 2,000 animals it housed probably didn't care
where the money came from. If they did, they would have
known that the zoo would be a tattered relic without the
efforts of the Lincoln Park Zoological Society.

The society had defined its mission in these words: "To
provide the funding and services required to operate the
zoo as a world class institution."

In practical terms, the society provided close to 50 percent of the total funding required to operate and improve
the zoo. The collaboration between the park district and
the zoo society enabled the zoo to sustain its reputation for
excellence, to modernize its facilities, and to remain free to
the public.

The zoo society, its civic-minded and influential board of
directors, the park district, and the zoo director, Les
Fisher, all played roles in achieving the objectives listed in
the society's annual report:

- Improve zoo buildings, provide excellent animal management facilities and outstanding exhibits for visitors.
- Beautify the zoo grounds, adding gardens and sculpture.
- Make improvements to facilitate public access, and improve parking areas.
- Provide resources to acquire additional animals and to care for all the animals properly.
- Enable the zoo to participate in international efforts to breed endangered species.
- Provide free services, including information, printed matter, and a library, to the public.
- Offer free educational services to school children and visitors, at the zoo itself and in outreach programs.
- Conduct research and conservation efforts to protect endangered animals, in captivity and in the wild.
- Inspire a flow of donated revenue to accomplish all of the society's goals.

In 1986, the park district provided the zoo with funds and services worth more than $4.5 million. The zoo society provided slightly more than $4 million.

At the heart of the society's effort was Barbara Whitney, its executive director. A forty-five-year-old Chicago-born divorcée and mother of three, Barbara grew up in the Chicago area, majored in English at Denison University in Ohio, married, and moved to New York. She spent two years as a researcher in the book division of Time Inc., returned to Chicago, had her children, and spent six years in suburbia.

When she was divorced in 1973, she realized that she needed a job; she didn't have the money to be self-sustaining. She did find work and moved to the first of several apartments within walking distance of the zoo. Over the years, she had volunteered for various causes. That experience made the zoo society an appealing possibility for her. In late 1975, she became its fourth executive director. The society had been formed in 1959, but had limped along

with just an executive director and a secretary for several
years until Barbara arrived.

After that, things changed.

Under Barbara's direction, the society membership went
from 2,200 when she arrived to 13,000 in 1987. The staff
grew to forty full-time and thirty part-time (in summer).
And donations to the zoo went from a trickle to a steady
and substantial flow. The names of well-known local business titans began to be engraved on the walls of new zoo
buildings: Pritzker on a new children's zoo; Regenstein on a
large mammal house; Kroc on a new hospital-commissary;
Crown and Field on the administration–zoo society building. The donations involved ranged from $500,000 to $2
million, and they highlighted the campaign to change the
face of the zoo, to modernize the venerable institution.

A tall (5'8") woman, trim and fashionable, with short
graying brown hair and hazel eyes, Barbara became the
ruler of a substantial empire. It included the board of
directors, the auxiliary board and the women's board—a
total of more than 250 volunteers dedicated to the progress
of the zoo. From her bright, modern, uncluttered office in
the Crown-Field Center, she functioned energetically.
Some of her associates saw her as "driven," an energized
director locked into a single cause. Those who appreciated
results didn't care how she might be defined.

She played a vital role in the renovations at the zoo, in
running the docent-volunteer programs (there were more
than 400 docents and volunteers at the zoo), in working
with Les Fisher and his staff, in guiding her own staff—
and in relating to the zoo society boards and philanthro-
pists in the outside world.

After she had been at the zoo for six years, Barbara
made a speech about her work. The message endured:

> My work at the zoo is not *with* the animals but it's *about*
> the animals and *for* the animals. My work is with people—
> literally thousands of them who make up this big family

that is called the zoo society. . . . They are investing in the future of the zoo. They are investing their money, and that equally valuable gift—their time. They are doing it so that the zoo will be here to make memories for the children of the future—memories of animals that are strange and wonderful and wild, from far-off lands they will never see.

She did not abandon that definition, but there were days when the demands of her packed schedule distracted her from such guiding abstractions. Much of her time was consumed by phone calls, meetings, dialogues with staff members, planning sessions, and more. The society's annual calendar was filled with events, mailings, publications, parties, fairs, conferences, picnics, dinners, luncheons, and zoo programs. Few pages in her desk diary were blank. She earned her $73,000 salary.

On one chilly Monday in October, she met with five staff members, one man and four women. (Men were underrepresented in the zoo society; so were minorities.) In a pink knit cardigan, trimmed in black with gold buttons, and a coordinated black knit skirt, she seemed dressed for action. But not necessarily for serious conversation, at least not immediately.

"Does anyone know what this meeting is about?" she asked, smiling. "Oh, well, it's Monday morning."

In truth, she knew quite well what the meeting was about. She wanted to talk about increasing the activity level of the committees of the board of directors. Among them: executive, architectural improvements, conservation, development, finance, programs, and visitor services. Each committee had a society staff member to depend upon. Barbara knew that much of the society's important work occurred in such committees. The staff members present were among those who worked closely with the committees.

"You must interact with them directly. We drown in details here, but they have general thoughts not obscured

by such details," she said. She knew that board members—
stockbrokers, industrialists, high-level executives—had an
expertise that the society lacked: how to succeed in business. And the society was a business.

"Set up your own relationship with the committee chairman," she urged. "Then work with me on an agenda. I
want to add my input. And remember, we need a report—a
written analysis of what goes on—or there's nothing to
discuss. The chairmen have full-time jobs, so they need
our staff support. Keep pushing forward. Keep them moving. Make sure that meetings happen.

"Let's pay attention to the board members. They have
credibility with their peers that we never have. But don't
forget that they don't spend twelve hours a day thinking
about the zoo, and we do. We can help them, and they can
help us."

The Landmark Campaign, to renovate zoo buildings and
add new exhibits, had gone along satisfactorily, given the
usual delays, construction impediments, and budget restrictions. Now, it was time for the society to look beyond
that major effort. Barbara knew that it took three years to
get a program in place. In the nonprofit arena, one had to
be patient or succumb to stomach acid.

There were plans for the future. She wanted to raise
funds to rehabilitate the aged reptile house, to repair the
sea lion pool. Above all, she wanted to honor the term
garden in "zoological garden."

"A half-million dollars could work wonders," she said. "It
would be easy to turn this zoo into a beautiful garden area,
with gardens all over the zoo. We could have garden cafés
and garden plazas. Yes, the animal areas are always our
first priority, but we've been dealing with that. Now we can
deal with other concerns.

"For example, we need more space for the administration. Can we solve that by renovating the basement of the
reptile house? Or do we need a new administration building? Will the society pay for it? The one we have now is on

valuable land. It may be too costly to house the administration, particularly when you consider that the visitors could
make use of it."

Planning—and talking about planning—never ceased.
When one program became a reality, it was time for
another. Someday, the perfect small zoo might manifest its
glory in Lincoln Park, but no one could imagine it. Work on
the future went on.

Barbara knew that the society depended on the board for
the success of such planning.

"Without the board, the society couldn't achieve its objectives," she said. "It's a dynamic. The board brings ideas
to us, and we bring ideas to them. It's the marriage that
creates good grant proposals, good presentations.

"We look ahead together. I spend an enormous amount
of time thinking about five years from now."

Nonprofit organizations hoped for one or more of the
three Ws from its board: wisdom, wealth, or work.

"You need a hard core—say twenty-five or thirty percent—that is active," Barbara noted. "If you have fifty
percent of the board members who are active, you're
lucky."

To tempt donors, the executive director had to be tactful,
cautious, considerate. Donors had to be courted.

"It's not a problem for me," Barbara said. "I have a weak
personality. That means I was taught to be nice, not con-
frontational. I've been a board member, so I can see matters from that point of view. And I like most of those
people I get to know in my job. It is my job to get to people
who don't even know my name, who look right through
me. Effort counts. The best people in this business are
those who make that extra phone call, who pay extra
attention to keep our 'family' together.

"You can raise money by begging, or you can raise
money by saying that a well-managed effort deserves support. We choose the latter course, a corporate image of
excellence, instead of need. We demonstrate permanence,
continuity, a plan—as a reality. Are we managing well?
That's the greatest weight I have to bear.

"A sense of style is important in everything we market. Printed materials. Events. We want to demonstrate a new energy. Excitement. Change. Being up-to-date. It's all a conscious effort on our part."

Barbara depended upon her staff to make that effort succeed.

Chuck Harris was one of her stalwarts. The short, bearded, tweedy project manager for the society, Chuck kept her posted on all the renovation and construction at the zoo. As winter invaded, he was preparing to escape to an African safari, a common respite for zoo staff members who could afford it. But first he met with Barbara and Les Fisher.

He told Barbara what to watch out for while he was away; he had done his best to prevent a calamity from occurring during his absence, but he couldn't be certain that calm would prevail. For a few moments, their roles were reversed. Barbara took notes; she wanted to be prepared.

There was a plan to erect a souvenir stand near the small mammal house. Could it be done by next summer, Barbara wondered. Chuck wasn't sure. The stand was needed by the society, which ran it; the revenue would be useful, particularly since the society's shop in the lion house would be shut down during that building's renovation.

Chuck would contact an architect and urge him to submit a concept for the stand by the time Chuck returned.

Various projects were subject to park district approval or consultation. Implied in that was an awareness of the personalities involved—and the power they wielded. Barbara and Les shared that awareness and spoke in a kind of bureaucratic shorthand about it.

As the meeting ended, Les got up and smiled at Chuck.

"Remember, once every three years a rhino charges a vehicle," Les told Chuck. "I just wanted to keep your adrenal glands from atrophying."

Les headed back to his office; Chuck went back to his cubicle. Barbara was left alone in her office, for a few minutes of silence before going to a meeting with several

354 ───────────────────────────── Zoo

members of the women's board, who were eager to discuss the future of the zoo.

It was a subject that consumed much of Barbara's time and concern. The zoo was a small zoo, just thirty-five acres, but it was a free zoo, open every day. In contrast to its 13,000 zoo society members, the San Diego Zoo had more than 120,000. And Lincoln Park had fewer personnel than most major city zoos. Those facts inspired perpetual reevaluations of goals.

No one wanted to initiate a fee to enter the zoo, but studies had indicated that zoos that did generated substantial revenue. In 1986, the San Diego Zoo had collected almost $15 million in admission revenue from its 3 million visitors. A projection of possible Lincoln Park revenues indicated that as much as $12 million might be gained from a $4 fee. What no one could know was how many people would not visit the zoo if they had to pay for it.

In the short term, Barbara had to help create and adhere to the society's annual budget. She kept it in mind. For the fiscal year ending in March 1988, the society projected revenues of more than $5 million and expenditures of more than $8 million. Fortunately, almost $5 million of the expenditures was for capital improvements and would be met by prior funding, already on hand, and pledges to be collected during the year.

In Barbara's view, there was much to be done. Suggestions, proposals, and hopes abounded.

It would be a good to convert the cramped Crown-Field Center—which housed the zoo's administrative staff and the zoo society staff, an auditorium, and a gift shop—into a public education center. That would mean that a new administration building would have to be built, or the basement of the reptile house converted to office space, not a solution guaranteed to improve staff morale. And the park district was not eager to endorse more new building at the zoo.

During the fiscal year, a number of projects would move toward fruition, and Barbara would have to attend to them, even as her thoughts headed beyond them. The children's zoo and the bird of prey area would be completed, if all went well. The lion house renovation would be 90 percent done, and the bird house 50 percent done. Architectural planning of the refurbished primate house would be completed, and the renovation of the farm would be finished.

The society hoped to begin a study of the renovation of the reptile house and the creation of a maternity area at the sea lion pool. Improvements were needed at the great ape house, and the new koala exhibit would have to be designed atop the Crown-Field Center, where a display of small mammals and a gift shop had been housed.

Barbara wanted gardens created throughout the zoo, and new sculpture added to the grounds.

Funds would be needed for education, conservation, research, graphics around the zoo, to enhance the animal collection—to purchase new animals and conduct expeditions to collect reptiles—and more. Those concerned with animal management needed a computer system; others needed new walkie-talkies. It would be useful to have a closed-circuit TV system to monitor the apes when they were in their outdoor habitat. And introducing the koalas to the zoo would cost money beyond the habitat.

The zoo's education program was wide-ranging. The society shared the cost of it with the park district. The program was essential. Barbara believed that the society had an obligation to make the zoo a satisfying place to visit, with information booths, free literature, attractive zoo merchandise, and bikes and roller skates for rent. Future plans included stroller rentals for parents with weary toddlers and operating the food service in the zoo. It was the society's intention to convert it from glorified hot dog stands to cafés and plazas offering good food in comfortable settings. In fact, the zoo society had won the bidding for the food services and planned to sublet them to a leading local restaurant chain.

For Barbara, these were the matters that kept her alert, when they weren't making her weary. With so many concerns, she had learned to delegate authority. Among the staff members reporting to Barbara were Mena Boulanger, the director of fund-raising, and Nancy Worssam, director of programs.

Mena, forty-six, was born in Seattle, Washington, and had come to the zoo in 1979. A wife, mother of two, and community activist wherever she had lived, she had a master's degree in communication from the University of Illinois. She was a short, neatly tailored blonde with glasses and an understated manner that concealed a quick mind and an ability to spot a donor on sight.

Although her office was a cramped cubicle down the curve from Barbara's office, her role was an essential one. She thought of what she did as "the art of persuasion."

"I studied persuasion in grad school," she said. "It involves identifying within an individual what he or she believes in. Our challenge is to identify a commitment to conservation, to children, to Chicago, to nature, to preservation—and to present the zoo to those people as the effective entity to support that commitment.

"I identify the donors, then we determine which member of the zoo family should present our case to that one person, one company, one family. Who's best to talk to donors? We do our research. Does Les Fisher go? Do we prepare a grant proposal? What form does our presentation take? We confer and we decide. It's important to talk to the right people in the right sequence."

Looking around the society's half of the Crown-Field Center, an observer did not have the sense of being at a zoo; the staff, almost all women, were well dressed, well educated, serious in their devotion. The impression was that of an upscale women's magazine, public relations agency, or any successful business run by women. Staffing the society—choosing the right people—was vital. Choices were not made casually or left to chance.

"We look for warmth, confidence, and more," Mena pointed out. "Education is a must."

In her private life—she lived in a western suburb—she

remained the activist, the partisan; she was a township committeewoman in the Democratic Party. At the zoo, she couldn't afford to be political. The zoo was her cause.

"Actually, it's not really that I have two sides to my life these days. I want to represent the zoo and nothing else. I'm fully involved in it. It's a big commitment.

"It takes time, plenty of time. I have to get volunteers involved, board members, community leaders. The art of fund-raising is conceptualizing a plan and linking it to the people who can make it happen.

"A major gift to the zoo requires a connecting link: a fully developed idea and a rationale for it. Not simply that the zoo needs money for its good intentions. It does, and some donors know that. But most of the time we need the specific project. Les Fisher had four years of conversations about his hopes for the new children's zoo. Then the Pritzkers gave us more than a million dollars.

"You have to spend money and thought to raise money. Friends bring friends to us. We make presentations, conduct tours, send out information. There's no boilerplate when you're obtaining major gifts.

"We need funds to guarantee the quality of the zoo, to create unbridled opportunities to educate. Four million people come through the gates every year. We can educate them right here at the zoo and through video and films as well. We can sponsor conferences.

"It all comes together. I got to go to Kenya with a group from the zoo, and that gave me a sense of connectedness of it all. When you do that, all the concepts that matter to us at the zoo come to life in the wild.

"Nature, the quality of life, it's all linked at the zoo and in Africa. I know I'm sounding existential, but that's where my head is at. At least once a week, I leave my office to visit the animals. I've been a gorilla nut since I was five. I know the animals in our zoo and the keepers, and I can even conduct tours. It's essential for me to get out of my office and see the animals. I don't want to forget them."

If Mena raised the funds, Nancy Worssam was the staff

member charged with figuring out how that money ought to be spent.

The park district took care of the basics, but the zoo society had to go beyond the basics, to improve the quality of life—for animals and staff.

Tall, chic, and understated in her manner, Nancy had a bachelor's degree in history from the University of Connecticut, a master's in anthropology from New York University, and two children from a marriage that ended in divorce.

She found herself working for the National Endowment for the Humanities in Washington, D.C., but concluded that "staying with the government for too long curdles the brain." So when the man with whom she lived had an offer to move to Chicago, they made it a joint decision, and Nancy looked for a job. An exploratory chat at the zoo society led to the creation (in 1986) of the job for Nancy, directing the flow of society funds to the needs of the zoo.

In her soft-spoken way, Nancy set out to understand and appreciate the needs of the members of the zoo staff, and the programs that needed financial transfusions. She quickly realized that while some of the zoo buildings seemed dated, the attitudes were not.

"This place has changed, dramatically, from what it once was," she said. "There's been an unbelievable amount of fund-raising. Now, it's time to take on the task of getting more members. We can use that kind of added support, getting more people involved in the zoo. The society supports all sorts of programs. Conservation. Animal management. Video. Research. Staff travel. Education. It's all program money, and that's what my title—director of programs—is really all about.

"We're working toward a comprehensive plan, an effort to control our own destiny, the zoo's destiny—a kind of financial oversight. In every department, people will tell us where they want to go. Then the zoo itself will have a direction. Growth is upon us. And that means that systems have to be in place before expansion takes place. We're catching up now, and I'm a part of the system. We're after excellence, and that wouldn't be apparent without the work of the zoo society.

"Our job is to make dreams come true. Les Fisher's dreams are shared by others, by curators and by keepers. A curator wants to get something done. He tells me. I take his message to the society. I try to answer the question, 'How can we make that happen?'

"Once you know what you want to do with the money, you can raise the money. My job is to define the path we take, to define the future of the zoo. It's growth in a coherent way. That's the best course."

What Nancy defined and Mena raised funds to support lent definition to Barbara's life. But she was in charge; no one made a major decision without Barbara's voice being heard. She had gone through a period of serious trial, raising money to renovate several old buildings and the farm, and wending her way through red tape to capture the right to provide better food for zoo visitors.

She knew that all major projects were costly. She antici-pated a cash squeeze down the road, and she wanted to be ready for it. She felt that the society had two years to prepare for that crunch; if it did not, important dreams would be thwarted.

It was time to create a new list of aims for the zoo, a shopping list to raise money.

In meetings with her staff, her crisp managerial stance was evident. "Impact" was one of her favorite verbs.

When she conferred with Mena, Nancy, and others, her advice surfaced again and again.

Certain maxims prevailed. Anticipate questions. Have answers ready. Plan whatever can be planned. The socie-ty's mission was not simply to raise cash for big projects. The zoo and the society were one in serving the people who came through the gates. Those people, many of them, might not be able to afford pets; their pets would reside in the cages at the zoo. The visitors' needs would have to be considered in everything the society did.

When the last meeting on a cold day had ended, Barbara sat behind her desk. She phoned one of her children to find out what was happening at home. She made a doctor's appointment. She collected a mass of paperwork to take home.

Several staff members stopped by on their way out. They clogged the doorway to her office. Barbara looked up at them and said, "It's all that, all that *stuff*, that sometimes keeps me awake at night and makes my stomach hurt." She waved an arm in the air, defining the invisible work load.

She smiled as she spoke, and everyone in the room knew that she wasn't complaining.

FIRST PERSON: BARBARA WHITNEY

I had animals when I was a kid. I had a pony, and I had a horse, and those were the important animals in my life. We always had dogs, we had cats from time to time when my mother didn't get her way, and then we had an assortment of fish and gerbils. I grew up out in the country, and I spent a lot of time during my childhood with my pony and my horse—that's what I did after school. So I spent a lot of time alone with that animal out in the fields, out in the country. That affinity was an extremely intense one, and that pony was as much a part of my life as my sisters were. But it never occurred to me to go into any kind of animal-oriented career.

However, there was a family tradition of being a volunteer. It was very strongly and directly taught by my mother, who volunteered for everything from school board to the PTA to the library board. And it was very simple. We have been given much, and we must give something in return. It probably grew out of the same streak that in my early years made me want to be Jane Addams or a nurse when I grew up. It was a belief in service, as I suppose it was for my mother, deeply rooted in the religion we grew up in. She was a genuinely Christian-oriented woman. We grew up in the Episcopal church, but it was more than going to Sunday School. I grew up believing. My mother also believed it was important to be interesting and try new things, and so she taught us that life was an avenue of experience, of learning about new things.

I'm a feminist, unofficially. I've never participated in feminist causes, in any way, shape, or form. But I am definitely a product of my time and have been for many years. I first recognized it in some things I wrote when I was maybe twenty-four or twenty-five years old. Actually I can recognize it earlier; I can recognize the anger I felt upon graduation from college that all the boys in my class could go out and get these high-paying jobs, maybe making twelve thousand dollars a year as salesman for a Fortune 500 company. And that I had to pass a typing test to get in the door anyplace. That was a very strong and visceral resentment that I remember to this day, sitting in New York City trying to speed up my typing so that I could get a job in publishing under the title of editorial assistant, which meant secretary. I resented that, and I flunked seventeen typing tests at seventeen different organizations before I got lucky and somebody overlooked the scoring.

I went into an organization in my first job where I was given enormous opportunity, and opportunity for growth very, very fast. And so the bitterness did not become deeply seated. So I never became a diehard feminist, and when I came back to Chicago, my recollection is that I still felt there was a whole world out there in which I could participate.

I really believe that what I brought with me here to the zoo, what I brought with me here that uniquely served me, were two or three things, maybe four. One thing I brought was that I was not a zoo person, I was a layperson. I was not an expert, I had not grown up next door to this zoo, and this zoo was not a household word in my life. As a matter of fact I remember bringing my kids to Lincoln Park Zoo, because after my husband left, I would try to find excursions on a Saturday morning to focus on. And I remember calling and trying to find out how you got to the zoo, and how much it cost, and that was only a couple years before I came to the zoo to work. I didn't even know whether there were gorillas at this zoo, let alone the best collection of gorillas in the world. So I think that that uninitiated vantage point served me very well.

But more directly, I think that my belief in communication skills served me, because I think I have communication skills—oral communication skills and written communication skills. I was not a marketing expert; I had not been in an ad agency, although I grew up with a Dad (and I do think that's important) who had been an advertising executive. He was the president of Leo Burnett. I grew up with that kind of conversation at the dinner table: communicate, communicate, communicate; tell them what you're going to tell, tell them, then tell them what you told them—that sort of old-fashioned American direct message stuff. And I believed it all, because I adored my father. I believed every word of it. So I was trained over the dinner table—we all were—to be communicators in one way or another.

There's another factor, an innate understanding of process. How to take an idea, something that is just ephemeral, and make it real.

We're very lucky here in that we have a product, if you will, the zoo, that sells itself. And so our job is only to make people aware of what this place is within the community, to the animals it serves, to the people it serves. Now, in fund language that's called the case statement. Uck, how dry, how awful. My experience here has been that you don't turn people into donors, that you introduce them to the zoo. The zoo turns them into donors. So my job is not fund-raising per se, it's friend-making. Get people on the premises face to face with animals; that is the best single thing we can do. Get people here, help them understand the needs of the institution, the complexity of the institution, the charm of what happens here between the visitors and the animals.

But it's very important to get them a step beyond the

visitors and the animals. This zoo was a very static experience compared to what I realized a zoo was when I saw it behind the scenes. The animals were there, and they existed in a vacuum. I didn't speak to any keepers, I didn't get to know any keepers, it was as if that didn't exist. I'd see animals munching some food, but they were just there. But the first time I came here and went behind the scenes, which was literally in conjunction with this job, and I saw the interaction of the animals and keepers back there, and walked through the commissary and realized the zillion kinds of food they need to stay alive and all the mechanics of this institution, I was blown away by them. I mean it's fascinating. People always say, "I had no idea all of this went on."

You introduce people to the zoo. Those people become converts. Converts become potential donors. But you must have a board of directors. A board of directors is not something that's just tolerated; a board of directors is an essential element in the process. I have enormous faith in the collective judgment of our board. And that's not an original quote from me; it came from Les. But it is a true statement that I often say and believe. I don't think I've ever seen our board make a bad collective judgment in the twelve years I've been here. I think the board's decisions have always been sound. And where a judgment was slow in forthcoming, it was only because the board members didn't have enough information, which is our responsibility, by the way.

One of the important functions of the board members is that they are the network into the community. It took me years before I appreciated what a strong tool that is. For years, people came up to me saying, "Well, I talked to Joe Blow—he's on your board, you know—and he was telling me this, and I didn't know that about the zoo." It works. There's much more of a sense of participating in the fate of the place here than I have discovered on boards of directors of corporations. The directors understand their role at this zoo. They know the zoo society doesn't run the zoo, and they aren't trying to run the zoo. I think they learn from us, and we learn from them.

The park district budget provides the employees who are needed to take care of the animal collection and the facility, the food for the animals, and equipment maintenance and repairs for the physical facility. We go beyond that and look at all the categories that have anything to do with travel, research, books for libraries—what we call here the frosting on the cake, but what in the past ten years has become an absolutely necessary ingredient in a zoo of the 1980s as opposed to a zoo of the 1920s. If the park district budget had to be cut 15 percent, it would be almost impossible to cut it, because you'd have to cut into diets or fire a lot of people.

Ninety percent of all the major physical changes we've made at this zoo have been on a matching basis, with public and private funds. Matching, not necessarily equal. Each campaign's been different. If Les goes to the park district and says, "The lion house is falling down. I need a new one," they won't say, "That's your problem," but because of the history that's behind us now, "Find out what you can get from the zoo society." It's almost a given now that the park district only takes on maintenance by itself. Cooperation with the zoo society is a given. There must be a tremendous temptation down at the park district to say, "Tell the zoo society to pay for that." Now with the farm, we did that. There was no money forthcoming from the park district, no money in the budget to renovate that farm. The farm, from an exhibit point of view, was in very bad shape; it was outdated and tired and run-down. And the zoo society took that on alone. The renovation of the children's zoo will cost roughly three and a half million dollars. We are paying seven hundred thousand dollars more than the park district. And all zoo society money is our donors' money.

When I first came here, I didn't understand why Les spent so much time teaching me about the history of the park district and all about the relationships with the commissioners and the staff and understanding that whole big complex chart. I came here with no understanding of that. And in the early days, there was a lot of frustration in trying to communicate. One of the beauties of being at any place long enough is that you either learn to accept that system and decide to spend your energy learning how to work within that system, or you probably wouldn't be there anymore. I genuinely believe that the park district makes every effort to support the goals of the zoo director, which are also the goals of the zoo society. There is certainly strong spiritual support for what we're all trying to achieve here. And there is financial support, as much as it can provide within reason, given its concerns, which stretch all over the city.

The zoo isn't finished being improved. We had a series of long-range planning meetings and came up with a list of probably ten to twenty million dollars' worth of additional improvements. The parking problem is going to cost millions of dollars to fix. The reptile house was not a part of this last campaign, and improvements are needed. More gardens and sculpture. And a solution to the space problem. The administration of a modern zoo simply takes more people, if you're going to go into research, conservation, all kinds of educational programming. And the facilities here are very limited.

The zoo's budget, in spite of the best efforts of the zoo society and the park district, is still severely constrained. We are probably underfinanced by three to five million dollars a year. We don't have enough people. When we did an informal survey of other zoos and the number of people they have on their staffs and the size of their budgets, what's accomplished here per dollar and per person is miraculous. The conservation and research programs could just eat money—five hundred thousand to a million dollars a year before you started scratching the surface. And that's a whole area that's going to become increasingly important, and possible, as we put behind us some of the major sums of money that had to be spent on buildings.

You must begin by spending your money on things that show for the visitors. Let them share the impact of the change. From there you can move to less visible projects, but in order to get fund-raising momentum going, you must have impact on the public so that they come in, see the results of the money, and that becomes the case for giving more money.

When you walk through the zoo now, it's turning into a beautiful place, and it was tired and run-down before. There is a real joy in seeing the animals outside against rocks and trees and in beautiful habitats. Each spring and each fall, more at the change of seasons than any other time, you walk through in the morning or in the evening when it's not crowded so you aren't looking at people, you're just looking at the place. And you say, "Not too bad; it's coming along." I guess that's what makes me proud.

Every time I've thought of giving up this job because it takes a lot out of me and makes me very tired, I try to think of anything that I could do that would be as challenging, as complex, as constantly changing as this is. I'm afraid I've become an excitement junkie or an energy junkie. There is an energy to this place, and to my task and my role in this place, that is constantly challenging. Something always needs to be done, that makes the job not finished, that makes you not want to move on. And the fact of the matter is, it will never be finished, and the day after I walk out the door, wonderful things will continue. It's not a sense of being indispensable. I have no illusions about that, I don't think any of us do around here. I mean, this place will be here, the zoo society will be here, and others will be doing what we're doing, differently but just fine.

I was recently at a park district meeting where some refinements—that's the nice word, cutbacks is the bad word—were being made to the bird of prey plans. And I looked around the table, and there were twelve men sitting around that table addressing this subject, all with goodwill, good faith, a lot of expertise, good spirit, trying to problem-solve. And it was a beautiful fall day, and I just glanced out the window, and it came over me in a flood, one of those little epiphanies that I have all the time around here: "God, am I lucky. Do you know how interesting this is, to be sitting here trying to solve this problem, a real problem that isn't ephemeral, isn't theoretical? Do you know how lucky you are? This is like going to college for the rest of your life, this is like being in a class." It's pretty exciting.

17

Doc

When those who admired zoo director Lester Fisher spoke about him, certain words were used: good, kind, folksy, benign, wise, compassionate, concerned. For them, he embodied the qualities John Leonard had once noted: "Naturalists in general seem so kindly disposed, so full of a sweetness of being, as to suggest that God is lucky they enlisted in His or Her cheerful service."

When his critics defined his style—and his critics were few in number and modest in influence—they were inclined to distort those virtues and term him vacillating, wimpish, nonconfrontational, corny, the Mister Rogers of the zoo world.

In reality, after twenty-five years as director of the zoo, Les was in charge gently; the style and the man were inseparable. His best dreams had been dreams about the future of the zoo; his understated determination had transformed the zoo from a small pastoral pocket in a big city to a perpetually revised haven for animals that required refuge in order to survive.

Les was not naive; he knew that in the best of worlds, animals would thrive in the wild. Yet he knew as well that the wild was vanishing. Human beings, who tried to protect animals in zoos, simultaneously had trashed the animals' own habitats. The critics of zoos had their reasons; so did the supporters. Les attempted to be a realist in the constant, and often abrasive debate.

To a degree, a feudal society existed at the zoo. The small kingdom was an enclave of lords and vassals, at least as perceived by the latter, the keepers.

Les was the lord of the manor, and his staff governed it. He was accessible to the keepers; when they found the curators to be too rigid in their rule, he listened. In the daily rituals of the zoo, however, the curators reigned. The keepers did not withhold their resentment. The struggle went on in subtle and nagging ways; there were no revolts to compare with the revolts of the outside world. In this sheltered society, conspiracies arose and vanished without overthrowing anyone.

It was not that Les was a despot, benevolent or otherwise. His manner was that of the concerned lord. He knew that things went wrong, that incompetence existed. He knew that there weren't enough dedicated bodies to do all the work efficiently. He tried to function, to be fair, within the system. It wasn't easy.

Les was unpretentious, diligent, and knowledgeable. His work ethic was a familiar one.

He was at his desk by 8 A.M., but he rarely spent more than a few hours behind it without heading to a meeting, a visit with keepers, or a stroll around the zoo. He was paid by the park district, and he had mastered the techniques of dealing with the bureaucracy, of getting done what must be done, and learning to avoid the delusion of instant gratification.

In discussions of the American dream, his career was a case in point.

His parents were immigrants from Czechoslovakia; his father was a butcher, and his parents raised four children on what the father could earn by selling meat. Les was born in 1921 in Chicago, the city that remained his home. As a child, he met food inspectors from the department of agriculture who visited his father's shop; in those days, food inspectors were veterinarians.

Those food inspectors had an impact on his own choice of career. He received his doctor of veterinary medicine from Iowa State University in 1943. World War II was on, and he was shipped to Europe as an army vet; he served as a food inspector as his unit moved across the continent from Brittany to Czechoslovakia. When the war ended, Les returned to Chicago, where he opened an animal hospital and became an attending vet at the zoo. In 1962, the park district board named him director, succeeding Marlin Perkins of TV's "Zoo Parade" fame. " 'Zoo Parade' put our zoo on the map nationally," Les remembered.

Over the years, he married twice, fathered two daughters, and participated in the work of countless zoological causes. Throughout the world of zoos, his name was familiar and respected.

His days at work were varied. On one winter morning, he got to work early from his lakefront high-rise apartment. He wore his typically Ivy League tweedy garb, with button-down shirt and one of his many animal motif ties. By 9 A.M., it was time to take a ride. He met curator of birds Kevin Bell and the associate executive director of the zoo society, Margo Morris, and they drove to the Hyatt Regency Hotel.

Margo had been in touch with the hotel's director of public relations, Nancy Ruth, who indicated that she and the hotel manager, Rodney Young, wanted to chat about the possibility of getting the zoo's help in erecting an aviary in the hotel's atrium.

Nancy, a chic blonde with an assured manner, and Rodney, a fastidiously tailored executive, were ready when Les, Kevin, and Margo arrived. Over coffee around a polished conference table in Rodney's office, the group discussed the project.

En route to the meeting, Les had alerted Kevin and

Margo, "We really can't get involved in the day-to-day operation in any way. Let's refer them to a veterinary practitioner and pull back and be there as a consultant." Tactfully, he repeated that message to Rodney and Nancy. They were not discouraged.

Rodney told Les that he was new to Chicago and didn't know much about the zoo.

"Well, we got started in 1868," Les said. "We might be the oldest zoo in America. In 1870 and 1872, we bought more animals and . . ."

"Is there a ranking of zoos?" Rodney interrupted.

"Sure, we're the best," Les said.

Rodney explained that a metal worker who had worked for Hyatt before was prepared to build a brass bird cage two stories tall. The hotel chain had such a cage in Atlanta, he pointed out. It was next to a bar, and the drinkers could feed their lemon peels and limes to the birds. On Sunday, when the bar was closed, the birds, suffering from alcohol deprivation, screamed for the handouts.

Les smiled.

"We are a public zoo," he said. "We can't directly run the exhibit. We can advise you. You really ought to know that, unlike years ago, when animals could be obtained easily, the movement of animals is difficult these days. And once you set it up, you'll probably have a bunch of agencies looking over your shoulder. Also, you should know that the availability of birds is limited, and the costs are high. So if it does come to be, it'll be your exhibit, not ours. If you do things right, fine. If you don't, you'll hear from someone for sure."

Rodney suggested that the cage might house macaws.

Kevin engaged in some cautious edification.

"Macaws can chew through most wire," he told Rodney. "Some birds can chew off fingers as well. Parrots chew up plants. But we can direct you to sources of birds for you to buy. What about doves? They're easier to manage, easy to get. And they're not loud. Of course, they're not as color-ful, either."

"Whatever we get, it's got to be unique," Rodney said. "I

want people to say, 'Look at those birds, aren't they great?' "

Nancy interrupted. "How can Hyatt help the zoo?"

It was a moment familiar to Les, used to courting potential donors. The zoo could use Hyatt funds, but Les didn't appear to be aggressive about it.

"You ought to get together with the zoo society," he suggested. "We're not here with hat in hand, but anything you can do to help us would be nice." He knew that the Pritzker family, which controlled the Hyatt chain, had already donated large sums to the zoo.

The group left Rodney's office to visit the atrium. A gray-haired, dapper pianist was playing florid music on a white Yamaha grand piano in the lobby.

Rodney pointed out the area that could be converted to an aviary.

"You'll need something relatively hardy," Les said. "There are considerations here. Temperature changes. Air currents. Traffic. Animals live in cycles every day, so the lighting would have to relate to their cycles."

"It could promote a lot of business for the zoo," Rodney said.

"Well, you are just a ten-minute cab ride from us," Les responded. "We'll go back home and do our homework. The challenge is real. It's interesting."

After the appropriate good-byes, back in the car heading to the zoo, Les turned to Kevin, smiled, and said, "Kevin, I give you seventy-two hours to come up with a master plan."

Kevin smiled reluctantly.

"You know, what we want is something the public enjoys that works for the birds, too," Les added.

"Yes," Kevin said stoically.

Les was in his office by 10 A.M. but didn't stay there long. He strutted out into the zoo grounds.

He walked toward the primate house, passing a young woman keeper, who waved at him.

"She had a relationship with a guy who works here that

wasn't too good for her," Les commented. "It's over, and I'm glad. She's a dedicated worker."

Inside the primate house, he went into a holding area. A young woman keeper was at work. He greeted her pleasantly and then asked her when the wire mesh on a cage would be repaired; it was ragged and might injure the monkey in the cage. The keeper assured Les that she'd follow up. He walked across the primate house to the kitchen to talk with keeper Pam Dunn.

Les told Pam that he was going to appear on a local children's TV show that afternoon and needed a well-behaved animal to appear with him. Pam took him to a cage containing a woolly opossum. She put on a pair of leather gloves and plucked the opossum out of the cage. The animal defecated but otherwise passed the test. Les would pick it up later for the show, which he did every other week.

At the great ape house, Les greeted senior keeper Pat Sass and several other keepers. One of them, Richard, was on his morning break, digging into a box of Ding Dongs.

"Want a Ding Dong?" Richard asked Les.

"I don't even know what a Ding Dong is," Les laughed.

Assistant vet Peri Wolff arrived, and the group went into a room off the keeper area, the room Pat devoted to young apes she was hand-raising. They gathered around an incubator-turned-crib for a small baby gorilla. The baby had been bitten by another gorilla and had been retrieved, treated, and returned to the gorilla exhibit. Then its mother neglected it, and another gorilla injured it, so it was pulled again for Pat to care for.

Pat noted, "There are some runny noses among the apes."

"Do we have that viral bug around again?" Les asked. On one occasion a virus, probably introduced by a human, had spread through the ape house.

"Let's hope this time it's not of the magnitude of the last outbreak," he added.

He looked at two baby chimps, happily playing with

stuffed animals. "The patients are looking good, so I feel good," he said.

He walked back to the zoo office in time for another meeting.

Months before, LuAnne Metzger, the farm curator, had been on a plane and had met the president of the National Livestock and Meat Board; he told her that he was interested in the farm. It occurred to her that the board could be helpful in funding the renovations at the farm.

The official and one of his aides would be arriving at the zoo for a tour of the farm. Getting ready for them involved Les, Barbara Whitney, and several other members of the zoo society, as well as LuAnne. They met in the Crown-Field conference room.

The entire visit had been outlined in a memo, and Les was ready. He was often pressed into service as lecturer, tour guide, and fund-raiser.

He pointed out that the National Livestock and Meat Board had been involved with the zoo before.

"We've often pursued them," he said.

"Fine, then it's time to forge a partnership," Barbara said.

Les had a few minutes before he had to join that effort. He went back to his office. A veteran keeper was standing at the door. He had been injured by a reindeer, he told Les. He had entered the yard to check the animal but had failed to carry a broom or a shovel, standard operating procedure. The animal attacked him. He grabbed its horns and held on. Eventually, the animal turned away, but the keeper did suffer a few minor bruises. He told Les that he was OK and would be back at work.

Les scowled, unhappy that an experienced keeper had put himself in a vulnerable position, but his words were consoling.

"Safety for the animals. Safety for the staff. Safety for the visitors. That's my main job," Les said.

The next morning, Les—his face reddened by the cold

wind—was at work early. He stood facing the stinging
breeze, in the middle of the zoo, surveying his domain for
a moment.

At 6'1" and 176 pounds, he was a conspicuous presence,
wearing his dark green parka with ZOO imprinted on the
back, and an expression of severe determination. He was on
a mission.

He went to the power house, the massive building constructed decades before by the park district to house the
heating system for the zoo, the electrical distribution
network for the area, and electricians' offices. The building
was so old that over the years it had gone from burning
coal to burning oil to burning gas.

At 8:15 A.M., he tracked down one of the electricians; he
made a point of knowing all of them, calling each by their
first name, being cordial and polite with them. He knew
that the zoo depended upon the cooperation of the trade
workers who serviced the vital systems.

In this case, Les needed help. A new copying machine
was going to be delivered to the zoo society. It would need
a separate power line. The electrician, a middle-aged man
and a veteran of zoo service, called Les "Doc," as many of
the laborers did, and assured him that the job would be
done on time.

Les walked out of the power house with a faint smile on
his face and moved into the chill wind. He seemed oblivious to the elements, tough in an inconspicuous way.

Back in his office, he noted that he was genuinely grateful that the electrician would be helpful. In the past, it
wasn't always that easy, when the patronage system sometimes put incompetents in place and let them live out their
careers to retirement without making many demands on
them to be efficient. Patronage remained, but it was not as
virulent as it had been.

"I try to keep the zoo neutral," Les said. "Politically
neutral. I let people know, in the bureaucracy, that it would
be sad, a setback, if there were people working at the zoo

who didn't deserve to work here. It would diminish our professionalism. Now, of course, most of our keepers are civil service."

At 9 A.M., he met with curator of mammals Mark Rosenthal, the zoo society's Margo Morris, and the park district's P.R. man, Don Garbarino. It was one of a periodic series of meetings to coordinate publicity for the zoo, a function shared by the park district and the zoo society.

What was newsworthy?

Bozie, one of the zoo's elephants, was being shipped to a zoo in Springfield, Missouri; the twelve-year-old, 6,000-pound female would be on a breeding loan.

A female gorilla was being transferred across town to the Brookfield Zoo for breeding purposes; the two Chicago area zoos often exchanged animals and expertise.

A University of Illinois architectural student had designed a module that would be placed in the great ape house, a module that would contain nuts and other treats and would tempt the apes to play with it and reward them for their dexterity. It was a safe form of play and intellectual stimulation for the animals.

When the meeting ended, Les attacked a small pile of phone messages and a large stack of unread mail. His office was filled with wildlife photos and drawings, framed awards, boxes of slides, family photos, animal sculptures. On one wall there was an African tribal mask from the Victoria Falls area and a spear and shield from the Masai.

That afternoon and evening, Les was set to attend a budget hearing at park district headquarters, a meeting of public library officials, and a meeting with the president of World Wildlife U.S.A. But first, he wanted to peek into the children's zoo, under construction and close to completion.

As he walked across the zoo, a group of preteenagers saw him and giggled.

"I saw him on TV," one laughed.

"Yes, that's the one. He's the man from the zoo," another said. "Should we get his autograph?"

Before they could vote on the matter, Les was into the children's zoo for a brisk walk-through.

His daily routine was a pragmatic, rather than a contemplative, one. There was much to do.

"I do try to stay abreast of medical matters, so I don't get lost," he said. "I'm not in practice now, but I take continuing education courses to keep my license. And there are dozens of institutions putting out publications that I feel I ought to scan. I still haven't figured out when I'm supposed to read a good book just for pleasure."

The meetings consumed his afternoon, and the next morning began with another.

At 9 A.M., he chaired his weekly staff meeting. Several curators were off on assignments. Present were Joan Friedman, assistant curator of education; Anne Boyle, director of graphics; Nancy Worssam, director of programs for the zoo society; reptiles curator Clarence Wright; farm curator LuAnne Metzger; and curator of education Judy Kolar.

Les consulted his notes.

He told them about the keeper who had been bruised by a reindeer. The keeper had seen Mark Rosenthal's slide presentation on safety for keepers, but hadn't been shielded from danger by it.

"Poor judgment," Les ruled. " And he paid a price. When you lose respect for an animal, you get hurt."

He announced that there had been a birth among a group of gorillas that Lincoln Park had sent to the St. Louis Zoo.

"A nice plus for us," he said. "Long-term conservation, a breeding program."

He told those present that Bozie would leave for the Springfield, Missouri, zoo within a few days, by special truck under the supervision of an elephant management specialist.

Later that day there would be a delegation from Citicorp, he announced. It would involve the "standard donor tour and lunch," and the group would be taken through the children's zoo, to which Citicorp had donated funds.

He had attended a budget hearing at park district head-quarters the night before, but hadn't been called to testify. As frustrating as the experience had been, he did feel that the zoo's budget request was in "a positive mode."

There was a new memo from park district headquarters about "Employee Disciplinary Procedures."

"Not much that we don't already know," he declared.

Nancy Worssam brought up the matter of a prominent donor who wanted to provide seed money for a program to install animal sculptures in the animal houses. On the surface, it seemed like an idea to enhance the appearance of the zoo buildings, but Nancy pointed out that it would involve a long-term commitment.

"How do we protect the sculptures?" Les asked, favoring pragmatism over art for the moment. "I do have a touch of concern about that. It has to be small-scale stuff, and small-scale stuff is easy to abuse. You can't put something big in our spaces, with our crowds. You've got to plan the displays in advance." He wanted to discuss the sculpture program again when more of the curators were present.

He reported on the construction-renovation of the children's zoo: "Sadly, the contractor is slowing down. The weather is getting sloppier, wetter, colder. I think it would be good to bring in some big trees before the big freeze. The so-called dedication of the completed children's zoo is still in question."

The zoo society would sponsor three African trips next year, he announced. All staff members, those who would be going and those who would not, should adjust their schedules to consider the dates of those trips.

Clarence Wright had bad news. A baby tortoise had been stolen from the reptile house. A plastic disposable razor and a can of shaving cream had been found, inexplicably, in a tortoise pen. Clarence had begun to change the locks at various doors to the reptile house holding areas.

"More and more incidents," he muttered, unhappily. "We have to look at it closely."

"You have to assume that ninety-eight percent of it is done by 'family,' " Les said to Clarence. "You know, you can accept silliness, but something that could be calamitous is always a threat."

"So many people pass through the house," Clarence lamented. "Even volunteers, docents picking up animals to take them to schools. Maintenance people pass through all the time."

"It could be angry employees getting back at the staff," Les theorized. "We've had that in the past."

The meeting ended at 10 A.M., and Les headed with LuAnne to the farm, to check on the work being done there.

Their faces were whipped by a painful wind as LuAnne drove an open electric cart from the Crown-Field Center to the farm. Winter had arrived. A few hardy visitors walked along the paths, but the sounds of gaiety that summer brought were no longer heard. The animals as well had retreated indoors, by choice or order.

At the farm, Les could see that an attempt to match paint on an exterior wall of the main barn had not succeeded. He cornered a friendly supervisor—who called him "Doc"— and chatted about correcting the mismatch. He cajoled in a most delicate way, expressing affection and respect even as he raised his cautiously stated demand for change. In a few minutes, the supervisor had gone from reticence about such a change to believing in the possibility of it.

Les moved on to the reptile house.

The evidence had been cleaned up; the tortoises were eating in their pen, minus the razor and the shaving cream. Art Maraldi, the keeper on duty in the basement, announced to Les that there was a moral to the story: "Never go out with an unshaven tortoise."

Art's joke made Les smile. He rushed out of the building with the smile intact.

After his lunch with the delegation from Citicorp, Les lingered in the reception area. A great ape keeper, Richard, came in, saw him, and let him know that about a third of the apes looked sick, with a possible flu bug. Peri Wolff had put them on antibiotics.

Trouble with apes, any trouble, was a personal matter for Les. He had spent years winning respect and admiration for the zoo's care and breeding of the great apes.

"A year ago, we lost an old chimp and a baby gorilla," he said. "They were zapped by acute viral pneumonia. What's scary is that the great apes can get almost everything we get."

It was time for him to make rounds, to roam around the zoo, to visit the animal houses and the keepers. He began in the small mammal house, where rodents had been a problem. Gene Brimer, responsible for exterminating them, had initiated a plan.

"Any rats around?" Les asked a keeper.

"The traps are out," she replied.

"Stay with it," he urged.

He remembered, with embarrassment, a tour he had conducted of the small mammal house with a prominent member of the park district hierarchy. Les showed the executive a cage, and the cage contained the proper animal plus a lively batch of invading mice. After that, he persuaded the park district to assign a pest control specialist to the zoo.

"I try to walk around and look at the zoo as a visitor would see it," he said.

He walked to the office and warehouse for the zoo society gift shops. He had his keys in hand, a sizable collection, but when he pushed the outer door, it opened. Money was kept inside the building—the proceeds from gift shop sales—and while it was in a locked safe in a locked office, unlocked doors bothered Les. He mentioned it to a staff member.

He strolled through the building, past stacks of animal toys and other gift items—including samples of stuffed koala bear toys; the gift shops would have to be ready.

At the hospital, all was in order. In a cage in the holding

area, one of the small monkeys screeched loudly. Not far away, in another holding area, a pair of mountain lions made their high-pitched whines. It reminded Les that these were creatures in from the wild and none too happy about it.

"Stress. People have it. Animals have it, too. They get it because they're away from what's familiar to them in the wild. Birds have died in my hands from stress," he said.

He moved on to the bear line, where behind the scenes a radio blared country music. A young, attractive keeper named Diana was at work hosing down the line; a few bear noses appeared in the slots of their dens.

"Look who's here," Diana announced to the bears, "The big cheese."

Outside, the polar bears—Chukchi and Thor—splashed and swam playfully in their pool, massive figures in slow motion when seen through the underwater viewing windows.

"They're probably the most dangerous animal in the zoo," Les said. "Even trained animal people can't get a feeling for their moods. They're totally impassive. No clues. The may be happy to see you or happy to eat you. They'll eat whatever they get."

He walked to the northern edge of the zoo, where the zoo met the traffic of civilization. Between the two was the zoo rookery. Les entered it, paused, and appreciated the setting.

"It's my personal joy," he said. "Quiet. Wonderful. Removed. A very special place."

In the large mammal house, he stopped behind the scenes to peer up at the giraffes, who peered down at him.

"They have extremely sensitive circulatory systems," he said. "They knocked down two of them at Brookfield, to examine them. They never got up. When you leave a giraffe down for an hour, an animal that tall, you run a risk."

He had commissioned a kind of squeeze cage for the

giraffes, so they could be examined without tranquilizing them, a large swinging gate that would enclose each giraffe when it had to be examined.

At the bird house, he made sure that there was a keeper on duty on the main floor, watching the birds in the free-flight area. He didn't want to have a bird stolen; it had happened. In fact, two keepers were on duty.

At 3 P.M. he returned to his office; his timing was fortunate. Standing in front of the building was a zoo society staff member with a couple who might become donors. She introduced them to Les, who responded with a short, lively lecture on the history of the zoo.

"We appreciate your interest and your support," he said. "We need your help."

He walked toward the door to the Crown-Field Center, then remembered a stop he had forgotten to make. He turned around and headed for the great ape house.

The apes on exhibit seemed sluggish, but he wasn't certain if that was due to sickness or if it was their "quiet time." Inside the core of the exhibit, he checked a baby chimp in a keeper's arms. For a moment, he was a vet again.

"Sounds nice and clean," he said, after tapping the chimp's back with his finger.

He spotted Pat Sass and walked over to her. They were standing in the inner core of the exhibit, with only wire mesh between them and the apes.

A large male gorilla, Koundu, slowly came over to where Les was standing. Koundu pushed a banana through the mesh, without bruising it, offering it to Les. It was an act of sharing, a wish for interaction, and Les recognized it. He took the banana, turned away pretending to take a bite out of it, then returned it to Koundu.

"I used to be able to tickle his tongue," Les said. "Now, he'd take my hand off."

He returned to his office, thinking about the apes.

"The line between a head cold and pneumonia is such a

thin one at times," he muttered. "It's so difficult to treat this situation. So difficult."

The next morning, Les was at work by 7:30 A.M., dressed in a light brown sport jacket, khaki slacks, and a blue plaid sport shirt. It was not likely garb for the winter climate in Chicago. But it was logical for his destination many hours later that day: Zimbabwe.

He was one of a group of zoo directors who had been invited by the government of Zimbabwe to spend two weeks touring that country. It was an effort to tempt them to return with others, as Les might on a zoo society safari. He had not been to Zimbabwe in years; he remembered it as a place hostile to some of the white natives, and he hoped that it had improved.

But before he could board the plane to England for the first leg of the trip, he had several meetings to attend.

At 8 A.M., he headed for the auditorium in the Crown-Field Center to chair the keepers' meeting. As usual, he brought the keepers up to date on developments that he felt mattered to them.

Budget hearings were going on, he told them, and "we're going to come out of them perfectly OK for this year's budget. We've built a solid case for the zoo, and the people at the park district respect that."

He asked vet Tom Meehan to speak to the keepers about a new program to use consultants to help improve the diets of the animals in the zoo. The consultants would do an in-depth analysis of present feeding practices, Tom said, and would discern problems and make suggestions for changes. To begin, Tom said, "we'll make a list of what the animals are fed now and what they actually eat—that's what is important."

"Diets evolve. Different approaches, different ideas," Les said. "Our work will be reflected in the animals' health. What do they really need? Now we'll have a scientific basis for that."

A park district executive with a concern for detail had visited the zoo unannounced and wondered if many keepers worked while dressed in outfits that weren't their proper uniforms. In very hot and very cold weather, variations abounded. Les urged the keepers to wear their uniforms, not to deviate from them. He did not appear to be insistent.

He encouraged all present to read the new park district pamphlet on disciplinary procedures.

"It's a system to potentially protect both sides, labor and management," he said. "I hope everyone understands it. See me if you have any questions."

He noted that 3,000 Girl Scouts would be visiting the zoo one day in three weeks. The audience produced a collective rumble in response to the news.

Workers were putting some finishing touches on parts of the children's zoo, he added, but completion was several months away. The main building might be opened during the winter, but opening the entire children's zoo might best be put off until the spring, when the weather would be cooperative.

Park district records indicated that zoo staff members were making a lot of long-distance calls. The bureaucrats kept their eyes—or, rather, their ears—open to such abuses.

"Don't go on for twenty or thirty minutes. Be mindful," he stressed.

The food concession at the zoo had been awarded to the zoo society, he announced. The keepers managed a mild cheer.

"It'll mean real good food at a fair price," he said. "It'll phase in during a two-year period. But by spring we'll have the new food available."

Mark Rosenthal, curator of mammals, was summoned to the podium by Les, to talk about the elephant shipment later in the week. Mark pointed out that Bozie would be in heat in two weeks, so "we'll see what happens when she gets there."

"We pay for any pregnancy that results, and a board fee," Les noted. "We continue to try. This is a long-term preservation program."

Les asked Kevin Bell, the curator of birds, to make an announcement. Kevin told the keepers that a pair of king penguins—larger, at four feet tall, than any of the penguins in the zoo—would be on loan from the Milwaukee Zoo while their habitat was being renovated. He was delighted.

The meeting ended just before 9 A.M., and Les went directly to the conference room for a staff meeting.

Assistant director Dennis Meritt, back from a trip to Africa, was there, along with education curator Judy Kolar, vets Tom Meehan and Peri Wolff, farm curator LuAnne Metzger, assistant education curator Joan Friedman, Mark Rosenthal, and the zoo society's Nancy Worssam.

Les ran down his agenda.

"The zoo food is number one in excitement," he said. "The zoo society got it. Very meaningful. Now we can get rid of those crappy signs and stands. The society has committed more than four million dollars to the project. A whole new world. The quality will change dramatically."

Joan Friedman filled in the others on the details of the Girl Scout walk through the zoo. It would indeed involve 3,000 girls, in seventy buses. Three zoo tours had been arranged for them, and it would all be done in about two hours.

Les ran down his stint at the budget hearings. "We're still in reasonably OK shape," he said. "Of course, they question every line item in our budget."

He repeated his message about phone abuse. "You can get a call done in five minutes," he implored. "I'm sure we're going to hear about it, so be helpful."

He talked about the keeper who had been careless with the reindeer. Something had to be done, some discipline imposed, he said. But what? He didn't want to suspend the keeper, who had been injured, though not severely. The point had to be made—that he knew better than to enter the pen without an implement, a broom or a rake or a shovel, to defend himself. Some reprimand was necessary, Les felt.

"He could have been dead potatoes," Dennis said. "He was lucky. Reindeer bash, but they really aren't fighters."

Mark suggested that a written reprimand might be enough. Mark had discussed safety with the keeper before; he would do so again.

"Well, there was no escape and no threat to the public, or anyone else injured," Les sighed. "I'll look into a written reprimand."

By 10 A.M. Les had gotten to the bottom of his pile of notes. It was time to go. By the end of the day, he would be flying east, to London and on to Zimbabwe, for two weeks without decisions about reckless keepers, bureaucrats, and hordes of Girl Scouts. As he left the conference room, his pace quickened.

FIRST PERSON: LESTER FISHER

I wasn't certain I wanted to be a vet. I had a high school chum, and he was going to go out to Ames, Iowa, to Iowa State to study animal husbandry. I had an interest in some such field. I had met a few veterinarians, some of the veterinarians who worked in the meat-packing plants. They were the food inspectors, then as now. When I decided to go to Ames, I thought that I would enroll in a preveterinary course, to see what it was like.

I had a unique exposure. There was a rooming house on the edge of town, a big old three-story green house, and one of the people living in it was a faculty man, Walter Anderson, who was in charge of the ambulatory clinic of the veterinary college. Whenever he had a call and I was home, he'd knock on my door and say, "Les, do you want to come along?" And after spending many months with him, I was pretty well convinced that I'd like to try for vet school.

I'm sure that he was a deciding person in my life because

at first I was an anachronism at college. I was the city kid; they were all country boys. Even though my grades were solid, I have to assume that Walter Anderson probably said a positive thing for me, and that must have helped me get into vet school.

While in vet school, I did what everyone did—took all four years of general courses, which included everything. Emphasis was on farm animals, certainly not on dogs and cats; the horse was our anatomy animal. It wasn't any secret that I was interested in small animals, but people couldn't quite understand that. I finished school, filled in for a vet for three months until he got called in the service, and then I went in the service.

When I got out of the army, Northwestern University was looking for a veterinarian to help their animal care program, someone who might be interested in further schooling. I came on board as head of the animal care program there, and took some graduate courses in physiology. It was there that I got the zoo connection. I met Marlin Perkins. I had bought a sheet metal shop that was for sale, and set up my practice. It was then that Marlin and I talked a bit about the possibility of my doing something with the zoo, and we agreed to an arrangement whereby half a day a week, every Wednesday morning, I'd come down and make rounds and take care of what needed doing, and emergencies. And so that started and kept on for fifteen years.

I thought zoo work would be fun. But I was thinking more in terms of zoo medicine, not being a zoo director. I enjoyed my practice, and I was very successful in my practice. So, up until the day that Marlin said, "Les, I'm leaving. I'm going back to St. Louis," I hadn't seriously thought about the possibility of zoo administration.

I had to think about it for a few months. It was one of the tougher decisions of my life. It was a great financial hardship; the job paid very little then, relatively speaking, and I was doing three to four times better than that in practice. But practice had lost its edge for me. Once you accomplish a goal, it's a little hard to get yourself up a bit. The zoo just seemed like a fresh challenge. I certainly had had enough years to get a feel for it. In fact, I even remember telling Marlin that I was going to apply. He said, "You must be nuts." He said, "You mean you want to put up with all this bureaucracy and take a cut in pay and everything?" And I said, "Well, I think so. I've thought and thought and thought and finally decided that I may want to apply." And so I finally went down to the district and put in an application.

I went down one time for an interview, and I remember very clearly, it was in June that one day I was making rounds here and got a phone call to go to the park district headquarters. So I finished up what I was doing. I went down there in my shirt sleeves; it was hot, and I'd been dirty and working, and all of a sudden, the man in charge said, "You're the new zoo director." I gulped; he already had alerted the media, and they were down there, and it was really an overwhelming kind of silliness the way it evolved.

Also, Marlin was still here. Marlin had served notice that he was going to leave in September. But there were some stresses between some of the commissioners and Marlin, and I think somehow they might have thought that it was a way to get him, to appoint the replacement zoo director. For me it was fine because it gave me a chance to work with Marlin more closely for a few months. We always got along great. He never tried to treat an animal, tell me medically what to do, and I repaid that kindness—I never told him how to run a zoo.

Marlin didn't have any degree. Marlin was one of these self-made naturalists. He started sweeping floors in the reptile house at St. Louis. He became a keeper and decided not to go back to school. He put Lincoln Park on the national map. He put the zoo on television. They started with a regular Sunday show here, and the NBC people would bring a trailer out, park it next to the reptile house, and the basement of the reptile house was a studio. After two, three years of local programming, they somehow got NBC to consider doing it on the network, and "Zoo Parade" was off and running. Marlin did some wondrous things.

I got to do some television work. But I think from day one when I took over the zoo, everyone kept saying, "Well, are you going to do TV like Marlin?" And I said, "No, I'm not Marlin. He's one of a kind, and he is television." For the first two years, I tried not to get involved with television. I wanted to do Les Fisher's thing and not Marlin Perkins's thing. But then I had a Saturday morning TV show, more of a kids' show. I did that for about a year and a half, two years. And one day they called me and said, "Les, sorry, we're going to bump you. Flash Gordon's coming on to take your spot." I said, "Well, that's too bad, but I like Flash," and that ended my brief solo show. Then they put me on with Ray Rayner on his morning show, and twice a week for about ten years we did the "Ark in the Park." Today I'm happy continuing my work here at the zoo and doing some TV spots. There's plenty to accomplish at the zoo.

I feel very fortunate, truly, that I've never been seriously injured at the zoo in all my years here. I have always been a very conservative doctor and very much aware of not underestimating an animal. And in the zoo, especially in those early years when I was awed by them all anyway, I wasn't about to go in with a bear or a lion or anything unless there was a reasonable method to handle it. In the lion house, we used to take a long pole, and we'd put a lariat on the end of it. We'd put it through the bars and drop it over the animal's head. The secret was not to just put it over the head, you had to get it under one or the other front leg, because when you went to pull the lariat, if it was just around the neck, the animal would choke before you could safely loosen it. You could do that in five minutes or an hour, it depended on how the luck went. And with some of the hoofed animals, we would get them in a stall, and we'd get a group of good people, keepers, and say, "You take the horn, you take the head, you take a hind leg, you

take a front leg, and when I say 'go, one-two-three' "—we
all grabbed hold of something and hoped that it worked.
We had different tools then, and we stressed animals and
took some chances, but I didn't bravely go into a cage with
a dangerous animal.

Today, we have our missions. The primary one is to save
the animals' habitats. There is no substitute for that. If it's
at all possible to preserve the wildlife in their home, that's
objective number one. Conservation. You preserve not an
individual animal but the whole ecosystem, the land, the
plants, the animals, you name it. And I think truly that the
zoo is a part of, or a supplement to, that. When you realize
that if you put all the zoos in the world together, their total
physical plant would still be a tiny space, you can see
there's only a certain number of animals that we can
handle. It'd be wrong to say the zoo breeding programs are
going to save x animals. To me, national parks, animal
reserves, and zoos are the main backup to the wild, to the
habitat. There are individual cases where the zoos have
saved some species, no question. And the classic American
buffalo, the bison story, is dramatic. The Bison Society and
the Bronx Zoo helped turn that program around when
hundreds of bisons were left, out of tens of millions. That
is a positive thing.

I think the zoo breeding program's important. The importance of it is varied. First of all, the zoo loves to have
babies; it's very exciting for our visitors to see youngsters.
Second, it's always been a historic benchmark for us, a sign
that maybe we're doing something right if we can breed
these animals in captivity. It's kind of a barometer of the
care we give. If you get down a second, third, fourth
generation of captive breeding, then you know you're doing
something right. I think the breeding programs in great
part hinge on a slowly evolving professionalism in the
management of the zoo animal.

And nutrition has to be one of the keys. Years ago we fed
what we thought was right, but there was no basis for it;
we fed meat eaters meat. Meat is not a balanced diet,

especially horse meat, which we fed to our cats. We started adding some calcium powder to the meat and cut a little pocket in there and put some powder in, and we started getting healthier animals. We were feeding frozen fish to a lot of animals, especially the seals and sea lions and that. And no one ever really researched what happens when you freeze a fish. We were feeding a thiamin-deficient diet to our seals, and we were losing some of them with neurological problems, and we didn't know why. And finally we did some research and now we put the B1, the thiamin tablets, down the mouth of the fish. We started balancing rations. Instead of the old days when we gave the hoofed stock a little ground corn and some hay and stuff like that, we now feed them grain rations that are nutritionally balanced, in addition to the hay and the rest. That probably did as much for the reproductive results as the other things.

The long-term hope for the survival of animals on earth is through education, there's no question about it. We have to get to the urban masses who are not able to personally experience the wild. We have to tell them the story, and that is one of the major justifications of a zoo. When you speak about the wild and a zoo and all the other things, there are people who say it's wrong to take an animal from the wild and put it in a zoo. Is the animal happier here? Who's to say? All I know is that if you just do today what we used to do—take an animal from the wild and put it in a cage and someone came and looked at it—and commented that it was either exciting or fun or silly or funny or whatever, it is not really a good justification.

We lost a lot of animals because we didn't have the facilities, we didn't have diets, we didn't have care, we didn't have a lot of things. But it seemingly wasn't serious because there was another animal out there that you could get and put in its place. So if a monkey died, you could contact someone and get another monkey. If it weren't for the long-term breeding programs, the conservation effort, if it weren't for the education department and its work here, if it weren't for some of the research we do to help the animals, I think the so-called recreation factor would be a weak one to justify taking these animals and putting them in a zoo. The fight that we wage to help animals in the world—and that comes through in our publications, our programs, our graphics—is to get people to be aware. Zoos don't do it alone, but they're a good part.

One has to try to separate emotionalism from realism. We in the animal world know that there is a balance of seals and so on in the world, and that if you don't harvest any, you may be creating a different situation than if you do. Everything ends up in a balance. Nature does balance things out, and that's one reason why in many wild animals there are multiple births. If you have thirty rattlesnakes hatched, maybe two are going to survive. Otherwise, you take thirty and keep multiplying them, and pretty soon you've got a world full of rattlesnakes.

We have more white-tailed deer in this country than we can handle. There's an annual hunt, and people pay to get a license, and that money goes into the conservation fund. Some hunters shoot deer for kicks; many shoot them for food. If we didn't hunt now, I think there'd be a tremendous die-off, due to the lack of food supply. The available food supply is what governs the number of animals that an area can hold. I am saying that I am comfortable with the fact that there is an annual hunt for deer. But there are people who say it's terrible to shoot a deer. And I can empathize with them; I understand why they say it. I'm not a hunter, I can't go out and shoot a deer. If I were starving and my family's life depended on my hunting and I had a chance to shoot a deer, I probably would do it. But I am saying that there are balances, and the business of all these save-the-whatevers, some of them make sense and some of them may not. It's an unending dialogue, and there are no easy answers.

When we say one of our justifications in these breeding programs is to have animals to reintroduce in the wild, in some places, there's no wild to reintroduce them to. Especially the large mammals and especially the predators and the more dangerous animals. You couldn't send a tiger back to India today. Where are you going to release it? There are a limited number of national parks there, and they are full to the carrying capacity of tigers. But in theory, sure, if there were some wipeout, for whatever reasons, the animals are still in a captive breeding program, and we could send them back.

Most of the animal releases that have been done have been reasonably successful, because they're done by professionals who know what they're doing, and they know where, how, and when to release them. Do they all survive? No. In a classic story about freedom in the wild, Joy Adamson wrote one of the world's great books. On the other hand when she gave it the name she did, *Born Free*, that was a tough title to those of us who are professional animal people, because the implication is that animals in the wild are free. They are and they're not. They have the same constraints that humans do. Consider their certain territories and certain available food supplies and certain natural disasters and certain predators and certain whatever, and the animal in the wild has relative freedom, primarily spatial. But beyond that, the *Born Free* syndrome is a tough one. It is and it ain't, and Joy's animals weren't in a sense free. Sure, she had a unique situation where they still could run around and do what they wanted and come back to her. I think Joy got carried away in the later years of her life; she was always out there looking for generations of Elsa, and people started questioning whether she was even being totally rational about her search.

My philosophy has always been to go ahead and treat people as adults. There's a job to do; I let them know what the job is and let them do it. I try to delegate, and I accept responsibility for the joys and the sorrows of whatever they do. I don't always agree with how they do it, and I might do it differently, but I can't do it. So I have to rely on staff, and I'm a great believer in that. I am very pleased with my staff because they are committed people, they are good people, they know their work, they are probably doing more than their counterparts in other zoos because of the small size of our staff.

I feel that I've been kind of privileged. I watched many of the young men that Marlin had when he was director; at that time Lincoln Park was one of the true training grounds for a zoo staff. Many zoologists came from college and spent a few years here with Marlin and moved on to other zoos. And that process continued after I became director. I'm always here and ready to encourage any of my staff who want to move on in their profession, because I believe in that. My door has always been open to anybody, whether it's the secretary, the keeper, the curator, the assistant director. I have great faith in people. I believe that I have to allow that kind of dialogue because that's part of the opportunity for me to be aware of what's happening in the zoo. As I make rounds or as I talk to people, I feel it's important that they're comfortable, that they can share things with me. And I tell them they can share it in two ways: they can share it in public or they can share it in private.

Dealing with people is the toughest part of anyone's life. It doesn't matter what the business is, it's the human factor. I try to listen to all sides, and I try to end up deciding what I believe is the right course. I never demean anyone in public; I always mediate in private. I try to resolve differences, because it's rare that something is totally black and white. I have to back my staff. I have to back the senior keeper over the keeper, I have to back the curator over the senior keeper and so on, but only if things are fair and correct. If there are animal things going on here—and it never ceases to be a source of concern, hopefully not contention—does the veterinarian pass judgment on a certain animal management matter, or does the curator or the animal management curator team do it? I don't favor anyone. If each staff member acts in a positive way, the animals benefit in every way. If they don't, then you have stress. The other extreme is a zoo where the curator

of mammals never goes in the bird section. The bird curator never goes in the reptile section, and it's just like a
compartmentalized ship; no one really knows what's going
on in the next compartment. I don't believe in that. One
reason I think a lot of fine young people got training here
and could move on was because they learned the whole
zoo. I think that's good.

I accept the system, the bureaucracy I work for. First of
all, I never looked upon the job as something that I had to
have. I looked upon this job as something important, but if
for whatever reason it didn't work out, I wasn't going to go
in a corner and cry. I'd do something else, either go back to
practice or some other job. So I didn't have that kind of
concern. Second, I have no civil service status; I'm here at
the will of the commission, as are some of my other staff. I
found that the people that I worked with at the park district
over the years were basically good people. I found that if I
treated people with respect, whether they were or weren't
empathetic to what I needed or was doing, they were there,
and they were doing whatever it was they were going to
do. I felt that I could either fight the bureaucracy as many
people tend to, or try to get it to work for me. I learned
patience. When I was in practice I made my own decisions
and I lived by them. Here many decisions are made for me.
I guess I was able to get through to the various people in
my early years that I wanted to do the best job I could, but I
wanted to do it my way. And as long as they respected my
job, as long as I did things that they could live with, then I
could survive all this other stuff. It is frustrating to see
some work orders sit around for a period of time, it is
frustrating to get things that aren't reacted to and so on,
sure it is. But to me the big picture is what counts, and the
big picture here is the zoo. And the zoo is what matters to
me. If I can see my animals getting cared for, if I can see
my visitors being treated properly, if I can see my employees doing their work properly, I think that's what's
important. The day-to-day problems drop a touch in perspective as time moves on and if you achieve the goal. And

the goal is to get the last of these animals out of these totally antiquated facilities. It's wrong. And so we have a commitment to them.

I never played politics. I have my own personal philosophy, and people that I respect more than others in the political scene. But I have always felt that the zoo is everybody's. Administrations come and go, and the zoo's had a long, proud history.

I travel and I look at other zoos. I react to them. I think the Basel, Switzerland, zoo is one of my personal joys. It's as small and compact as we are, beautifully landscaped, fine animal collection. The National Zoo's always been a source of concern and interest to me. I feel it's part of my zoo. I keep reminding people at the National Zoo it ain't their zoo, it's our zoo. It's the *National* Zoo. And the nice thing is that by happy coincidence, our congressman helped that zoo. Sid Yates from the Ninth District here sits on the budget committee of Interior. Sid and I have known each other twenty-five years, and Sid has an interest in Lincoln Park Zoo; he's become very aware of the role of zoos. And whenever the hearings would come up in Washington for the Smithsonian, of which the National Zoo is part, I think Sid looked out very strongly and kindly for them. So I'd like to think that whatever it is, twenty to fifty million dollars' worth of work that's gone on there in the last fifteen or twenty-five years, is in part due to that man's help, and I'd like to think I had a little piece of it. The National Zoo's very important, and like ours, it's come from pretty sad to real good.

The Bronx I've always had great respect for, not only because of the zoological job they do, but because they're concerned with international and national conservation and wildlife. They have historically done more than all the other zoos in America combined in that area. There are two major zoos in the world that have done that, Frankfurt and the Bronx. San Diego is a great zoo, and everyone mentions it. Part of it is the mystique of marketing. They sold that zoo. After the war there was this zoo, and it was a relatively small one, in some ways analogous to Lincoln Park, but it was in a lovely site, with a lot of topography and terrain. The thing that made San Diego great in its earlier years was the fact that it had the best climate in America, and everything there would grow in terms of flowering plants. Therefore you could take a facility perhaps no different from some of mine here, antiquated, outmoded, you name it, but you put flowers, plants in front of it, in back of it, on top of it, around it. So it really became a true zoological garden, and about ten, fifteen years ago they did an inventory, and I think the plants were worth ten times what the animals were worth.

The other thing that happened was Los Angeles, its closest neighbor, had literally no zoo up to fifteen years ago. There was a little collection, a dozen cages, on the side of Griffith Park, nothing to promote. San Diego wisely started marketing: "Come to our zoo." And people did, and do, and so the mystique developed. And then when they did the wild animal park on top of it, two thousand acres, thirty-five miles out, they proceeded to use the "Johnny Carson Show." Their budget for marketing and PR at one time was almost the same as my whole direct zoo operating budget, several million dollars. Well if you tell a story often enough and do it well and have good reason, people will accept it. So the mystique started and kept on that San Diego was America's number one zoo. And I accept that, with their combined collections, but once Los Angeles got into the business, and once they became good and professional at it, they're on the same level professionally as San Diego. At first, all the things that could go wrong did go wrong there. They had so many mistakes they brought in consultants on top of consultants to try to straighten things out, in terms of animal habitats and so on. It took some years, but finally it's a lovely landscaped garden of its own, much more compact than some zoos, not one of these two-hundred-acre things.

It would be wrong not to say Brookfield's one of my

398 —————————————————————————————— Zoo

favorite zoos. My kids were brought up in Brookfield, and I took care of some of their animals and got to know the people well. When it opened, it was one of the state-of-the-art zoos with open space and so on. Brookfield's always had a strong commitment to science, and I've always respected them for that. That's one of the things that we are playing a little bit of a slower role in, because our board, the park district, is park commissioners; they're not necessarily interested in research and academic things. Whereas some of the Brookfield board historically has been scientists, and so they've been able to do that.

There are other zoos. I think San Francisco is coming along. The Detroit Zoo was built by a landscape architect; at one time it was one of the prettiest zoos in America. It had its bad days, and now I think it's coming back strongly. I think a lot of zoos are changing. I think the Minnesota State Zoo and the North Carolina State Zoo are two important collections in our country. St. Louis and Cincinnati are meaningful collections that I have respect for. Denver's come a long way in recent years.

I think you have to have Regent's Park in London in there; it's one of the meaningful zoos. Antwerp has to rate as one of the fine collections in Europe. Amsterdam and Rotterdam are very good collections. Cologne. Berlin certainly, the old tiergarten, even though the wall split it, and they have two zoos in Berlin now, East and West. But West Berlin is one of the early great zoos of the world. They're one of the collectors, very interested in diversity of species.

The naturalistic setting isn't necessarily good for the animal. After all, no one's ever really figured out what the animal thinks on the other side of the bars. The tendency is to provide better spaces, give animals what is biologically important to their needs. But in my old monkey house, for example, for forty, fifty years on the west side of the building there were outside cages, and on the east side there were none. From a health standpoint, I never saw any difference if the animals got outside or not. As long as we had ultraviolet lights, as long as we balanced the diet, from the standpoint of health, longevity, reproduction, I saw no difference. Sure, sunshine is important. But that convinced me that you could do a good job of maintaining animals inside, if you gave them a total proper environment. Animals make peace with their cages, because that's their home.

When animals escape in a zoo, unlike a human escaping from a jail, they don't want to get away from anything. They're out, and once they're out, they're perplexed and concerned and excited as to what's what, because they've lost the security of their home. And more often than not, if wild animals are given a chance in a zoo, they'll go back to the place they escaped from. The problem is that it's hard for them to ever do that because people are after them. And it'd be kind of simplistic to say, "Well, if everyone just sits back, you know, that tiger's going to go back into his cage." You worry where that tiger might go, and therefore you'd better catch it, before it gets in trouble. But it is a fact that animals look upon their cage as their home; they're secure in there. And part of the secret of good cage design is to know the needs of the kind of animal. Some animals need space, some animals don't need a lot of space. One animal has to literally touch the walls of its cage; for others, the more space the better. That's part of good cage design. We always keep the animals in mind.

The great cats have a certain beauty to them that is special, because it isn't just that they're pretty in the usual sense of the word, but it's a fabulous machine that nature has evolved—the way that animal can have the ability to hunt, the way it can move around. There's just something about a cat, the great cats especially, that's very special.

Antelope, you look at those sable antelope, you look at the adra gazelles, you look at the zebra. They are all wondrous creatures, with a dignity befitting them. And the primates—I guess most people relate to them because we anthropomorphize, and if I go through the monkey house and the wanderoo macaque will sort of grimace when I grimace at him, and there's a recognition factor, that's special. When they get excited when you come, it makes you feel good.

You can go to a circus and see a pig doing certain tricks, and someone will say it's an intelligent animal. You can see a horse doing certain tricks, or a dog, but regarding total true intelligence, I think there's no question that at the top of the heap in the animal collection in the zoo are the three great apes, the chimp, orang, and gorilla. You just have to observe them a while, and you start wondering, "What are they thinking about?" And you get eye contact, and you know that there's something going on there.

When I make rounds, especially with a lot of the mammals, certainly more than the birds or reptiles, and then with some of the primates and great apes more than other mammals, there's no question that most of them tell me they're kind of glad to see me, as I am to see them. But there are times when I sense they're not at all happy with whatever it is that's going on at that particular moment. You can see it in the way they walk around, the way they sit, the way they look.

Many times the great apes will come to whatever the barrier is, the wire mesh, the glass, and try to interact. Many times they'll pick up things in their cage and hand them to me through the wire. I think it's one of the tricks that has both pleased me and saddened me that Koundu would do for years. He and I played games through the wire mesh. I'd hand him something, he'd hand me something, I'd reach through and touch him, tickle his tongue. That went on for years. One day all of a sudden I realized he's getting in his terrible teens, and he was ready to nail me. And now he sets you up. He'll start handing you something through that wire mesh, and if you're not careful his fingers are there to grab you. Most of the animals in the great ape house would not hurt people they knew, unless there was some reason for it. But with the adult males—it doesn't matter if it's chimp, orang, gorilla—

I think potentially they could do something untoward.

I've had emotional attachments to animals. The massive gorilla, Bushman, was one of a kind during his time. I was privileged to know him and to care for him during the last three, four years of his life. He's the only animal I think that I ever used to dream about. Occasionally when I'd make night calls to the old monkey house at two in the morning, I would open the doors and look to see if Bushman was out there waiting for me somewhere. There were all kinds of thoughts and feelings in those early years that if he really wanted to, he could get out of that cage. I'd dream about the old guy, in there, waiting.

Judy, the elephant, was one of my special animals. She was here forty, fifty years. She was a big, wonderful creature, and I was awed by this mass and the fact that she was basically a reasonably good animal. She had some tricks, and if you ever got between her and a wall, she'd just slowly lean and get you in there. I had a couple of close calls until I learned that. Once someone hollered in time, and I dropped down as she hit the wall.

Sinbad, the gorilla, was a special animal to me because I took care of him when he first came and he was just a little tyke, about a year old. So I interacted with him all those years. He wasn't necessarily friendly to me, but I guess I was honored because I was one of the few people that he never threw anything at. With most people, over a period of time, he'd throw anything from food to feces to you-name-it at them. That was one way he expressed displeasure. I never had that. He was around a long time and was a cornerstone animal.

Mike, the polar bear, also had been here many years. I got a mate for Mike, and she came as a little polar bear, and I thought, "Well, she's going to grow," but she never did. She remained about one-third or one-fourth the size of Mike. And I remember when the day came that I had to decide to get rid of one of them or try them together. And with great trepidation, I had them pull the transfer door, and big Mike walked into her cage, and I thought, "With one swipe of the paw, he could heave her right out of the whole cage." And she just barked at him and put a paw in his face, and he backed down. From that moment on, they got along just great. He never bothered her, and she got along with him. That was a classic case where I said, "Wow, am I lucky. That worked." We've been fortunate with most of our introductions in the zoo. We've had very few tragedies. It's not unusual in the zoo world for animals that are introduced to hurt each other or kill each other. And it's a worry we always have. But we've been lucky here.

I have great respect for animals and love them, but I still look upon them as animals. Even my family pets at home over the years—I've had wonderful dogs and I had a few cats—I don't look upon them as my children. I don't look upon one of the zoo animals on the same level that I would equate with a human. I still am able somehow to put it in perspective.

Millions of people in metropolitan Chicago might never have had a firsthand experience with these wild creatures if they weren't in a zoo. I don't care what you say about films and TV and slides and you name it, they're no substitute for being able to see, to smell, to hear, to be near this animal, to look at a giraffe firsthand and to be close and look up at it and see it. Even though I'd love to have enough space for all the animals to be in their natural homes, some specimens have to become goodwill ambassadors to tell their story.

I think this zoo will get more involved in conservation around the country and the world. I think this zoo will get more involved in research with its animals, continuing behavioral research, nutritional research, reproductive biology. I think these are important things, and this zoo should be doing more. I think as we get more financial support and get more staff, that's going to be the future for the zoo. I think its education programs will continue to grow, as they tie in more with the school systems. I think that people will take it for granted, finally, that the zoo is a classroom.

Once I get the last of these kids out of their inadequate facilities, the zoo is fixed, the plan—down the road, when and where and how we can do it—is to have a farm somewhere, some space out in the country, where, for example, we can maintain a small herd of zebras and bring one or two in for exhibition. I don't envision a two-thousand-acre thing. I'm thinking of a one- to two-hundred-acre space somewhere that would be a supplement to the zoo. There's no possibility that the zoo itself would or should expand. I think the collection should scale down to the zoo size rather than the zoo trying to expand.

I think we have a moral responsibility to these animals, and I believe that very strongly. On the other hand, part of the joy to me is to see the public use this place. I can't tell you what great inner satisfaction I get watching people visit the zoo, and watching them interact with the collection and watching them have fun or learn or whatever. As each generation of young people comes along, you see it all over again. Watching parents with their kids here, and watching the kids and listening to the conversation and seeing all segments of society here is to me a great, great source of contentment. It's not an achievement, because I didn't bring it about. Maybe I helped. I feel strongly about that. It's part of my inner satisfaction about being here.

Within a few years, if everything goes well and I retain my health, I probably will retire. I'm not certain what I'll do. I'll probably want to visit some parts of our country. Believe it or not, I've been to very few national parks; I've always flown over them or gone around them or something, I've never made time to enjoy them. There are a lot of wonderful books that I want to read. I'll keep busy. The old zoo and the collection here are part of an extended family, and to just cut them off would probably be hard. I used to think about doing things in other parts of the country. I always travel and come back and make peace. Chicago is my home.

By 5 P.M., many of the animals have come in. Some are eager to retreat from the advancing night. Some, like the lions, move at their own pace. Inside, at night, they are safe from that occasionally nasty predator, the human, who may taunt them with rocks. The gates to the zoo are locked; it is possible to leave through a turnstile, but not to enter.

The keepers have gone for the day; the buildings close at five, and the grounds are secured fifteen minutes later. Only a few night keepers patrol the zoo after hours. They walk around, from building to building, checking on the animals, making sure that everything that should be locked is locked. By the time the sun sets, there are no joggers, no businesspeople, no giggling children in the zoo. Only the animals and the night keepers. The nocturnal animals come alive in their cages; those that thrive in sunlight wind down.

A curator may work late. A zoo society worker may stay on at a desk until the sun is gone, and beyond. By late evening, all of them are gone, and the place is quiet. The sounds of animals—roars, growls, howls, whines, chattering, the secret vocabulary of the zoo—punctuate the sounds of the city itself.

Those who live in the nearby high-rise apartments wonder, "Was that sea lion calling out to someone?"

No one knows.

ACKNOWLEDGMENTS

I want to thank all of those mentioned in this book, for their candor and their patience. They permitted me to be a part of their daily lives at the zoo. There are others to thank as well: Keeper Norm Andresen, in particular, and all the other keepers who tolerated my presence with goodwill. All of the zoo's administrative staff, including Lois Stanley, Marybeth Gilchrist, Teresa Duffy, Kathleen Marshall, and Joanne Earnhardt. The zoo society staff members who were helpful, including Marge Morra, Lynn James, Maggie Schmid, Tina Koegel, Jennifer Marx, Susie Reich, and Lynne Yamaguchi. Volunteer coordinators Susan Young and Lois Wagner and all the docents and volunteers I encountered. John Fennessey of the park district power house staff.

Special gratitude goes out to Lucy Bukowski, who transcribed my tapes and made sense out of my editing with accuracy, speed, and good cheer; Karen Schenkenfelder, a gifted and supportive copyeditor; and thanks to Bernard Shir-Cliff, an amiable, caring, and skilled editor.